Production System Models of Learning and Development

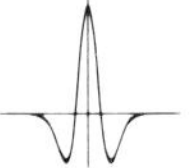

Computational Models of Cognition and Perception

Editors

Jerome A. Feldman
Patrick J. Hayes
David E. Rumelhart

Parallel Distributed Processing: Explorations in the Microstructure of Cognition. Volume 1: Foundations, by David E. Rumelhart, James L. McClelland, and the PDP Research Group

Parallel Distributed Processing: Explorations in the Microstructure of Cognition. Volume 2: Psychological and Biological Models, by James L. McClelland, David E. Rumelhart, and the PDP Research Group

Neurophilosophy: Toward a Unified Science of the Mind-Brain, by Patricia Smith Churchland

Qualitative Reasoning about Physical Systems, edited by Daniel G. Bobrow

Induction: Processes of Inference, Learning, and Memory, by John H. Holland, Keith J. Holyoak, Richard E. Nisbett, and Paul R. Thagard

Minimal Rationality, by Christopher Cherniak

Vision, Brain, and Cooperative Cognition, edited by Michael A. Arbib and Allen R. Hanson

Production System Models of Learning and Development, edited by David Klahr, Pat Langley, and Robert Neches

Production System Models of Learning and Development

edited by
David Klahr
Pat Langley
and Robert Neches

The MIT Press
Cambridge, Massachusetts
London, England

This book was set in Times New Roman by Asco Trade Typesetting Ltd., Hong Kong, and printed and bound by Halliday Lithograph in the United States of America.

Library of Congress Cataloging-in-Publication Data

Production system models of learning and development.

(Computational models of cognition and perception)
Includes bibliographies.
1. Learning, Psychology of. 2. Human information processing. 3. Cognition.
I. Klahr, David. II. Langley, Pat. II. Neches, Robert. IV. Series.
BF318.P73 1987 153 86-27638
ISBN 0-262-11114-4

Contents

List of Contributors

John R. Anderson
Carnegie-Mellon University

Yuichiro Anzai
Hokkaido University

Kevin Bluff
Deakin University

David Klahr
Carnegie-Mellon University

Pat Langley
University of California, Irvine

Clayton Lewis
University of Colorado

Robert Neches
Information Sciences Institute

Allen Newell
Carnegie-Mellon University

Stellan Ohlsson
University of Pittsburgh

Paul Rosenbloom
Stanford University

Iain Wallace
Swinburne Institute of Technology

Introduction

In the past two decades cognitive psychologists have started to adopt *production systems* as the principle theoretical medium in which to cast complex theories of human intelligence. Production systems are a class of computer simulation models that are stated in terms of condition-action rules, and that make strong assumptions about the nature of the cognitive architecture. The initial use of production systems was to provide theoretical accounts of human performance on a variety of tasks. However, one fundamental feature that distinguishes production systems from most other forms of cognitive simulation is their capability for self-modification. Because of this feature it quickly became apparent that they were eminently well suited for dealing with issues of development and learning.

During this period of growth many papers describing, using, proposing, and extolling production systems have appeared. However, those papers have been the product of many different researchers operating relatively independently and have appeared in widely disparate forms and forums. There has been no single volume exclusively devoted to production-system models of human cognition. For this reason we came to feel that a volume that enables readers to compare and contrast those research efforts would have special importance.

All of the chapters in this book deal with the issues that arise when one constructs self-modifying production systems. The book should be of interest to any cognitive scientist interested in the processes underlying the acquisition of knowledge and skills, particularly researchers in psychology with an information-processing orientation, as well as cognitively oriented researchers in artificial intelligence. (There remains an unmet need for a "how-to" text on cognitive modeling that would lay out the basic mechanisms of the production-system framework, focusing on performance models and emphasizing the details of formulation, design, programming, and debugging of such models.)

In planning this book, we sought to accomplish for the production-system paradigm what *Explorations in Cognition* did for the LNR Group, or what *Scripts, Plans, Goals and Understanding* did for the Yale AI group. That is, we have tried to provide a single volume that provides access to state-of-the-art research results and does so in a way that allows readers to gain some perspective on the underlying research approach. Unlike those other volumes, the relatedness of the work presented in this book is an emergent property developed through informal intellectual interactions, rather than the planned product of a formally constituted research group.

We did not limit ourselves to any particular laboratory or research project. Our only criterion was that the papers present a theoretical perspective on implemented self-modifying production systems. Although it turns out that most of the authors have at one time or another been affiliated with the Department of Psychology at Carnegie-Mellon University (in fact, when this project started, all three of the editors were at CMU), this was as much an effect as a cause of their interest in this kind of work. Carnegie-Mellon has a long history of providing a particularly fertile environment for computational studies of human intelligence.

As the chapters in this volume attest, this common heritage did not produce a homogeneous and constrained view of cognitive simulation. Instead, it generated a rich and contentious diversity of opinion about what it means to adopt production systems as a medium for theorizing about cognitive processes. As editors, we have not tried to paper over this diversity but have sought to provide some structure to it that will make it meaningful and, we hope, useful to the reader.

In the first chapter we attempt to lay out the fundamental issues that are involved in this endeavor, with a particular emphasis on the theoretical power that production systems bring to issues of learning and development and, conversely, the challenge that learning and development pose for production-system architectures. This overview chapter is followed by a set of substantive research-oriented papers.

In chapter 2 Anzai describes a theory of learning by doing and learning by understanding. He considers a number of related components of the learning task, ranging from the construction of an initial problem space, the acquisition of "negative" heuristics for avoiding undesirable moves, the generation of "positive" heuristics for proposing desirable moves, and the discovery of useful subgoals. He examines three tasks—the Tower of Hanoi puzzle, a seriation task, and the complex task of steering a ship—examining each of these in terms of the four types of learning.

In the third chapter Langley presents a theory of discrimination learning, in which one begins with overly general rules and generates more conservative variants as errors of omission occur. He compares discrimination learning with generalization-based approaches and applies the method to four different tasks—learning concepts from examples, learning search heuristics, the acquisition of grammatical expertise, and development on the balance scale task. The first two systems are not intended as models of human behavior; the latter two systems attempt to account for well-established stages that children traverse during the course of development.

In chapter 4 Neches describes his theory of strategy transformation, in which well-defined, but inefficient, procedures are gradually transformed into more efficient procedures. The theory includes a principled representation of procedural knowledge, the notion of memory traces for goals and for productions that have applied, a version of spreading activation that is sensitive to currently active goals, and the use of different conflict resolution strategies for different classes of productions. Neches applies the theory to procedural learning in the domain of simple addition, accounting for a number of phenomena reported in the educational literature.

In the fifth chapter Rosenbloom and Newell discuss the power law of practice, an empirical generalization that summarizes a wide range of speedup phenomena. They propose a theory of learning by chunking to account for the power law, and apply the theory to simulate learning on a task originally studied by Seibel (1963). The model is embedded in XAPS2, a production-system architecture that assumes a limited form of parallelism. The chunking process is intimately linked to the goal hierarchies used in carrying out a given task, and leads to chunks with three components—an encoding rule, a decoding rule, and a rule connecting these two.

The chapter by Ohlsson proposes the *rational learning* thesis—that declarative knowledge plays a central role in procedural learning. The author contrasts the production-system formalism with the notion of logical implication and examines ways in which the latter can be used to aid the acquisition of productions. Ohlsson argues that Neves and Anderson's (1981) notion of proceduralization is too weak and that additional constraints must be placed on the conditions for rule learning. He proposes four heuristics for when to construct productions—the rule of relevance, the rule of differentiation, the rule of specification, and the rule of generalization. He implements these heuristics within PSS, a production-system theory of the human cognitive architecture, and describes a model of learning on three-term series problems.

In chapter 7 Lewis considers in some detail the mechanism of learning by composition, in which two or more productions are combined to form a more powerful rule. He reviews the psychological phenomena that this method explains and provides some examples of the mechanism at work. Lewis then presents a formal analysis of the composition technique, introducing the notion of *safety* in which a new rule is guaranteed to produce the same behavior as the rules from which it was constructed. Briefly, he finds that knowledge of production syntax is insufficient for safety; this also requires information about the semantics of the productions.

In the eighth chapter Wallace, Klahr, and Bluff describe a model of cognitive development called BAIRN. Their architecture involves a hierarchically organized set of "nodes" (each a production system) with the ability to activate multiple nodes in parallel. The developmental theory includes mechanisms for constructing new nodes from episodic sequences of the system's previous behavior, and they show how these methods account for observed development on quantification and conservation tasks.

In the final chapter of the book Anderson reviews his ACT* theory and discusses its relevance to intelligent tutoring systems. The central learning mechanism of ACT* is a process of knowledge compilation that transforms general rules and declarative knowledge into more specific procedural knowledge. In addition Anderson presents the model-tracing paradigm of instruction and considers its use in a computer-based system for tutoring LISP programming skills. He argues that ACT* has four implications for tutorial action—relating to instruction, the correctness of declarative encodings, limitations on working memory, and the strength of productions—and discusses each of these in some detail.

Although the research described in this book does not exhaust the work on production-system models of learning and development, we feel that it includes many of the best examples of this paradigm. And though we would not claim that any of the following chapters presents a complete theory of human learning, we do believe that each makes a significant contribution toward this common goal. Certainly the achievement of this goal lies in the distant future, but we believe that the production-system approach has already given us a deeper understanding of the nature of learning and development.

David Klahr
Pat Langley
Robert Neches

Production System Models of Learning and Development

1 Learning, Development, and Production Systems

Robert Neches, Pat Langley, and David Klahr

The fields of cognitive science and artificial intelligence attempt to understand the *mechanisms* underlying intelligent behavior. However, many different approaches are consistent with this general goal, and various frameworks have been proposed for explaining intelligence. In this book we focus on one such approach, known as *production systems*, that has received considerable attention both within cognitive psychology and artificial intelligence. Moreover, we will limit our attention to production system models of learning and development, since this has been an active area of research that we feel has considerable long-term significance.

In the current chapter we will introduce the production-system framework and argue for the importance of studying learning phenomena. We base our discussion on the assumption that our understanding of the psychological phenomena can be advanced by constructing and evaluating computational models of intelligent behavior. Although some readers may question this assumption, we do not have the space to defend it here. However, we refer interested parties to treatments of the issue by Newell and Simon (1972) and Anderson (1976).

Even when applied to relatively circumscribed domains, and even without the added complexity of self-modifiability, production systems are difficult to formulate and to understand. It is not surprising therefore that after almost two decades, only a handful of psychologists have attempted to use them. For some investigators, production systems have a forbidding aura of esoteric mystery and complexity. For others, they seem to represent an unconstrained proliferation of arbitrary assumptions and idiosyncratic notations. The "cost" of production systems is obviously high, and the "benefits" have not been immediately apparent.

In this chapter we will attempt to clarify the benefit and, to some extent, reduce the cost by explaining the basics of production systems and discussing their relation to other areas of psychology and artificial intelligence. As editors, we are well aware that many of the subsequent chapters in this book are not easy reading. However, we will make a case for why they are worth the reader's effort. The central argument has two parts. First, learning and development are the fundamental issues in human psychology. Second, self-modifying production systems, although admittedly complex entities, represent one of the best theoretical tools currently available for understanding learning and development.

In making this argument, it is important to distinguish between two related but necessarily distinct views of the role of production system models. The first framework treats production systems as a formal *notation* for expressing models. Viewed in this way, it is the content of the models, rather than the form of their expression or their interpretation scheme, that is the object of interest. For example, one might characterize the rules a person uses to perform some task in terms of a production system. This type of modeling represents an attempt to formally specify the allowable "behaviors" of a system just as a grammar is intended to define the legal sentences in a language. Other formalisms for expressing the same content are possible (e.g., scripts, LISP programs, and flowcharts), and one can debate their relative merits (see Klahr and Siegler 1978).

In contrast, the second view treats the interpreter of a production system as a highly specific theory about the architecture of the human information processing system.[1] In its strongest form, this view asserts that humans actually employ the functional equivalent of productions in reasoning, understanding language, and other intelligent behavior. This second view also attributes great importance to the ability of production systems models to modify themselves in ways that capture many of the central features of learning and development.

We believe that it is the second view, originally put forward by Newell (1967) and most extensively applied by Anderson (1983), that provides the major justification for the use of production systems in modeling human behavior. In other words, if we are simply interested in the content of a domain, then in many cases the complexity of a production system formulation may just not be worth the effort. On the other hand, if we view the production system framework as a serious assertion about the fundamental organization of performance and learning processes, then the effort is justified.

Even the earliest production system models were designed to capture the characteristic features of the human cognitive architecture. Efforts to explore those characteristics at deeper and more concrete levels led—not surprisingly—to the discovery of technical and theoretical problems concerning management of search and control of attention. Efforts to address those problems, within both the community of production system builders and the closely related community of rule-based expert system builders, have fed back into the search for architectures that more closely reflect properties of human cognition. Issues of learning and human development have been a major forcing function in the definition of the problems and have served as a crucial testing ground for proposed solutions. The resulting architectures have implications not only for learning, but also for the broader nature of intelligent behavior and the structure of intelligent systems.

We begin the chapter with an introduction to production systems, using a simple example from the domain of multicolumn subtraction, and follow this with a brief history of the development of production systems in psychology. We then consider some phenomena of learning and development, and review some of the mechanisms that have been proposed to account for these phenomena within the production-system framework. In closing, we discuss some implications of learning issues for production-system models.

1.1 An Overview of Production Systems

Before moving on to the use of production systems in modeling learning and development, we should first introduce the reader to the concepts and mechanisms on which they are based. In this section we outline the basic components of production system architectures and follow this with an example of a simple production system program for solving multicolumn subtraction problems. After these preliminaries we review some of the arguments that have been made in favor of production system models and consider exactly what we mean by a production system "architecture."

The Components of a Production System

The basic structure of production system programs (and their associated interpreter) is quite simple. In its most fundamental form a production system consists of two interacting data structures, connected through a simple processing cycle:

1. A *working memory* consisting of a collection of symbolic data items called working memory *elements*.

2. A *production memory* consisting of condition-action rules called *productions*, whose conditions describe configurations of elements that might appear in working memory and whose actions specify modifications to the contents of working memory.

Production memory and working memory are related through the *recognize-act* cycle. This consists of three distinct stages:

1. The *match* process, which finds productions whose conditions match against the current state of working memory; the same rule may match against memory in different ways, and each such mapping is called an *instantiation.*
2. The *conflict resolution* process, which selects one or more of the instantiated productions for applications.
3. The *act* process, which applies the instantiated actions of the selected rules, thus modifying the contents of working memory.

The basic recognize-act process operates in cycles, with one or more rules being selected and applied, the new contents of memory leading another set of rules to be applied, and so forth. This cycling continues until no rules are matched or until an explicit halt command is encountered. Obviously this account ignores many of the details as well as the many variations that are possible within the basic framework, but it conveys the basic idea of a production system.

A Production System for Subtraction

Now that we have considered production systems in the abstract, let us examine a specific example from the domain of arithmetic. Multicolumn subtraction problems are most naturally represented in terms of rows and columns, with each row-column pair containing a number or a blank. The basic operators in subtraction involve finding the difference between two numbers in a given column, decrementing the top number in a column, and adding ten to the top number in a column. However, the need to borrow forces some sort of control symbols or goals, in order to distinguish between the column for which one is currently trying to find an answer and the column from which one is currently trying to borrow.

Before considering our production system for subtraction, we should consider the representation used for elements in working memory against which our rules will match. Suppose we have the problem 87 − 31, before the system has started trying to find an answer. We will represent this as a number of separate propositions, one for each number. For instance, the fact that the number 8 occurs in the top row and the leftmost column would be stored as (8 in column-2 row-1), in which the names for columns and rows are arbitrary. The positions of the remaining numbers would be represented by the elements (3 in column-2 row-2), (7 in column-1 row-1), and (1 in column-1 row-2). Since the position for each column's result is blank, the elements (blank result-for column-2) and (blank result-for column-1) would also be present.

Three types of relations must also be stored in memory. The first two involve the spatial relations *above* and *left-of*, and are used in elements like (row-1 above row-2) and (column-2 left-of column-1). These translate into English as "row-1 is above row-2" and "column-2 is left of column-1", respectively. Naturally the arguments of *above* are always rows, whereas the arguments of *left-of* are always columns. The final predicate is the *greater-than* relation, which takes two numbers as its arguments. This relation occurs in elements such as (3 greater-than 1), which means "3 is greater than 1."[2]

One must also be able to distinguish between the column for which we are currently computing a result and the column that is the current focus of attention. We will use the label *processing* for the first and the label *focused-on* for the second. Since one always starts subtraction problems by working on the rightmost column, and since the initial focus of attention also resides there, we would begin with the additional elements (processing column-1) and (focused-on column-1).

Now let us examine the productions that operate on this representation. We will present an English paraphrase of each rule and consider the role played by each condition and action. Italicized terms in the paraphrased rules stand for variables, which can match against any symbol as long as they do so consistently across conditions. In our discussion of a given production we will refer to specific conditions by their position in the rule. For instance, the parenthetical expression (2) will stand for the second condition in a production. After we have described each of the rules individually, we will examine the manner in which they interact during two sample runs.

The most basic action in subtraction problems involves finding the difference between two digits in the same column. The FIND-DIFFERENCE rule is responsible for implementing this behavior and matches when the column currently being processed (1) contains a top number (2, 4) that is greater than or equal to (5) the bottom number (3, 4). Its actions include computing the difference between the two numbers and writing the difference as the result for that column. We are assuming that the system has the primitive capability of correctly finding the difference between two digits.

FIND-DIFFERENCE
IF you are processing *column*,
 and *number1* is in *column* and *row1*,
 and *number2* is in *column* and *row2*,
 and *row1* is above *row2*,
 and *number1* is greater than or equal to *number2*,
THEN compute the difference of *number1* and *number2*,
 and write the result in *column*.

Once the result for the current column has been filled in with a digit (i.e., when the current column has been successfully processed), it is time to move on. If there is a column to the left of the current column (3), then the rule SHIFT-COLUMN matches, shifting processing and the focus of attention to the new column. Thus this rule is responsible for ensuring that right to left processing of the columns occurs.

SHIFT-COLUMN
IF you are processing *column1*,
 and you are currently focused on *column1*,
 and the result in *column1* is not blank,
 and *column2* is left of *column1*,
THEN note that you are now processing *column2*,
 and note that you are focusing on *column2*.

A special operator is needed for cases in which the bottom row in a column is occupied by a blank (since one can only find differences between numbers). The FIND-TOP rule handles this situation, matching in any case involving a number above a blank (2, 3, 4) in the column being processed (1). On application, the rule simply stores the top number as the result for that column. This will only occur in the leftmost columns of certain problems, such as 3456 − 21.

FIND-TOP
IF you are processing *column*,
 and *number* is in *column* and *row1*,
 and *column* and *row2* is blank,
 and *row1* is above *row2*,
THEN write *number* as the result of *column*.

In cases where the top number in a column is smaller than the bottom number, the ADD-TEN rule must add ten to the top number (2, 3) before the system can find an acceptable difference for the column currently in focus (1). However, this rule will only match if the system has just applied its DECREMENT operator (4), and finding a column from which one can decrement is not always a simple matter, as we will see.

ADD-TEN
IF you are focusing on *column1*,
  and *number1* is in *column1* and *row1*,
  and *row1* is above *row2*,
  and you have just decremented some number,
THEN add ten to *number1* in *column1* and *row1*.

Before the ADD-TEN rule can apply, the system must first apply the DECREMENT rule. This matches in cases where the system has shifted its focus of attention away from the column currently being processed (1, 2), and the top number in the new column is greater than zero (3, 4, 5). Upon firing, the rule decrements the top number by one and returns the focus of attention to the column immediately to the right (6). A negated condition (7) prevents DECREMENT from applying more than once in a given situation.

DECREMENT
IF you are focusing on *column1*,
  but you are not processing *column1*,
  and *number1* is in *column1* and *row1*,
  and *row1* is above *row2*,
  and *number1* is greater than zero,
  and *column1* is left of *column2*,
  and you have not just decremented a number,
THEN decrement *number1* by one in *column1* and *row1*,
  and note that you have just decremented a number,
  and note that you are focusing on *column2*.

However, before the system can decrement the top number in a column, it must first be focused on that column. The rule SHIFT-LEFT-TO-BORROW takes the first step in this direction, matching in precisely those cases in which borrowing is required. In other words, the rule applies if the system is focused on the column it is currently processing (1, 2), if that column contains two numbers (3, 5), if the bottom one larger than the top one (4, 6), and if there is another column to the left (7) from which to borrow. A negated condition (8) keeps this rule from matching if DECREMENT has just applied, thus avoiding and infinite loop. Under these conditions SHIFT-LEFT-TO-BORROW shifts the focus of attention to the adjacent column.

SHIFT-LEFT-TO-BORROW
IF you are focused on *column1*,
  and you are processing *column1*,
  and *number1* is in *column1* and *row1*,
  and *number2* is in *column1* and *row2*,
  and *row1* is above *row2*,
  and *number2* is greater than *number1*,
  and *column2* is left of *column1*,
  and you have not just decremented a number,
THEN note that you are focusing on *column2*.

For many borrowing problems (e.g., 654 − 278) the SHIFT-LEFT-TO-BORROW rule is quite sufficient, since one can borrow from the column immediately to the left of the one being processed. However, if the column to the left contains a zero as its top number, one must search further. The rule SHIFT-LEFT-ACROSS-ZERO handles cases such as these, matching if the system has shifted its focus of attention (1, 2), if it has found a zero (3) in the top row (4) of the new column, and if there is another column to the left (5). When these conditions are met, the rule shifts attention to the column immediately to the left. Again this will not occur if DECREMENT was just applied (6), since this would cause an infinite loop. On problems involving multiple zeros in the top row (e.g., 10005 − 6), SHIFT-LEFT-ACROSS-ZERO will apply as many times as necessary to reach a number which it can decrement.

SHIFT-LEFT-ACROSS-ZERO
IF you are focused on *column1*,
  and you are not processing *column1*,
  and the number in *column1* and *row1* is zero,
  and *row1* is above *row2*,
  and *column2* is left of *column1*,
  and you did not just decrement a number,
THEN note that you are focusing on *column2*.

The preceding rules handle the major work involved in multicolumn subtraction, but the system must also have some way to know when it has completed solving a given problem. The rule FINISHED is responsible for noting when there is no longer a blank (3) in the result position of the leftmost column (1, 2). In such cases this rule fires and tells the production system to halt, since it has generated a complete answer to the problem.

FINISHED
IF you are processing *column1*,
  and there is no *column2* to the left of *column1*,
  and the result of *column1* is not blank,
THEN you are finished.

A Simple Subtraction Problem

Now that we have examined each of the rules in our system, let us consider its behavior on some specific subtraction problems. Presented with the problem 87 − 31, the system begins with the problem representation we described earlier.[3] This consists of 10 basic working memory elements:

(8 in column-2 row-1)
(7 in column-1 row-1)
(3 in column-2 row-2)
(1 in column-1 row-2)
(processing column-1)
(focused-on column-1)
(blank result-for column-2)
(blank result-for column-1)
(column-2 left-of column-1)
(row-1 above row-2)

We are assuming here that greater-than relations are tested by LISP predicates rather than being explicitly represented in memory, but the relations above and left-of are stored directly. Note that the rightmost column **(column-1)** is labeled for processing first, and that this column is also the initial focus of attention.

Given this information, the rule FIND-DIFFERENCE matches against the elements **(processing column-1)**, **(7 in column-1 row-1)**, **(1 in column-1 row-2)**, **(row-1 above row-2)**, and **(7 greater-than 1)**. The action side of this production is instantiated, computing the difference between **7** and **1**, and the number **6** is "written" in the results column. This last action is represented by the new element **(6 result-for column-1).**

Now that there is a result in the current column, the rule SHIFT-COLUMN matches against the elements **(processing column-1)**, **(focused-on column-1)**, and **(column-2 left-of column-1)**. Although this production has four conditions, only the first, second, and third are matched, since the third is a negated condition that must not be met. Upon application, the rule removes the elements **(processing column-1)** and **(focused-on column-1)** from memory, and adds the elements **(processing column-2)** and **(focused-on column-2)**. In other words, having finished with the first column, the system now moves on to the adjacent one.

At this point, the conditions of FIND-DIFFERENCE are again met, though this time they match against a different set of elements: **(processing column-2)**, **(8 in column-2 row-1)**, **(3 in column-2 row-2)**, **(row-1 above row-2)**, and **(8 greater-than 3)**. As before, the rule computes the difference of the two digits and adds the element **(5 result-for column-2)** to working memory. The presence of this new element serves to trigger the conditions of FINISHED, since both columns now have answers. Having generated a complete answer to the problem (56), the system halts.

A Complex Subtraction Problem

Since the preceding problem involved no borrowing, we saw only a few of the rules in action, so let us now turn to the more difficult problem 305 − 29. At the outset of this task, working memory contains the following elements:

(blank in column-5 row-2)
(3 in column-5 row-1)
(column-5 left-of column-4)
(2 in column-4 row-2)
(0 in column-4 row-1)
(column-4 left-of column-3)
(9 in column-3 row-2)
(5 in column-3 row-1)
(focused-on column-3)
(processing column-3)
(row-1 above row-2)

If we measure complexity by the number of elements in memory, this problem is only slightly more complex than our first example. However, the manner in which these elements interact with the various productions leads to significantly more processing than in the earlier case.

As before, the system begins by attempting to process the rightmost column. Since the *greater-than* condition of FIND-DIFFERENCE is not met (5 is not greater than 9), this rule can not apply immediately. Instead, the production SHIFT-LEFT-TO-BORROW matches, and shifts the focus of attention to the column to the left **(column-3)**. On many borrowing problems the system would apply DECREMENT at this point, but the conditions of this rule are not met either (zero is not greater than zero). However, the conditions of SHIFT-LEFT-ACROSS-ZERO are met, and this leads to system to move its focus even further left, to column-5.

Finally, the system has reached a column in which it can apply DECREMENT, and in doing so, it replaces the element **(3 in column-5 row-1)** with the element **(2 in column-5 row-1)**. This rule also moves the focus back one column to the right, making **column-4** the center of attention. Given this new situation, ADD-TEN matches and the **0** in the middle column is replaced with the "digit" **10**. This is accomplished by replacing the element **(0 in column-4 row-1)** with the new element **(10 in column-4 row-1)**.

Now that the system has a number larger than zero in the middle column, it can decrement this number as well. The DECREMENT production matches against the current state of memory, replacing the recently generated **10** with the digit **9**. In addition the rule shifts the focus of attention from the middle column **(column-4)** back to the rightmost column **(column-3)**. Since the system has just decremented a number in the adjacent column, the rule ADD-TEN now replaces the **5** in the rightmost column with the "digit" **15**. This in turn allows FIND-DIFFERENCE to apply, since the number in the top row of this column is now larger than the number in the bottom row. The effect is that the difference **6** (i.e., 15 − 9) is added as the result for **column-3**.

The presence of a result in the current column causes SHIFT-COLUMN to match, and both the processing marker and the focus of attention are shifted to the center column. Since the top number in this column is larger than the bottom number (from our earlier borrowing), FIND-DIFFERENCE matches and computes 9 − 2. The resulting difference **7** is "written" as the result for the middle column, and this in turn leads SHIFT-

COLUMN to fire again, shifting processing and attention to the rightmost column.

In this case the bottom row of the current column is blank, so the only matched production is FIND-TOP. This rule decides that the result for the rightmost column should be **2** (the digit in the top row), and since all columns now have associated results, the rule FINISHED applies and the system halts, having computed the correct answer of 276.

Comments on Subtraction

Although we hope that our program for subtraction has given the reader a better feel for the nature of production system models, it is important to note that it makes one major simplification. Since only one rule (and only one instantiation of each rule) matches at any given time, we were able to ignore the issue of conflict resolution. Although this was useful for instructional purposes, the reader should know that there are very few tasks for which it is possible to model behavior in such a carefully crafted manner, and conflict resolution has an important role to play in these cases.

Our choice of subtraction as an example gives us some initial insight into the advantages of this framework, which we consider in more detail shortly. Brown and Burton (1978) and Brown and VanLehn (1980) have made significant strides in classifying children's subtraction errors, and in accounting for these errors using their "repair theory." However, Young and O'Shea (1981) have proposed an alternative model of subtraction errors based on a production system analysis. They account for many of the observed errors by omitting certain rules from a model of correct behavior. Langley and Ohlsson (1984) have taken this approach further, accounting for errors only in terms of incorrect *conditions* on the rules shown here. Within this framework they have developed a system that automatically constructs a model to account for observed errors. This is possible only because of the inherent modularity of production system programs.

Before closing, we should point out one other feature of the production system approach—it does not completely constrain the systems one constructs any more than other computer programming languages. For example, Anderson (1983) has presented a production system model of multicolumn addition that is organized quite differently from our subtraction system, despite the similarity of the two tasks. The point is that there is considerable room for different "programming styles" within the production system framework, since people can employ quite different representations and control structures. Thus Anderson's model makes heavy use of explicit goals that are held in working memory; our "processing" and "focus" elements play a similar role but organize behavior in a different fashion.

Advantages of Production-System Models

Now that we have seen an example of a production-system model, it is appropriate to consider the advantages of this approach. The fact that production systems allow one to carry out subtraction or any other behavior is not sufficient—most programming languages are equivalent in computational power. However, Newell and Simon (1972) have argued that production systems have a number of features that recommend them for modeling human behavior. Let us recount some of these characteristics:

1. *Homogeneity.* Production systems represent knowledge in a very homogeneous format, with each rule having the same basic structure and carrying approximately the same amount of information. This makes them much easier to handle than traditional flow diagram models.

2. *Independence.* Production rules are relatively independent of each other, making it easy to insert new rules or remove old ones. This makes them very useful for modeling successive stages in a developmental sequence and also makes them attractive for modeling the incremental nature of much human learning.

3. *Parallel/serial nature.* Production systems combine the notion of a parallel recognition process with a serial application process; both features seem to be characteristic of human cognition.

4. *Stimulus-response flavor.* Production systems inherit many of the benefits of stimulus-response theory but few of the limitations, since the notions of stimuli and responses have been extended to include internal symbol structures.

5. *Goal-driven behavior.* Production systems can also be used to model the goal-driven character of much human behavior. However, such behavior need not be rigidly enforced; new information from the environment can interrupt processing of the current goal.

6. *Modeling memory.* The production-system framework offers a viable model of long-term memory and its relation to short-term memory, since the matching and conflict resolution process embody principles of retrieval and focus of attention.

Taken together, these features suggest the production system approach as a useful framework within which to construct models of human behavior. Of course, this does not mean that production systems are the *only* such framework, but there seems sufficient promise to pursue the approach vigorously.

As we will shortly see in the historical section, production systems have been used successfully to model human behavior on a wide range of tasks. As we will also see, Newell and Simon's initial ideas on the nature of the human cognitive architecture have been revised along many dimensions, and many additional revisions will undoubtedly be required before we achieve significant understanding of human learning and performance. This observation leads us back to the issue of viewing production systems as cognitive architectures, to which we now turn.

Production Systems as Cognitive Architectures

The term "cognitive architecture" denotes the invariant features of the human information processing system. Since one of the major goals of any science is to uncover invariants, the search for the human cognitive architecture should be a central concern of cognitive psychology. The decision to pursue production system models involves making significant assumptions about the nature of this architecture, but within the boundaries defined by these assumptions there remains a large space of possibilities.

In later chapters we will see many different instantiations of the basic production-system framework, but let us anticipate some of these variations by considering the dimensions along which production-system architectures may differ:

Working Memory Issues

1. *The structure of memory.* Is there a single general working memory, or multiple specialized memories (e.g., data and goal memories)? In the latter case, which are matched against by production memory?

2. *The structure of elements.* What is the basic form of working memory elements (e.g., list structures, attribute-value pairs)? Do elements have associated numeric parameters, such as activation or recency?

3. *Decay and forgetting.* Are there limits on the number of items present in working memory? If so, are these time-based or space-based limitations?

4. *Retrieval processes.* Once they have been "forgotten," can elements

be retrieved at some later date? If so, what processes lead to such retrieval? For example, must productions add them to memory, or does "spreading activation" occur?

Production Memory Issues

1. *The structure of memory.* Is there a single general production memory, or are there many specialized memories? In the latter case, are all memories at the same level, or are their organized hierarchically?

2. *The structure of productions.* Do productions have associated numeric parameters (e.g., strength and recency) or other information beyond conditions and actions?

3. *Expressive power of conditions.* What types of conditions can be used to determine whether a rule is applicable? For example, can arbitrary predicates be included? Can sets or sequences be matched against? Can many-to-one mappings occur?

4. *Expressive power of actions.* What kind of processing can be performed within the action side of an individual rule? For example, can arbitrary functions be evoked? Can conditional expressions occur?

5. *Nature of the match process.* Are exact matches required or is partial matching allowed? Does the matcher find all matched rules, or only some of them? Does the matcher find all instantiations of a given production?

Conflict Resolution Issues

1. *Ordering strategies.* How does the architecture order instantiations of productions? For example, does it use the recency of matched elements or the specificity of the matched rules?

2. *Selection strategies.* How does the architecture select instantiations based on this ordering? For example, does it select the best instantiation, or does it select all those above a certain threshold?

3. *Refraction strategies.* Does the architecture remove some instantiations permanently? For example, it may remove all instantiations that applied on the last cycle, or all instantiations currently in the conflict set.

Self-Modification Issues

1. *Learning mechanisms.* What are the basic learning mechanisms that lead to new productions? Examples are generalization, discrimination, composition, proceduralization, and strengthening.

2. *Conditions for learning.* What are the conditions under which these learning mechanisms are evoked? For example, whenever an error is noted, or whenever a rule is applied?

3. *Interactions between mechanisms.* Do the learning mechanisms complement each other, or do they compete for control of behavior? For example, generalization and discrimination move in opposite directions through the space of conditions.

To summarize, the basic production-system framework has many possible incarnations, each with different implications about the nature of human cognition. The relevance of these issues to enduring questions in the psychology of learning and development should be obvious. The chapters in this volume represent only a small sample from the space of possible architectures, although they include many of the self-modifying production systems that have been proposed to date. Before elaborating some of the issues involved with the formulation of learning systems, we will digress slightly in order to establish some historical context for production systems.

1.2 The History of Production-System Models

Although they have their roots in the formalisms of computer science and mathematics, the relevance of production systems to psychology began some 20 years ago, when Newell (1967) first proposed them as one way to formulate information processing theories of human problem-solving behavior. Their initial use was to provide theoretical accounts of human *performance* on a variety of tasks, ranging from adults' behavior on various puzzles (Newell and Simon 1972) to children's responses to class-inclusion questions (Klahr and Wallace 1972). However, it soon became apparent that they were eminently well suited for dealing with issues of *development* (Klahr and Wallace 1973, 1976) and *learning* (Anderson, Kline, and Beasley 1978; Anzai and Simon 1979; Langley, Neches, Neves, and Anzai 1980). In this section we review the history of these efforts, including specific models and general production system architectures.

Specific Production-System Models

The early production-system models were not implemented on a computer and required "hand simulation" in order to determine their consequences.

The first running production system appears to have been Waterman's (1970) poker-playing program. It is interesting to note that this was also a learning system, though it was not an attempt to model the human learning process.

Soon thereafter, Newell (1972) described the implementation of a general purpose production-system interpreter (PSG) that could be applied to a wide range of cognitive domains. Newell's first two applications of PSG were atypical of the subsequent use of production systems. The first (Newell 1972) focused on stimulus encoding, and the second (Newell 1973) modeled performance on the Sternberg memory-scanning paradigm. Both papers presented a much finer-grained analysis than the majority of production system models have employed. Klahr's (1973) model of basic quantification processes was also designed to account for very fine-grained encoding processes.

A few years later, Waterman (1975) reported new results with adaptive production systems. One of these systems implemented EPAM-like discrimination networks as production rules, and another focused on sequence extrapolation tasks. Again, neither was intended as a cognitive simulation, but both were interesting in their adaptive characteristics. One year later Rychener (1976) completed a thesis in which he reimplemented a variety of well-known AI systems as production systems. This work convincingly demonstrated that the production system framework was as powerful as other existing representational schemes and that it was a useful framework for implementing complex models of intelligence.

Anderson, Kline, and Lewis (1977) went on to use production systems to model the complexities of natural language understanding, and Anderson (1976) also applied the approach to a variety of other information processing tasks. Thibadeau, Just, and Carpenter (1982) went even further, showing how production-system models could account for reaction time phenomena in reading tasks. Finally, Ohlsson (1980b) employed the production system framework to model detailed verbal protocols on transitive reasoning tasks. Since 1980 the use of production systems in modeling human performance has spread, but since performance is not our central concern, let us turn our attention to other matters.

In addition to Waterman's early concern with learning, a number of early researchers employed production systems in modeling cognitive development. However, rather than develop models of the transition process at the outset, they constructed models of behavior at successive developmental stages. Klahr and Wallace (1973, 1976) carried out the earliest work of this type, constructing stage models of behavior on a variety of Piagetian tasks, including class inclusion and conservation of quantity. The basic approach involved modeling behavior at different stages in terms of production-system programs that differed by only one or a few rules.

Baylor, Gascon, Lemoyne, and Pother (1973) extended this approach to Piagetian length and weight seriation tasks, and Young (1976) carried out an even more detailed analysis of length seriation in his thesis research. Klahr and Siegler (1978) developed similar production-system stage models for Piaget's balance scale task, combining this with detailed empirical studies of children's behavior on the task. Larkin (1981) used a comparable framework to model adult expert-novice differences in physics problem solving, and Ohlsson (1980a) modeled similar differences in ability on his transitive reasoning tasks.

These stage models were tantalizing, in that they explained behavioral differences at successive stages in terms of slightly different rule sets, but yet provided no *mechanisms* to account for the transition process. (The work by Klahr and Wallace did eventually lead to a transition model, as we will see in chapter 8.) After Waterman's early forays the first truly adaptive production-system models were reported by Anderson, Kline, and Beasley (1978); these employed mechanisms of generalization, discrimination, and strengthening, which will be discussed further by Langley in chapter 3.

Shortly thereafter, production-system models of learning became an active research area. For instance, Anzai (1978) reported a model of human learning on the Tower of Hanoi puzzle, and Neves (1978) proposed a model of algebra learning. At about the same time, Langley (1978) developed an adaptive production system for concept attainment, sequence extrapolation, and simple empirical discovery, and McDermott (1979) described a production system approach to reasoning by analogy. (However, neither Langley nor McDermott's systems were concerned with modeling human behavior in any detail.) Finally, Lewis (1978) introduced the mechanism of composition, which he describes in more detail in chapter 7.

Research on adaptive production systems continued into the 1980s, with Neves and Anderson (1981) extending Lewis's notion of composition and introducing the mechanism of proceduralization. Neches (1981a, 1981b) took a quite different approach in his theory of strategy transformation (see chapter 4), and Newell and Rosenbloom (1981) proposed a theory of learning by chunking (see chapter 5). Since then research in production-

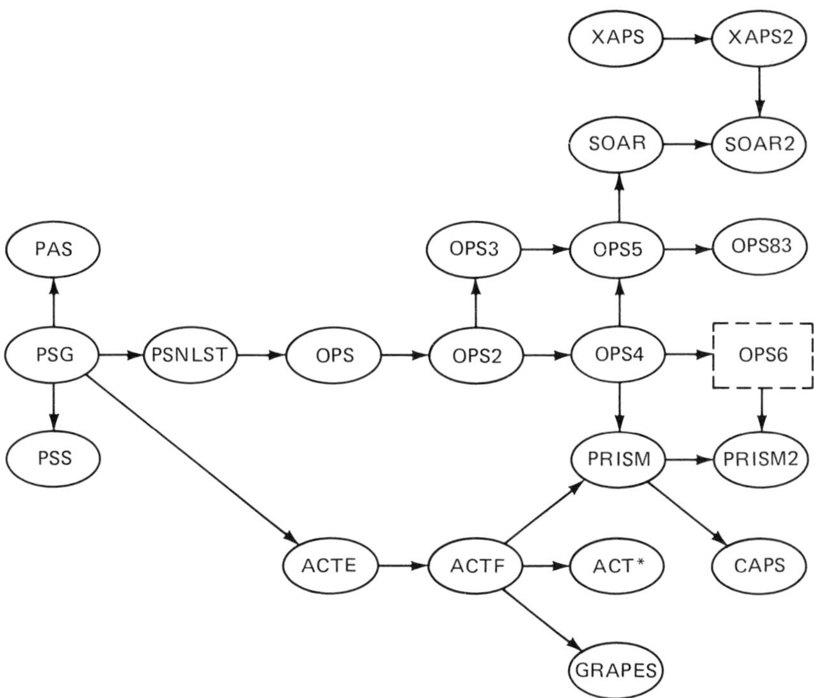

Figure 1.1
Development of production-system architectures

system models of learning has continued unabated, and many of the researchers in the new field of machine learning have taken a closely related approach.[4]

Research on Production-System Architectures

Our treatment of production systems would not be complete without some discussion of the history and development of production system architectures and their implementations as programming languages. On examining the history of research on production systems, one is struck by an obvious trend—nearly every researcher who has developed production system models of significant complexity has developed his own architecture and associated language. However, many of these architectures are very similar, and it is worthwhile to trace their evolution over time. Figure 1.1 summarizes this evolutionary process.

The first widely used production system programming language was PSG (Newell and McDermott 1975). Rather than embodying a single architecture, PSG provided a number of parameters that defined an entire *class* of architectures. Thus the modeler could explore different memory limitations, alternative conflict resolution schemes, and similar issues. However, PSG did assume a "queue" model of working memory, with elements stored in an ordered list. Many of the early production-system models were implemented in PSG, including Newell's (1973) model of the Sternberg phenomenon and Klahr and Wallace's (1976) developmental stage models.

Another early production-system language was Waterman's PAS. This was not intended as a serious model of the human cognitive architecture, but it did have some primitive learning capabilities.[5] Conflict resolution was based on the order of productions, and working memory was stored as a queue. Ohlsson (1979) developed a similar production system language called PSS, which he used in his models of transitive reasoning. This was very similar to PAS in that it used production order for conflict resolution and a queue-based model of short-term memory; however, one could also divide production rules into a number of sets that were organized hierarchically.

Rychener's PSNLST (1976) incorporated a number of novel features. First, the main conflict resolution method was based on recency, with preference being given to instantiations that matched against more recent elements. Rychener used this bias to ensure that subgoals were addressed in the desired order. Second, PSNLST dynamically reordered productions according to the number of times they had been placed on the candidate match list. This led the architecture to prefer rules that had recently shown promise and had a quite different flavor from the static ordering schemes that had prevailed in earlier languages.

The history of production systems took another significant turn when Forgy and McDermott (1976) developed the first version of OPS. This language was the vehicle of the Instructable Production System project at Carnegie-Mellon University, led by Allen Newell. The most important feature of OPS was its pattern matcher, which allowed it to compute efficiently the matched instantiations of all productions. This in turn made possible experiments with different conflict resolution strategies and made the notion of refraction tractable. OPS also assumed a working memory of unlimited size, with the associated theoretical claim that human memory only *appeared* limited due to a recency-based conflict resolution scheme (similar to that used by PSNLST).

Forgy's initial version of OPS was followed by OPS2 (1977) and OPS4 (1979a), which were minor variations implemented in different programming languages. By OPS4, the basic conflict resolution strategies had stabilized, with refraction given first priority, followed by recency of the matched elements and specificity of the rules. Rychener's (1980) OPS3 was a descendant of OPS2 that stored elements in terms of attribute-value pairs in an effort to provide greater representational flexibility.

The next incarnation, OPS5 (Forgy 1981), also used an attribute-value scheme, but in a much less flexible manner than OPS3 did. However, the main goal of OPS5 was efficiency, and along this dimension it succeeded admirably. Over the years, it has become one of the most widely used AI languages for implementing expert systems, but it was never intended as a serious model of the human cognitive architecture. We direct the reader to Brownston, Farrell, Kant, and Martin (1985) for an excellent tutorial in OPS5 programming techniques. More recently, Forgy (1984) has developed OPS83, a production-system language with many of the features of PASCAL, making it an even less plausible cognitive model than was OPS5 (though again, this was not its goal).

Although never implemented, OPS6 (Rosenbloom and Forgy, personal communication) included a number of ambitious ideas. For instance, both lists and sets were to be supported as basic data structures in both working memory elements and productions. In addition, multiple working memories and production memories were to be allowed, each having its own sub-architectural characteristics. This flexibility was in direct contrast to the restrictions imposed for the sake of efficiency in OPS5.

In parallel with the work at "Carnegie-Mellon University," Anderson and his colleagues at Yale were developing ACTE (1976), a production-system framework that was intended to model human behavior. This architecture included two declarative respositories—a long-term memory and an "active" memory that was a subset of the first. Productions matched only against elements in active memory, but these could be retrieved from long-term memory through a process of spreading activation. Conflict resolution was tied to the strength and specificity of rules, and to the activation levels of the matched elements; moreover, the final selection of instantiations was probabilistic. Its successor was ACTF (Anderson, Kline, and Beasley 1978), an architecture that included mechanisms for learning through generalization, discrimination, and strengthening of rules. Methods for learning by composition and proceduralization were added later (Neves and Anderson, 1981).

When Anderson moved to Carnegie-Mellon University in 1978, a new generation of languages began to evolve that incorporated Forgy's matcher. Two architectures—ACTG and ACTH—existed only in transitory form, but these were followed by GRAPES (Sauers and Farrell 1982), a production-system language that placed goals in a special memory. Methods for learning by composition and proceduralization were also included in GRAPES, and were closely linked to the processing of goal structures.

Concurrently with the GRAPES effort Anderson (1983) developed ACT*, apparently the final installment in the ACT series of architectures. This framework employed the notion of excitation and inhibition among the conditions of various productions, and implemented a partial matching scheme based on a variant of Forgy's matcher. ACT* also employed three forms of declarative representation—list structures (like those used in most production systems), spatial structures, and temporally ordered lists. The architecture also supported a variety of learning methods carried over from ACTF, though the notion of spreading activation differed considerably from earlier versions.

The short-lived ACTG was developed by Langley, but a collaboration with Neches led to PRISM (Langley and Neches 1981), a production-system language that supported a *class* of cognitive architectures in the same spirit as PSG. PRISM incorporated some features of OPS4, ACTF, and HPM (Neches, chapter 4), including two declarative memories, mechanisms for spreading activation, and methods for learning by discrimination, generalization, and strengthening. Since it employed the OPS4 matcher, the language provided considerable flexibility in conflict resolution. Based on the PRISM code, Thibadeau (1982) developed CAPS, an activation-based architecture that employed a notion of thresholds and allowed rules to fire in parallel.

PRISM's major limitation was the large number of unstructured parameters used to specify a given architecture. In response, the researchers developed PRISM2 (Langley, Ohlsson, Thibadeau, and Walter 1984), which organized architectures around a set of schemas, each with a few associated parameters. This language was strongly influenced by the Rosenbloom and Forgy OPS6 design, and allowed arbitrary sets of declarative and production memories, each with its own characteristics (e.g., decay functions and conflict resolution schemes).

Rosenbloom's interest in motor behavior led to XAPS (1979) and XAPS2 (see chapter 5), architectures that allowed parallel application of productions. The first of these was activation based, and the distinguishing feature of the second was its method for learning by chunking. Laird (1983) developed SOAR, an architecture that combined the production system framework with Newell's (1980) problem space hypothesis. Finally, Laird, Rosenbloom, and Newell (1984) reported SOAR2, an architecture that combined the problem-solving features of SOAR with the chunking abilities of XAPS2.

We have attempted to summarize the developmental influences among these architectures in figure 1.1. For instance, the sequence of OPS languages descended directly from one another, though OPS3 and OPS4 should be viewed as coexisting rather than as parent and child. ACTF and OPS4 were the main influences on the initial version of PRISM, whereas PRISM2 derived from PRISM and the OPS6 design. We have not attempted to give an exhaustive treatment here. However, the architectures we have reviewed seem to be the mainstream of production system research, and most of the architectures described in this book can be traced back to one of the frameworks we have described.

1.3 The Nature of Learning

The term "learning" is similar to the term "art," in that it is very difficult to generate a satisfactory definition of either term.[6] Learning is clearly a multifaceted phenomenon that covers a variety of quite different behaviors. Perhaps the most commonly accepted "definition" is that learning is "the improvement of performance over time." However, other researchers view learning as "increased understanding," while still others view learning as involving "data compression" or the summarization of experience.

Examples of Learning

Rather than attempt to define such an ambiguous term, let us consider some examples of learning "tasks" that have been discussed in the literature of cognitive psychology and artificial intelligence. The most common of these is the task of "learning from examples," in which one is presented with positive and negative instances of some concept, and attempts to formulate some general description that covers the positive instances but none of the negative instances. For this class of tasks, improvement consists of increasing one's ability to correctly predict exemplars and nonexemplars of the concept. Chapter 3 gives a fuller treatment of this problem, which has a long history within both psychology and AI. In many ways this is the simplest of the learning tasks that has been studied (Winston 1975; Hayes-Roth and McDermott 1978; Anderson and Kline 1979; Michalski 1980).

A more complex task is that of "learning search heuristics," in which one is presented with a set of problems that require search in order to find the solution. After suitable practice on these tasks the learner is expected to acquire heuristics that reduce or eliminate the search he must carry out in solving the problems. This task has received considerable attention within AI in recent years and is also discussed in greater detail in chapters 2 and 3. The vast majority of work in this area has been within the production system framework (Brazdil 1978; Neves 1978; Langley 1983; Mitchell, Utgoff, and Banerji 1983), though only a few researchers have attempted to model human learning in this domain (Anzai 1978; Ohlsson 1983).

In the heuristics learning task the notion of improvement involves a reduction in search. On another class of procedural learning tasks improvement consists of reduction in the amount of time required to carry out an algorithmic procedure. Chapters 4, 5, and 7 focus on how such speedup effects can result from practice. In general, the mechanisms proposed to account for speedup have been quite different from those posited to account for reduced search (Lewis 1978; Neches 1981a; Neves and Anderson 1981). However, Laird, Rosenbloom, and Newell (1984) have recently outlined a production system theory that accounts for both using the same mechanism.

The task of language acquisition has also received considerable attention, though most work in this area has focused on the subproblem of grammar learning (Hedrick 1976; Berwick 1979; Anderson 1981; Langley 1982). In this task, the learner hears grammatical sentences from the language to be acquired, together with the meanings of those sentences.[7] The goal is to generate rules for mapping sentences onto their meanings, or meanings onto grammatical sentences. In the grammar learning task, improvement involves generating ever closer approximations to the adult grammar. This task is described in more detail in chapter 3.

The final class of tasks we will consider (though we have not attempted to be exhaustive) is that of cognitive development. Obviously this term covers considerable ground, but in this context we assume a fairly specific meaning. Cognitive developmental researchers have studied children's behavior on a variety of tasks, many originally invented by Piaget. There is considerable evidence that children progress through identifiable stages on each of these tasks, and one would like some theory to account for this progression. In this case, improvement consists of changes that lead toward adult behavior on a given task. Relatively few learning models have been proposed to account for these data, but we will see two of them in chapters 3 and 8.

In addition to accounting for improvement, models of human learning should also account for side effects of the learning process. For example, one effect of speedup seems to be a lack of flexibility in the resulting procedure. Neves and Anderson (1981) have shown that such phenomena arise naturally from their composition model of speedup, leading to *Einstellung* in problem-solving behavior. The list of such successful predictions is small, but at this stage in the development of our science, even theories that account for the fact of improvement must be considered major advances.

The reader may have noted that we have focused on learning from experience, as opposed to learning from instruction or learning by deduction. Similarly, we have focused on the acquisition of procedures, rather than the acquisition of declarative knowledge. This reflects a bias of the editors, and this bias is reflected in the following chapters (the chapter by Wallace, Klahr, and Bluff is the exception, addressing non-procedural issues). We will not attempt to justify this bias, for certainly non-procedural, non-experiential learning is equally a part of the human condition and must ultimately be included in any integrated model of human behavior. However, we should note that our emphasis on procedural, experience-based learning reflects current trends in cognitive science and AI, so we feel our bias is representative of these fields.

Components of Learning

Now that we have examined some examples of learning tasks, let us turn to some common features of these tasks. In particular, within any task that involves learning from experience, one can identify four component problems that must be addressed:[8]

1. *Aggregation.* The learner must identify the basic objects that constitute the instances from which he will learn. In other words, he must identify the *part-of* relations, or determine the appropriate *chunks*.

2. *Clustering.* The learner must identify which objects or events should be grouped together into a class. In other words, he must identify the *instance-of* relations, or generate an *extensional* definition of the concept.

3. *Characterization.* The learner must formulate some general description or hypothesis that characterizes instances of the concept. In other words, he must generate an *intensional* definition of the concept.[9]

4. *Storage/indexing.* The learner must store the characterization in some manner that lets him retrieve it, as well as make use of the retrieved knowledge.

We would argue that any system that learns from experience must address each of these four issues, even if the responses to some are degenerate. In fact, we will see that many of the traditional learning tasks allow one to ignore some of the components, making them idealizations of the general task of learning from experience.

For instance, the task of learning from examples can be viewed as a degenerate case of the general learning task, in that the tutor solves the aggregation and clustering problems by providing the learner with positive and negative instances of the concept to be learned. In addition, since only one (or at most a few) concept(s) must be acquired, there is no need to index them in any sophisticated manner—a simple list is quite sufficient. Thus, the task of learning from examples can be viewed as "distilled" characterization, since this is the only component of learning that must be addressed. This simplification has proved quite useful to learning researchers, and many of the characterization methods that were initially developed for the task of learning from examples have been successfully transferred to more complex problems.

Similarly the task of heuristics learning ignores the issue of aggregation, assuming that individual problem states constitute the objects on which learning should be based.[10] However, methods for heuristics learning must directly respond to the clustering issue because no tutor is available to identify positive and negative instances. In fact, within the framework of learning search heuristics, the clustering problem is identical to the well-known problem of credit and blame assignment. Methods for heuristics learning must also address the characterization problem because one must generate some general description of the situations under which each operator should be applied. Finally, the storage issue has generally been ignored in research on heuristics learning because relatively small numbers of operators have been involved.

Many of the models of speedup involve some form of chunking, and this approach can be viewed as another variant on the general task of learning from experience. In this case the structure to be learned is some sequential or spatial configuration of perceptions or actions. Unlike the tasks of learning from examples and heuristics learning, chunking tasks force one to directly address the *aggregation* issue because one must decide which components to include as parts of the higher-level structure. However, in most chunking methods the *characterization* problem is made trivial because new rules are based directly on existing rules, for which the level of generality is already known. Also even in methods that address issues of characterization, chunks are based on single instances, so that the *clustering* problem is also bypassed.

Finally, the grammar learning task can be viewed a fourth variant on the general problem of learning from experience. Like the chunking task, it forces one to respond to the problem of *aggregation* because it must form sequential structures such as "noun phrase" and "verb phrase." Like the heuristics learning task, it requires one to address the *clustering* problem because it must group words into disjunctive classes like "noun" and "verb" without the aid of a tutor. It also forces one to deal with characterization issues, though in some approaches the set of chunks in which a class like "noun" occurs can be viewed *characterization* of that class. Storage is also a significant issue in grammar learning because many rules may be required to summarize even a small grammar.

It is interesting to note that production system models of learning sometimes provide their own answer to the storage/indexing problem because the conditions of productions can be efficiently stored in a discrimination network that both reduces space requirements and speeds up the matching process. Forgy (1982) has described this storage scheme in some detail, and many of the models described in this book rely on Forgy's approach. Thus, one can argue that within the production system framework, only the issues of aggregation, clustering, and characterization must be addressed. Although some readers may disagree with this assumption, most of the chapters in this volume adopt it either implicitly or explicitly.

Mechanisms of Learning

In the preceding sections we considered the learning *phenomena* that require explanation, followed by the *components* of learning that any model must address. In this section we consider various *mechanisms* that have been proposed to account for the learning process, both in the following chapters and elsewhere in the literature.

Within the production-system framework the nature of the recognize-act cycle constrains the points at which learning can have an effect. There are three such choice-points; a production system's repertoire of behaviors can be changed by affecting the outcome of (1) the process of matching productions, (2) the process of conflict resolution, and (3) the process of applying productions. Let us examine different mechanisms that have been proposed in terms of the manner in which they affect the recognize-act cycle.

The most obvious way to affect the set of applicable productions found by the matching process is to add new productions to the set. However, this makes certain assumptions: matching must either be exhaustive, or the new production must be added in such a way that guarantees it will be considered by the matcher. Waterman's (1970, 1975) early work took the latter approach, adding new rules above those productions they were intended to mask (since rules were matched in a linear order). The work on stage models of development (Young 1976) employed similar methods. After Forgy (1979b) presented an efficient method for computing all matched instantiations, the exhaustive scheme became more popular.

The earliest approach to creating new rules employed a production-building command in the action side of productions. This function took an arbitrary condition-action form as its argument and, whenever the rule containing it was applied, would instantiate the form and add a new rule to production memory. Of course, simple instantiations of a general form are not very interesting, but one could use other productions to *construct* more useful rules, which were then passed to the production-building rule. The OPS family of architectures called this function *build*, while the ACT family used the term *designate*. Although this method was quite popular in the early work on adaptive productions, it has now been largely replaced by other methods.

Another way to affect the set of matched productions is to modify the conditions of existing rules or to construct variants on existing rules with slightly different condition sides.[11] In practice, most researchers have opted for the latter approach, sometimes to model the incremental nature of human learning and other times to respond to complexities in the learning task such as the presence of noise. In such approaches, the generation of variants must be combined with methods for modifying the conflict resolution process, so that better variants eventually come to mask the rules from which they were generated.

Two obvious methods present themselves for modifying the conditions of productions. Although these mechanisms had been present in the AI literature for some time, Anderson, Kline, and Beasley (1978) were the first to use them in models of human learning, labeling them with the terms *generalization* and *discrimination*. The first process involves creating a new rule (or modifying an existing one) so that it is *more* general than an existing rule, meanwhile retaining the same actions. The term "generalization" has also been used to denote *any* process for moving from data to some general rule or hypothesis, but Anderson intended a much more specific sense. The second process of discrimination involves the creation of a new rule (or modifying an existing one) so that it is *less* general than an existing rule, while still retaining the same actions. The two mechanisms lead to opposite results, though in most models they are not inverses in terms of the conditions under which they are evoked.

Within production-system models there are three basic ways to form more general or specific rules, each corresponding to a different notion of generality. First, one can add or delete conditions from the left-hand side of a production. The former generates a more specific rule, since it will match in fewer situations, while the latter gives a more general rule. The second method involves replacing variables with constant terms, or vice versa. Changing variables to constants reduces generality, whereas changing constants to variables increases generality. The final method revolves around the notion of class variables or is-a hierarchies. For example, one may know that both dogs and cats are mammals and that both mammals and birds are vertebrates. Replacing a term from this hierarchy with one below it in the hierarchy decreases generality, while the inverse operation increases generality.

These techniques have been used in programs modeling behavior on concept acquisition experiments (Anderson and Kline 1979), language comprehension and production at various age levels (Langley 1982; Anderson 1981), geometry theorem proving (Anderson, Greeno, Kline, and Neves 1981), and various puzzle-solving tasks (Langley 1982). We will not elaborate on these learning mechanisms here; Langley describes them in considerable detail in chapter 3.

Note that methods like discrimination and generalization directly respond to the characterization issue we described in the last section. Both methods require instances that have been clustered into some class, and both attempt to generate some general description of those classes based on the observed instances. As one might expect, these methods were first proposed by researchers working on the task learning from examples (Winston 1975; Hayes-Roth and McDermott 1978; Mitchell 1982; Brazdil 1978).

Once a set of matching rule instantiations have been found, a production-system architecture still must make some determination about which instantiation(s) in that set will be executed. Thus, conflict resolution offers another decision point in the recognize-act cycle where the behavior of the system can be affected. This turns out to be particularly important because many models of human learning attempt to model its incremental nature, assuming that learning involves the construction of successively closer approximations to correct knowledge over a series of experiences.

The knowledge represented in new production rules are essentially hypotheses about the correct rules. A learning system must maintain a balance between the need for feedback obtained by trying new productions and the need for stable performance obtained by relying on those productions that have proved themselves successful. This means that a learning system must distinguish between rule *applicability* and rule *desirability*, and be able to alter its selections as it discovers more about desirability. Production systems have embodied a number of schemes for performing conflict resolution, ranging from simple fixed orderings on the rules in PSG (Newell and McDermott 1975) and PAS (Waterman 1975), to various forms of weights or "strengths" (Anderson 1976; Langley, chapter 3), to complex schemes that are not uniform across the entire set of productions as in HPM (Neches, chapter 4). Combined with certain timing assumptions, these schemes can be used to predict speedup effects as well as affect more global behavior.

Any production-system model of learning must take into account the parameters used during conflict resolution. This concern goes beyond learning models, since any system with multiple context-sensitive knowledge sources may have overlapping knowledge items that conflict.[12] However, the problems of conflict resolution are exacerbated in a learning system because the knowledge items being resolved may change over time and because new items must be added with consideration for how conflicts with existing items will be handled. Later in the chapter, we will return to the constraints that learning imposes on acceptable conflict resolution mechanisms.

After conflicts have been dealt with, the instantiation(s) selected for execution are applied. Although the opportunities arising at this point largely parallel those involved in matching, there is little parallel in the methods that have been proposed. For instance, one can imagine methods that add or delete the actions of existing rules, but we know of only one such suggestion in the literature (Anderson 1983).

However, three additional learning mechanisms have been proposed that lead to rules with new conditions *and* actions. The first of these is known as *composition*, and was originally proposed by Lewis (1978) to account for speedup as the result of practice. Basically, this method combines two or more rules into a new rule with the conditions and actions of the component rules. However, conditions that are guaranteed to be met by one of the actions are not included. For instance, if we compose the rules **(AB → CD) and (DE → F)**, the rule **(ABE → CDF)** would result. Of course, the process is not quite this simple; most composition methods are based on instantiations of productions rather than the rules themselves, and one must take variable bindings into account in generating the new rule. The presence of negated conditions also complicates matters.

Note that composition is a form of chunking, and thus is one response to the aggregation problem we discussed earlier. However, the combination procedure outlined here is not sufficient; this must be combined with some theory about the conditions under which such combinations occur. Some theories of composition (Lewis 1978; Neves and Anderson 1981) assume that composition occurs whenever two rules apply in sequence, while others (Anderson 1983) posit that composition transpires whenever some goal is achieved. Naturally, different conditions for chunking lead to radically different forms of learning. The chapter by Lewis describes the composition process in more detail.

Newell and Rosenbloom (1981) have proposed another response to the aggregation issue in their theory of learning by chunking, showing that the learning curves predicted by their model are quite similar to those observed in a broad range of learning tasks. Rosenbloom and Newell (chapter 5) present results from this approach to modeling practice effects.

Yet another mechanism for creating new rules has been called *proceduralization* (Neves and Anderson 1981). This involves constructing a very specific version of some general rule, based on some instantiation of the rule that has been applied. Ohlsson (chapter 6) has used a similar mechanism to model learning on transitive reasoning tasks. In some ways, this method can be viewed as a form of discrimination learning because it generates more specific variants of an existing rule. However, the conditions for application tend to be quite different, and the use to which these methods have been put have quite different flavors. For instance, discrimination has been used almost entirely to account for reducing search or eliminating errors, whereas proceduralization has been used to account for speedup effects and automatization. But perhaps these are simply different names for the results of the same underlying phenomena.

Additional Learning Mechanisms

Langley, Neches, Neves, and Anzai (1980) have argued that self-modifying systems must address two related problems: including *correct* rules for when to perform the various actions available to the system and developing *interesting* new actions to perform. However, most of the models that have been developed in recent years have focused on the first of these issues, and some researchers (e.g., Anderson 1983) have asserted that mechanisms such as composition, generalization, and discrimination are sufficient to account for all learning.

Nevertheless, evidence is starting to build up that these processes, although apparently necessary components of a computational learning theory, are by no means sufficient. The evidence for this comes from a number of recent studies that have tried to characterize differences between the strategies employed by experts and novices. For example, Lewis (1981) has documented differences between expert and novice solution methods for algebra expressions, and shown that the differences could not have been produced by composition. Lewis' argument consists of a demonstration that the procedures produced by a process of composition would not apply correctly in all cases. To ensure that a new procedure would work correctly, additional rules must be produced by some process other than composition.

Another example of complex expert strategies appears in Hunter's (1968) analysis of the procedures employed by a "mental calculator," a subject with highly exceptional skills at mental arithmetic. There appear to be a number of aspects to the subject's special abilities. Some, such as his large collection of number facts, might be explained in terms of mechanisms like the Neves and Anderson (1981) "knowledge compilation" model. However, there are many aspects of the subject's performance for which it is very difficult to see how syntactic learning mechanisms could have produced the observed results.

For instance, Hunter found that his subject's superior ability to mentally solve large multiplication problems was due to a procedure that performed the component multiplications in left-to-right order while keeping a running total of the intermediate products. This contrasts to the traditional pencil-and-paper algorithm in which columns are multiplied right-to-left, with the subproducts written down and totaled afterward in order to compute the product. The left-to-right procedure, which drastically reduced the working memory demands of any given problem, requires a massive reorganization of the control structure for the traditional multiplication procedure.

The reorganization involves much more than refinements in the rules governing when suboperations are performed. Such refinements could presumably be produced by generalization and discrimination mechanisms. However, producing this new procedure requires the introduction of new operations (or at least new goal structures), such as those involved in keeping a running total of the subproducts. Those new operations, and the control structure governing the sequence of their execution, require the introduction of novel elements or goals—something that generalization, discrimination, and composition are clearly not able to do.

Similar conclusions can be drawn from studies on expert/novice differences in physics problem solving (Simon and Simon 1978; Larkin 1981). A general observation in those studies is that experts rely on working-forward strategies while novices are much more inclined to use means-ends analysis. Generally, the mechanism used to explain this relies on a method first developed by Anzai called "block-elimination" (Anzai and Simon 1979). In this method one remembers a state S in which some desired action (operator) A cannot be executed because its preconditions are not met. If heuristic search later generates another action B that eliminates the blockage (enabling A to be applied), then a new rule in constructed. This rule has the form: "If you are in state S and you want to apply action A, then try to apply action B." In other words, this approach leads to new subgoals and to rules that propose when they should be generated.

The examples presented thus far provide motivation for seeking learning mechanisms beyond composition, proceduralization, generalization, and discrimination. However, our argument has rested on cases in which no evidence was available about the intermediate forms of the acquired procedures. There are very few studies in which learning sequences, and the intermediate procedures produced within them, have been directly observed. Fortunately, a similar picture emerges from two studies in which those observations could be made.

In the first of these studies, Neches (1981b) traced procedure development in the command sequences issued by an expert user of a computer graphics editing system. In doing this, he found a number of changes that involved reordering operations and replanning procedure segments on the basis of efficiency considerations. In the second study, Anzai and Simon (1979) examined a subject solving and re-solving a five-disk Tower of Hanoi puzzle. They found a number of changes in procedure that seemed inconsistent with strict composition / generalization / discrimination models. These included eliminating moves that produced returns to previously visited problem states, establishing subgoals to perform actions that eliminated barriers to desired actions, and transforming partially specified goals (e.g., moving a disk off a peg) into fully specified goals (e.g., moving the disk from the peg to a specific other peg).

A key observation about these examples is that the learning appears to involve reasoning on the basis of knowledge about the structure of procedures in general, and the semantics of a given procedure in particular. In each of the examples we have considered, procedures were modified through the construction of novel elements rather than through simple deletions, additions, or combinations of existing elements. This leads us to believe there exist important aspects of learning that involve the use of both general and domain-specific knowledge about procedures. Neches (chapter 4) examines this form of learning in more detail.

1.4 Implications of Learning for Production-System Architectures

In the preceding sections, we have been concerned with the mapping between learning phenomena (viewed from a psychological perspective) and explanations of these phenomena in terms of production systems. Attempts to build production-system-based learning models have led, among other things, to a much better understanding of what does and does not work in production-system architectures. In this section, we try to summarize the lessons that that have been learned for three major aspects of production systems.

Pattern Matching

In practice, languages for expressing production conditions generally turn out to be fairly simple. In particular, they generally rely on pattern-matching rather than the testing of arbitrary predicates. That is, the language of condition sides describes abstract configurations of data elements. A production's conditions are said to be satisfied when data in working memory instantiates the described configuration in a consistent manner. This means that the condition side specifies a pattern consisting of constants and variables, and the data in working memory matches that pattern by utilizing the same constants in the same places as they appeared in the pattern, with constants that correspond to variables in the pattern appearing consistently in the same places as those variables.

The description in the preceding paragraph may seem both obvious and redundant, given our discussion of production systems. However, note that rule-based systems need not operate within a pattern-matching paradigm. In principle, the condition sides of production rules could be arbitrarily complex and have arbitrarily powerful predicates.[13] From a logical standpoint, any class of expressions that evaluated to true or false (applicable or not applicable) could serve to specify production conditions. It is worthwhile to examine the advantages of the pattern-matching paradigm. We will argue that there are three constraints on production systems that have emerged from learning research and that the pattern-matching paradigm serves to satisfy:

1. *Efficiency and adaptivity.* Since the grain size of productions is relatively small (i.e., little happens with each production firing), and since humans are real-time systems that must make timely responses to external events, it is important to iterate through the recognize-act cycle as quickly as possible.

2. *Even granularity.* Learning mechanisms often depend on taking fragments of different existing rules, making inferences about the contribution of those fragments to the "success" or "failure" of the rule, and modifying rules by adding or deleting those fragments. Therefore, it is important that those fragments all represent small and approximately equal units of

knowledge. If a fragment represents too large a decision, then the reasoning that went into that decision is not accessible to learning mechanisms. This means that that reasoning cannot be re-used elsewhere if it is correct, and cannot be corrected if it is not.

3. *Analyzability.* As just mentioned, learning mechanisms operate by manipulating fragments of rules (or instantiations of rules), either to construct new rules or to "edit" existing rules. This can only occur if the mechanisms can predict the effect their manipulations will have on behavior, and this in turn requires that there be consistent principles about the nature of conditions and the effects of altering them. Put another way, for learning mechanisms to operate in a domain-independent way (i.e., without built-in knowledge about the domain in which learning is taking place), these mechanisms must operate on the structure or syntax of productions rather than on their content or semantics.

To understand the implications of these constraints, let us first consider why they rule out the extreme opposite of pattern matching: using the connectives of first-order predicate calculus to combine predicates implemented as functions that return a truth value. In a rule-based system that allowed such conditions, one could generate rules with condition sides that required extremely long (if not infinite) amounts of time to test, thus violating the efficiency constraint. It would be possible to (in fact, it would be difficult *not* to) have a set of predicates that differed widely in their complexity, sophistication, and generality, thus violating the granularity constraint. The absence of restrictions on the form of expressions (much less the content of the predicates) would make it very difficult to predict the effects of any but the simplest changes to a condition side. This means that two syntactically equivalent modifications could have semantically quite different effects, due to differences between predicates. Thus, the analyzability constraint is also violated.

Conflict Resolution

Something like the analyzability constraint for pattern matching applies to conflict resolution as well. In order for learning mechanisms to alter behavior, the productions they generate must be applied, which in turn means that they must be selected for application. Frequently, to achieve the desired effect of altering behavior, the new rule must "mask" some other rule that previously would have fired in the current circumstances; in other words, the new rule must be selected in place of the old rule. This means that the mechanisms that create and modify new rules must be designed with significant respect for the mechanisms of conflict resolution, and vice versa.

The earliest versions of production systems relied on a conflict resolution policy called "production ordering," in which the set of productions was completely ordered by each rule's position in a list. The highest-ranked production whose conditions were satisfied was selected for firing. In some variants on this approach, productions were only partially ordered; these systems assumed that the conditions on the unordered productions would be mutually exclusive. Lacking any efficient method for computing all matches, this conflict resolution scheme was a natural approach.

Difficulties arose for this approach when a new production was added to the set, since some mechanism had to decide the position of the new production in the ordering. One solution was to blindly add the new production to the top of the list. Waterman (1975) employed a more sophisticated method, adding a new rule immediately above the highest existing rule that shared a condition element with the new rule. The reasoning behind this heuristic was that any rules sharing a common condition were likely to be related, and that old rules should be masked by new rules since the new rules are likely to be improvements.

The problem with this approach (and others we will be considering) is that it still has only a weak notion of which rules are related in the masking sense. Consider the following example from Neches's goal-oriented HPM system (chapter 4). At any point in time, a number of different goals may be "active," which means that they are posted as requiring attention. To avoid a proliferation of goals, the system must terminate unnecessary or unachievable ones as early as possible. Productions that do so will appear to have much in common with productions that help process such goals. Yet, if the system acquires a new goal-processing production, this rule should not mask any goal-terminating productions. The syntactic nature of production-ordering methods makes it difficult to find a place to add new rules that will respect such constraints.

Production ordering also fails to satisfy a number of other criteria for an effective conflict resolution policy. The most important is maintaining balance between persistence on existing goals and sensitivity to changes in the environment. (For a more thorough discussion of these issues, see McDermott and Forgy 1978.) The production system must give enough priority to the results of its own recent activity to focus on a goal and carry it through to completion (as opposed to oscillating between many different goals while only slowly making progress on any given goal). At the same time, humans must interact with an external environment, and this requires that production system models of human behavior be able to shift attention in response to events in the outside world.

In order to meet these demands, production systems generally employ a hybrid approach, in which the set of applicable productions is whittled down by applying a sequence of conflict resolution policies, rather than a single all-encompassing policy. OPS2 (Forgy and McDermott 1977) is an example of this approach. The OPS2 conflict resolution scheme operates in five successive stages:

1. *Refraction.* Once executed, an instantiation of a given production may not be executed again (until one of the matched elements has been deleted and readded to working memory).

2. *Recency.* Production instantiations matching recently asserted data should be selected over those matching older data.

3. *Specificity.* Instantiations of productions with the greatest number of condition elements and constant terms should be selected.

4. *Production recency.* Instantiations of recently created productions should be selected over those from older productions.

5. *Random selection.* If the preceding rules were not sufficient to produce a unique selection, then a production instantiation should be chosen at random.

These policies were intended to satisfy a number of concerns. Refraction ensured that the system would move on to new tasks and would not tend to enter infinite loops. Recency ensured that the system would not tend to oscillate between goals but would focus on the most recent one, attending to that goal until it was accomplished. At the same time, this policy still allowed for switching attention in response to external events, since those also would entail new data in working memory.

The third criterion, specificity, attempted to ensure that the "best" production would be selected. Since rules containing more conditions and more constant terms tend to be more specific than those with fewer conditions or constants, and therefore the one most closely tailored to fit the current situation, they should be most appropriate. The criterion of production recency was intended to favor the results of learning. Much like the notions behind production ordering, the assumption was that new rules were likely to be improvements over old rules and therefore should be given an opportunity to mask the prior ones. The final policy of random selection was intended to ensure that the system would only fire one production per cycle; in parallel systems that allow more than one production to be executed in a cycle, it is possible to execute productions that are at cross-purposes.

Policies like those in the OPS family of languages have generally been successful at controlling production systems which do not change greatly. They have been used in practical applications, such as McDermott's (1982) R1 expert system, involving large numbers of productions and calling for a high degree of efficiency. However, though they are clearly an improvement, such policies have not proved completely satisfactory where learning is concerned. Fortunately, Forgy's (1979b) work on matching provides a method for efficiently computing all matched rules. This in turn provides considerable flexibility in the conflict resolution process, so that one is not locked into a particular set of decision criteria.

One early target of dissatisfaction concerned criteria that favored newly acquired rules over older rules. Such policies ignored the need for learning mechanisms that relied on incremental refinement of rules. Any policy that always favors new productions ignores the possibility that intermediate stages of learning might produce errorful rules. Furthermore, such a policy provides no help in selecting between multiple variants of an existing rule which are generated by some learning mechanisms. Langley's work on the AMBER and SAGE systems (chapter 3) illustrates both the problems and the general approach taken toward solving them in many recent production system architectures.

The basic idea was to introduce a notion of production *strength* as a factor in conflict resolution. The strength (or weight) of a production is a parameter that is adjusted to indicate the system's current confidence in the correctness and/or usefulness of that rule. There have been a number of different approaches taken in various production system architectures toward making use of this general concept. In some variants, the strength or weight of productions are subject to a threshold; rules below the threshold simply are not considered. In other variants, the strength is a positive factor in selection; "stronger" rules are preferred over weaker ones. In still other variants, the notion of strength is used to make selection less deterministic; strength is treated as a measure of the probability that a rule will fire given that its conditions are satisfied.

Although these variants all make different statements about the precise usage of production strength, the particular mechanisms all serve a common purpose—enabling a phase of evaluation and testing for proposed rules, rather than forcing an all-or-nothing decision about them. To this end, mechanisms for affecting the strength of a rule are needed. Some researchers have postulated automatic mechanisms. For example, in Langley's AMBER and SAGE systems a rule is strengthened each time a learning mechanism rediscovers it; thus, more weight is given to rules that have been learned a number of times, even if they have been created by different learning methods.

Although the notion of production strength is probably the major change in production system architectures that has resulted from research on learning, other problems have also received attention. In particular, Neches (1981b) has argued that a uniform conflict resolution scheme places an excessive burden on learning mechanisms. (By a uniform conflict resolution scheme, we mean a set of conflict resolution policies that are applied consistently to all applicable productions with no special exceptions.) The argument, which is only briefly touched on in his chapter in this volume, is that a uniform conflict resolution scheme forces several different kinds of knowledge to be confounded in the conditions of productions. Three kinds are particularly important:

1. Conditions that define the context in which the production is applicable—in other words, knowledge about the circumstances in which it is meaningful to execute the production.
2. Conditions that enable processing on the action side of a rule, usually by causing values to be assigned to variables that are referenced on the action side—in other words, knowledge about prerequisite information for operations on the right-hand side.
3. Conditions that serve to affect flow of control by causing otherwise applicable productions to be inapplicable or by affecting the ranking of applicable productions during the selection process—in other words, heuristic knowledge about desired sequencing of productions.

In response to these observations, Neches has proposed having different conflict resolution associated with different *classes* of rules, with each class being responsible for different aspects of behavior.

Working Memory

All modern notions of the human information processing architecture, although differing in their details, agree on the importance of distinguishing two aspects of memory. On the one hand, there seems to be a limited capacity working memory that changes rapidly over time. Working memory plays the same role for humans as input/output buffers and processing registers play for computers. On the other hand, there is also a large capacity, long-term memory that is much more stable. We have already seen how production system models instantiate this distinction.

The production system for subtraction that we presented earlier was quite simple, requiring only a few types of working memory elements. However, this was a performance model, and learning systems require more information than is strictly necessary for performance.[14] This extra information must be retained somewhere, and the most likely place is working memory. Thus, a focus on learning imposes constraints on models of working memory that would not arise from a concern with performance alone.

The state of the art is not sufficiently advanced that we can exhaustively list all of the different kinds of information used by learning mechanisms, but we can extract a partial list from the mechanisms discussed elsewhere in this chapter. For example, the minimum information requirements of composition methods are behavioral records (in the form of at least two production instantiations), along with temporal information (in the form of the sequential ordering between the two instantiations).

Generalization and discrimination methods require more information, including knowledge of the success/failure of rules and the context in which that success or failure occurred. In simple tasks such as learning from examples, immediate feedback is provided to the learner. However, more complex learning tasks require the system to *infer* the success or failure of individual rules; Minsky (1963) has called this the *credit assignment* problem. Moreover, since credit or blame may not be assigned to a rule until long after it has applied, the context of that application (generally the state of working memory at that point) must be stored for later retrieval.

For example, when generalization and discrimination methods are used to determine heuristic conditions for problem-solving operators (Sleeman, Langley, and Mitchell 1982), the learning system must retain information about its search toward a problem solution. After the problem is solved by weak search methods, feedback is obtained by asking whether or not actions that were tried were on the final solution path. Credit assignment is performed by attributing success to the productions that suggested actions on the solution path, and by attributing failure to productions that suggested actions leading off the final solution path. In these more sophisticated models, information must be retained about the sequential ordering of previous knowledge states, as well as the states themselves.

Similar themes can be found in Anzai's work on "learning by doing," which is reviewed as part of chapter 2. Anzai models a number of complementary processes that contribute to the development of procedures for solving problems that can initially only be solved by general search methods. His view of learning involves several phases. In the first phase a system learns to a narrow the search space by avoiding unproductive branches in the search tree ("bad moves"). The key to this phase is the use of heuristics for identifying bad branches, such as noting action sequences that return a problem solution to a previous state. This first phase involves retaining much the same sort of knowledge as required by generalization and discrimination.

In Anzai's second phase of learning, a system attempts to infer subgoals ("good moves"). This depends on noting actions that cannot be carried out when they are first proposed because some preconditions are violated but that are applied later, after another action has satisfied those preconditions. This second phase of learning requires information that goes beyond that needed for the first phase, since it must retain in memory both unsatisfied goals and the reasons they were not satisfied. More generally, the kind of information being retained has to do with planning, that is, the consideration of actions separate from the performance of those actions.

Anzai's later phases of learning involve acquiring associations between action sequences and the subgoals learned in the second phase, as well as grouping sequences into useful units. Thus, the subgoals acquired in the preceding phase now become additional information items that must be retained.

The developmental mechanisms described in chapter 8 on BAIRN by Wallace, Klahr, and Bluff rely on analyzing and comparing multiple sequences of actions. The information required to do so is organized primarily at the level of "nodes," which are groups of related productions. (Nodes may be loosely analogized to Anzai's subgoals, but are much more fundamental to the BAIRN architecture.) A "time line" represents the chronological sequence of node activations, along with the activating input, the resulting state, and a flag for cases of unexpected results. (Thus, information about expectations is an additional implicit aspect of the information demands of their learning model.) If a node is in "focal consciousness" (i.e., in the foreground of conscious attention), then information is also retained about the sequence of productions fired in the course of processing that node. In addition to this information, the learning mechanisms also make use of an "experience list" associated with each node, which contains the memory of action sequences that commonly follow the given node. BAIRN also makes use of information about the applicability conditions of nodes, and about their superordinate/subordinate relationships to other nodes.

The strategy transformation model described in Neches' chapter focuses on the refinement and optimization of procedures that are already well defined. His approach postulates a set of heuristics for detecting opportunities to improve the cognitive efficiency of procedures. After analyzing the information requirements of these heuristics, he proposed 11 information categories utilized by his learning mechanisms.[15] Most of the cases described here also seem to fit into these categories:

1. *Goals and procedures.*
2. *Episodes*—the structure representing a single problem solution.
3. *Events*—individual instances of goals with particular inputs.
4. *Inputs*—internal concepts or representations of external states considered by a goal.
5. *Results*—concepts or state representations resulting from a goal.
6. Relationships between *goals* and their *subgoals.*
7. The *effort* associated with achieving a goal.
8. *Temporal orderings* of events (or production firings).
9. *Processing information* (size of working memory, presence in working memory, etc.).
10. *Descriptive information*—assertions about properties associated with a concept.
11. *Frequency information*—knowledge about how frequently a concept is accessed.

The work by Neches and others indicates the large variety of information that is prerequisite to learning. This also has implications for the sheer *amount* of information that a learning/performance system must be able to sift through. Models of performance, or even of particular learning mechanisms, can gloss over this issue by considering only the information relevant to the topic being modeled. However, a complete model of an information-processing system must handle the entire range of information categories.

Since a system cannot know in advance what information it will need in order to learn, it must be prepared to cope with all information that it is likely to need. There are two ways in which it could do so. One is a strategy of neglecting some of the information available, perhaps even on a random basis, and relying on the large number of learning opportunities presented by the world to ensure that important aspects that are missed on one trial will be found on another. The other is a strategy of retaining all sorts of information and relying on strong attention-focusing processes to sift out information that will lead to productive learning. The distinction between these two approaches centers on whether the amount of potential information is reduced to manageable quantities by refusing to represent the full set to begin with, or by attending to items selected from a relatively larger pool.

We have just seen that the range of information required for learning can be rather broad. Mechanisms of the first sort, those which try to neglect information, would have to be very weak and would have to be designed to err in the direction of keeping unnecessary information. Any other alternative risks eliminating juxtapositions in memory of information items critical to learning. Therefore, mechanisms for controlling focus of attention—already an important issue in production system architectures because of the data-driven nature of such systems—become a vital concern in production system architectures for learning. This is particularly so when we wish to map such production system architectures back to models of human information architectures.

There are a number of critical choice points in the design of a production system architecture where the attention-focusing issue must be addressed (Neches 1982). These primarily fall into two classes: processes governing the contents of working memory and processes governing conflict resolution. Processes involved in conflict resolution contribute primarily in an indirect way, by enabling processes that manage working memory to be designed in ways that minimize working memory size.[16] For example, as Neches argues in his chapter, systems that allow multiple productions to fire within a single cycle reduce the amount of time that data must reside in memory before receiving attention. This allows data to be moved out of working memory sooner than would otherwise be possible, thereby reducing the amount of information requiring space in working memory at any given point in time.

As the size of working memory grows, so do the difficulties of a system trying to select productions and maintain a consistent pattern of behavior, simply because the number of distracting alternatives increases. Therefore, it is important to keep working memory relatively small. The processes that move information into working memory have to be oriented toward entering as little as possible. Processes that remove items from working memory need to be oriented toward eliminating as much as possible and toward doing this as soon as possible.

1.5 Summary

The goal of this chapter has been to provide both an overview of production-system architectures and a perspective on the issues that arise in applying them to the areas of learning and development. We have attempted to provide readers with a framework for understanding the different systems described in this book in terms of the issues that each system was designed to address. Our framework rests on three fundamental premises:

1. *The structure of production-system architectures provides insight into the nature of the human information-processing system architecture.* This premise derives from observations about similarities in terms of both structural organization and behavioral properties. Structurally, production systems provide analogies to (and, in fact, have helped fuel) modern cognitive psychology's notions about the relationship between long-term memory and short-term working memory, and about the interaction between procedural and declarative knowledge. Behaviorally, strong analogies can be seen between humans and production systems with respect to their abilities to mix goal-driven and event-driven processes, and with their tendency to process information in parallel at the recognition level and serially at higher cognitive levels.

2. *Learning is the fundamental aspect of intelligence; we cannot say that we understand intelligence, or the structure of the human mind, until we have a model that accounts for how it learns.* Although the first 20 years of the information-processing approach to psychology paid little attention to

learning, in recent years its centrality has been reasserted by many researchers (cf. Anderson 1982; Langley and Simon 1981).

3. *All information-processing-system architectures, whether human or artificial, must obey certain constraints in order to facilitate the process of learning.* It is these constraints that give rise to the seemingly complex particulars of individual production system architectures. Thus, following from our second premise, an understanding of production-system models of learning and development is not just a step toward understanding of machine learning. It is a step toward understanding the nature of human learning and, by extension, a necessary step toward a complete understanding of both human and machine intelligence.

Given these premises, the starting point for discussion has been the adaptation of the generic architecture of production systems to the specific needs of learning. All production systems consist of a working memory, a collection of condition-action rules that apply to and operate upon that memory, and a processor that executes the *recognize-act cycle* of selecting productions to apply and evaluating them to determine their effect upon the working memory. In considering the learning-relevant specializations of this generic description, we emphasized two broad topic areas: *the nature of the learning task*, and the *choice-points for introducing learning mechanisms into production-system architectures.*

The Nature of the Learning Task

Throughout this chapter we reiterated two different, but complementary, themes about the design issues that researchers in learning must face when building a particular learning model. We urge readers to consider the following chapters with respect to the checklist of issues that can be constructed from these two themes. The first theme was essentially oriented toward characterizing the methods necessary in a complete learning system. The second was concerned with the goals of learning systems.

First, under the rubric of "components of learning," we presented some assertions about *requirements* for learning systems. We argued that there were four subproblems that all learning researchers must address—either by providing mechanisms in their model, or by narrowing their self-assigned mission so as to render the requirement moot. *Aggregation* is the problem of identifying the data from which learning will be done, separating signal from noise. *Clustering* is the problem of developing extensional definitions for concepts based on those data (e.g., recognizing positive and negative instances of a concept). *Characterization* is the problem of developing intensional hypotheses or descriptions of concepts and classes identified in clustering, so that instances not previously encountered can be recognized and utilized. *Storage/Indexing* is the problem of saving those characterizations so that they can be retrieved and applied in appropriate situations.

Second, under the various headings of "*correct versus interesting*" or "*applicability versus desirability*," we suggested that learning is focused toward some purpose. Learning systems must address two concerns. They must ensure that the conditions of their new rules are (or eventually will become) correct, in the sense that the rules are applicable whenever appropriate and not applicable under any other circumstances. They must also ensure that the actions of these rules are useful, in the sense that there is some criteria by which the system is better off for having behaved according to its new rules rather than its old ones. Not everything that could be learned is worth learning; therefore mechanisms that produce correct rules do not necessarily produce useful rules.

Introducing Learning Mechanisms into Production-System Architectures

Operationalized into production-system terms, a system has "learned" if, as a result of experience, it comes to apply a different production in some situation than it would have applied in the equivalent situation at an earlier point in its lifetime. Given the processing cycle of production-system architectures, all learning mechanisms can be characterized as seeking to accomplish this goal by manipulating one or more of the following processes within that cycle: production matching, conflict resolution, and application.

We also presented several constraints to which learning systems are subject, and argued that the natures of both learning mechanisms and production-system architectures are shaped by the need to interact in ways that satisfy these constraints. Among the constraints considered were *efficiency and adaptivity*, *even granularity* of rules, and *analyzability* of rules. In preceding sections, we indicated how these constraints have led modern production-system theories in particular directions. These include favoring exhaustive pattern-matching processes over other possible ways of stating and testing production conditions, moves toward refined conflict resolution techniques involving notions like "strength" of production rules, and an increased emphasis on building a sensitivity to goals into the architecture for both conflict resolution and control of working memory contents.

We hope that the present chapter has provided a useful overview of production systems and their role in modeling learning and development. As we will see in the following chapters, different researchers have taken quite different paths in developing self-modifying production systems. However, underlying these differences are a common set of goals and a common framework, and it is these common concerns that we have attempted to present. We believe that the production-system approach holds great promise for understanding the nature of human learning and development, and we hope that future researchers will build upon the excellent beginning described in the chapters that follow.

Notes

Preparation of this chapter was supported in part by a grant from the Spencer Foundation to David Klahr, and in part by Contract N00014-85-15-0373 from the Personnel and Training Research Program, Office of Naval Research, to Pat Langley. We would like to thank Mike Rychener and Jeff Schlimmer for comments on an earlier version of the chapter.

1. We use the term "production system" in two distinct senses. The first refers to a *theory* of the cognitive architecture, independent of particular programs that are implemented within this framework. The second refers to specific sets of condition-action rules that run within such an architecture. In general, the intended meaning should be clear from the context. Within artificial intelligence the term "production system" sometimes includes backward chaining rule-based systems, such as that used in MYCIN (Shortliffe 1976). However, we will use the term in the more limited (forward chaining) sense.

2. Since there are ten digits, some 45 binary *greater-than* relations exist. Rather than storing these explicitly in working memory, one might insert a LISP function in the condition side to test whether this relation is met. Although this is not psychologically plausible, it considerably simplifies the implementation.

3. This representation may be provided directly by the programmer, or it may be generated automatically by the system from linear input, using another set of rules. In any case, we will ignore this pre-processing stage to keep our example as simple as possible.

4. For instance, nearly all work on heuristics learning has represented procedures in terms of condition-action rules or productions.

5. However, PAS aided the cognitive simulation effort indirectly because Waterman and Newell (1972) used it to construct a semiautomatic system for analyzing verbal protocols.

6. Bundy (1984) discusses the difficulties of defining "learning" in some detail.

7. Typically, these are presented as sentence-meaning pairs, though it is theoretically assumed that the child must infer the meanings from context.

8. Fisher and Langley (1985) have used some of these components to analyze methods for "conceptual clustering," while Easterlin and Langley (1985) have examined their role in concept formation.

9. This is often called the "generalization" problem, but since this word has an ambiguous meaning, we will avoid its use here.

10. This is not completely true, as we will see in chapter 3, but it has been true of the majority of work on learning search heuristics.

11. For this to be different from simply adding a new production, another constraint is required: the conditions must be composed of simple parts, rather than invocations to very powerful predicates. If such predicates were allowed, one might change the matched set by redefining some predicate in an arbitrary manner. Although theoretically possible, this scheme would make the learning process hopelessly complex.

12. The traditional example used to illustrate this point contrasts the two pieces of decision-making advice: "Look before you leap" and "He who hesitates is lost."

13. For an extreme example of this approach, see Lenat (1977).

14. For example, Neches (1981b) compares a production system for learning an addition procedure (also described in chapter 4) with another production system that was adequate for performing the task but that did not carry the information needed for his learning mechanisms to operate. Although the number of productions contained in the two systems was approximately the same, the "complexity" of the productions needed in the learning system was almost three times greater for both of two different measures. (Complexity was measured by the number of symbols and the number of propositions appearing in the production.)

15. There is an implied twelfth category: information about production instantiations, i.e., linkages between concepts referenced in a production's condition side and to the concepts resulting from its action side.

16. At first blush, it might seem that attention focusing could also be aided by mechanisms that did not have to exhaustively consider all production matches. However, as we have seen elsewhere in this chapter, such mechanisms greatly increase the difficulty of adding new productions, and thus seem inappropriate for intelligent learning systems.

References

Anderson, J. R. 1976. *Language, Memory, and Thought.* Hillsdale, N.J.: Lawrence Erlbaum Associates.

Anderson, J. R. 1981. A theory of language acquisition based on general learning principles. In *Proceedings of the Seventh International Joint Conference on Artificial Intelligence*, pp. 165–170. Vancouver, B.C., Canada.

Anderson, J. R. 1983. *The Architecture of cognition.* Cambridge, Mass.: Harvard University Press.

Anderson, J. R., Greeno, J. G., Kline, P. J., and Neves, D. M. 1981. Acquisition of problem-solving skill. In J. R. Anderson (ed.), *Cognitive Skills and Their Acquisition.* Hillsdale, N. J.: Lawrence Erlbaum Associates.

Anderson, J. R., and Kline, P. J. 1979. A learning system and its psychological implications. *Proceedings of the Sixth International Joint Conference on Artificial Intelligence*, pp. 16–21. Tokyo, Japan.

Anderson, J. R., Kline, P. J., and Beasley, C. M. 1978. *A theory of the acquisition of cognitive skills.* Technical Report No. ONR 77–1. Department of Psychology, Yale University.

Anderson, J. R., Kline, P. J., and Lewis, C. 1977. A production system model for language processing. In P. Carpenter and M. Just (eds.), *Cognitive Processes in Comprehension.* Hillsdale, N.J.: Lawrence Erlbaum Associates.

Anzai, Y. 1978. Learning strategies by computer. *Proceedings of the Second Biennial Conference of the Canadian Society for Computational Studies of Intelligence*, pp. 181–190. Toronto, Ontario, Canada.

Anzai, Y., and Simon, H. A. 1979. The theory of learning by doing. *Psychological Review* 86, 124–140.

Baylor, G. W., Gascon, J., Lemoyne, G., and Pother, N. 1973. An information processing model of some seriation tasks. *Canadian Psychologist* 14, 167–196.

Berwick, R. 1979. Learning structural descriptions of grammar rules from examples. *Proceedings of the Sixth International Conference on Artificial Intelligence*, pp. 56–58. Tokyo, Japan.

Brazdil, P. 1978. Experimental learning model. *Proceedings of the Third AISB/GI Conference*, pp. 46–50. Hamburg, West Germany.

Brown, J. S., and Burton, R. R. 1978. Diagnostic models for procedural bugs in basic mathematical skills. *Cognitive Science* 2, 155–192.

Brown, J. S., and VanLehn, K. 1980. Repair theory: a generative theory of bugs in procedural skill. *Cognitive Science* 4, 379–427.

Brownston, L., Farrell, R., Kant, E., and Martin, N. 1985. *Programming Expert Systems in OPS5: An Introduction to Rule-Based Programming*. Reading, Mass.: Addison-Wesley.

Bundy, A. 1984. *What has learning got to do with expert systems?* (Research Paper No. 214). Department of Artificial Intelligence, University of Edinburgh.

Easterlin, J. D. and Langley, P. 1985. A framework for concept formation. *Proceedings of the Seventh Conference of the Cognitive Science Society*, pp. 267–271. Irvine, Calif.

Fisher, D. and Langley, P. 1985. Approaches to conceptual clustering. *Proceedings of the Ninth International Joint Conference on Artificial Intelligence*, pp. 691–697. Los Angeles, Calif.

Forgy, C. L. 1979a. *OPS4 user's manual*. Technical Report. Department of Computer Science, Carnegie-Mellon University.

Forgy, C. L. 1979b. *On the efficient implementation of production systems*. Dissertation. Department of Computer Science, Carnegie-Mellon University.

Forgy, C. L. 1981. *OPS5 user's manual*. Technical Report. Department of Computer Science, Carnegie-Mellon University.

Forgy, C. L. 1982. Rete: A fast algorithm for the many pattern/many object pattern match problem. *Artificial Intelligence* 19, 17–37.

Forgy, C. L. 1984. *The OPS83 report*. Technical Report. Department of Computer Science, Carnegie-Mellon University.

Forgy, C. L., and McDermott, J. 1976. *The OPS reference manual*. Technical Report. Department of Computer Science, Carnegie-Mellon University.

Forgy, C. L., and McDermott, J. 1977. *The OPS2 reference manual*. Technical Report. Department of Computer Science, Carnegie-Mellon University.

Hayes-Roth, F., and McDermott, J. 1978. An interference matching technique for inducing abstractions. *Communications of the ACM* 21, 401–410.

Hedrick, C. 1976. Learning production systems from examples. *Artificial Intelligence* 7, 21–49.

Hunter, I. M. L. 1968. Mental calculation. In P. C. Wason and P. N. Johnson-Laird (eds.), *Thinking and Reasoning*. Baltimore: Penguin Books.

Klahr, D. 1973. A production system for counting, subitizing, and adding. In W. G. Chase (ed.), *Visual Information Processing*. New York: Academic Press.

Klahr, D., and Siegler, R. 1978. The representation of children's knowledge. In H. Reese and L. P. Lipsitt (eds.), *Advances in Child Development*, Vol. 12. New York: Academic Press.

Klahr, D., and Wallace, J. G. (1972). Class inclusion processes. In S. Farnham-Diggory (ed.), *Information Processing in Children.* New York: Academic Press.

Klahr, D., and Wallace, J. G. 1973. The role of quantification operators in the development of conservation of quantity. *Cognitive Psychology* 4, 301–327.

Klahr, D., and Wallace, J. G. 1976. *Cognitive Development: An Information Processing View.* Hillsdale, N.J.: Lawrence Erlbaum Associates.

Laird, J. E. 1983. *Universal subgoaling.* Dissertation. Department of Computer Science, Carnegie-Mellon University.

Laird, J. E., Rosenbloom, P. S., and Newell, A. 1984. Towards chunking as a general learning mechanism. In *Proceedings of the National Conference on Artificial Intelligence*, pp. 188–192. Austin, Tex.

Langley, P. 1978. BACON.1: A general discovery system. *Proceedings of the Second Biennial Conference of the Canadian Society for Computational Studies of Intelligence*, pp. 173–180. Toronto, Ontario, Canada.

Langley, P. 1982. Language acquisition through error recovery. *Cognition and Brain Theory* 5, 211–255.

Langley, P. 1983. Learning search strategies through discrimination. *International Journal of Man-Machine Studies* 18, 513–541.

Langley, P., and Neches, R. T. 1981. *PRISM user's manual.* Technical Report. Computer Science Department, Carnegie-Mellon University.

Langley, P., Neches, R. T., Neves, D., and Anzai, Y. 1980. A domain-independent framework for learning procedures. *International Journal of Policy Analysis and Information Systems* 4, 163–197.

Langley, P., and Ohlsson, S. 1984. Automated cognitive modeling. *Proceedings of the Fourth National Conference of the American Association for Artificial Intelligence*, pp. 193–197. Austin, Tex.

Langley, P., Ohlsson, S., Thibadeau, R., and Walter, R. 1984. Cognitive architectures and principles of behavior. *Proceedings of the Sixth Conference of the Cognitive Science Society*, pp. 244–247. Boulder, Colo.

Langley, P., and Simon, H. A. 1981. The central role of learning in cognition. In J. R. Anderson (ed.), *Cognitive Skills and Their Acquisition.* Hillsdale, N.J.: Lawrence Erlbaum Associates.

Larkin, J. H. 1981. Enriching formal knowledge: A model for learning to solve textbook physics problems. In J. R. Anderson (ed.), *Cognitive Skills and Their Acquisition.* Hillsdale, N.J.: Lawrence Erlbaum Associates.

Lenat, D. B. 1977. Automated theory formation in mathematics. *Proceedings of the Fifth International Joint Conference on Artificial Intelligence*, pp. 833–842). Cambridge, Mass.

Lewis, C. 1978. *Production system models of practice effects.* Dissertation. Department of Psychology, University of Michigan.

Lewis, C. 1981. Skill in algebra. In J. R. Anderson (ed.), *Cognitive Skills and Their Acquisition.* Hillsdale, N.J.: Lawrence Erlbaum Associates.

McDermott, J. 1979. Learning to use analogies. *Proceedings of the Sixth International Joint Conference on Artificial Intelligence*, pp. 568–576. Tokyo, Japan.

McDermott, J. 1982. R1: A rule-based configurer of computer systems. *Artificial Intelligence*, 19, 39–88.

McDermott, J., and Forgy, C. L. 1978. Production system conflict resolution strategies. In D. A. Waterman and F. Hayes-Roth (eds.), *Pattern-Directed Inference Systems*. Orlando, Fla.: Academic Press.

Michalski, R. S. 1980. Pattern recognition as rule-guided inductive inference. *IEEE Transactions on Pattern Analysis and Machine Intelligence* 2, 349–361.

Minsky, M. 1963. Steps toward artificial intelligence. In E. A. Feigenbaum and J. Feldman (eds.), *Computers and thought*. New York: McGraw-Hill.

Mitchell, T. M. 1982. Generalization as search. *Artificial Intelligence* 18, 203–226.

Mitchell, T. M., Utgoff, P., and Banerji, R. B. 1983. Learning problem solving heuristics by experimentation. In R. S. Michalski, J. G. Carbonell, and T. M. Mitchell (eds.), *Machine Learning: An Artificial Intelligence Approach*. Palo Alto, Calif. Tioga Publishing.

Neches, R. (1981a). A computational formalism for heuristic procedure modification. *Proceedings of the Seventh International Joint Conference on Artificial Intelligence*, pp. 283–288. Vancouver, B.C., Canada.

Neches, R. 1981b. *Models of heuristic procedure modification*. Dissertation. Department of Psychology, Carnegie-Mellon University.

Neches, R. 1982. Simulation systems for cognitive psychology. *Behavior Research Methods and Instrumentation* 14, 77–91.

Neves, D. M. 1978. A computer program that learns algebraic procedures by examining examples and working problems in a textbook. *Proceedings of the Second Biennial Conference of the Canadian Society for Computational Studies of Intelligence*, pp. 191–195. Toronto, Ontario, Canada.

Neves, D. M., and Anderson, J. R. 1981. Knowledge compilation: Mechanisms for the automatization of cognitive skills. In J. R. Anderson (ed.), *Cognitive Skills and Their Acquisition*. Hillsdale, N. J.: Lawrence Erlbaum Associates.

Newell, A. 1967. *Studies in Problem Solving: Subject 3 on the Crypt-Arithmetic task Donald + Gerald = Robert*. Technical Report. Center for the Study of Information Processing, Carnegie Institute of Technology.

Newell, A. 1972. A theoretical exploration of mechanisms for coding the stimulus. In A. W. Melton and E. Martin (eds.), *Coding Processes in Human Memory*. Washington, D.C.: Winston.

Newell, A. 1973. Production systems: Models of control structures. In W. G. Chase (ed.), *Visual Information Processing*. New York: Academic Press.

Newell, A. 1980. Reasoning, problem solving, and decision processes: The problem space hypothesis. In R. Nickerson (ed.), *Attention and Performance*, Vol. 8. Hillsdale, N.J.: Lawrence Erlbaum Associates.

Newell, A., and McDermott, J. 1975. *PSG manual*. Technical Report. Department of Computer Science, Carnegie-Mellon University.

Newell, A., and Rosenbloom, P. S. 1981. Mechanisms of skill acquisition and the law of practice. In J. R. Anderson (ed.), *Cognitive Skills and Their Acquisition*. Hillsdale, N. J.: Lawrence Erlbaum Associates.

Newell, A., and Simon, H. A. 1972. *Human Problem Solving*. Englewood Cliffs, N.J.: Prentice-Hall.

Ohlsson, S. 1979. *PSS3 reference manual*. Technical Report. Department of Psychology, University of Stockholm.

Ohlsson, S. 1980a. *A possible path to expertise in the three-term series problem*. Technical Report. Department of Psychology, University of Stockholm.

Ohlsson, S. 1980b. *Competence and strategy in reasoning with common spatial concepts: A study of problem solving in a semantically rich domain.* Dissertation. Department of Psychology, University of Stockholm.

Ohlsson, S. 1983. A constrained mechanism for procedural learning. In *Proceedings of the Eighth International Joint Conference on Artificial Intelligence*, pp. 426–428. Karlsruhe, West Germany.

Rosenbloom, P. S. 1979. *XAPS reference manual.* Technical Report. Department of Computer Science, Carnegie-Mellon University.

Rosenbloom, P. S. 1983. *The chunking model of goal hierarchies: A model of practice and stimulus-response compatibility.* Dissertation. Department of Computer Science, Carnegie-Mellon University.

Rychener, M. D. 1976. *Production systems as a programming language for artificial intelligence applications.* Dissertation. Department of Computer Science, Carnegie-Mellon University.

Rychener, M. D. 1980 *OPS3 production system language: Tutorial and reference manual.* Unpublished manuscript. Department of Computer Science, Carnegie-Mellon University.

Sauers, R., and Farrell, R. 1982. *GRAPES user's manual.* Technical Report. Department of Psychology, Carnegie-Mellon University.

Seibel, R. 1963. Discrimination reaction time for a 1,023 alternative task. *Journal of Experimental Psychology* 66, 215–226.

Shortliffe, E. H. 1976. *MYCIN: Computer-based medical consultations.* New York: Elsever.

Simon, D. P., and Simon, H. A. 1978. Individual differences in solving physics problems. In R. Siegler (ed.), *Children's Thinking: What Develops?* Hillsdale, N.J.: Lawrence Erlbaum Associates.

Sleeman, D., Langley, P., and Mitchell, T. 1982. Learning from solution paths: An approach to the credit assignment problem. *AI Magazine* 3, 48–52.

Thibadeau, R. 1982. CAPS: A language for modeling highly-skilled knowledge-intensive behavior. *Proceedings of the National Conference on the Use of On-line Computers in Psychology.* Minneapolis, Minn.

Thibadeau, R., Just, M. A., and Carpenter, P. A. 1982. A model of the time course and content of reading. *Cognitive Science* 6, 157–203.

Waterman, D. A. 1970. Generalization learning techniques for automating the learning of heuristics. *Artificial Intelligence* 1, 121–170.

Waterman, D. A. 1975. Adaptive production systems. *Proceedings of the Fourth International Joint Conference on Artificial Intelligence*, pp. 296–303. Tbilisi, USSR.

Waterman, D. A., and Newell, A. 1972. *Preliminary results with a system for automatic protocol analysis.* Technical Report CIP No. 211. Department of Psychology, Carnegie-Mellon University.

Winston, P. H. 1975. Learning structural descriptions from examples. In P. H. Winston (ed.), *The Psychology of Computer Vision.* New York: McGraw-Hill.

Young, R. M. 1976. *Seriation by Children: An Artificial Intelligence Analysis of a Piagetian Task.* Basel: Birkhauser.

Young, R. M., and O'Shea, T. 1981. Errors in children's subtraction. *Cognitive Science* 5, 153–177.

2 Doing, Understanding, and Learning in Problem Solving

Yuichiro Anzai

Learning is ubiquitous, and mechanisms of learning are many. We learn by being told, from written instructions, from worked-out examples, by doing, and so on. This chapter aims particularly at a description of the information-processing theory and models of learning by doing. Learning by doing is one of the central concerns in psychological learning theory. The maze learning of rats in behaviorism, and simple parameter learning in mathematical psychology, are manifestations of learning by doing through repetitive trials. Human learning by doing, however, involves more than what is treated in those traditional paradigms. In this chapter, two other aspects are discussed in detail.

First, I consider learning of cognitive strategies by repeatedly solving a problem-solving task. As examples, I take the Tower of Hanoi puzzle and a seriation task. These tasks are well-structured, and allow clearcut modeling of the process of learning by doing. I describe how the learning process can be explained by adaptive production-system models.

Although the models convey the underlying basic idea in a theoretically acute manner, the tasks are so simple that they miss many psychologically interesting points. One such point is understanding. Understanding well-structured problems is not difficult, especially if the problem instructions are stated clearly. On the other hand, if the problem is ill-structured, that is, if the problem solver does not know what an adequate problem space is, he needs to make an effort to understand the problem before developing efficient strategies. A theory of learning by doing should not neglect this prerequisite understanding stage.

So, second, I consider understanding by working on a problem-solving task. As an example domain, I take the manual control task of steering a ship. This task has rarely been treated in cognitive psychology, but has much in common with the Tower of Hanoi and seriation.

The sections following begin with a description of the basic mechanisms for strategy acquisition. Next, I present examples from the Tower of Hanoi puzzle and a seriation task in order to illustrate models for the mechanisms. Then, I describe an extension of our theory that includes the understanding process, and illustrate it with an example from a model of strategy acquisition for the ship steering task. Rather than taking into account all the psychological aspects of learning and understanding by doing, this chapter is concerned with specific mechanisms modeled by adaptive production systems. So, finally, I give some comments on the implications of our theory and models in a more general context.

2.1 General Mechanisms of Learning by Doing

Differences between cognitive strategies of experts and novices in problem-solving tasks have recently received much attention (e.g., Larkin, McDermott, Simon and Simon 1980). The question to be asked, now, is how the differences come about.

How do experts acquire strategies? One basic idea is that experts solve similar problems repeatedly, and learn efficient strategies through that experience. Our theory asserts that this strategy acquisition process begins with construction of the initial problem space, proceeds to formation of weak strategies such as avoiding poor moves, and then to generation of strong ones like means-ends strategies (Anzai and Simon 1979). This section explains briefly the essence of this theory of learning by doing.

Construction of the Initial Problem Space

The adequacy of using the problem-space concept for a theory of problem solving is well established (Newell and Simon 1972). As for generation of problem spaces, an important source of information for the problem-space construction is problem instructions. For problems with well-structured instructions, an internal representation for a proper space can be generated by simply interpreting those instructions (Hayes and Simon 1974).

However, even with simple well-structured problems, the initial space may be updated by using information made available by solving the problem. A typical example is formation of subgoals. It is often the case that useful subgoals cannot be determined by only reading the problem instructions before starting to solve the problem. In complex problems, the goal structure is elaborated gradually during the problem-solving process, and thus knowledge states are updated continually. Another example is acquisition of operator application rules. Their complete specifications, especially situation-specific conditions for when to apply operators, are not usually obtained from the instructions, and the problem solver needs to learn them through experience. Learning by doing is, in this sense, accompanied by learning proper problem spaces.

Collection of Bad Instances

The process of problem solving begins with a search for better states in the initial problem space. Even when problem solvers do not yet have an efficient strategy, they must manage somehow to try to reach a solution. It is reasonable to believe that people have the strategy of general and weak trial-and-error search. That is, they pick one operator from the initial set almost arbitrarily, apply it to the present knowledge state, and evaluate the resulting state. If they believe that the resulting state is good, they continue the search, but if they consider it bad, they return to the previous state and try another operator.

If problem solvers are unfamiliar with the task, their manner of evaluating knowledge states or applied operators must necessarily be crude at this point. However, the trial-and-error search strategy puts a great burden on their limited capacity for processing symbolic information. It is indispensable for them to evoke general evaluation heuristics for detecting good or bad instances of the state.

Typical examples of bad-instance detection heuristics are returning to a previously visited state and taking operators leading to a state that can be reached by another shorter route. Both of these heuristics indicate to the problem solver that he did not reduce the difference between the present and goal states. Actually, any heuristic employing a criterion of failure to reduce the difference can be used for detecting bad instances.

This is not the case, however, for detection of good instances. If a problem solver lacks knowledge about the task, it is difficult for him to decide whether the current application of a particular operator reduces the difference of the present and the goal states. Thus our theory predicts that problem solvers with limited knowledge about the task start not by collecting good instances but by gathering information about bad instances.

Acquisition of Procedures for Avoiding Bad Instances

Let us denote by *S* the state encountered prior to the state evaluated as bad, and denote by *O* the operator applied to *S* that produced the bad state. Then, a general procedure for avoiding the bad state next time can be constructed easily:

If the present knowledge state is *S*,
and if *O* has not been applied to the present state,
then note that *O* should not be applied to the present state.

If the reader is familiar with search algorithms, this production is readily seen to be a procedure for pruning a particular branch at a particular node in the search space. It should be noted that this production can be built entirely from the information available when a bad instance is detected, if information about the previous state and the operator applied to it is encoded and remembered.

Productions for avoiding bad instances are relatively powerful. They are helpful for pruning unnecessary paths in the search space, and thus for making trial-and-error search more efficient.

Collection of Good Instances and Building Subgoal Generation Procedures

Narrowing the search is a necessary condition for discovering good instances. After the search is narrowed, recognition of desirable states is made by various heuristics. One heuristic is to use analogy: if a problem solver knows what the final state looks like, he believes a state analogous to it to be a good state. Another example is to locally evaluate the difference between the present and the goal states: if a problem solver believes that moving to the present state has greatly decreased the difference from the goal state, then he evaluates the present state as good.

Detected good states are soon converted to internal subgoals. The problem solver then tends to search for those subgoals instead of the final goal. It is not likely, however, that those subgoals form a well-organized strategy from the initial moment. Most of them are found independently and piecewise in the course of searching the state space by weaker strategies. Usually they are only weakly related: for example, they may be organized merely by order of application. In such cases, gaps between the subgoals must be filled systematically, and furthermore, the problem solver needs to create procedures to generate the subgoals so as to satisfy this systematic organization. One possible general mechanism for this is as follows (Anzai 1978a).

First, suppose that the problem solver has a production that generates an already known subgoal G_1:

IF the conditions $C_1, \ldots, C_m$ are satisfied,
THEN generate the subgoal G_1.

This production implies that if the conditions C_i, $i = 1, \ldots, m$, are all met, then G_1 is generated. Now suppose further that at least one C_j among those conditions is not satisfied at the present state. At this point, the problem solver stores the information:

(CONDITION: NOT (C_1 & ... & C_m)).

After depositing the list into memory, the problem solver continues to work on the problem by using weak strategies. Then, when he comes to the state where G was attained, he recalls the knowledge state G_2 immediately preceding G_1 and uses it to store the new information:

(ACTION: generate G_2).

Now, since candidates for CONDITION and ACTION reside in memory, the following new production may be created:

IF at least one of $C_1, \ldots, C_m$ is not satisfied,
THEN generate G_2.

Actually, this production is somewhat too general. A more restricted production takes the form:

IF only one of $C_1, \ldots, C_m$ is unsatisfied, [A]
THEN generate G_2.

This production would fire when the present knowledge state is close to a state satisfying the subgoal G_1.

If operator application rules are provided (or understood by the problem solver) in the form of productions, the conditions in this production may be identified with conditions in one of the application rules. Thus, if m productions are created, where the jth production takes the form

IF $C_1, \ldots, C_{j-1}, C_{j+1}, \ldots, C_m$ are satisfied,
but C_j is unsatisfied,
THEN generate G_2,

for the previously violated operator application rule, and if the problem solver has already stored, for example, the information

(CONDITION: NOT (C_j)),

after the application rule violated because of the violation of the condition C_j, then these m productions work equivalently to the production [A]. This avoids testing conditions in a combinatorial way, if the number of conditions, m, is not large.

Productions built by this subgoal generation algorithm work generally as a means-ends strategy. That is, subgoals are generated successively to form a stack, based on the present-state information. However, the learned productions respond to the violation of the operator application rules and not to the difference between the goal and the present state. This distinction is not accidental. The problem solver is still in the process of organizing independently discovered subgoals, and it is not easy for him to evaluate the difference between the goal and the present state. In contrast, the operator application rules are always at hand once they are understood, and are usable at any time.

Pattern Discovery in Subgoal Structure

If the strategy acquired by the preceding productions is sufficiently effective, the problem solver may be able to reach the final goal without many errors or even directly without search. In the process he may discover a steady pattern in the sequence of operators or states in the solution path. He will then develop a set of new subgoals based on the discovered pattern and chunk old subgoals. The problem solver will now proceed forward using the pattern-based strategy rather than the subgoal-generation strategy. The pattern-based strategy, because of the efficient way it can be stored in memory, may generate an entire sequence of necessary operators at the initial state before the actual problem-solving process is begun.

2.2 Example from Tower of Hanoi Puzzle

In this section, I will use the five-disk Tower of Hanoi puzzle to illustrate the general mechanisms mentioned in the previous section. The psychological investigations into strategy learning in the task (Anzai and Simon 1979), and detailed computational results (Anzai 1978b), are provided elsewhere. The purpose of this discussion is to show how the general mechanisms are adapted to an actual task, by describing an adaptive production-system model of the strategy acquisition process for the Tower of Hanoi problem. The model explained here was written for a production-system interpreter developed by the author, and initially included about 160 productions.

Construction of the Initial Problem Space

First, the initial knowledge state includes descriptions of the initial and desired final disk configurations for the puzzle. It also contains a description of the current disk configuration, presently the same as the initial configuration. Each of these three kinds of information is represented as a list of three sublists. Each sublist corresponds to an ordered set of the names of disks on pegs *A*, *B*, and *C* from the left to the right. For example, the list ((3 4 5) (1) (2)) indicates that disks 3, 4 and 5 are at peg *A* in that order from the top, disk 1 is at peg *B*, and disk 2 is at peg *C*. If no disk resides at some peg, it is represented by NIL. For instance, ((1 2 3 4 5) NIL NIL) represents the initial disk configuration in which all the disks are at peg *A*.

Also the knowledge state includes various kinds of perceptual information. For example, the model is able to attend to some particular peg or to search for a move from some peg to another.

The elements described above are all represented as declarative information residing in the working memory of the model. The model also contains some functional knowledge. For example, it has a function taking a peg $*P* and the disk configuration ($*A* $*B* $*C*) as arguments, where $*P*, $*A*, $*B*, and $*C* are variables, and returning the name of the top disk at $*P* as the value: if no disk is on $*P*, it returns NIL. [In this chapter we assume that a variable is denoted by an atom headed by "$." Thus, ($*A* $*B* $*C*) is a disk configuration with $*A*, $*B*, and $*C* as variables indicating ordered sets of disks on pegs *A*, *B*, and *C*. As a convention I use $*A*, $*B*, and $*C* for disk configurations on pegs *A*, *B*, and *C*; $*P*, $*Q*, and $*R* for (different) peg names; and $*X* and $*Y* for (different) disk names.]

Another example of procedural knowledge is a predicate that is true if and only if the disk $*Y* is smaller than $*Z*, or $*Y* is bound to NIL. Still another is a function for updating the disk configuration. Actions permitted in productions are either of depositing an element into working memory, removing an element from working memory, or other simple functions such as exemplified earlier.

Basic problem operators transfer a disk from some peg to another, but additional operators are needed to perform the task. An operator application rule is, for example, defined in the production form:

IF the present disk configuration is ($*A* $*B* $*C*),
  and the peg $*P* is currently attended to,
  and a move from $*P* to the peg $*Q* is searched for,
  and the top disk at $*P* is smaller than the top disk at $*Q* or no disk is on $*Q*,
THEN deposit into working memory the information that the top disk at $*P* can be moved from $*P* to $*Q*.

Finally, procedural knowledge for finding an initial solution by trial-and-error search is, of course, stored in the form of productions.

Collection of Bad Instances

Using the knowledge just described, the model is able to start its search through the problem space. As mentioned earlier, states are evaluated at least initially by general evaluation heuristics. In the Tower of Hanoi puzzle, one such heuristic can be paraphrased as follows:

IF the present disk configuration is ($*A* $*B* $*C*),
and one of the past disk configurations is ($*A* $*B* $*C*),
THEN deposit into working memory the information that the present state is bad.

This production is a realization of the avoid-loop heuristic noted earlier.

Acquisition of Procedures for Avoiding Bad Instances

As an example, let us consider generation of a production for avoiding loop moves. Suppose that the model finds that the present configuration of ((3 4 5) (1) (2)) was bad. At that point, it tries to recall recent moves, which we suppose are moving disk 2 from peg *A* to peg *C*, moving disk 1 from peg *B* to peg *A*, and moving disk 1 from peg *A* to peg *B*. Then it creates a production instance of the following form:

IF the present disk configuration is ((1 3 4 5) NIL (2)),
and the next-to-last move was moving disk 2 from peg *A* to peg *C*,
and the last move was moving disk 1 from peg *B* to peg *A*,
and moving disk 1 from peg *A* to peg *B* has not yet been tried,
THEN deposit into working memory the information that moving disk 1 from peg *A* to peg *B* was already tried at the disk configuration of **((1 3 4 5) NIL (2)).**

The production is a procedure for avoiding the return of disk 1 from peg *A* to peg *B*. It can be stored in production memory in a more general format by replacing constants with variables:

IF the present disk configuration ($*A* $*B* $*C*),
and the next-to-last move took disk $*X* from peg $*P* to peg $*Q*,
and the last move was moving disk $*Y* from peg $*R* to peg $*P*,
and moving disk $*Y* from peg $*P* to peg $*R* is not yet tried at the disk configuration of ($*A* $*B* $*C*),

THEN deposit into working memory the information that moving disk $Y from peg $P to peg $R at the configuration ($A $B $C) was already tried.

Collection of Good Instances and Building Subgoal Generation Procedures

The model has a production that deals with the subgoal information:

IF the present disk configuration is ($A $B $C),
and there exists a subgoal to move disk $X from peg $P to peg $Q in working memory,
and disk $X is at the top of peg $P in the configuration ($A $B $C),
and disk $X is smaller than the disk at the top of peg $Q, or no disk is on peg $Q in the configuration ($A $B $C),
THEN deposit into working memory the information that disk $X can be moved from peg $P to peg $Q.

Using this production, the model is able to create a set of productions for the means-ends strategy. For example, suppose that the present disk configuration is **((4 5) (1 2) (3))**, and the subgoal at the top of the goal stack is "Move disk 4 from peg *A* to peg *B*." Then, among four conditions in the preceding production the first three conditions are satisfied, but the fourth is not. The system now remembers that it has *almost* satisfied the conditions for attaining the subgoal, by depositing into working memory the information that an "almost satisfying" state was encountered when the following conditions held: the disk configuration was **((4 5) (1 2) (3))**, the subgoal was to move disk 4 from peg *A* to peg *B*, disk 4 was at the top of peg *A*, and disk 4 was *not smaller than* the disk at the top of peg *B*. The system keeps the deposited information in working memory, and when the condition "disk 4 is smaller than the top disk at peg *B*" is satisfied, it remembers via the following production that the operator that transferred the previous state to that state is a good *subgoal*:

IF the present disk configuration is ($A $B $C),
and the past operator was to move disk $Y from peg $R to peg $S,
and the information that disk $X was not smaller than the disk at the top of peg $P in the disk configuration of ($D $E $F) is already stored in working memory,
and disk $X is now smaller than the disk at the top of peg $P in the disk configuration of ($A $B $C),

THEN deposit into working memory the information that moving disk \$*Y* from peg \$*R* to peg \$*S* is a good subgoal,
and deposit into working memory the information that the subgoal must be generated only when it is not yet stored in working memory.

In the actual simulation it was the move of disk 2 from peg *B* to peg *C* that made true the condition "disk 4 is smaller than the top disk at peg *B* in the configuration (\$*A* \$*B* \$*C*)." Thus, the model creates the following new production at that time:

IF the present disk configuration is ((4 5) (1 2) (3)),
and the present subgoal is to move disk 4 from peg *A* to peg *B*,
and disk 4 is at the top of peg *A* in the configuration of ((4 5) (1 2) (3)),
and disk 4 is not smaller than the top disk at peg *B* in the configuration of ((4 5) (1 2) (3)),
and there is no subgoal of moving disk 2 from peg *B* to peg *C* in working memory,
THEN deposit into working memory the subgoal of moving disk 2 from peg *B* to peg *C*.

The production in this example is generalized immediately by relating all the elements appearing in the right-hand side to the elements in the left-hand side, and then substituting variable symbols into specific values. The model has some functions for relating elements. The resulting generalized production looks like this:

IF the present disk configuration is (\$*A* \$*B* \$*C*),
and the present subgoal is to move disk \$*X* from peg \$*P* to peg \$*Q*,
and disk \$*X* is at top of peg \$*P* in the configuration of (\$*A* \$*B* \$*C*),
and disk \$*X* is not smaller than the disk at the top of peg \$*Q* in the configuration of (\$*A* \$*B* \$*C*),
and there is no subgoal to move the disk next smaller than \$*X* at peg \$*Q* in the configuration of (\$*A* \$*B* \$*C*) from peg \$*Q* to the peg other than \$*P* or \$*Q*,
THEN deposit into working memory the subgoal of moving the disk next smaller than \$*X* at peg \$*Q* in the configuration of (\$*A* \$*B* \$*C*) from peg \$*Q* to the peg other than \$*P* or \$*Q*.

In building this production, two functions for relating elements were used. One was **next-smaller**, which returns the name of the disk next smaller than the specified disk. For instance, in the configuration **((4 5) (1 2) (3))**, **2** is **next-smaller** than **4** at peg *B*. The other was **other**, which takes two same sets of atoms, except that the first set has one atom less than the second, and returns the atom included in the first but not in the second. For example, if the first set is the set of the names of the three pegs *A*, *B*, and *C*, and the second is the set of *A* and *B*, then **other** returns *C*.

The foregoing new production plays a powerful role in the Tower of Hanoi puzzle solving. Along with other productions created in similar fashion, it constitutes a means-ends strategy for the task.

Pattern Discovery in Subgoal Structure

The strategy just acquired is sufficient to produce a unique path to the goal after the first move. The model should then be able to discover a specific pattern in the path. For example, if the present disk configuration is **((5) (4) (1 2 3))**, and if the present subgoal is to move disk 5 from peg *A* to peg *C*, the model is likely to *perceive a pyramid* consisting of the three disks, 1, 2, and 3 at peg *C*. Such a perception will lead the model to create a new type of subgoal—a *pyramid subgoal*.

However, because move operations always involve only single disks, the model must develop procedural knowledge to decompose a pyramid subgoal into a sequence of one-disk-move subgoals. Acquisition of this kind of knowledge can be done while solving the problem. The model first remembers the pyramid, and then records its moves while trying to find a move sequence that transfers the whole pyramid to another peg. When it succeeds, it creates a production that relates the move sequence to the pyramid subgoal.

One such production, after generalization, takes this form:

IF the present disk configuration is ($*A* $*B* $*C*),
  and the present subgoal is to move the pyramid $*X* from peg $*Q* to peg $*R*,
  and disks, 1, . . . , $*X*, are on $*Q* in the configuration of ($*A* $*B* $*C*),
  and there is no subgoal to move the disk next smaller than $*X* to peg $*R* from the peg other than $*Q* or $*R*,
  and there is no subgoal of moving the disk at peg $*Q* next smaller than disk $*X* from peg $*Q* to the peg other than $*Q* or $*R*,

THEN deposit into working memory the subgoal of moving the pyramid next smaller than $*X* to peg $*R* from the peg other than $*Q* or $*R*,

and deposit into working memory the subgoal of moving disk $\$X$ from peg $\$Q$ to peg $\$R$,
and deposit into working memory the subgoal of moving the pyramid next smaller than disk $\$X$ on peg $\$Q$ in the configuration of ($\$A$ $\$B$ $\$C$) from peg $\$Q$ to the peg other than $\$Q$ or $\$R$,
and delete from working memory the present subgoal of moving the pyramid $\$X$ from peg $\$Q$ to peg $\$R$.

It is easily seen that this production constitutes the core of the well-known recursive strategy for the Tower of Hanoi puzzle.

As described earlier, the strategy acquisition process for our task is helped by many kinds of a priori knowledge. The system should have learning competence in this sense. Among them, knowledge relating to perception and goal manipulation is particularly important. This is not peculiar to the Tower of Hanoi puzzle, but holds generally for strategy acquisition in problem-solving tasks.

Summary

The adaptive production-system model acquires three different strategies for the Tower of Hanoi puzzle in the order predicted by the general mechanisms for learning by doing mentioned in the previous section. First, by using a primitive trial-and-error search, the model learns a strategy for avoiding bad moves in the form of a set of productions with which it prunes the search tree. This lets the model efficiently detect good subgoals. Then, the model tries to organize these subgoals, and as a result learns a strategy which generates them. This second strategy generates a sequence of subgoals without redundancy, which enables the model to induce a particular pattern of subgoals in that sequence. This, in turn, leads the model to a third strategy, well known as the recursive strategy for the Tower of Hanoi puzzle. The model in this case is concerned only with the five-disk problem; no extension to the general *N*-disk problem is made. Amarel (1983) provides in a different context a more formal treatment on the representational structure of the *N*-disk Tower of Hanoi problem. The strategy acquisition process for our task depends on many kinds of prior knowledge. Most important is knowledge concerning perception, trial-and-error search, and goal manipulation.

Acquisition of subgoal-based strategies is closely related to cognitive mechanisms for organizing discovered subgoals. I have described in this section an example of such a mechanism that detects an almost satisfied subgoal and waits and sees if the subgoal is satisfied. Note that this *wait-and-see* mechanism presumes the model's ability to remember time traces of some specific information.

The characteristics pointed out here are not peculiar to the Tower of Hanoi task. Rather, they are general properties of learning by doing in problem-solving tasks. In the following section, I provide a model for another example of learning by doing.

2.3 Example from a Seriation Task

As a second example of the general mechanisms for learning by doing, this section will describe strategy acquisition in a seriation task.

Children about five years of age may need an experimenter's help to complete a length seriation task using blocks. However, they soon get used to the task and acquire procedures for seriating randomly provided blocks. The model of strategy acquisition presented below simulates this short-term procedure learning process.

The problem we are concerned with here is an abstract version of seriation tasks. It is a generalized version of tasks such as length seriation (Young 1973) or weight seriation (Baylor and Gascon 1974). The problem in its abstract form can be stated as follows:

> Suppose that S is a set of n linearly ordered elements. For simplicity, assume that i denotes the ith maximal element in S. Find a procedure to arrange the n elements from n to 1 in their linear order (i.e., from largest to smallest). You can put an element from (to) S to (from) an array A in which elements are to be placed in order, recognize and evaluate the order of two elements adjacent in A, and change the positions of two adjacent elements in A.

I will start by describing how the general mechanisms for learning by doing apply to the acquisition of strategies for this task, illustrating my points by explaining a production-system model that I have constructed. In order to delineate clearly the mechanisms for learning embedded in the model, I have postponed the explanation of the model structure itself to the end of this section.

Construction of the Initial Problem Space

The knowledge states for our problem consist of configurations of elements in S and A. There are two move operators: the transfer of an element from (to) S to (from) A, and the exchange of an element in S with another element in A. An operator can be applied to any state if all elements concerned are located at an appropriate place (S or A).

For instance, the initial state is the set of the following elements for the problem with three elements:

(3 LARGER-THAN 2): Element 3 is larger than element 2.
(3 LARGER-THAN 1): Element 3 is larger than element 1.
(2 LARGER-THAN 1): Element 2 is larger than element 1.
(TIME-TOKEN N1): **N1** denotes the time.
(POINTER N1): The present time is **N1**.
(N1 SET 3): Element 3 is in the set S at time **N1**.
(N1 SET 2): Element 2 is in the set S at time **N1**.
(N1 SET 1): Element 1 is in the set S at time **N1**.
(N1 SUCCESSOR INITIAL): The time previous to **N1** is INITIAL.

Notice that time is crucial in this representation. The reason is that remembering the time trace of a cognitive performance is essential for learning, especially for learning based on causal inference. All the models described in this chapter include a representation of time, and the ability to remember and use time traces.

The operator application rules are embedded in productions. An element to be moved from S to A can be chosen, for example, by the following move-generating production:

IF the present time is $*TIME2*,
  and the element *L* is in the set *S* at time $*TIME2*,
  and $*TIME1* is the time previous to $*TIME2*,
  and the element *L* is not yet moved at time $*TIME2*,
  and the element *L* is not yet attended to as an element that can be
    moved at time $*TIME2*,
THEN note that *L* can be moved at $*TIME2*.

In this production, and in all the productions described in this section, the expression "note that..." is used for simplicity instead of "deposite into working memory the information that...."

If the production fires, a candidate for the next move is deposited into working memory. After that, new state will be generated by the execution of assorted state-changing productions. These productions may move an element (e.g., element 1) from S to A, change the present time to *N2*, note that *N1* is the time previous to *N2*, remember that element 2 is in *S* at time *N2*, and element 3 is also in *S* at time *N2*. After such state changes, suppose that element 3 was randomly chosen from *S* and moved to the end of *A*. This could be done by the same move-generating production mentioned earlier. When the program tries to generate a new state at this point, it will recognize the wrong order of elements 1 and 3 in *A*, because a production for detecting bad patterns will apply. Thus, constructs the initial state, and applying operators for generating moves and states naturally leads to discovery of bad instances.

It should be noted that the structure of the problem space is so simple only because our problem is the abstract seriation task. If we want to model a concrete version of the task, then we must consider the processes of perceptually encoding as a knowledge state the configuration of objects being seriated and of retrieving and performing complex operations. For instance, in a length seriation task using blocks, the processes of attending to specific objects in the spatially distributed blocks, or of changing the order of more than two specific blocks not necessarily adjacent in the array, might play decisive roles in performance of the task. The additional complexity of concrete tasks appears not only in the construction of the problem space but also in every aspect of the strategy acquisition process. I will refer to it in appropriate places but will generally focus on the abstract task to keep the discussion simple.

Collection of Bad Instances

The model begins the task with a weak trial-and-error strategy using two operators. The first operator moves an element between *S* and *A*, and the second evaluates the order of two adjacent elements in *A*. With these operators the system can perform the task by putting at the end of *A* an element randomly selected from *S* and evaluating the order of that element in relation to the one previously located at the end of *A*. The new element is moved back to *S* if the order is recognized to be bad.

The order of a pair is detected as bad if an element i is placed before another element j in *A*, and if $i < j$. This is the only heuristic used for recognizing a bad instance. Children usually have a greater number of perceptual heuristics for detecting bad instances. For example, in a length seriation task, if the block being considered for placement in the line is far larger than the block at its end, a child will return it immediately to the pile. I consider only one heuristic here for simplicity of explanation.

The following production is an example of such pattern-recognizing productions:

IF the present time is $*TIME2*,
  and the element $*L* is in *A* at time $*TIME1*,
  and the element $*M* is in *A* at time $*TIME2*,
  and $*TIME1* is the time previous to $*TIME2*,
  and $*M* is the element moved at time $*TIME1*,
  and $*M* is smaller than $*L*,
  and now the state is being updated from one at $*TIME1* to one at $*TIME2*,
THEN note that the most recently arranged element $*M* is smaller than the next-to-most-recent element $*L*,
  and note that the state at the previous time $*TIME1*, or the move made at $*TIME1*, was bad.

Consider the situation mentioned in the preceding subsection when elements 1 and 3 (in that order) are located in *A* and element 2 remains in *S*. This production can fire in that situation. It will note that either moving element 1 from *S* to *A* at the previous time (the value bound to $*TIME1*) was bad, or the state at that previous time was itself bad.

Acquisition of Procedures for Avoiding Bad Instances

When a bad pattern is detected, the problem solver tries to infer its cause. The inference mechanism in the model is a simple backtracking algorithm. That is, the program tries to infer the cause of the bad occurrence by using the information collected when the bad pattern was recognized. The inference mechanism is very simple. If there is an alternative move at the previous state to the one detected as bad, then the detected bad move is inferred to be bad. If there is no such move, then the previous state is assumed to be bad. In the latter case, the causal inference mechanism works recursively for past states and operators.

For example, the following production infers that the operator applied to the previous state was bad:

IF the present time is $*TIME2*,
  and $*TIME1* is the time previous to $*TIME2*,
  and the operator applied at time $*TIME1* was moving the element $*N* from *S* to *A*,

and the element \$*M* is in *S* at time \$*TIME1*,
and \$*M* is not equal to \$*N*,
and \$*M* was not moved at time \$*TIME1*,
and either the state at \$*TIME1* or the operator applied at
\$*TIME1* was bad,

THEN create a new time, \$*TIME3*,
and note that the present time is \$*TIME3*,
and note that \$*TIME1* is the time previous to \$*TIME3*,
and note that moving the element \$*M* was the operator applied
at time \$*TIME3*,
and note that \$*M* is in *A* at time \$*TIME3*,
and note that \$*N* is in *S* at time \$*TIME3*,
and note that moving \$*N* from *S* to *A* was already tried at \$*TIME1*,
and note that "\$*TIME1* is the present time" may be a condition for a
new production since \$*TIME1* was the time when the bad operator
was applied,
and note that "moving \$*N* from *S* to *A*" may be an action for a new
production since \$*N* was a bad operator that should be avoided,
and forget all the information related to the time \$*TIME2*.

When this production is applied, the system infers that the operator applied to the previous state is bad, and another operator applicable to the previous state is selected. Say that elements 1 and 3 are placed in array *A*, the order is recognized as bad, and the system has not yet tried moving element 2 from *S* to *A*. Then moving 3 at the previous state would be inferred to be bad, and the production would consider putting 3 back to *A* and moving 2 to *A*.

The following production infers that the previous state itself was bad:

IF the present time is \$*TIME3*,
and \$*TIME2* is the time previous to \$*TIME3*,
and \$*TIME1* is the time previous to \$*TIME2*,
and the state at time \$*TIME2* or the operator applied at time \$*TIME2*
was bad,

THEN note that the present time is \$*TIME2*,
and note that the state at time \$*TIME1* or the operator applied
at time \$*TIME1* was bad,
and forget all the information related to the time \$*TIME3*.

The model ensures that this production can fire only when the former production for inferring bad operators does not fire. When this production fires, the previous state is inferred to be bad, and the inference process backtracks one step to the state preceding the previous state and the operator applied to it. For example, assume that element 1 is in array *A*, and that element 3 was once returned to *S* from *A* based on the causal inference made by the former production. If element 2 is then put next to 1 in *A*, the order of 1 and 2 in *A* is recognized as bad, and then the latter production will fire and infer that the previous state (in which only 1 was in *A*) was already bad.

Once a plausible cause is determined by such productions, the program tries to build a production that generates actions for avoiding that cause. It starts by determining conditions for the to-be-built production. In the present version, two kinds of processes are involved: collecting candidates for conditions, and adding relations among them as condition candidates.

To collect appropriate conditions for the to-be-built production, it is necessary for the program to understand the semantics of atoms included in the initial productions, such as *set*, *array*, and *operator*. For this, the program retains in its working memory what we call here problem-solving schemata. For example, *operator* is semantically related to *state* by the relation *applied-to* in the problem-solving process. Since *state* is represented in the initial productions by *time-token*, it is also related semantically to time-token by the relation *isa*. These two problem-solving schemata are represented in working memory in the following form, respectively:

(SCHEMA PROBLEM-SOLVING OPERATOR APPLIED-TO STATE)
(SCHEMA PROBLEM-SOLVING STATE ISA TIME-TOKEN).

Such schemata are used in some productions for selectively collecting conditions for the to-be-built production.

After the collection of condition candidates is completed, their relations are inferred and added as further condition candidates. For example, if *the element* $M *is in the set* S and *the element* $N *is in the set* S are collected candidates for conditions, and if $*M* and $*N* are found not to be equal, then the information $M *and* $N *are not equal* is added as a condition candidate.

The condition candidates generated by these two processes are deposited in working memory. Next, productions for building new rules try to build a new production. The condition side primarily consists of the condition candidates held in working memory. Additional conditions check that certain information, to be deposited by the actions of the new production, does not already reside in working memory. (The latter conditions are added to avoid refractory loops of the matching-execution cycle.) The action side of the new production is composed of the action candidates that were generated and retained in working memory in the process of causal inference. Finally, all specific instances of times and elements in the newly built production are generalized into variables.

For example, when the operator of moving element 3 from *S* to *A* is inferred as bad at the state in which element 1 was in *A*, the following new production for avoiding such a bad move at that state is created:

IF the present time is $*V1*,
  and the element $*V2* is in *S* at time $*V1*,
  and the element $*V3* is in *S* at time $*V1*,
  and the element $*V4* is in *A* at time $*V1*,
  and $*V5* is the time previous to $*V1*,
  and $*V2* is larger than the element $*V4*,
  and $*V2* is larger than $*V3*,
  and $*V2* is not equal to $*V3*,
  and the operation of moving $*V2* from *S* to *A* has not yet tried
    at time $*V1*,
THEN note that the operator of moving $*V2* from *S* to *A* was
  already tried at time $*V1*.

Note that the action of this new production—that of claiming that the operation of moving a certain element from *S* to *A* had already been tried at a certain time—actually means that this operator should not be considered at that time. Thus, if this production fires, it will cause the model to search for some operator other than the one indicated by the production's action side.

Another example is the situation where element 1 is in *A*, the operators of moving elements 3 and 2 from *S* to *A*, respectively, are recognized as bad, and thus the state where 1 was moved from *S* to *A* is inferred to be bad, which leads to the inference that the operator of moving 1 was itself bad. In this case the following type of new production is created:

IF the present time is $*V1*,
  and $*V2* is the time previous to $*V1*,

and the element $*V3* is in *S* at time $*V1*,
and the element $*V4* is in *S* at time $*V1*,
and the element $*V5* is in *S* at time $*V1*,
and $*V4* is larger than $*V3*,
and $*V5* is larger than $*V3*,
and $*V5* is not equal to $*V4*,
and the operation of moving $*V3* from *S* to *A* has not yet tried at time $*V1*,

THEN note that the operation of moving $*V3* from *S* to *A* was already considered at time $*V1*.

Newly created productions for avoiding negative moves, once acquired, constitute a strategy for avoiding bad instances. The strategy is important in pruning the search space. For instance, consider the seriation problem with three elements. Once the new productions for the negative-move-avoidance strategy are generated, they fire at the initial moment to avoid moving elements 1 and 2 from *S* to *A*. Thus the only remaining operator, moving element 3 from *S* to *A*, is applied to the initial state. Next, with element 3 in *A*, the strategy works to avoid moving 1 from *S* to *A*. This makes moving 2 from *S* to *A* the only remaining operator applicable to that state. Then, with elements 3 and 2 placed in order in *A*, moving 1 from *S* to *A* completes the task.

Collection of Good Instances and Building Subgoal Generation Procedures

As this last example illustrates, the strategy for avoiding bad moves, once acquired, actually selects good operators for achieving the goal of the task. Then the program is able to work on the next step in strategy acquisition: if an operator considered at some state is known to be good, then it should be selected when that state is encountered. A production for selecting a particular good operator can be built easily at the time when such a state is encountered, by placing information about the current state in the condition side of the to-be-built production, and the action of choosing the operator in its action side.

For example, assume that in the seriation task with three elements, the program is at the initial state and has a strategy for avoiding bad operators. Using this strategy, it starts by choosing the operator of moving element 3 from *S* to *A*. At that point the following production can be created as part of the strategy for selecting good operators:

IF the present time is \$*V1*,
 and \$*V2* is the time previous to \$*V1*,
 and the element \$*V3* is in *S* at time \$*V1*,
 and the element \$*V4* is in *S* at time \$*V1*,
 and the element \$*V5* is in *S* at time \$*V1*,
 and \$*V5* is larger than \$*V3*,
 and \$*V5* is larger than \$*V4*,
 and \$*V3* is not equal to \$*V4*,
 and the operation of moving \$*V5* from *S* to *A* has not yet tried at time \$*V1*,
THEN apply the operator of moving \$*V5* from *S* to *A* at time \$*V1*.

Positive evaluation of operators is done after the problem has been solved by the strategy for avoiding bad instances. Since the problem solver knows that the path selected by the strategy leads to the goal, any operator on that path is considered to be good for the state to which it is applied. The productions built in this way constitute the strategy of choosing a good move at the present state. Note that this is not a case of means-ends backward generation of subgoals but a forward generation strategy based only on current state information.

Adaptive Production-System Model

An adaptive production-system model was constructed to simulate the strategy-learning process for our seriation problem, along the lines explicated in the preceding discussion. The program was written in a production-system language developed by our group (Anzai, Mitsuya, Nakajima, and Ura 1981), and contained 31 productions before learning. It successively learned two different strategies; one for avoiding bad moves and the other for selecting good moves. Since the working mechanisms of the program were explained above, we consider now the global structure of the model and its general performance.

The initial 31 productions could be classified functionally into the following nine subsets:

1. INITIAL—Preparation and initiation of problem solving.
2. MOVEGEN—generation of move operators.
3. STATEGEN—updating of problem states.
4. PATTERN-DETECTION—detection of specific pattern in problem states.

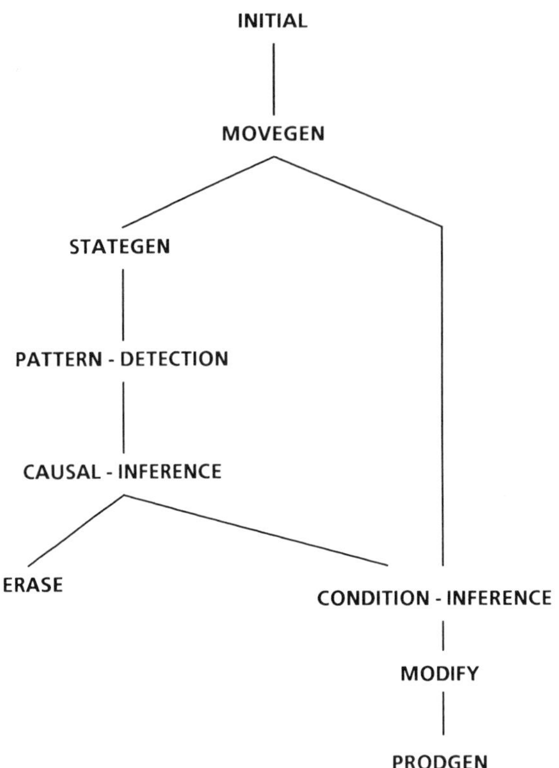

Figure 2.1
Relations among production subsets for strategy acquisition in the seriation problem

5. CAUSAL-INFERENCE—casual inference of occurrence of detected pattern.
6. CONDITION-INFERENCE—inference of condition sides of to-be-created productions.
7. MODIFY—modification of inferred conditions.
8. PRODGEN—generation of new productions.
9. ERASE—erasing unnecessary information from working memory.

These nine sets of productions are related hierarchically as shown in figure 2.1. Any transfer from an upper-level set to a lower-level one is made by depositing specific elements into working memory. For instance, depositing into working memory the assertion that element 3 was moved from *S* to *A* at time **N1** causes control to transfer from MOVEGEN to STATEGEN. Control is returned to the upper-level set when the deposited control information is deleted.

In figure 2.1 the control transfer from STATEGEN to PATTERN-DETECTION is the only case of data-driven transfer. That is, PATTERN-DETECTION is evoked not by depositing a special control element into working memory, but by attending to specific pattern in the contents of working memory.

There are several interesting features to the model. First, as the figure shows, MOVEGEN plays an important role in controlling not only MOVEGENeration but also causal inference and condition inference. Second, ERASE is called only from CAUSAL-INFERENCE; that is, unnecessary information is detected only if causal inference is made. Also, PATTERN-DETECTION is called only if control is moved from MOVEGEN to CAUSAL-INFERENCE. On the other hand, CONDITION-INFERENCE, MODIFY, and PRODGEN are always called, since CONDITION-INFERENCE can be called directly from MOVEGEN or indirectly through STATEGEN. This means that inference and modification of condition elements, and generation of new productions, are considered whenever learning is attempted.

The structure of figure 2.1 shows that there are two ways of creating productions in the system. One is by detecting a pattern in a problem state, inferring the cause of the pattern, and then inferring appropriate new productions. The other is by directly inferring condition elements for new productions by examining move operators.

The model acquired two different strategies for solving the problem, based on these two different paths of control. The pattern-detection-based learning led to the *poor-move-avoidance* strategy (PMAS), and the direct-condition-inferring learning led to the *good-move-generation* strategy (GMGS). At each choice point, PMAS rejects poor moves and selects the remaining move. To learn PMAS, the model needs to perform trial-and-error search and to recognize undesirable patterns in problem states. In Contrast, GMGS proposes a good move based on the current state information; to learn GMGS, the model needs only to find how move operators are related to problem states.

For the seriation problem with three elements, the model's initial solution required 196 production firings to achieve the final goal, while creating four new productions that constitute PMAS. Using this new strategy, the model then solved the same problem once again. The second solution required 94 production firings while generating three new productions that correspond to the main part of GMGS.

It should be noted that the three productions created in the second round of problem solving do not completely define GMGS. Some of the four productions built in the first round are also used for GMGS. Thus, the simulation suggests that the process of acquiring new strategies is not merely a matter of creating disjoint sets of new productions, each corresponding to a new strategy. Rather, newly acquired strategies are functionally interdependent.

Note also that the model is limited by lacking generalized concepts. Thus all newly built productions were dependent on the number of elements. For example, because the model had no concept of *largest element*, it was prevented from learning a new production for selecting the largest element remaining in the set *S*, which would have led to the acquisition of a new strategy independent of the number of elements.

Summary

The computational mechanism underlying learning strategies for the seriation task is very simple: it is basically a simple backtracking algorithm with some extra machinery. This simplicity stems only from the purpose of the work here: I have not tried to present a procedure-learning algorithm for broad application but just a basic example for a particular task that fits the general learning-by-doing mechanisms proposed earlier in this chapter.

Although the model did not simulate acquisition of strategies based on subgoal patterns such as induced in the last stage of the strategy acquisition process for the Tower of Hanoi puzzle, it generated two different strategies, one that chooses operators by avoiding bad moves and the other that plans forward by selecting good moves, in the order predicted by the general mechanisms for learning by doing.

The model described here for the seriation task, though simpler than the model for the Tower of Hanoi task explained in the previous section, helps clarify what mechanisms are necessary for learning by doing. For instance, the model for the seriation task explicitly indicates the significance of remembering time traces of states and operators, causal inference of bad patterns, and inference of conditions to be included in a newly built production. All these factors are crucial in learning by doing.

2.4 Understanding by Doing

I have described the basic mechanisms for learning by doing, along with two examples. However, I do not claim that the theory described above explicates the whole story. Learning by doing is a complex process, and we need to extend the theory in several directions to capture the essence of the learning process. In this section I review one such direction: understanding by doing.

The notion of understanding in problem solving is based at least partially on a long tradition of Gestalt psychology, but has gained a much firmer basis in the recent development of cognitive psychology. It is treated in information-processing terms sometimes very specifically (Hayes and Simon 1974), and sometimes very generally (Greeno 1980). It is concerned mainly with the construction of new internal representations related to a task. Hayes and Simon were the first to define clearly what understanding in problem solving means. For them, "understanding" is internal construction of a problem space appropriate for subsequent problem solving. This definition allows precise formulation of the understanding process, if the problem space can be defined without vagueness. Greeno asserts that understanding in the information-processing paradigm is essentially equivalent to learning in the sense that both understanding and learning refer to construction of new representations and their reorganization. Learning by doing, then, is the same as understanding by doing because learning by doing also involves the generation of new representations.

However, the foregoing part of this chapter, as well as the work of Greeno, and of Hayes and Simon, misses one important aspect: how the internal problem space is transformed into a more adequate one based on information obtained by working on the problem that is, how understanding develops through doing. Especially when a task is too complex or too vague to make direct contact with a problem solver's knowledge, the might start the task without much insight into what is the best problem space or what is the best set of move operators.

In the following section, I present an example of a learning task that illustrates understanding by doing and describe a production-system model of the acquisition of strategies for the task.

2.5 Example from a Ship-Steering Task

Perception and action are the fundamental ways of interacting with the environment. We often assume that our action in an environment causes a change in our perception of it. For example, if we turn our car's steering wheel to the right, we expect that this action will cause a change in the view outside the car window. If we find that this causal relationship between action and perception does *not* hold, we will be surprised and will try to understand this queer world by acquiring new causal knowledge about pairings between an action as a cause and a perception as an effect. This knowledge constitutes the initial representation of the problem. We consider an example of the acquisition of a problem representation in the form of this kind of causal knowledge. The example uses a task akin to that of steering ships.

Large oil tankers, submarines, or chemical plants usually have long exponential time lags, that is, system output follows an input only after a significant delay. Because of this characteristic, control of these systems is a difficult task for novices. Although this fact has been known for some time, no detailed analysis has been made of the strategy acquisition process necessary for development beyond the novice level.

Anzai (1984) analyzed the initial cognitive stages of skill learning for ship steering using a simple laboratory simulator and found that there exists essentially the same strategy acquisition sequence as observed in the Tower of Hanoi and the seriation tasks.

Anzai's subjects were required to use a dial to control the direction of a point moving at constant speed on a display, so as to guide the point through several gates in a specified order. One of the experiments for this task concerned cognitive differences of expert and novice strategies. The result showed that experts are apt to use goal-oriented strategies based on locally created plans, while novices were usually absorbed in perceiving and evaluating the immediate consequence of their action. This suggests that novices use most of their cognitive resources for trying to understand the man-machine interface, while experts have already developed efficient strategies, such as entering a gate from outside to inside so that the ship be able to go directly to the next destination.

Another experiment, using the same task to examine one particular subject's learning over repeated trials, showed that several different strategies were discovered and employed, along with gradually developed understanding of the man-machine interaction. Among the discovered strategies, a strategy for planning when to initiate turns was acquired first, then a strategy for steering the ship straight, and then a goal-oriented strategy paraphrased as *to pass through that gate, reach this point first; to reach this point, turn the control dial here to a particular direction.*

The biggest difference between novices and experts seemed to be that novices do not have much task-specific knowledge about the man-machine interface. For example, they did not know how much, and how late, the ship would change its direction when they turn the dial to a particular direction. In our theoretical terms, novices do not know the operator application rules in the problem space that they had represented.

Based on these observations, Anzai (1984) constructed a production-system model that explains how strategies are developed in the ship-steering task. Unlike the Tower of Hanoi and seriation task examples described in the preceding sections, the ship-steering model does not incorporate detailed mechanisms for creating conditions and actions of each new production. Rather, it emphasizes the sequence in which new operator application rules are acquired while working on the task repeatedly.

The general mechanisms for learning by doing apply to the strategy acquisition process in the ship-steering task. The production-system model I use to explain these mechanisms was written in OPS5 (Forgy 1981), and included about 100 initial productions. This initial set of productions reflects general procedural knowledge that people may already possess before encountering the task. Naturally, it is not possible to include here all the details of the declarative and procedural representations employed in the model. See Anzai (1984) for their details.

Construction of the Initial Problem Space

The ship-steering task is ill-structured in the sense that the controller does not know beforehand, and cannot obtain from the instructions, an adequate initial knowledge base, an initially available set of operators, or operator application rules for solving the problem efficiently.

However, it is also not true that the controller is completely without knowledge about these three things. Rather, his general knowledge is more sophisticated than one might first expert. For instance, it is likely that a controller's initial representation will consider the current direction of the ship, relative direction to the next gate, and the shape of the trajectory as components of a problem state. It is also likely that the representation will define directions and rotation angles of the control dial as the set of problem operators. The crude goal structure, such as the ordered sequence of the given gates, also is likely to be encoded as soon as the controller sees the gate configuration and understands the task instructions. As a matter of fact, for those kinds of problem-state information, use of general knowledge is sufficient to construct a fairly simple problem space. The controller also knows crude operator application rules, based on the predefined problem space and operators. For example, if the operator of rotating the control dial to the right is applied to a current state where the ship is heading north, the state will be changed to one in which the ship's direction is to the northeast or east.

Part of the difficulty of the ship-steering task stems from the fact that, although the problem states and operators can be represented at least crudely, there remain many degrees of freedom in construction of adequate operator application rules. For instance, the controller does not know beforehand *how much* the ship will turn to the right when he turns the dial to its rightmost limit. Nor, does he know *exactly when* the ship will start to turn after turning the control dial, since the ship has a long exponential time lag which causes a long delay in the ship's response to the control input. Learning involves continually updating the operator application rules, starting from the crude one that most novices have: if you turn the control dial to the right or left, the ship will turn immediately to the right or left. The computer model also starts with this rule and tries to elaborate it through experience.

Operator application rules take the form, "*if a particular control action is taken for a particular problem state, then the state is changed to another particular one.*" The controller needs to record the causal relation between his control input and the resultant behavior of the ship in order to continually update the rules. To do this, the model has abilities for perceiving specific patterns in the past control action and also specific patterns in the ship's trajectory. It then tries to relate them in the rule form just stated. For instance, suppose that the ship was heading east, started to turn to the left at time 5, and then ceased turning and began heading north at time 9. Also suppose that the action of turning the control dial to the left was started at time 3, and then the action was changed to turning the dial to the right at time 7. Then, if the model remembers all these, it deposits into working memory the relation among the ship's initial state of going to the east, action of turning the dial to the left, and the ship's resulting state of going to the north, in the rule form mentioned previously. The following production is responsible for constructing this rule:

IF there is in memory a sequence of past controls* of the same value,
  and there is also in memory a sequence of past states* of the
    same value for the attribute shape**,
  and the values for the controls* and the states* match,
  and the sequence of states* started after, and ended after, the
    sequence of controls*,
THEN construct a rule in memory from the information in the
  sequence of controls* and states* by using basic procedures***,
  and delete the two sequences from memory.

In this production, *control(s)** and *state(s)** are not physical controls and states but *mentally represented* control actions and states. Shape** refers to shapes of the ship's trajectory, mentally represented as part of states, and *basic procedures**** refer to perceptual and motor procedures that are not represented as productions but packed as actions in productions. The acquisition of causal knowledge in this way continues throughout the repetitive trials, even after the model has reached an expert level.

Collection of Bad Instances

Because of the long time lag in the ship-steering task there exists a representative type of bad instance: overshooting. Even if the pilot turns the control dial to the left while the ship is moving round to the right, the ship does not react immediately: it keeps moving to the right for a while and then starts to turn to the left. Less-skilled subjects in our experiments showed overshooting very frequently.

In the model overshooting is perceived and collected in memory by recording and comparing the two (past and present) pairs of the ship's current direction and the direction to the next gate. If the present directional difference is larger than the previous one, the model decides that the ship's trajectory is overshooting.

The evaluation of overshooting is not necessarily performed only when overshooting occurs. The future trajectory can be predicted by using operator application rules acquired as causal knowledge. For instance, suppose that we regard each of acquired operator application rules as a triple of the initial state, applied action, and end state. Then, if the present state matches the initial state of one of acquired rules, the future direction of the ship can be predicted as the direction specified in the end state of the rule. The following production takes care of such predictive evaluation.

IF the present state∗ is in memory,
 and there also is in memory a rule whose initial state matches the state∗,
THEN evaluate the difference between (1) the difference between the direction to the next gate and the ship's direction and (2) the difference between the ship's future direction specified by the end state of the rule and the ship's present direction.

The result of the evaluation by this production is one of the tokens *large*, *medium*, or *small*. If the result is *small*, then the model selects the control action specified in the rule whose initial state matched with the present state. But if it is *medium* or *large*, the model tries to build productions for avoiding bad instances. This process is explained below.

Acquisition of Procedures for Avoiding Bad Instances

When the model collects a bad instance, typically involving overshooting, it remembers that the operator *O* generating the instance should not be applied at the state *S* to which *O* was once applied. But, unlike the simpler Tower of Hanoi or seriation task, the set of operators for the steering task is potentially large or even infinite, and so there remains the problem of how to select an operator other than *O*.

However, people usually possess a good heuristic for this: if you want the ship to turn round to the opposite direction, turn the control dial to that direction *well before* the planned turning point. The model includes productions that generate new productions for choosing a good operator for a planned turning point based on such a heuristic. One production that generates productions for avoiding bad instances is shown next:

IF the present state∗ is in memory,
 and there is in memory a rule whose initial state matches the state∗,
 and the evaluated result of the difference between the two directional differences is *large*,
THEN build a production of the form:

IF a state∗ is in memory,
 and there is in memory a rule whose initial state matches the state∗,
THEN evaluate the difference between the two directional differences,

and build a production of the form:

IF a state* is in memory,
  and there is in memory a rule whose initial state matches the state*,
  and the evaluated error for the difference between the two directional differences is *large*,
THEN set the value of future control* to the one recommended in the rule,
  and compute its duration by basic procedures,
  and extend the duration to the intended length by appending controls* of the opposite value,
  and deposit into memory the sequence of the future control* values.

Note that new productions to be generated for coping with overshooting are already embedded in this production-generating production. In this regard, new productions are not being constructed, since they already reside in complete form in the initial knowledge base. However, it should be noted that the production-generating production may fire only after the model has collected bad instances of overshooting. The model potentially knew how to prevent overshooting but could only make procedures for it after it encountered and remembered bad instances.

The strategies for avoiding bad instances acquired in this manner are called the *locating* and *canceling* strategies. The locating strategy is for determining an appropriate point to start a turn well before the actual turn of the ship. The canceling strategy is for making the ship proceed in a straight line. The canceling strategy is actually a composition of both strategies: for instance, turning the dial at proper points to the right, to the left and then to the right would make the ship go straight. Making the ship go along a straight line is actually not an easy matter for novices, but it can be accomplished by acquiring the canceling strategy through repetitive use of the locating strategy to compensate for overshooting.

It should also be noted here that prediction of a future turning point, as well as determination of the time period specified by the term *well before*, depends causal knowledge acquired as operator application rules. Only with such rules is the model able to predict a future trajectory of the ship. Thus the acquisition of the operator application rules described earlier is indispensable for the acquisition of strategies for avoiding bad instances.

Collection of Good Instances and Building Subgoal Generation Procedures

Acquisition and use of the strategy for making the ship go straight gives the model a good chance of passing successfully through a gate. It then gives valuable information about what is a good strategy of passing through the next gate, such as a strategy to enter the next gate from the direction leading most readily to the gate following it. Choosing an *out-in* curve when about to enter the first target gate is generally a good strategy for taking a suitable direction toward the second target gate. A similar situation occurs in driving a car through a steep curve: one detours toward the outer curb before the curve, entering into it toward the inner curb. People are generally acquainted with this strategy through everyday experience, and their acquisition of this strategy for our particular task mainly involves comprehending the time lag and trajectory patterns used in the strategy.

To choose an appropriate pattern for the future trajectory through the next target gate, the model needs to locate a proper point well before the gate to initiate a particular action. This can be done by using operator application rules. If the trajectory pattern specified at the end state of some rule matches the pattern needed at the gate coming next, then the appropriate point for initiating action, as well as the particular control action to be taken at that point, can both be estimated by examining that rule's initial state and action taken. Using this *reversal extrapolation* (estimating the initial state by matching the end state), the model is able to generate a subgoal for passing through the next target gate, which includes an intermediate point to pass through and an action to be taken at that point. This point is not a physical gate but is used similarly as a spatial subgoal, specifying an intermediate destination of the ship. Thus the point is called a *mental gate*.

A mechanism for acquiring the *subgoal-generating* strategy is incorporated in the model. It can be summarized more abstractly as follows. First, good instances (i.e., good ways of entering gates) are collected. Let us denote such an instance as S_1. Then a subgoal S_2 is generated such that S_1 and S_2 are the end and the initial states specified in some operator application rule memorized by the model. This subgoal generation process can be repeated recursively as long as the model possesses appropriate rules. The mental gates specified in $S_1, S_2, \ldots,$ are to be used as new (intermediate) destinations of the ship.

The model includes productions for evaluating how well the ship entered into a gate. An example of these productions is as follows:

IF the ship succeeded in passing through a gate,
  and the next gate exists,
  and the present state* is in memory,

THEN evaluate the difference between the ship's direction to the next gate and its present direction given in the state*.

When the difference between the two directions is found to be *large* by productions such as this one, the model tries to create productions for generating subgoals. The subgoal-generating productions are generated by rules such as the following:

IF the result of evaluating the difference between the goal and the present directions after passing through a gate is *large*,
and the next gate exists,
and the present state* is in memory,
THEN build a production of the form:

IF two consecutive gates, *GATE1* and *GATE2*, exist,
and the present state* is in memory,
but no goal is in memory for *GATE1*, the current target physical gate,
THEN generate a goal by computing values for the attributes by basic procedures**, using the information in the two gates, *GATE1* and *GATE2*, and the state*,

and build a production of the form:

IF a goal is in memory,
and there is in memory a rule whose end state matches the goal,
and there are two consecutive gates,
and the present state* is in memory,
THEN generate another goal by computing the values of the attributes by basic procedures**, using the information in the existing goal, the rule, the state*, and the two gates.

New productions generated by executing productions such as these may create a sequence of subgoals and thus constitute a subgoal-generating strategy. Note that, as shown in the above production, new productions for the subgoal-generating strategy are actually embedded in the production-generating productions and no sophisticated mechanism for constructing new productions is involved. However, it should also be noted that the new productions for the subgoal-generating strategy can be created only after good instances are collected by the model. The new strategy can be used only with the already acquired operator application rules, by which generation of new mental gates is possible.

Summary

Starting with the initial set of productions, the model was able within several trials to generate the locating, canceling, and subgoal-generating strategies (in that order). With each of these newly acquired strategies, the model's performance changed radically. The process of strategy acquisition generally followed the predictions of the general mechanisms for learning by doing presented at the beginning of this chapter. The process of pattern discovery in subgoal structure was not simulated by the model, though in my experiments some experienced problem solver tried to find a strategy for generating such a pattern, that is, a long complex pattern of the future trajectory.

The information-processing analysis of the ship-steering task is more difficult than that of the Tower of Hanoi puzzle or the seriation task. Many details in designing the production system model are left open. However, the purpose of studying the ship-steering task was to explore a theory of learning by doing that also incorporates understanding by doing. This goal has been attained, at least to some extent, by this study.

2.7 Discussion

I have described production-system models for the theory of learning by doing using three example tasks. The examples show that the strategy acquisition process in learning by doing involves a complex interaction between already possessed knowledge and knowledge newly acquired. In this section, I present some implications from the study, including theoretical discussions and arguments on computer implementation.

Learning by Doing and Understanding by Doing in Problem Solving

The theory of learning by doing not only explicates the process of acquiring new strategies, but also shows that it can be formalized in terms of conventional theories of problem solving.

It is by now generally accepted that the generation of problem spaces and the search for goals in them constitute the central scheme for human problem solving. Given this basic scheme, our theory of learning by doing can be stated relatively simply: if the problem solver is capable of constructing (any crude) initial problem space and performing (any weak, e.g., trial-and-error) search in the space, learning by doing consists of acquiring strategies for pruning particular parts of the search space. This leads to discovering good subgoals in the course of the search and, later, to efficient planning strategies that organize those subgoals. Also, if it is difficult to represent precisely the initial problem space at the beginning, learning by doing must include understanding by doing, that is, acquisition in the course of working on the problem of knowledge for constructing problem spaces. The strategy acquisition process involved in all three examples given here illustrates the process of learning by doing in this sense. Acquisition of causal knowledge in the ship-steering task can be regarded as understanding by doing in the theory.

This account, based on the search theory of problem solving, is more important than might appear at first because the phenomenon itself—the change of behavior from trial-and-error search to goal-directed procedures in solving problems—is an everyday phenomenon that can be easily observed in many cases. However, its explanation, in terms of the faculties and mechanisms involved in generating such behavioral change is far from trivial. The change actually involves complex cognitive processes that can only be explained rigorously through an approach such as the computational theory and models provided here.

Generality of the Theory

The three tasks covered in this chapter differ in several aspects. To evaluate the generality of the theory, it is helpful to consider the properties of these tasks and the differences between them.

A characteristic of the Tower of Hanoi puzzle is that the number of move constraints, or operator application rules, is very small, and these constraints are easily understood. Also, the number of possible moves is always very small (only two or three). This means that condition sides of newly created productions (which correspond to descriptions of situations for taking particular actions) may be generated fairly easily using relatively small amounts of information. In other words, it seems fairly easy to determine what information to use and what to omit in new condition sides. When we solve the Tower of Hanoi problem, explicit error moves (i.e., moves violating the move constraints) are rather infrequent. Similarly the production system model described here does not learn from explicit error moves but rather from moves thought to be inefficient based on some general heuristics for evaluating move efficiency.

In the seriation task, on the other hand, many moves are often possible, and the move constraint (i.e., the ordering of elements in the line) may frequently be violated. Thus, unlike the model for the Tower of Hanoi puzzle, the model learns new strategies by examining explicit bad moves that violate the move constraint. In this task, encoding the condition sides of newly acquired productions is not a trivial matter. How the state of the elements remaining in the set is perceived in each problem-solving situation raises some fairly subtle issues. It is possible that only part of the information is represented as the present state and used in creating new condition sides. This encoding issue is not treated in the model presented here. The model encodes all information literally available in the problem.

The ship-steering task is more complex than the other two tasks. It involves a virtually infinite number of possible moves, and each of the moves may change the present state in a different way. Thus, the number of operator application rules is infinite. Also, there is a large number of degrees of freedom in how to represent problem states; it is to a large extent dependent upon the pilot's knowledge and perceptual/motor abilities, although there exist some constraints on representation (e.g., encoding change of acceleration is fairly difficult for humans). Because of these characteristics, an adequate representation of the problem space can be learned only by working repeatedly on the task. Furthermore, the ship-steering task involves *real time*, which allows little time for deeper or broader search; the other tasks are *discrete*, which means the problem solver can take virtually unlimited time to select a next move. Because of this, the model for the ship-steering task incorporates almost no search, and relies heavily on acquired causal knowledge to generate plans for moves.

Thus, the three tasks have very different characters. Despite these differences, our theory of learning by doing generally applies to all these tasks. The reason is simple. It is because we can assume that humans possess general capacities for (1) mentally representing tasks as well-structured problems, (2) searching for goals in the represented problem space, (3) constructing procedures for avoiding occurrences of bad instances (4) discovering good subgoals, (5) organizing these subgoals to construct procedures for generating the subgoals, and (6) acquiring knowledge to make these processes more efficient and to integrate them in systematic ways that would accomplish the task. These kinds of competencies may apply to a broad spectrum of problems from the simple Tower of Hanoi to complex ship steering.

Changing Problem Representations by Doing

A production specifies actions to be executed when a particular situation, represented as the production's conditions, is encountered. There are various algorithms known for learning a new production by specifying conditions and related actions. Among the best known algorithms for learning productions are generalization and discrimination (e.g., Anderson 1983). The models presented in this chapter use some additional algorithms for learning productions that, along with generalization and discrimination, are important as computational devices for creating new productions. However, there remain some fundamental issues regarding what is involved in learning a new production. For example, how does a production system program encode information about the present situation relevant to solving the problem? How is such information represented as conditions of a production? The models presented in this chapter more or less avoid these issues by presupposing the representations of problem spaces.

These questions are important, since internal representations of a problem solver are very sensitive to information provided in a particular situation. For example, Anzai and Yokoyama (1984), using elementary mechanics problems, showed that an initial problem representation may rapidly change to another when just a little additional relevant information is given but might not change when another kind of information is provided. What kind of additional information contributes to the abrupt representational shift, and what does not, depends on the relationship between three factors: the problem solver's current internal representation of the problem, his or her knowledge about the domain, and the contents of the additional information given from the outside. Because the representation process is very sensitive to changes in the task situation, determination of the condition side of a to-be-built production must take account of this sensitive process of changing representations. This would require more capabilities than the currently known algorithms for learning new productions provide.

Of course humans are able to change, or revise, problem representations using knowledge acquired by repeatedly solving problems. One of my experiments shows this empirically (Anzai 1982). For about one month in this experiment, a novice subject repeatedly solved a set of about 25 mechanics problems three or four times while thinking aloud. A figure was drawn each time a problem was solved, so it was possible to compare the figures drawn for the same problem to infer how the representation for the problem changed. The results show that the representation changed drastically for some problems. This process of revising representations by repeatedly solving problems is an important facet of learning by doing, since, as the experimental results suggest, a good representation leads to a good solution, and vice versa.

Computer Implementation: Its Significance and Present Limitations

The three production system models presented here all are implemented as working computer programs. The most significant result from this effort of computer implementation was that our theory of learning by doing could be embedded rigorously in a well-established computational theory of problem solving. Phenomena to be explained by our theory can frequently be observed in everyday situations, but implementation of working models on the computer can explain these everyday phenomena in a psychologically plausible computational problem-solving framework.

The models implemented as computer programs are detailed enough so that their structures can be compared. This makes possible a relatively precise analysis of the mechanisms necessary for working on the three tasks. For instance, the three models employ different mechanisms to construct condition sides of new productions. In the model for the Tower of Hanoi task, the wait-and-see algorithm is used with a set of incomplete move constraints defined as productions. In the model for the seriation task, candidates for new conditions are collected by using problem-solving schemata, in the model for the ship-steering task, causal knowledge is used extensively to generate new productions, and their condition sides include acquired causal knowledge. These different mechanisms for creating condition sides reflect possible task-specific aspects in learning by doing.

Unfortunately implementation in a production-system architecture currently explains only part of the cognitive process in learning by doing. There should be more attention given to such issues as how condition sides are encoded and how action sides are decoded. These processes are not serious issues as far as discrete puzzlelike problems such as the Tower of Hanoi and the seriation task are concerned. They become important issues, however, for real-time control tasks like the ship-steering task.

To construct a model of cognitive processes for this kind of task, we need to consider how the rapid perceptual/motor system is related with the cognitive system. While cognitive research on puzzle problem solving and learning has not been concerned with the perceptual/motor system, traditional research on modeling the perceptual/motor system for controlling rapidly moving objects (e.g., Adams 1976) has largely ignored cognitive aspects of the problem-solving and learning processes. Our work on the ship-steering task considers both systems and their relations, though the perceptual/motor system is treated relatively crudely. For instance, one of our experiments shows that experts and novices in the ship steering task differ in the performance of subconscious perceptual/motor system tasks: the experts showed skill in minute, high-frequency tuning of the control dial, while novices' control operations were rough and restricted to a few distinct (e.g., right and left extreme) values of the control angle. Our computer model addresses these differing capabilities, although it does not explain how a novice learns the tuning operations necessary to become an expert.

Instructional Implications

The processes of learning by doing and understanding by doing are constrained by many different information sources including problem instructions, perception of external environments, general heuristic knowledge, subgoals, and problem-solving traces. Even if the fundamental process of learning by doing is as described in this chapter, we may still be able to alter its outcomes by controlling these constraints.

There are, however, many levels to the strategy acquisition process. Thus discussion of the conditions for acquiring new problem-solving strategies must look at these levels separately. Two important levels are the *behavioral level* (i.e., what kinds of strategies are acquired in what order) and the *computational level* (i.e., how a new strategy is acquired by using the currently available strategies). Let us take a brief look at the work on strategy acquisition in problem solving from this viewpoint.

Among the work on acquisition of problem-solving strategies, most of psychology-oriented research has been concerned with the behavioral level. The concept of advance organizers developed by Ausubel (1968), and the emphasis on interaction between instructions and learning processes such as zones of proximal development by Vygotsky (1962) are examples of early, but rather vague, precursors in this direction. More recent work has been done mostly in the information-processing paradigm. For example, the attempt of Simon and Reed (1976) to provide an explicit hint about good subgoals for the Missionaries and Cannibals problem succeeded in shifting their subjects to a more efficient problem-solving. McDaniel (1981) sought to test experimentally whether or not a direct hint about a good strategy for the Hobbits and Orcs problem, a problem isomorphic to the Missionaries and Cannibals problem, would lead to the subjects' acquisition of new strategies and thus change their problem-solving performance. The percentage solved by the shortest path was larger in initial trials for the group with the hint, but in later trials was asymptotic for the two groups with and without the hint. His results also show that, although the two groups acquired the same efficient strategy after a sufficient number of trials solving the same problem, the hint had virtually no influence on the number of legal moves taken by the subjects. McDaniel argues that the hint for the strategy worked as a constraint for the problem-solving search process, which led to different initial overall performance for the two groups. The hint seemed to be irrelevant to final performance, possibly because the learning processes continued along essentially the same lines in later stages.

These experimental studies as well as several others, suggest that explicit structions about strategies would lead to the acquisition of efficient strategies under certain conditions. However, the studies are mainly concerned with the effects of hints on acquisition of strategies, or at most with what sort of strategies are learned in what order. They are not concerned with how each strategy shift actually occurs. In other words, they are concerned with explanation and prediction at the behavioral level, not the computational level.

In the field of artificial intelligence, there is some work on computer acquisition of problem-solving strategies. For example, Mitchell, Utgoff, and Banerji (1983) built a system that acquires new strategies for solving symbolic integration problems. Carbonell (1983) was concerned with a system that uses past experience solving analogous problems to acquire new problem-solving strategies. Langley (1985) conducted computational experiments on a system that applies task-independent heuristics for learning search strategies in various puzzle-solving tasks. These and other studies done mainly in the area of machine learning are helpful in explaining the process of strategy acquisition at the computational level. These studies, however, are not concerned with how the process generally proceeds—that is, the behavioral level of explanation and prediction.

There is also some work related more to cognitive psychology than AI which touches on the computational level of strategy acquisition processes.

For example, Anderson, Greeno, Kline, and Neves (1981) presented a computer model for how strategies for solving geometry proof problems are acquired. They pointed out that there are many different process components in learning to prove geometry problems: analogy, schematization, proceduralization, generalization, compilation, and subsumption, to list a few. Their model shows how these components are intertwined in the learning process, and thus explains and predicts the student's behavior at the computational level. It is not very concerned, however, with the behavioral level of learning—that is, how the application of those process components changes due to acquisition of more knowledge. Neches (1981) presented a computational formalism for acquiring strategies for simple arithmetic addition by using a set of domain-independent heuristics for learning procedures. His model explains computationally how children acquire efficient strategies for addition, without explicit instructions from a teacher, by using those heuristics on problem-solving traces. His formalism provides an explanation at the behavioral level concerning what kind of strategies are acquired in what order. However, such explanations are still restricted to small domains like simple addition and need to be extended to other domains while keeping computational-level descriptions.

Our theory, in contrast, concerns multiple levels. It explains and predicts both what kinds of strategies are acquired in what order and how a specific new strategy is acquired from currently available strategies. Furthermore, the theory applies across a wide variety of domains, as shown by the three different tasks described in this chapter.

In general, explanations at the behavioral level focus on macroscopic accounts of the problem solver's learning behavior, whereas the computational level approach focuses on the minute details of how the problem solver's cognitive processes work to learn a new strategy from old ones. Both accounts are indispensable when we apply a cognitive theory of learning to an instructional situation: the macroscopic, behavioral account points out exactly where in the whole process of learning the problem solver is at present and predicts what comes next in learning, and the microscopic, computational account detects, explains, and predicts each action, such as how an error is utilized in learning. Hence I believe that focusing on two different levels of explanation and prediction is an important necessary condition for a cognitive theory to be applied successfully to instructional situations. Our theory appears to satisfy this condition.

Although our theory has not yet been tested in a real instructional situation, it may be useful for designing hints and other instructional programs. For example, when is the best time for giving hints about the subgoal strategy in the process of training for the ship-steering task? Out theory suggests that the best time is just after acquisition of the canceling strategy because the subgoal strategy requires making the ship go straight, which can not be achieved until after the canceling strategy is acquired. It is hardly plausible that hints about a more advanced strategy prompt acquisition of less-advanced strategies if no such strategies are yet acquired. For instance, hints about the subgoal strategy for the ship-steering task would not help acquisition of the canceling strategy because the acquisition of the subgoal strategy presupposes the possession of the canceling strategy.

Although we need more empirical clarification of the relationship between instructions like hints and our theory of learning processes, the theory seems to provide reliable implications for instructions and predictions of their results at both the behavioral and computational levels, which makes it useful for instructional or training situations.

References

Adams, J. A. 1976. Issues for a closed-loop theory of motor learning. In G. E. Stelmach (ed.), *Motor Control: Issues and Trends*. New York: Academic Press.

Amarel, S. 1983. Problem of representation in heuristic problem solving: related issues in the development of expert systems. In R. Groner, M. Groner and W. F. Bischof (eds.), *Methods of Heuristics*. Hillsdale, N. J.: Lawrence Erlbaum Associates, pp. 245–349.

Anderson, J. R. 1983. *The Architecture of Cognition*. Cambridge, MASS.: Harvard University Press.

Anderson, J. R., Greeno, J. G., Kline, P. J., and Neves, D. M. 1981. Acquisition of problem-solving skill. In J. R. Anderson (ed.), *Cognitive Skills and Their Acquisition*. Hillsdale, N.J.: Lawrence Erlbaum Associations, pp. 191–230.

Anzai, Y. 1978a. How one learns strategies: processes and representation of strategy acquisition. *Proceedings of the 3rd Artificial Intelligence and Simulation of Behavior Conference*, pp. 1–14, Hamburg, West Germany.

Anzai, Y. 1978b. Learning strategies by computer. *Proceedings of the 2nd Canadian Society for Computational Studies on Intelligence Conference*, pp. 181–190, Toronto, Canada.

Anzai, Y. 1982. Role of problem solving knowledge in understanding problems. CIP Paper No. 440. Department of Psychology, Carnegie-Mellon University.

Anzai, Y. 1984. Cognitive control of real-time event-driven systems. *Cognitive Science* 8, 221–254.

Anzai, Y., Mitsuya, Y., Nakajima, S., and Ura, S. 1981. LPS: A rule-based, schema-oriented knowledge representation system. *Journal of Information Processing* 4, 177–185.

Anzai, Y., and Simon, H. A. 1979. The theory of learning by doing. *Psychological Review* 86, 124–140.

Anzai, Y., and Yokoyama, T. 1984. Internal models in physics problem solving. *Cognition and Instruction* 1, 397–450.

Ausubel, D. P. 1968. *Educational Psychology: A Cognitive View*. New York: Holt, Rinehart and Winston.

Baylor, G. W., and Gascon, J. 1974. An information processing theory of aspects of the development of weight seriation in children. *Cognitive Psychology* 6, 1–40.

Carbonell, J. G. 1983. Learning by analogy: Formulating and generalizing plans from past experience. In R. S. Michalski, J. G. Carbonell, and T. M. Mitchell (eds.), *Machine Learning: An Artificial Intelligence Approach*. New York: Springer-Verlag, pp. 137–161.

Forgy, C. L. 1981. OPS5 User's Manual. Report No. CMU-CS-81-135. Department of Computer Science, Carnegie-Mellon University.

Greeno, J. G. 1980. Psychology of learning, 1960–1980: One participant's observations. *American Psychologist* 35, 713–728.

Hayes, J. R., and Simon, H. A. 1974. Understanding written problem instructions. In L. W. Gregg (ed.), *Knowledge and Cognition*. Hillsdale, N.J.: Lawrence Erlbaum Associates, pp. 167–200.

Langley, P. 1985. learning to search: from weak methods to domain-specific heuristics. *Cognitive Science* 9, 217–260.

Larkin, J., McDermott, J., Simon, D. P., and Simon, H. A. 1980. Models of competence in solving physics problems. *Cognitive Science* 4, 317–345.

McDaniel, M. A. 1980. *Bottom-up and top-down acquisition of expertise on rivercrossing problems*. Dissertation. Department of Psychology, University of Colorado.

Mitchell, T. M., Utgoff, P. E., and Banerji, R. B. 1983. Learning by experimentation: Acquiring and refining problem solving heuristics. In R. S. Michalski, J. G. Carbonell, and T. M. Mitchell (eds.), *Machine Learning: An Artificial Intelligence Approach*. New York: Springer-Verlag, pp. 163–190.

Neches, R. 1981. A computational formalism for heuristic procedure modification. *Proceedings of the Seventh International Joint Conference on Artificial Intelligence*, pp. 283–288.

Newell, A., and Simon, H. A. 1972. *Human Problem Solving*. Englewood Cliffs, N.J.: Prentice-Hall.

Simon, H. A., and Reed, S. K. 1976. Modeling strategy shifts in a problem-solving task. *Cognitive Psychology* 8, 86–97.

Vygotsky, L. S. 1962. *Thought and Language*. Cambridge, Mass.: MIT Press (first Russian version published in 1934).

Young, R. M. 1973. *Children's seriation behavior: a production-system approach*. Dissertation. Department of Psychology, Carnegie-Mellon University.

3 A General Theory of Discrimination Learning

Pat Langley

One of the major goals of any science is to develop general theories to explain phenomena, and one may ask what general mechanisms have so far been uncovered to explain the nature of intelligent behavior in man and machine. Early research in cognitive science and artificial intelligence focused on this issue, and systems like the General Problem Solver (Newell, Shaw, and Simon 1960) were the result. These programs employed techniques like heuristic search and means-ends analysis to direct attention down promising paths, and such methods have proved to be very general indeed. In contrast to these early efforts, recent work has emphasized the importance of domain-specific knowledge (Feigenbaum, Buchanan, and Lederberg 1971; Pople 1977), and much of the current research focuses on expert systems for particular fields of knowledge. While these systems perform admirably in their areas of expertise, they fare very poorly on the dimension of generality.

We hope that our final theory of intelligence will consist of more than a few basic search techniques, along with the statement that domain-specific knowledge can be used to direct one's search. In addition Langley and Simon (1981) have proposed that we look for generality in the *learning mechanisms* through which such domain-specific knowledge is acquired. They have argued that because learning theories should be able to account for both novice and expert behavior, as well as the transition between them, such theories are inherently more general than performance theories alone. Moreover, there is the chance that a single learning theory can be used to explain the transition process for a number of different domains. Given this generality, learning has a central role to play in any theory of cognition, and in this chapter we present a general theory of learning that is stated in the language of adaptive production systems.

We will not attempt to justify our choice of production systems as the formalism in which to cast our models of learning and development, since that issue has been addressed elsewhere in this volume. As we have seen, the natural way to model learning in a production system framework is by the creation of new condition-action rules or productions. The appropriate actions of these new rules can often be determined rather easily, since analogous actions can be observed in the environment. However, the conditions under which these actions should be applied is seldom so obvious. In this chapter we address the issue of how one determines the correct conditions on productions. We review some earlier research that has been concerned with condition finding and outline a theory of discrimination learning that begins with overly general rules and that creates variants of these rules with additional conditions when these rules lead to errors. After this we consider how the theory can be applied to explain learning and development in four rather different domains; these include concept attainment, strategy learning, first language acquisition, and development on a Piagetian task. Finally, we evaluate the theory along a number of dimensions, including its generality.

3.1 Previous Research on Condition Finding

The problem of determining the correct conditions on a rule is not limited to the production-system framework, and much of the research on learning in both artificial intelligence and cognitive science has focused on condition-finding methods. In this section we review some of the earlier work on this topic. We begin by describing some systems that learn through a process of generalization, after which we review some limitations of the generalization-based approach. Finally, we consider a number of systems that learn through an alternative process of discrimination.

Learning Concepts through Generalization

The majority of research on condition finding has incorporated techniques for *generalization*, and the bulk of work on generalization has focused on the problem of learning the definition of a concept from a set of positive and negative examples. In this paradigm the learning system begins by assuming that all aspects of the first positive instance are relevant to the concept and then systematically removing conditions as they fail to occur in new examples. The basic insight is that one can determine the relevant conditions on a concept by finding those features or structures that are held in common by a set of positive examples. Below we review a number of systems that learn by generalization, and we will see a few of the many variations that are possible within this basic framework. In each case, we describe the learning task, and discuss two key features of the particular learning method–the manner in which the space of rules is searched, and the use that is made of negative instances.

Bruner, Goodnow, and Austin (1956) carried out one of the earliest studies of concept learning, working with concepts that could be represented in terms of simple attribute-value pairs. Although their primary concern was with human behavior on concept-learning tasks, they completed detailed task analyses that could have been easily cast as running programs. Many subjects employed a *focusing* strategy for determining the conditions defining a concept.[1] This approach started with a positive example of a concept, such as a *large blue square*, and initially assumed that all features were relevant to the concept's definition. As new positive instances were encountered, they were used to eliminate some of the features. For example, if a *large red square* were also an example of the concept, then the color dimension would be deemed irrelevant. Such comparisons continued until each of the attributes had been varied; those attributes whose alteration led to negative instances were retained, and all others were eliminated. Although this strategy works well with conjunctive concepts like *large and square*, it cannot be used to learn disjunctive concepts like *large or square*. An important feature of this strategy was that for concepts defined as conjunctions of attribute-value pairs, no real search was involved in their determination. Given the current hypothesis as to the concept's definition (some features of which were known to be relevant, and others still in question) and a new positive instance, only a single generalization could result, leading to the removal of the varied attribute from the hypothesis. We shall see that in learning tasks involving more complex representations, life is not so simple, and negative instances play a more important role than in Bruner et al.'s concept attainment tasks.

Winston (1970) extended this approach to learning structural concepts such as *arch*. His system was given a sequence of structural descriptions, each with an associated classification, with the goal of determining the conditions that would allow the proper classification of new examples. On first encountering a positive instance of a concept, the program included every aspect of the description in its initial definition of the concept. For example, the initial definition of *arch* might state that two standing blocks supported a third block, that the two standing blocks were not in contact, and that each block had certain features of its own. When the system was given another positive example of the same concept, it would find a mapping between the current definition and the new example; this specified the structures held in common by the definition and the example, and the concept was redefined in terms of these common structures.

For instance, if the original arch had a brick as its top block, while another arch used a pyramid in this position, then the shape of the top block would be removed from the definition. This approach was very similar to that described by Bruner et al., except that because of the more complex representation being used, in some cases more than one generalization was possible. Since the program considered only one of these possibilities, it can be viewed as carrying out a *depth-first* search through the space of possible concepts. And since there was no guarantee that the program would always select the right generalization, it required the ability to backtrack through this space as well, and it was in such cases that negative instances came into play. When the definition of a concept led the system to incorrectly predict that a description was an example of that concept, Winston's program backtracked to an earlier, more specific concept definition. The system also used negative instances to identify 'emphatic' conditions such as 'must support.' To ensure that the system did not also have to search for the conditions it should add, Winston presented it only with *near misses*; these were negative instances that differed from positive exemplars by only a few features.[2] Although Winston's learning heuristics were potentially very general, he never seems to have extended them beyond his blocks world.

Hayes-Roth and McDermott (1976) have described SPROUTER, another program that learned concepts from a series of exemplars. This system used a technique called *interference matching* that was similar to Winston's method for finding common properties between positive examples. However, where Winston used relatively ad hoc rules for selecting the appropriate generalization, SPROUTER carried out a systematic *beam search* through the space of possible mappings. This was a version of breadth-first search in which multiple mappings were entertained simultaneously; when the number of alternative generalizations exceeded a reasonable bound, the search tree was pruned and only the best hypotheses were retained. In making this decision, generalizations that contained few nodes but many relations between them were preferred to generalizations that consisted of less dense structures. SPROUTER focused on positive instances, but negative instances also had an important role in directing the search process. If a generalization was formed that covered nonexamples of the concept in addition to positive examples, then it was considered overly general, and that hypothesis was dropped from consideration. As a result whole branches of the search tree could be abandoned, and attention focused in more profitable areas. The system also searched the space of examples, selecting those most likely to provide new information. SPROUTER showed its generality by learning a number of concepts, including the structural description for *chair*.

One advantage of breadth-first generalization strategies is that they need not retain any positive instances of a concept since they need never backtrack. However, negative instances must still be retained if they are to be used in rejecting overly general rules. Mitchell (1977) has done away with the need for negative information as well with his version space technique. In addition to maintaining a set of generalizations or *maximally specific versions* (MSVs) of a concept, his system maintained a set of *maximally general versions* (MGVs). New positive instances led to more general MSVs with fewer conditions, which corresponded to the process of generalization in earlier programs. New negative instances led to more specific MGVs with additional conditions.[3] If a negative instance was encountered that an MSV successfully matched, that MSV was removed from further consideration (much as in SPROUTER). Similarly, an MGV was removed from the competition when a negative instance was found that it failed to match. The main use of Mitchell's system was within the meta–DENDRAL program, in the discovery of conditions for predicting peaks in mass spectrograms. However, the learning heuristics were implemented in a very general manner, and were applied to Winston's arch-learning task as well.

The programs described here certainly do not exhaust the generalization learning paradigm. The interested reader is directed to Vere (1975) for an excellent formal treatment of breadth-first strategies for generalization. Mitchell (1979) provides an interesting overview of work in this area relating the various approaches and evaluating them in terms of their search strategies and memory requirements. Although most work on condition finding has been concerned with concept learning, Hedrick (1976) has employed generalization techniques in modeling language acquisition, Vere (1977) has considered the generalization of procedures stated as condition-action rules, and Mitchell, Utgoff, and Banerji (1981, 1983) have applied the version-space method to learning heuristics for directing search.

Drawbacks of the Generalization Approach

There is little doubt that progress has been made since the early work of Bruner, Goodnow, and Austin. The most recent generalization learning systems are considerably more general than the earliest programs, in that they can deal with structural and relational representations as well as attribute-value pairs. In addition they are more robust than their ancestors in that they take advantage of negative information to reduce the search that results from more complex representations, and they organize this search more efficiently. However, this basic approach has a number of drawbacks that limit its value as a path to knowledge acquisition. First, because they examine features that are held in common between examples, generalization-based strategies do not lend themselves to the discovery of *disjunctive* concepts (e.g., *large or red*). When confronted with positive examples of disjunctive rules, these systems overgeneralize (removing those features not held in common by the disjuncts) and cannot recover. Iba (1979) has extended Winston's depth-first search approach to handle disjunctive concepts, but this method is very costly in terms of computation time.

Second, generalization-based learning systems have difficulty handling errorful data. As before, this results from their dependence on finding commonalities in a number of examples. If even one of these examples is faulty, then the entire learning sequence is thrown into confusion. Again we are not claiming that one cannot in principle modify generalization-oriented strategies to respond to noise; rather, we would claim that these strategies do not lend themselves to handling noisy environments. For example, Mitchell (1978) has proposed an extension to his version-space technique that can deal with isolated errors. However, such a system would pay a high price for maintaining the additional hypotheses that would be necessary to recover from even a single faulty piece of information.

One final drawback is closely related to the issue of noise. Any program that learns through generalization would have serious difficulty responding to an evironment in which the conditions predicting an event actually changed over time. For example, if a tutor decided to modify the definition of a concept in the middle of a training session, a system that searched for common features would rapidly become very confused. Of course one would not expect a learning system to note such a change immediately, since it must gather evidence to determine whether its errors were due to random noise or to an actual shift. However, the ability to recover gradually from changes in its environment would be a definite advantage in real-world settings, where such changes are all too common. In summary, generalization-based approaches to condition finding have a number of disadvantages. Next we review five systems that learn through discrimination, an approach to knowledge acquisition that has the potential to overcome these difficulties.

Finding Conditions through Discrimination

Although the majority of research on condition finding has employed generalization–based methods, some research has been carried out with techniques for discrimination. Members of this class of learning methods start with very general rules containing few conditions and introduce new constraints as the need arises. Positive and negative examples are used in a quite different manner from the way they are used in generalization-based strategies. Rather than looking for features held in common by all positive instances, these methods search for *differences* between positive and negative instances. These differences are then used to further specify the conditions under which a concept or rule should apply. Let us consider five systems that learn in this manner.

Feigenbaum (1963) has described EPAM, a computer simulation of verbal learning behavior in humans. This model learned to associate pairs of nonsense syllables such as DAX and JIR through a process of discrimination; using the same mechanism, it was also able to memorize sequences of nonsense syllables. EPAM learned by constructing a discrimination net for sorting different stimuli and responses. Tests bifurcated the tree and specified which path should be taken, while nonsense syllables were stored at the terminal nodes of the tree. This tree was initially very simple, but new branches and their associated tests were inserted as new syllables were encountered. For example, *JIR* would first be stored below a branch taken if *J* were the first letter of a syllable; however, once the syllable *JUK* was encountered, a new branch would be introduced that tested whether the third letter was *R*, and *JIR* would be restored on this branch. The particular letter EPAM focused on was determined by the position that had been most recently found to be useful in discriminating between syllables. Associations between stimuli and responses were encoded by storing enough information at a stimulus' terminal node to allow retrieval of the associated response. EPAM's discrimination process accounted for a number of well-known verbal learning phenomena, including stimulus and response generalization, oscillation and retroactive inhibition, and the forgetting of seemingly well-learned responses.

Hunt, Marin, and Stone (1966) described a set of programs that applied EPAM-related ideas to the task of concept learning. They focused on concepts such as *large and red*, in which instances could be represented as attribute-value pairs. Concepts were represented as discrimination nets, with each branch in the tree testing the value of one of the attributes and each terminal node stating whether or not the instance was an example of the concept. The basic learning strategy was to search for attribute–value pairs common to all positive or negative instances. If this failed, then the attribute–value pair occurring most frequently in either the positive or negative class was chosen as the test for a new branch in the tree for the concept.[4] The same heuristic was then applied recursively to the instances satisfying this test, until a tree was constructed that divided the instances into sets that were exclusively positive or exclusively negative. The researchers carried out a number of experiments with this approach. For example, they found minimal effects as the number of irrelevant attributes and values were increased, but significant effects as the complexity of concepts grew. Limiting memory for past instances increased the number of instances required to determine the correct rule, but an overall saving in computation time resulted because less information had to be taken into account in forming the discrimination tree. Another interesting finding was that the ability to select instances intelligently did not result in a significant improvement over random selection. Because in general the expression *not [A and B]* is equivalent to the expression *not [A] or not [B]*, Hunt, Marin, and Stone's systems could learn disjunctive concepts simply by viewing positive instances as negative instances, and vice versa. Since their approach did not exclusively rely on finding common features, it should also have lent itself to dealing with noisy data, but they did not address this issue.

Langley (1978, 1979) has described BACON.1, a discovery system that operated in the domains of concept attainment, sequence extrapolation, and the induction of mathematical functions. The central heuristic of this program was to search for constant values of dependent terms and then attempt to determine the conditions under which these constancies held. For example, when presented with a standard Bruner et al. concept attainment task, BACON.1 would systematically vary the independent attributes (e.g., color, size, and shape) and observe the feedback associated with each combination of values. Upon encountering two cases in which the feedback was *yes* (i.e., two situations that were examples of the concept), the system would immediately conclude that *all* combinations would lead to this feedback (i.e., that everything was an example of the concept). However, it would continue to gather additional data, and if it came upon a combination with an unpredicted feedback (e.g., *no*), it would realize that it had overgeneralized and attempt to correct its error through a simple discrimination process. BACON.1's recovery heuristic was stated as a condition-action rule that searched for some attribute that had the same value in two of the correctly predicted situations, but a different value in two of the incorrectly predicted cases. When such a difference was discovered, the distinguishing attribute-value pair was included as an additional condition on the hypothesis. Since it based its discriminations on only *two* good and bad instances, BACON.1 was able to learn disjunctive concepts like *large or red* as well as conjunctive rules like *large and red.*

Brazdil (1978) has discussed ELM, a PROLOG program that learned from sample solutions in the domain of simple algebra and arithmetic. The system began with a set of rules for associativity, for adding the same number to both sides, and so forth. It was then given a set of practice problems, along with their solution paths. For each problem ELM went through each step of the solution, comparing the step it would have made with the corresponding step of the known solution. Since the system had no priority ordering for its rules at the outset, it tried all rules that were applicable to the current problem state. However, only one rule application agreed with the solution trace, so the corresponding rule was given priority over its competitors; in the future this rule was selected in preference to the others. In this way ELM established a partial ordering on its rule set. Difficulties arose when one problem suggested a certain ordering, and another problem suggested a different one. In such cases Brazdil's system invoked a discrimination process to create more constrained versions of the competing rules with additional conditions on their application. The new conditions were selected by finding predicates that were true when the rule should have been applied but false when another rule should have been preferred. The new rules were added to the priority ordering above the rules from which they were generated, so the more conservative rules would be preferred in the future.

Anderson, Kline, and Beasley (1978, 1980) have described ACT, a production system formalism that has been used to model a wide range of cognitive phenomena. Anderson and his colleagues have applied their theory to many aspects of learning, and we cannot review all of them here. Instead, we will focus on a paper by Anderson and Kline (1979), in which they summarize ACT's learning mechanisms and their use in simulating the process of concept attainment. The authors divided their learning model into three major components. The first of these consisted of a generalization process much like those reviewed here, in which positive instances of the concept were compared, and more general rules (in this case stated as productions) were created with conditions removed or with constants replaced by variables. However, Anderson and Kline also recognized the possibility that this process could lead to overgeneralizations, and they included a discrimination mechanism to direct the recovery process. This discrimination technique compared a good application of a rule (when the correct classification was made) to a bad application (when an incorrect application was made) and, based on the differences it found between these two cases, constructed a less general version of the rule by replacing variables with constants.[5] Finally, the model employed a strengthening process that incremented the strength of a production if it was applied correctly or if it was relearned. Along with a bias toward more specific productions, the strength of a rule was used in deciding which production should be selected at any given time. Taken together, the three ACT learning methods accounted for data from various concept learning experiments with humans. In addition, the discrimination process let the model acquire disjunctive concepts as well as conjunctive ones.

3.2 An Overview of the Discrimination Learning Theory

In the previous section we examined a number of systems that learned through generalization. In finding the definition of a concept, these programs initially assumed that all conditions were relevant and systematically removed these conditions when they failed to occur in new examples. However, we also saw that an alternative approach to condition finding is possible. Instead of starting with all conditions, one initially assumes that *none* of the potential conditions are relevant. If the resulting rule is overly general and leads to errors, then one inserts new conditions that make the rule more conservative. This *discrimination learning* approach provides an interesting alternative to the more traditional generalization paradigm. As with generalization-based condition finding, a discrimination-based strategy can be implemented in many different ways. In this section we outline a theory of discrimination learning that we feel has considerable potential, beginning with a discussion of PRISM, the formalism in which the theory is stated. While our approach shares some features with the earlier work on discrimination, it has some important differences as well.

The PRISM Formalism

Our theory of discrimination learning is implemented in PRISM, a production-system language that was designed as a tool for exploring different architectures and their relation to learning mechanisms. PRISM is a very flexible language through which the user can create any of a large class of production-system architectures. Thus the particular architecture in which the discrimination learning theory has been implemented is only one of many possible PRISM-based schemes. However, since we have found this particular framework to be the most useful for building actual learning systems, we will focus on its characteristics here.

We will not review the basic production-system cycle, since that has been covered elsewhere in this volume. However, the PRISM conflict resolution procedure is worth some discussion, since it interacts with the various learning mechanisms. On every cycle PRISM applies the following (ordered) sequence of conflict resolution principles:

1. *Refraction.* Eliminate from consideration every instantiation that has already been applied; this lets the system avoid simple loops by forcing it to focus on new information.

2. *Production strength.* From the remaining instantiations, PRISM selects those matched by productions with the greatest *strength*; this serves to focus attention on rules that have been successful in the past or that have been learned many times.

3. *Recency.* From the revised set, PRISM selects those instantiations that match against the most *recent* elements in working memory; this serves to focus attention on recently established goals in preference to older ones.

4. *Random selection.* If multiple instantiations still remain at this stage, PRISM selects one of them at random. Thus one and only one production instantiation is applied on each cycle.

These particular conflict resolution strategies are far from new. For example, Forgy (1979) has used both refraction and recency in his OPS4 production system language, and Anderson et al. (1980) have relied on strength in their ACT models. The preceding combination of strategies was determined partially by analysis, and partially by trial and error, to be the most useful in constructing robust adaptive production systems. Refraction is foremost because trivial looping must be avoided. Strength is second in line because some measure of a rule's usefulness or success is essential to direct search through the large space of productions that could conceivably be constructed. Recency is essential for domains such as strategy learning and language acquisition, where the order in which goals have been added to memory can be used to order behavior. Finally, random selection is required if one wishes to retain the standard assumption of the serial application of productions.

PRISM also includes a number of mechanisms for modeling learning phenomena. The most basic of these is the *designation* process, which allows the creation of a new production as the action of an existing rule. By including the general form of a rule in its action side, a designating production matching against a particular situation can carry over variable bindings to its action side, and in this way it creates a specific rule based on the general form. A second process lets PRISM create generalizations of existing rules when it discovers two productions in its memory that have isomorphic structures; the resulting rule includes variables in places that the two specific rules had differing constants, and so it can match in situations that the less-general versions could not. (The PRISM–based learning systems that we will be discussing in later sections do not take advantage of this capability.) PRISM also has the ability to strengthen or weaken productions and so affect their order of preference during the conflict resolution stage. Rules are strengthened whenever they are re-created by any of the learning mechanisms, but they can also be strengthened (or weakened) explicitly by the action side of an arbitrary production. Finally, PRISM incorporates a *discrimination* process that can be used to recover from overly general rules; we discuss this learning mechanism in some detail below.

Finding New Conditions

We will begin our discussion of discrimination learning in terms of a simple example, and introduce complexities as we proceed. Consider a concept learning task like that studied by Bruner et al., in which we have four potentially relevant attributes—size (*large* or *small*), color (*blue* or *red*), shape (*circle* or *square*), and thickness of the lines making up the shape (*thick* or *thin*). Also suppose that we start with a rule that predicts that every combination of values is an example of the concept:

IF you have a combination of values,
  and you have not yet made a prediction,
THEN predict that the combination is an example.

Clearly this overly general rule will lead to many errors, but suppose that our concept is *large and square* and that initially the system is presented with the combination *large thick red square*. In this case the rule will produce a correct prediction, and this information would be stored for future reference. Now suppose that the next combination is *large thick red circle*, which is not an example of the desired concept. In this case our initial rule will make a faulty prediction, indicating that it lacks one or more relevant conditions.

When such an error is noted, the discrimination process is evoked to produce more conservative variants on the original rule. To accomplish this, the learning mechanism retrieves information about the situation in which the faulty rule was last correctly applied and compares it to the current situation, which led to an incorrect application. The goal is to dicover differences between the good and bad situations, and in this case only one difference is noted: in the good case the shape was square, while in the bad case the shape was circle. Accordingly the discrimination process constructs a variant on the original rule with a new condition:

IF you have a combination of values,
and you have not yet made a prediction,
and the shape is square,
THEN predict that the combination is an example.

This rule is guaranteed to match in the correct situation but will fail to match in the incorrect one, avoiding the error made by its predecessor. In order to select between competing productions, each rule is given an an associated *strength*. When a variant rule is first created, it may be weaker than the more general one from which it was created, but if the same rule is learned many times, it will eventually come to exceed its ancestor. The initial strength of a rule is controlled by a user-modifiable parameter, as is the amount by which rules are strengthened upon recreation. In addition to strengthening a rule each time it is relearned through discrimination, a faulty rule is weakened when it leads to an error. Since stronger rules are preferred to their competitors, these strengthening and weakening strategies bias the learning system in favor of more successful productions, so that useful variants eventually come to mask the rules from which they evolved.[6]

Although this second rule is better than the original version, it still does not represent the entire concept *large and square*. Before the complete concept is acquired, another error must occur. Suppose our second rule has gained sufficient strength to mask its ancestor, and the combination *small thick red square* is presented. In this case the variant rule will apply, incorrectly predicting that this combination is an example of the concept. Again discrimination is evoked, this time comparing the combinations *large thick red square* and *small thick red square*. As before, only a single difference is noted, and a still more conservative rule is created:

IF you have a combination of values,
 and you have not yet made a prediction,
 and the shape is square,
 and the size is large,
THEN predict that the combination is an example.

Once this rule has been learned enough times to mask its predecessors, our system will always correctly predict whether a combination is an instance of the concept. Although it should have helped to clarify the basic nature of discrimination learning, this example oversimplifies the process along a number of dimensions. For example, it assumes an attribute-value representation rather than more general (and complex) relational structures. Also we have ignored the possibility of learning negated conditions through discrimination, and we have omitted the details of learning from far misses, in which one must consider a number of alternative variants. Below we discuss each of these complications on the basic discrimination learning method.

Finding Negated and Complex Conditions

One extension of the basic method concerns the acquisition of rules with negated conditions. In the preceding example, including the condition that *the size is not small* would be equivalent to the condition *the size is large*. However, this results from the fact that each attribute took on only two values; if we had allowed the size to take the value *medium* as well, then the two conditions would have quite different meanings. The discrimination learning mechanism can be easily extended to allow the discovery of negated conditions. In the previous example, if a fact was present during the good application and absent during the bad application, then it was included as a positive condition in a new variant rule. But the reverse reasoning holds equally well: if a fact was present during the bad application but absent during the good application, then it should be included as a *negated* condition in a new rule. This means that variants with positive and negative conditions may be created in response to the same error, but since one cannot distinguish between them on the basis of a single example, this is a reasonable decision. If one of the rules is more useful than the other, then it should be created more often and eventually come to mask its competitor.

A second extension allows the discovery of many conditions at the same time. This can occur in the context of structural or relational representations, when a single fact is not sufficient to distinguish between a good and bad application. As an example, suppose that our system is learning the concept *uncle* but starts with an overly general rule that believes the uncle relation holds between any two people. Suppose further that it correctly predicts that *Joe* is the uncle of *Sam* but incorrectly predicts that *Jack* is the uncle of *Steve*. Upon examining the information associated with each of these situations, it finds that both *Sam* and *Steve* have a parent; thus this condition in itself is not enough to predict the uncle relation in one case but not the other. But on continuing its search, the discrimination process finds that *Joe* is the brother of *Sam*'s parent, while *Jack* is not the brother of *Steve*'s parent. Thus the *conjunction* of the parent and brother relations is sufficient to tell between the two instances, and these two relations would be included as conditions in a variant on the original rule. Analogous situations can lead to a conjunction of negated conditions; a rule containing such a conjunction will match if any subset of its negated conditions match but not if all of them are true simultaneously. In principle, this approach may be used to find variants with an arbitrary number of new conditions; in practice, the search must be constrained to a reasonable depth, allowing no more than four or five conditions to be found simultaneously.

Selecting between Alternative Variants

The reader may have noted the careful crafting of the above examples, so that only one difference occurred in each case. This meant that the relevant conditions were obvious, and the discrimination mechanism was not forced to consider alternative corrections. Unfortunately one cannot always depend on a benevolent tutor to present an ideal sequence of examples. Accordingly, when an error is detected, the discrimination process considers all differences between the correct and incorrect situations and constructs *all* of the corresponding variants. For example, suppose the good case was *large thick blue circle*, while the bad case was *small thin red square*. Here four rules would be created, one with *large* as a new condition, one with *thick*, one with *blue*, and one with *circle*.[7] Some of these differences may have nothing to do with the actual concept, but each of the rules is initially given a low strength. Only if the same rule is constructed many times will it have a chance to play a role in the decision process.

The strengthening process is the key to focusing attention on promising variants. Even if a variant rule is still overly general, it will tend to be created more often than other variants in which the wrong conditions were inserted. This means that it will be selected in preference to its competitors and lead to errors of its own. When this occurs, the discrimination mechanism will generate variations on this rule with still more conditions, which in turn may generate their own errors and lead to even better rules. Thus, though the discrimination process may generate many completely spurious rules, these tend to be ignored and only the most promising variants are considered further. The entire process may be viewed as a *beam search* through the space of rules, in which only a few nodes are chosen for expansion at any given depth. This strategy makes for much slower learning than occurs in generalization-based approaches, but the strategy is also much more robust than the more traditional methods.

The Advantages of Discrimination Learning

In the previous section we discussed some drawbacks of generalization-based learning methods. We found that generalization ran into difficulties when confronted with disjunctive rules, noisy environments, or rules that change over time. In contrast, a discrimination learning technique like the one just outlined responds comparatively well in these situations. Because our discrimination process compares only a single good situation to a single bad situation, disjunctive concepts can be easily acquired. The disjunct that is learned in a particular case depends on the good situation that is examined, but since the most recent good situation is used, each of the disjuncts will eventually be found. The combination of discrimination and strengthening allows learning in noisy environments, since the occurrence of occasional errors will have little effect on a learning algorithm that sums across many different examples. Finally, the weakening of faulty variants provides a natural mechanism for backing up through the space of rules, should this ever be necessary due to a change in the environment.

In summary, the proposed discrimination learning theory appears to embody a very robust approach to learning that deserves further exploration.

Relation to Earlier Research on Discrimination

Although the majority of condition-finding research has been concerned with techniques for generalization, we have seen that a few researchers have employed discrimination-based learning methods. At least some of these researchers have realized the potential of discrimination to deal with the issues we have discussed. Hunt, Marin, and Stone used their technique to learn disjunctive concepts by viewing positive instances as negative instances, and vice versa. Anderson and Kline used discrimination to learn disjunctive rules when overgeneralizations occurred, and they seemed to realize the importance of a strengthening component for dealing with noisy environments. However, to our knowledge they have not explored these issues in any detail. Thus our theory should not be viewed as an entirely new approach to the task of determining relevant conditions. Rather, it is an attempt to extend a promising approach to learning that has received relatively little attention and to cast this approach in sufficiently general terms that it can be applied to a variety of domains.

Since our learning method bears a close resemblance to that employed by Anderson and Kline, we should spend some time discussing the differences. First, the earlier researchers used discrimination mainly to recover from overgeneralizations, while we are exploring discrimination separately from generalization-based approaches. Second, Anderson and Kline's version of discrimination created only a single variant whenever it was evoked, while the proposed method constructs a different variant for each difference that is found. Thus the earlier technique can be viewed as carrying out a depth-first search through the space of possible rules, while our method carries out a beam search that should be able to discover all useful variants. Finally, Anderson and Kline's variants differed from their predecessors by including only one additional condition.[8] In contrast, our discrimination mechanism can discover more complex differences that lead to the addition of multiple conditions, and to the addition of negated conjunctions that constrain the variant in complex ways. This allows the discovery of rules that, as far as we can determine, cannot be learned with any of the existing generalization-based or discrimination-based methods. Thus, while the new method has many similarities to Anderson and Kline's earlier technique, there are some important differences as well.

3.3 Learning Concepts through Discrimination

The majority of research on condition finding has taken place in the context of concept attainment tasks. Therefore this was a natural area in which to begin our exploration of discrimination learning. And because concept attainment tasks deal with condition finding in its purest form (since no additional learning issues are involved), this was an ideal domain for testing our major claims about the new approach. Accordingly we set out to construct a general system that could learn a variety of concepts when presented with examples and nonexamples of those concepts. Below we present an overview of this system, after which we discuss some empirical explorations of the program's behavior.

An Overview of the Program

The program's task is to learn the conditions that correctly predict all positive instances of a concept, without predicting that any negative instances are examples. Since it must have data on which to base its learning, the system begins by selecting an example at random from user-supplied lists of good and bad instances. (The probability of choosing a good instance is 50 percent.) Once an instance is available, the system makes a prediction about whether that instance is good or bad. When no other rule is available or preferred, a default rule cautiously decides that the instance is not an example of the concept[9]. Next the program compares its prediction to the correct answer. Errors of *omission* occur when the program fails to correctly predict a positive instance. In such cases the system designates a new very general rule that predicts *any* situation to be a positive instance. This will be the first learning response of the program, since it can only make negative predictions at the outset.

When the system correctly predicts a positive instance, it stores the instantiation of the rule that made that prediction. This information is used in recovering from errors of *commission*, which occur if the system predicts a positive instance when a negative instance actually occurs. When such an error is noted, the program evokes the discrimination process in an attempt to generate more conservative variants of the responsible rule (whose strength is decreased). As we have seen, this routine compares the bad instantiation of the rule that made the faulty prediction to the most recent good instantiation of the same rule. For every difference that is found, a variant of the overly general rule is created which includes that difference as an extra condition. When a variant is rebuilt, its strength is increased so that it has a greater priority. If any of these variants are still too general, they will produce their own errors of commission and lead to even more conservative variants. Thus the discrimination process can be viewed as carrying out a breadth-first search through the space of rules, considering simpler variants before more complex ones.

To summarize, our concept learning system has six distinct components, each stated as a separate PRISM production. These components are:

1. A production that selects an instance at random from the space of possible instances.
2. A production that asks the tutor whether an instance is an example of the concept to be learned (i.e., a rule that gathers feedback).
3. A default production that predicts that an instance is *not* an example of the concept when no other prediction has been made.
4. A designating production that creates a rule for predicting that all instances are examples whenever an error of omission occurs.
5. A production that notes when a correct prediction has been made and that assigns credit to the responsible rule.
6. A production that notes errors of commission and evokes the discrimination process in an attempt to construct more conservative variants of the responsible rule.

The production system itself is quite simple, since the real power of the program lies in the discrimination process that is called when overly general rules lead to faulty predictions. In the following pages, we see how the overall system learns different concepts under various conditions.

Learning Conjunctive Concepts

Since most research on concept learning has focused on conjunctive rules, it seemed reasonable to first see if the model could acquire such concepts. Rules stated in terms of attribute-value pairs are the simplest, so our initial runs were on concepts such as *large* and *large-and-thick*. The learning path in these runs was much as expected. Since no rule for predicting examples of the concept existed at the outset, errors of omission led the system to create such a rule. Once this became strong enough, it led to errors of commission and a call on the discrimination process. As a result variants with single

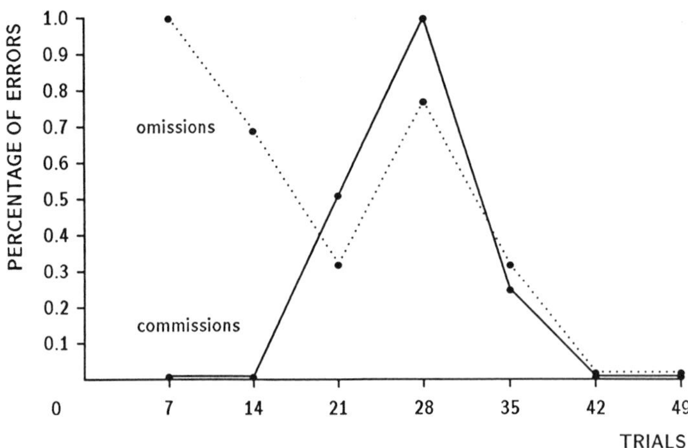

Figure 3.1
Errors in learning a single-condition concept

conditions were constructed, with those containing useful conditions eventually exceeding threshold after they had been built repeatedly. When these overly general rules led to errors, productions containing a second condition were generated, again with useful variants eventually exceeding threshold. This process continued until the correct rule gained sufficient strength to be selected, after which no additional errors were made.

Figure 3.1 presents the errors made by the system as a function of time while learning the concept *blue*. As one would expect, errors of omission abound at the beginning of the run, but they become fewer as experience is gained (growing again at one point), until eventually they disappear. Errors of commission are initially absent, but they grow to a peak at the center of the figure as overly general rules become stronger. However, as the dominant rules become more specific, such mistakes drop off and finally disappear as well. Figure 3.2 presents the trials to criterion (the number of examples until no errors occur) for conjunctive concepts of varying complexity. Since the discrimination process moves from general to more specific rules, simpler concepts with fewer conditions are mastered more rapidly than more complex ones.[10] Although one might expect a linear relationship, it does not occur. This results from the fact that as the system masters more of the conditions in a concept's definition, the chance for errors of commission decreases, since the dominant rules are more nearly correct. Since variants are created or strengthened only when errors of

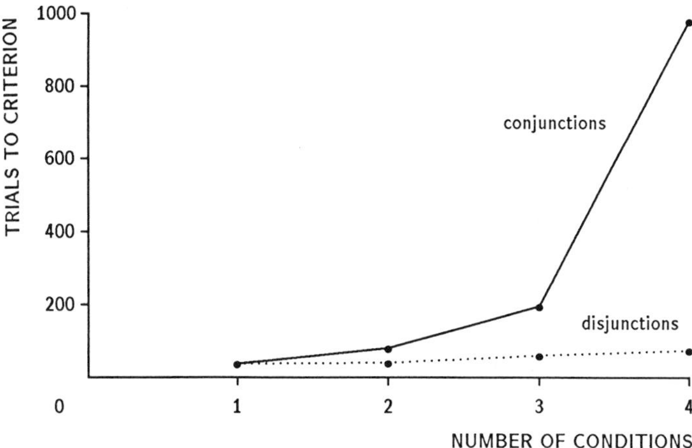

Figure 3.2
Learning speeds for conjunctive and disjunctive concepts

commission occur, the learning process slows down as the correct rule is approached. The effect is more pronounced when the correct rule includes many conditions, since a larger fraction of the instances are correctly classified when the concept is nearly learned than would be the case if a simpler concept were nearly learned. One solution to this problem is to let the program select its own instances, with a preference for those which it would predict as examples of the concept.

The reader will recall that the discrimination process is not restricted to learning concepts based on attribute-value pairs. In addition it can discover rules incorporating complex structures, such as *uncle-by-marriage* (i.e., the husband of a parent's sister). Rather than applying to a single object, this concept concerns a relationship between two people. Moreover this concept cannot be described in terms of a simple conjunction of features; these features must be related to one another in certain ways as well. This means that the discrimination process will sometimes be required to discover complex differences between good and bad instances. We do not have the space to trace the system's evolution on such concepts, though it has successfully learned them.

Learning Disjunctive Concepts

In addition to learning conjunctive concepts, discrimination can also master disjunctive rules. This results from the breadth-first nature of the mechanism's search through the space of possible conditions. Let us trace the system's progress on a simple disjunct like *large or red.* Suppose the program first encounters a positive exemplar that is *large and blue* (along with a number of other features) and later encounters a negative instance that is *small and blue* instead. Upon noting the differences, the discrimination mechanism will construct a variant with *large* in its condition side (and perhaps others as well). Now suppose the system meets with another positive instance containing the features *small and red,* followed by a negative example that is *small and blue.* In this case discrimination will create a variant with *red* as an extra condition. In summary, the method is capable of learning disjunctive rules because it focuses on a single positive and a single negative instance at a time. The particular pair it examines will determine which of the disjuncts will be found in that case. This is in sharp contrast to generalization-based approaches, which rely on finding features common to all positive instances to determine the appropriate conditions.

Besides summarizing the system's behavior on conjunctive rules, figure 3.2 also graphs the complexity of disjunctive concepts against their learning time. This curve is also nonlinear, but it is considerably less steep than its conjunctive counterpart. The reason for this lies in the strategy used to search the space of concepts. Because disjunctive concepts are stated as separate rules, and because the space is searched in a breadth-first manner, disjunctive rules can be found more or less in parallel. However, since generally only one of the disjuncts can be strengthened when an error of commission occurs, one might expect a linear relationship.[11] But as with conjunctive concepts, fewer useful negative instances occur in later stages of the learning process. Of course the system can also discover disjunctive relational concepts like *uncle,* which can be restated as *uncle-by marriage* or *uncle-by-birth.* The complexity of such disjunctions cannot be treated as strictly cumulative, since they share some conditions, such as the fact that the uncle must be male.

Dealing with Noise

The strengthening process has proved very useful in directing search through the space of concepts, but one can imagine a discrimination-based learning system that makes no use of strength and is still capable of learning conjunctive and disjunctive rules. However, when one introduces noise into the environment, ordering rules along some measure of success becomes

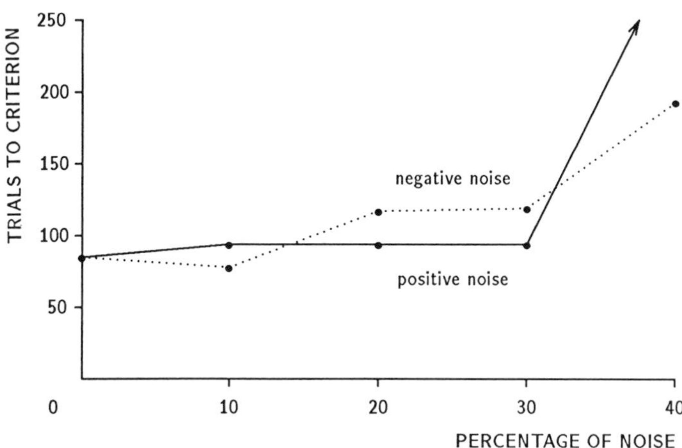

Figure 3.3
Effect of noise on learning a two-condition concept

much more important. On reflection it becomes apparent that two forms of noise are possible: a positive instance may be marked as a negative instance (positive noise), or a negative instance may be marked as a positive instance (negative noise). The effects on discrimination learning are different in these two situations. In the case of positive noise, a positive prediction is incorrectly marked as an error of commission; discrimination will be evoked, and since two positive instances are being compared, any variants are guaranteed to be spurious. A negative prediction in this case is less serious, since the system will simply fail to note an error of omission, and the general rule normally designated in such situations will not be strengthened. In the negative noise case, a negative prediction is incorrectly marked as an error of omission. The resulting construction of an overly general rule will in itself do little harm, but the "good" instantiation stored with it will actually be a bad instantiation. Accordingly, when the next error of commission occurs, two bad instantiations will be compared for differences, and again any resulting variants will be incorrect. Since a good instantiation remains with a production until it is replaced by another, this second type of noise may have cumulative effects. If instead the system makes a positive prediction, it will not be detected as an error of commission, and an opportunity for creating or strengthening useful variants will be lost.

Figure 3.3 presents the trials to criterion for a two-condition conjunctive concept with varying levels of noise. A noise level of 0 represents no noise, while a noise level of 0.5 represents maximum noise or perfect randomness.[12] Separate curves are shown for two types of noise. The system was never presented with both forms of error in the same run. One would expect the system's performance to degrade gracefully as more noise was introduced, but this does not appear to be the case. Instead, the program's behavior was largely unaffected by noise in the 0 to 30 percent range, and then was affected drastically when the noise rose above this level. Whether these results are due to the chance order in which the data were presented in these runs, or whether this is a basic characteristic of the system, can only be determined by further experiments with the program. Still, it is clear that the discrimination learning approach, combined with a strengthening mechanism to focus attention on promising variants, is capable of discovering concepts despite significant amounts of noise.

Adapting to a Change in the Concept

The strengthening mechanism has not only proved useful for learning concepts in the presence of noise but also in the process of recovering from a change to a well-learned concept. Any intelligent system must be capable of revising its prediction rules as change occurs in the environment. For example, suppose that tomorrow our traffic laws were changed so that the color of stop lights became blue instead of red. Presumably we would learn to stop when the light turned blue. The concept learning program has succeeded on a similar task in which it must alter the conditions under which it predicts an example of a concept. The system is presented with instances of one concept until it achieves criterion performance at predicting that concept. Then the concept is changed, and the program must revise its prediction rules in order to regain its previous level of success.

Figure 3.4 describes the program's performance on this task, mapping the percentage of errors of omission and commission made against the number of trials. For the first 40 trials, the learning system is presented with positive and negative examples of the concept *blue*. This process is similar to that described earlier in reference to simple conjunctive concept learning. The criterion of perfect performance is reached by trial 30, and the subsequent 10 trials are predicted correctly. At this point the system's strongest rule states that if the color of a token is *blue*, then the token is an example of the concept. This rule fires on all positive instances so that no errors of omission are made. The next to strongest rule is the default rule, which makes negative predictions. This production fires on all the negative in-

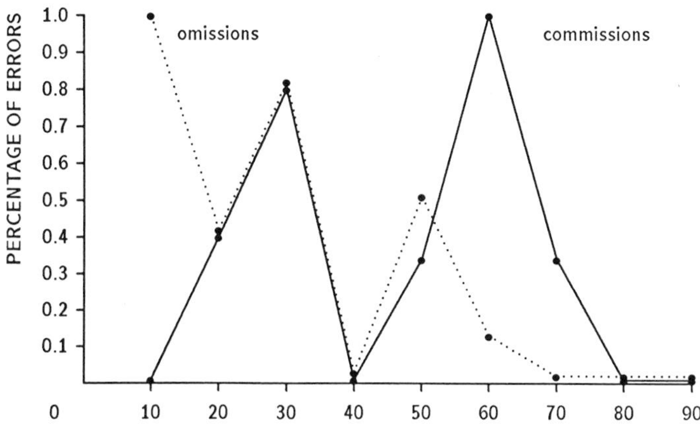

Figure 3.4
Errors with a change of concept on trial 40

stances, so no errors of commission are made, either. A number of weaker rules created in the process of learning the concept *blue* are also present, but they are not strong enough to compete with the other two and do not fire.

At trial 41 the concept is changed to *square* and the program's current set of rules becomes insufficient for continued perfect performance. Errors of commission are made in response to instances that are *blue* but not *square*, causing the *blue* rule to be weakened and variants to be created. Errors of omission are made when the program is presented with examples that are *square* but not *blue*, resulting in the strengthening of the most general prediction rule by designation. Note that errors of both types increase rapidly following the change of the concept, with omission errors reaching a peak at trial 50. Errors of commission rise even higher after the overly general rule becomes strong enough to fire. This rule consistently makes commission errors, and variants, including the *square* rule, are created (or strengthened, if they were created while learning the concept *blue*). Errors decrease gradually as the system revises its rules until at trial 80, both types of errors have diminished to nothing, and perfect predictive power has been achieved again.

Summary

In conclusion, the discrimination-based approach to condition finding provides a viable alternative to the more traditional generalization-based paradigm. Discrimination can be used to learn conjunctive concepts, including those composed of complex relational terms. And because it compares a single good instantiation to a single bad instantiation, the technique can discover disjunctive concepts as well. Finally, when combined with a strengthening process, discrimination can successfully learn the desired conditions in the presence of noise and can recover from changes in the environment. One limitation of the program revolved around its inability to intelligently select instances that might lead to errors of commission, and this is an obvious direction in which the concept learning system should be extended. Although we do not wish to detract from the excellent work on generalization, we believe that the discrimination learning approach offers some distinct advantages, which we will explore further in the following sections.

3.4 Learning Search Strategies through Discrimination

Upon first encountering a problem-solving situation, humans engage in search; however, once they have gained experience in an area, their search is much more directed and in some cases may disappear entirely. The domain of strategy learning is another field in which discrimination learning techniques can be applied. This results from the fact that search can be cast as the successive application of operators that transform one state into another, in the hopes of achieving some goal. The novice may possess the *legal* conditions for applying the operators in some task but may lack the heuristically useful conditions under which those operators should be applied. The discovery of such useful conditions can be cast in a form analogous to that for finding the conditions on concepts. However, though the assignment of blame and credit is trivial in the concept learning paradigm, it becomes considerably more complex when search is involved.

Sleeman, Langley, and Mitchell (1982) have discussed an apparently general solution to the credit assignment problem in the context of strategy learning. If one is willing to find the solution to some problem by trial and error, or if a sample solution is provided by a tutor, then one can use the known solution path to determine the appropriateness of an operator as soon as it has been applied. Thus, one can easily distinguish between good and bad instances of an operator, and the task of learning the heuristically useful conditions under which these operators should be applied is reduced to a task very like that of learning concepts. Brazdil (1978) has employed this approach, along with a discrimination like learning mechanism, to discover strategies from sample solutions, while Mitchell, Utgoff, and Banerji (1981) have explored strategy learning from self-generated solution paths, using Mitchell's (1977) version-space technique. Langley (1982, 1983) has described these systems and their approach to strategy learning in greater detail.

In this section we describe SAGE, an adaptive production system that operates in a similar fashion. The system that starts with legal operators for some task (stated as productions), finds a solution path by trial and error, and then attempts to learn from this solution path. Upon trying the same problem a second time, it can tell immediately when it has applied the incorrect operator. Such an error implies that the responsible rule is overly general, and discrimination is used to generate more conservative variants. This process continues (with relearned variants being strengthened) until the problem can be solved without errors. SAGE has many similarities to Brazdil's ELM and Mitchell, Utgoff, and Banerji's LEX, but there are some important differences as well. Like the concept learning program described in the previous section, SAGE is not intended as a detailed model of human strategy acquisition. Let us consider the system's behavior on a simple puzzle known as slide-jump.[13]

The Slide-Jump Puzzle

Like many puzzles the slide-jump task appears deceptively simple on the surface but is fairly difficult for humans to solve. In this puzzle one starts with equal numbers of two types of coins (e.g., quarters and nickels) set in a row. All quarters are on the left, all nickels are on the right, and the two sets are separated by a blank space. The goal is to interchange the positions of the quarters and nickels. However, quarters can move only to the right, while nickels can move only to the left. Two basic moves are allowed: a coin can *slide* from its current position into an adjacent blank space, or it can *jump* over a coin of the opposite type into a blank space.[14] Table 3.1 presents one solution path for the four-coin problem.

Figure 3.5 shows one-half of the state space for the four-coin puzzle (the other half is simply a mirror image of that shown). Dead-end states are represented by squares, and the solution path is shown in bold lines. We will refer to the numbers on the states later in the section. SAGE starts this task with one condition-action rule for sliding and one for jumping, as well as some additional rules that support the search for a solution. The initial rules are correct in that they propose only *legal* moves, but they lack

Table 3.1
Solution path for the four-coin slide-jump puzzle

QQ–NN	Initial state
Q–QNN	Slide a quarter from 2 to 3
QNQ–N	Jump a nickel from 4 to 2
QNQN–	Slide a nickel from 5 to 4
QN–NQ	Jump a quarter from 3 to 5
–NQNQ	Jump a quarter from 1 to 3
N–QNQ	Slide a nickel from 2 to 1
NNQ–Q	Jump a nickel from 4 to 2
NN–QQ	Slide a quarter from 3 to 4

conditions for distinguishing *good* moves from *bad* moves. As a result the program makes many poor moves on its first pass and is forced to back up whenever it reaches a dead end.

However, SAGE does eventually solve the problem in this trial-and-error way. At this point it attempts a second solution, but this time it has the initial solution to guide its search. When one of the move-proposing rules is incorrectly applied, the system knows its mistake immediately. If such an error occurs, SAGE calls on the discrimination process to compare the last correct application of the offending production to the current incorrect application. The resulting variants contain additional conditions that prevent them from firing in the undesired case. The program continues to learn in this fashion, constructing more conservative rules when errors are made and strengthening rules when they are relearned, until it traverses the entire solution path with no mistakes.

The reader may wonder why the program should bother to improve its rules once it knows the solution to the puzzle. The reason is simple: there is a chance that these revised productions will also be useful in related problems for which the solution path is *not* available. As we shall see later, the heuristics SAGE learns on the four-coin puzzle let it solve the six-coin puzzle immediately, without backtracking.

Representing Problem States and Operators

Any problem solver must have some *representation* to work upon, as well as operators for transforming the *initial state* into the *goal state*. Although SAGE necessarily uses different representations for the different tasks it attempts, they all have one major feature in common: each problem state is

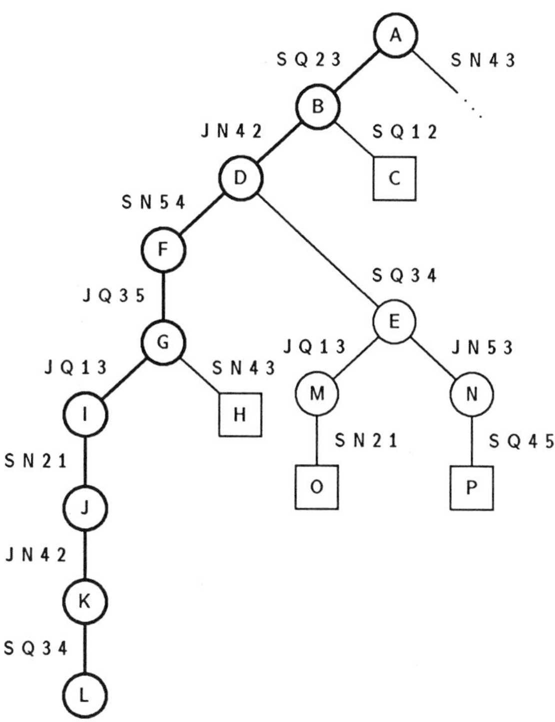

Figure 3.5
State space for the four-coin slide-jump puzzle

represented as a number of *distinct* elements in working memory. SAGE's operators are implemented in such a way that they affect only some of these elements, so the entire problem state need not be respecified each time a move is made. Instead, those elements that have become true are added to memory, while those that are no longer true are removed. Also, this composite representation allows partial information about the problem state to be included as conditions on a move-proposing rule to the exclusion of less relevant information.

For example, consider the representation for the four-coin slide-jump puzzle. Table 3.2 presents the initial state for this task. The first column states that a quarter is in position one, another quarter is in position two, a blank is in position three, and so forth. Note that each of these facts is

Table 3.2
Initial state for the four-coin slide-jump task

(Quarter one)	(One is left of two)	(Five is right of four)
(Quarter two)	(Two is left of three)	(Four is right of three)
(Blank three)	(Three is left of four)	(Three is right of two)
(Nickel four)	(Four is left of five)	(Two is right of one)
(Nickel five)	(Nickel moves left)	(Quarter moves right)

stored as a separate element. Thus, if SAGE slides a quarter from two to three, it simply removes the elements (QUARTER TWO) and (BLANK THREE), and adds the elements (BLANK TWO) and (QUARTER THREE); nothing else must be altered. The remaining columns state the spatial relations between the positions, along with the directions in which each coin may move; these facts remain unchanged throughout the problem.

The composite representation SAGE uses for problem states leads naturally to the rules for proposing moves between those states. These rules incorporate the legal conditions for applying an operator in their left-hand sides and include a proposal to apply that operator in their action sides. When one of these productions is selected, it inserts a goal to apply the associated operator; when this operator is applied, it removes some elements from working memory and adds others. For example, the basic *slide* production can be stated:

SLIDE-1
IF a *coin* is in *position1*,
  and *position2* is to the *direction* of *position1*,
  and *position2* is blank,
  and that *coin* can move to the *direction*,
THEN consider sliding that *coin* from *position1* to *position2*.

This production will match whenever a coin is next to the blank space and the coin is allowed to move in that direction; it will work for either coin and for any pair of adjacent positions.[15] Once a goal has been set, another production is responsible for updating the problem state by actually adding and deleting elements from memory. This division of labor simplifies matters in later runs when the solution path is known, for an incorrect goal may be caught before it is implemented. Also, the goals provide a trace of what has been done, which can prove useful in stating more heuristics for directing the search process.

Controlling the Search

Before SAGE can learn from its mistakes, it must be able to identify those mistakes. The most obvious way to distinguish good moves from bad moves is by examining the correct solution path to a given problem.[16] And to find a solution using the very weak move-proposing rules it has at the outset, the system must search. In addition to rules for suggesting moves, effective search requires the ability to eventually recognize a fruitless path and the ability to backtrack once such a path is recognized. SAGE carries out a form of *depth-first* search in each of the tasks it attempts, and learning consists of constructing more specific move-generating rules that direct the search down fruitful paths.

When SAGE decides it has reached a bad state or dead end, it backtracks to the previous state. This is possible only because the system keeps a trace of all previous moves made along the current path. This trace serves a second purpose in that it provides a record of the solution path once the goal has been reached. During the initial search SAGE also remembers bad moves it has made along the current path, so that it can avoid making these moves a second time. However, this negative information is removed once the solution is reached.

SAGE employs a single production for recognizing the solution state. The rule for slide-jump may be paraphrased:

SOLVED
IF a *coin1* moves to the *direction1*,
  and a *coin2* moves to the *direction2*,
  and *position* is blank,
  and no *coin1* is to the *direction2* of *position*,
  and no *coin2* is to the *direction1* of *position*,
THEN you are finished.

The goal-recognizing rules for other tasks are necessarily different, but they are always stated as single productions in much the same spirit as the above rule. Below we trace the details of SAGE's improvement on the slide-jump puzzle.

Learning Search Heuristics

SAGE was initially presented with the four-coin slide-jump task. After finding the solution path by depth-first search, a second attempt was made to solve the same problem. SAGE's first proposal was to slide a quarter from 2 to 3; this move is represented by the line connecting states *A* and *B* in figure 3.5, where *A* stands for the initial state and *B* for the resulting state. Since this move lay upon the known solution path, the system implemented its plan and stored the latest instantiation of slide-1 as a good instance of that rule.[17] However, this was immediately followed by a proposal to slide a quarter from 1 to 2, which would have led to state *C* in the figure. Since this move lay off the known solution path, it was deemed an error and the discrimination routine was called to compare the instantiation of slide-1 that proposed this action to the good instantiation that had just been stored. In this case the discrimination process discovered two differences, and so two variants of the slide-1 production were created. One of these was based on the fact that the correct move was the first that was made, while the incorrect one occurred in the context of an earlier move. The result was a production that would apply only on the first move of every task (the discriminant condition is shown in bold italics):

SLIDE-2
IF a *coin* is in *position1*,
  and *position2* is to the *direction* of *position1*,
  and *position2* is blank,
  and that *coin* can move to the *direction*,
  and you have not made any previous moves,
THEN consider sliding that *coin* from *position1* to *position2*.

Unfortunately this rule contains no information in its conditions to direct the search down useful paths, since only slide moves are possible from the initial state. The second variant was based on information about the particular type of move that had occurred before the bad slide move; the resulting production included more specific information in its new negated condition:

SLIDE-3
IF a *coin* is in *position1*,
  and *position2* is to the *direction* of *position1*,
  and *position2* is blank,
  and that *coin* can move to the *direction*,
  and you did not just slide a *coin* ***from*** *position2* ***to*** *position3*.
THEN consider sliding that *coin* from *position1* to *position2*.

This second variant is more selective than slide-2; it would not have proposed moving a coin from position 1 to 2, provided that coin had just been moved from 2 to 3, and so it would have avoided the error produced by slide-1. In general, it would not slide a coin *into* a position which had just been vacated by another slide.

Still at state *B*, SAGE next considered jumping a nickel from 4 to 2; this agreed with its previous experience, so the suggestion was carried out, leading to the state labeled *D* in figure 3.5. On the following move, slide-1 (which was still stronger than the two variants) proposed sliding a quarter from 3 to 4, which would have led off the path to state *E*. Again the program decided it had made an error, and the responsible instantiation of slide-1 was compared to the same good instantiation that was used earlier (since no new good instances of the rule had occurred in the meantime). This time discrimination reproduced the variants slide-2 and slide-3, causing them to be strengthened; in addition a new production was constructed, based on the jump that had just been made:

SLIDE-4
IF a *coin* is in *position1*,
  and *position2* is to the *direction* of *position1*,
  and *position2* is blank,
  and that *coin* can move to the *direction*,
  and you did not just jump the *other* ***coin from*** *position2* ***to*** *position3*.
THEN consider sliding that *coin* from *position1* to *position2*.

This rule states that one should not slide a coin *into* a position from which one has just jumped the other brand of coin. Note that this production may still propose those moves avoided by the slide-3 variant, while the earlier version may still propose this type of sliding move. In their current forms both rules are overly general.

At this point SAGE considered sliding a nickel from 5 to 4 (still via the original rule slide-1), which would have led to state *F* in the figure. Since this agreed with the known path, the proposal was implemented, giving the system a new good instantiation of the responsible production to consider in subsequent discriminations. Next the system correctly jumped a quarter from 3 to 5 (leading to state *G*), but this was followed by a proposal to slide a nickel from 4 to 3. This would have led off the solution path to state *H*, and so discrimination again searched for differences, this time generating a fourth variant:

SLIDE-5
IF a *coin* is in *position1*,
and *position2* is to the *direction* of *position1*,
and *position2* is blank,
and that *coin* can move to the *direction*,
***and you have just jumped a** coin **from** position2 **to** position3*,
THEN consider sliding that *coin* from *position1* to *position2*.

Here we have a positive condition included in the variant, suggesting that slides should occur after a jumping spree has been completed, and in the same direction. In addition discrimination produced four other less useful variants that made reference to moves earlier in the problem. By now SAGE had reached the halfway point for the problem. Since only one move was possible at each step from this point onward, the program finished with no more mistakes.[18] However, earlier errors had been made, so the system tried the problem a third time. In this run identical mistakes occurred, and each of the variants was strengthened.

The program continued along these lines, until during the fifth run the second variant, slide-3, came to surpass the original rule in strength. After this the more conservative production was applied whenever possible. When slide-3 proposed sliding a quarter from 3 to 4 while the system was at state *D* (recall that slide-1 made this same mistake earlier, leading slide-4 to be learned), discrimination resulted in a variant of slide-3 that contained yet another condition (shown in bold italics) for directing search down fruitful paths:

SLIDE-6
IF a *coin* is in *position1*,
and *position2* is to the *direction* of *position1*,
and *position2* is blank,
and that *coin* can move to the *direction*,
and you did not just slide a *coin* from *position2* to *position3*,
***and you did not just jump the** other **coin from** position1 **to** position3*,
THEN consider sliding that *coin* from *position1* to *position2*.

This rule includes the negated conditions of both slide-3 and slide-4 stating that one should not propose a slide if *either* condition is met. Other variants were created as well but never gained sufficient strength to have any effect on the system's performance.[19] After five more runs SLIDE-6 rule acquired more strength than its precursor, and on its eleventh run SAGE

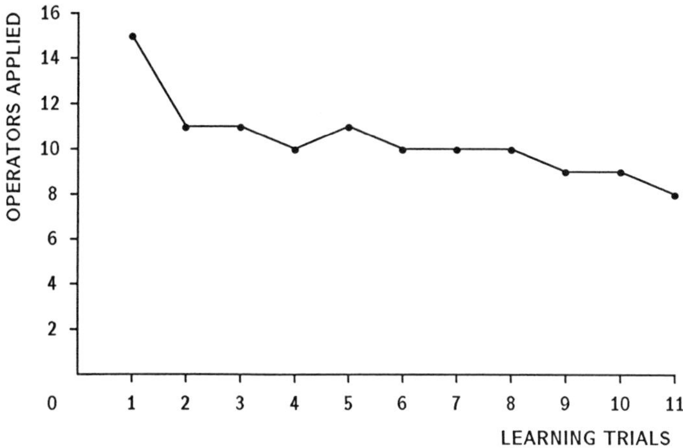

Figure 3.6
Learning curve for the slide-jump task

reached the goal state (marked L in the figure) without error. In addition, when the system was presented with the six-coin task, the system successfully applied its heuristics to direct search, so that it solved the problem on its first attempt with no backtracking.

Figure 3.6 presents SAGE's learning curve on the four-coin slide-jump task. The graph plots the number of moves that were considered before the solution was reached, against the order in which each run occurred. The drop between the first and second trials results from knowledge of the solution path and so does not reflect the system's progress in developing useful heuristics. However, the slow improvement from the second trial onward shows that the system was gradually narrowing its search. And since the solution path was not needed in the eleventh and final run, it is appropriate to compare the number of moves on this trial to that on the first run. This comparison reveals that the variants on the slide-1 production, with their heuristically useful conditions, reduced the number of moves from the initial 15 to the optimum number 8.

Summary

In summary, SAGE is an adaptive production system that improves its search behavior by adding heuristically useful conditions to rules that initially contain only the legal conditions for applying operators. Presented with the slide-jump task, it solves the problem first by trial and error, and then attempts to learn from the solution sequence using the discrimination process. The system learns a number of useful variants, including one that allowed it to solve the four-coin and six-coin tasks with no errors. SAGE has also learned heuristics for solving algebra problems in one variable, and for ordering blocks according to their lengths. Although the performance rules for these cases differ, all versions of the system share a common core of adaptive productions that direct the learning process. Although SAGE is not intended as a model of human learning, it does shed light on one important way in which strategies can be improved.

Future research with SAGE should concentrate on testing the system in additional domains. These tasks should include other puzzles for which the problem spaces are well understood, such as Tower of Hanoi or Missionaries and Cannibals. However, it is also important to test the learning system in domains involving many operators and large search spaces, such as symbolic integration or geometry theorem proving. The first of these is especially attractive, since it would allow direct comparision of SAGE's behavior to Mitchell, Utgoff, and Banerji's LEX system. In addition to further testing the program's generality, other methods should be explored for solving the credit assignment problem without resorting to complete solution paths. For example, one should be able to modify Anzai's loop move and shorter path heuristics so as to determine good and bad applications of an operator, and so allow discrimination learning to occur before a complete solution has been found. Such an approach would be particularly useful for learning in domains with very large problem spaces, where the search involved in finding a solution entirely by trial and error would be prohibitive.

3.5 A Model of First-Language Acquisition

Children do not learn language in an all-or-none fashion. They begin their linguistic careers uttering one word at a time and slowly evolve through a number of stages, each containing more adultlike speech than the one before. In this section we present a model that attempts to explain the regularities in children's early syntactic development. The model is called AMBER, an acronym for Acquisition Model Based on Error Recovery. AMBER learns grammar by comparing its own utterances to those of adults and attempting to correct any errors, and discrimination plays an important role in AMBER's learning scheme. The model focuses on the omission of content words, the occurrence of telegraphic speech, and the order in which function words are mastered. Before considering AMBER in detail, let us first review some major features of child language, along with some earlier models of these phenomena.

Around the age of one year the child begins to produce words in isolation and continues this strategy for some months. At approximately 18 months he starts to combine words into meaningful sequences. In order-based languages such as English, the child usually follows the adult order. Initially only pairs of words are produced, but these are followed by three-word and later by four-word utterances. The simple sentences occurring in this stage consist almost entirely of content words; grammatical morphemes such as tense endings and prepositions are largely absent. During the period from about 24 to 40 months the child masters the grammatical morphemes that were absent during the previous stage. These "function words" are learned gradually; the time between the initial production of a morpheme and its mastery may be as long as 16 months. Brown (1973) has examined the order in which 14 English morphemes are acquired, finding the order of acquisition to be remarkably consistent across children. In addition those morphemes with simpler meanings and involved in fewer transformations were learned earlier than more complex ones. These findings place some strong constraints on the learning mechanisms one postulates for morpheme acquisition.

Although language learning has been a popular topic in artificial intelligence, only a few researchers have attempted to construct plausible models of the child's learning process. For example, Kelley (1967) has reported on a system that modeled the omission of content words and the gradual lengthening of utterances. However, in order to move between stages, the program had to be told about new syntactic classes by the programmer, making it less than satisfactory as a model of first-language learning. Selfridge's CHILD (1981) was much more robust than Kelley's program and is unique in modeling children's use of nonlinguistic cues for understanding. However, CHILD's explanation of the omission of content words—that those words are not yet known—was implausible, since children often omit words that they have used in previous utterances. Reeker's PST (1976) explained this phenomenon through a limited memory hypothesis, which is consistent with our knowledge of children's memory skills. Still, PST included no model of the process through which memory improved; in order to let the system master more complex constructions,

Reeker would have had to increase the system's memory size himself. Both CHILD and PST learned relatively slowly and made mistakes of the general type observed with children. Both systems learned through a process of error recovery, starting off as abominable language users but getting progressively better with time. This is a promising approach, and in this section we develop it in its extreme form.

An Overview of AMBER

Although Reeker's PST and Selfridge's CHILD address the transition from one-word to multiword utterances, problems exist with both accounts. Neither of these programs focus on the acquisition of function words, and their explanations of content word omissions leave something to be desired. In response to these limitations the goals of the current research are three:

1. Account for the omission of content words, and the eventual recovery from such omissions.
2. Account for the omission of function words, and the order in which these morphemes are mastered.
3. Account for the gradual nature of both these linguistic developments.

In this section we provide an overview of AMBER, a model that provides one set of answers to these questions. Since more is known about children's utterances than their ability to understand the utterances of others, AMBER models the learning of generation strategies, rather than strategies for understanding language.

Like Selfridge's and Reeker's models, AMBER learns through a process of error recovery.[20] The model is presented with three pieces of information: a legal sentence, an event to be expressed, and a main goal or topic of the sentence. An event is represented as a semantic network, using relations like agent, action, object, size, color, and type. The specification of one of the nodes as the main topic allows the system to restate the network as a tree structure, and it is from this tree that AMBER generates a sentence. If this sentence is identical to the sample sentence, no learning is required. If a disagreement between the two sentences is found, AMBER modifies its set of rules in an attempt to avoid similar errors in the future, and the system moves on to the next example.

AMBER's performance system is stated as a set of productions that operates on the goal tree to produce utterances. Although the model starts with the *potential* for producing (unordered) telegraphic sentences, it can initially generate only one word at a time. To see why this occurs, we must consider the three productions that make up AMBER's initial performance system. The first of these (the *start* rule) is responsible for establishing subgoals. Matching first against the main goal node, it selects one of the nodes below it in the tree and creates a subgoal to describe that node. This rule continues to establish lower-level goals until a terminal node is reached. At this point a second production (the *speaking* rule) retrieves the word for the concept to be described, and actually says the word. Once this has been done, a third rule (the *stop* rule) marks the terminal goal as satisfied. Moreover, since the stop rule is stronger than the start rule (which would like to create another subgoal), it marks each of the active goals as satisfied, and AMBER halts after uttering a single word. Thus, although the model starts with the potential for producing multiword utterances, it must learn additional rules (and make them stronger than the stop rule) before it can generate multiple content words in the correct order.

In general, AMBER learns by comparing adult sentences to the sentences it would produce in the same situations. These predictions reveal two types of mistakes—errors of *omission* and errors of *commission*. We begin by discussing AMBER's response to errors of omission, since these are the first to occur and thus lead to the system's first steps beyond the one-word stage. We consider the omission of content words first, and then the omission of grammatical morphemes. Finally, we discuss the importance of errors of commission in discovering conditions on the production of morphemes, and it is here that our theory of discrimination will be required.

Learning Preferences and Orders

AMBER's initial self-modifications result from the failure to predict content words. Given its initial ability to say one word at a time, the system can make two types of content word omissions—it can fail to predict a word *before* a correctly predicted one, or it can omit a word *after* a correctly predicted one. Rather different rules are created in each case. For example, imagine that Daddy is bouncing a ball, and suppose that AMBER predicted only the word "ball" while hearing the sentence "Daddy is bounce ing the ball." In this case the system notes that it omitted the content word "Daddy" before the content word "ball", and an agent production is created:

AGENT
IF you want to describe *event1*,
and *agent1* is the agent of event1,
THEN describe *agent1*.

A similar rule for describing actions results from the omitted "bounce." Note that the production does *not* give AMBER the ability to say more than one word at a time. It merely increases the likelihood that the program will describe the agent of an event instead of the action or the object.

However, as AMBER begins to prefer agents to actions and actions to objects, the probability of the second type of error (omitting a word after a correctly predicted one) increases. For example, suppose that Daddy is again bouncing a ball, and the system says "Daddy" while it hears "Daddy is bounce ing the ball." In this case a slightly different production is created that is responsible for *ordering* the creation of goals. Since the agent relation was described but the object was omitted, an agent-object rule is constructed:

AGENT-OBJECT
IF you want to describe *event1*,
and *agent1* is the agent of *event1*,
and you have described *agent1*,
and *object1* is the object of *event1*,
THEN describe *object1*.

Together with the AGENT rule, this production lets AMBER produce utterances such as "Daddy ball." Thus the model provides a simple explanation of why children omit some content words in their early multiword utterances. Such rules must be constructed many times before they become strong enough to have an effect, but eventually they let the system produce sentences containing all relevant content words in the standard order and lacking only grammatical morphemes.

Learning Suffixes and Prefixes

Once AMBER begins to correctly predict content words, it can learn rules for saying grammatical morphemes as well. As with content words, such rules are created when the system hears a morpheme but fails to predict it in that position. For example, suppose the program hears "Daddy * is bounce ing * the ball" but predicts only "Daddy bounce ball." In this case the following rule is generated:[21]

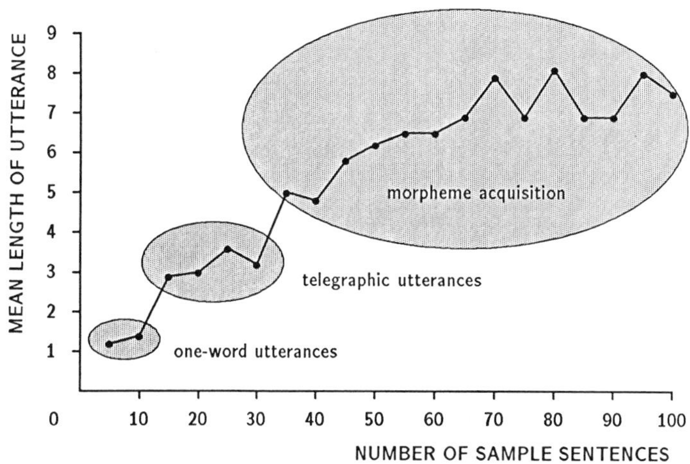

Figure 3.7
Mean length of AMBER's utterances

ING-1
IF you have described *action1*,
  and *action1* is the action of *event1*,
THEN say ING.

As stated, this production is overly general and will lead to errors of commission. We consider AMBER's response to such errors in the following section.

The omission of prefixes leads to very similar rules. In the preceding example, the morpheme "is" was omitted before "bounce," leading to the creation of a prefix rule:

IS-1
IF you want to describe *action1*,
  and *action1* is the action of *event1*,
THEN say IS.

Note that this rule will fire *before* the action has been described, while the rule ing-1 can apply only *after* the goal to describe the action has been satisfied. AMBER uses such conditions to control the order in which morphemes are produced.

Figure 3.7 shows AMBER's mean length of utterance as a function of the number of sample sentences (taken in groups of five) seen by the program.

As one would expect, the system starts with an average of around one word per utterance, and the length slowly increases with time. AMBER moves through a two-word and then a three-word stage, until it eventually produces sentences lacking only grammatical morphemes. Finally, the morphemes are included, and adultlike sentences are produced. The temporal positions of these three stages are shown by the successive regions in the figure; although the stage boundaries are not so distinct as indicated, the regions should give some idea of the relative time the model spends in mastering various aspects of syntax. The incremental nature of the learning curve results from the piecemeal way in which AMBER learns rules for producing sentences, and from the system's reliance on strengthening.

Recovering from Errors of Commission

Errors of commission occur when AMBER predicts a morpheme that does not occur in the adult sentence. These errors result from the overly general prefix and suffix rules that we saw in the last section. In response to such errors, AMBER calls on the discrimination routine in an attempt to generate more conservative productions with additional conditions.[22] Earlier, we considered a rule (is-1) for producing "is" before the action of an event. As stated, this rule would apply in inappropriate situations as well as correct ones. Suppose that AMBER learned this rule in the context of the sentence "Daddy *is* bounce ing the ball." Now suppose the system later uses this rule to predict the same sentence but that it instead hears the sentence "Daddy *was* bounce ing the ball."

At this point AMBER retrieves the rule responsible for predicting "is" and lowers its strength; it also retrieves the situation that led to the faulty application, passing this information to the discrimination routine. Comparing the earlier good case to the current bad case, the discrimination mechanism finds only the difference—in the good example, the action node was marked *present*, while no such marker occurred during the faulty application. The result is a new production that is identical to the original rule, except that a present condition has been included:

IS-2
IF you want to describe *action1*,
and *action1* is the action of *event1*,
you** action1* ***is in the present,
THEN say IS.

This new condition will let the variant rule fire only when the action is marked as occurring in the present. When first created, the is-2 production is too weak to be seriously considered. However, as it is learned again and again, it will eventually come to mask its predecessor. This transition is aided by the weakening of the faulty is-1 rule each time it leads to an error.

Once the variant production has gained enough strength to apply, it will produce its own errors of commission. For example, suppose AMBER uses the is-2 rule to predict "The boy s *is* bounce ing the ball" while the system hears "The boy s *are* bounce ing the ball." This time the difference is more complicated. The fact that the action had an agent in the good situation is no help, since an agent was present during the faulty firing as well. However, the agent was *singular* in the first case but not during the second. Accordingly the discrimination mechanism creates a second variant:

IS-3
IF you want to describe *action1*,
  and *action1* is the action of *event1*,
  and *action1* is in the present,
  and** agent1* ***is the agent of *event1*,
  and** agent1* ***is singular,
THEN say IS.

The resulting rule contains *two* additional conditions, since the learning process was forced to chain through two elements to find a difference. Together these conditions keep the production from saying the morpheme "is" unless the agent of the current action is singular in number.

Note that since the discrimination process must learn these sets of conditions separately, an important prediction results: *the more complex the conditions on a morpheme's use, the longer it will take to master*. For example, multiple conditions are required for the "is" rule, while only one condition is needed for the "ing" production. As a result the former is mastered after the latter, just as found in children's speech. Thus the discrimination process provides an elegant explanation for the observed correlation between a morpheme's semantic complexity and its order of acquisition. As we noted earlier, a generalization-based learning system would master more complex rules before learning simpler ones and so would predict exactly the opposite of the observed correlation.

Unfortunately parents seldom present sentences in an ideal order, so that the relevant conditions are obvious to the child. In order to more closely

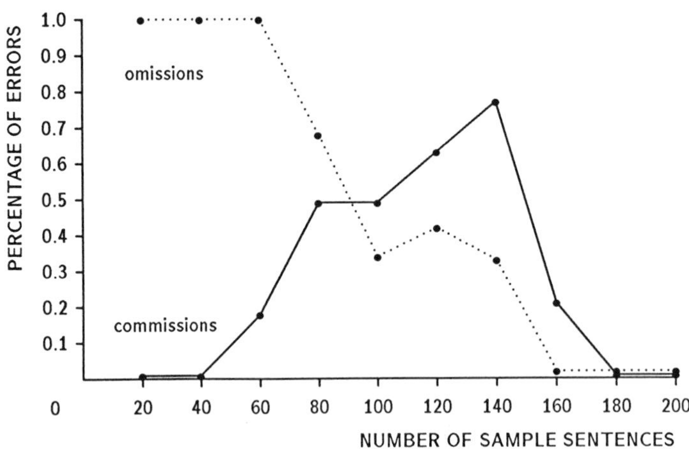

Figure 3.8
AMBER's learning curves for the morpheme "ing"

model the environment in which children learn language, AMBER was presented with randomly generated sentence/meaning pairs. Thus it was usually impossible to determine *the* correct discrimination that should be made from a single pair of good and bad situations. As in other domains the strategy of strengthening relearned rules and weakening faulty versions was sufficient to focus attention on useful variants. Figure 3.8 presents the learning curves for the "ing" morpheme. Since AMBER initially lacks an "ing" rule, errors of omission abound at the outset, but as the "ing" rule and its variants are strengthened, these errors decrease. In contrast, errors of commission are absent at the beginning, since AMBER lacks an "ing" rule to make false predictions. As the morpheme rule becomes stronger, errors of commission grow to a peak, but they disappear as discrimination takes effect.

Summary

In conclusion, AMBER provides explanations for several important phenomena observed in children's early speech. The system accounts for the one-word stage and the child's transition to the telegraphic stage. Although AMBER and children eventually learn to produce all relevant content words, both pass through a stage where some are omitted. Because it learns sets of conditions one at a time, the discrimination process explains the order in which grammatical morphemes are mastered. Finally, AMBER learns *gradually* enough to provide a plausible explanation of the incremental nature of first-language acquisition. Thus the system constitutes a significant addition to our knowledge of syntactic development.

Of course AMBER has a number of limitations that should be addressed in future research. For example, the current model cannot master irregular constructions like "ate" and "feet," and this is another area where discrimination would seem to have an important role to play in recovering from overgeneralizations. Another application of this learning mechanism lies in the acquisition of word order, since there is no reason in principle why the conditions on rules such as the agent-object production could not be learned through a discriminationlike process. The solutions to other limitations are not so apparent. For instance, the existing program models only the earliest stages of language acquisition, and major extensions may be necessary to replicate later developments. As it stands, AMBER says nothing about the relation between generation and comprehension, and the model's strategies for error recovery have only been used to learn rules for generation. Finally, the system has been tested only on English, and it is not clear how relevant the model's learning mechanisms will be for languages in which word order plays a less important role. But despite these limitations, AMBER has helped to clarify the incremental nature of language acquisition, and future versions should further our understanding of this complex process.

3.6 Modeling Cognitive Development

A final area of application lies in the domain of cognitive development. Most researchers in this field have been strongly influenced by the early work of Piaget (1969). Although the majority of research in cognitive development has been experimentally oriented, recent efforts have been made to explain some developmental trends in information-processing terms. Production systems have been a popular framework for modeling behavior at different stages, partially because their modularity allows the statement of successive models that differ by only one or two productions. For example, Baylor, Gascon, Lemoyne, and Pother (1973) have constructed production system models of children at various stages on Piaget's weight seriation task, and Young (1976) has devised similar models for the related length seriation task. The most comprehensive work along these lines has been carried out by Klahr and Wallace (1976), who have proposed production system models of children's behavior at various stages on tasks ranging from quantification to class inclusion. The next step is to construct models of the transition process that account for the movement between these stages. These models can be stated as adaptive production systems, and it is here that our theory of discrimination learning has an important role to play.

The Balance Scale Task

Klahr and Siegler (1978) have studied children's development on a variant of Piaget's balance scale task. In this task the child is presented with a two-arm balance, with several pegs spaced evenly along each arm. Small disks of equal weight are placed on the pegs (only one peg on each side has weights), and the child is asked to predict the direction in which the scale will move when released. The standard method for correctly making this prediction involves the notion of torque. The number of weights on a peg is multiplied by that peg's distance from the center. If one side has the greater product, that side will go down; if the products are equal, the scale will remain balanced.

Despite the apparent simplicity of this rule, Klahr and Siegler found their subjects using quite different prediction schemes. Also these schemes differed systematically with the age of the child. Four basic stages appeared to exist, and the researchers successfully modeled each stage as a simple production system. Table 3.3 presents the productions used to model the first three stages, paraphrased in English. Since each successive stage differs from the previous model by the inclusion of only one or two new productions, we have grouped the rules according to the stage at which they were introduced. We have omitted the productions required for the final stage, which include rules for computing torque and responding appropriately.

The model of the initial stage consists of two simple productions. The first rule, P1, predicts that the scales will balance if the weights are the same on both sides. Similarly, P2 predicts that if the weights are different, the side with the greater weight will go down. The model of the second stage requires only one new production, P3, which predicts that if the weights are equal but the distances differ, the side with the greater distance will descend. Since Klahr and Siegler were assuming that conflicts between productions would be decided in favor of specific rules over more general ones, the new production would be preferred to P1 whenever both matched. However, P1 would still be selected in cases where both weights and distances were equal (since P3 would not match in this situation), correctly

Table 3.3
Klahr and Siegler's model of behavior on the balance scale task

STAGE 1	P1 IF you have a balance with *side*, and the weights are equal, THEN predict the sides will balance.
	P2 IF you have a balance with *side*, and *side* has the greater weight, THEN predict *side* will go down.
STAGE 2	P3 IF you have a balance with *side*, and the weights are equal, and *side* has the greater distance, THEN predict *side* will go down.
STAGE 3	P4 IF you have a balance with *side*, and *side* has the greater weight, and *side* has the lesser distance, THEN muddle through.
	P5 IF you have a balance with *side*, and *side* has the greater weight, and *side* has the greater distance, THEN predict *side* will go down.

predicting a balance. Modeling third-stage behavior required two new rules, labeled P4 and P5 in the table.[23] The first of these applies only when the weight and distance cues conflict. Klahr and Siegler called these "conflict problems," and they were especially difficult for the subjects. Accordingly the action associated with this rule is to "muddle through," which seemed to be a way of incorporating random behavior into the model. The final rule, P5, applied whenever the weight and distance cues were greater on the same side, and predicted that side would go down.

Although Klahr and Siegler's models were very simple, they accounted for much of the variance observed in children's behavior on the balance scale task. As we have noted, successive models differed by only one or two productions. Thus, while the authors did not propose a mechanism to account for the transition between these stages, their analysis must be viewed as taking us a major step in that direction. Below we present a slightly revised stage model that brings us even closer to that goal.

A Revised Stage Model

Table 3.4 summarizes our revised model of successive stages on the balance scale task. In addition to the three stages shown in table 3.3, we have also included a random stage. Taken together, the first pair of productions (BALANCE-1 and DOWN-1) randomly predict that one of the two sides will go down, or that the sides are balanced.[24] Klahr and Siegler found no evidence for this stage, presumably because their subjects had moved beyond the random strategy at an earlier age. When the second pair of rules (BALANCE-2 and DOWN-2) is added to the first pair, the resulting system behaves exactly as Klahr and Siegler's model of stage 1, *provided* the new rules are stronger than the first pair (and so will always be preferred, since we are assuming PRISM's conflict resolution principles). Upon adding the third pair of productions (BALANCE-3 and DOWN-3), we have a model of stage 2 behavior, provided that both of these rules are stronger than the production BALANCE-2. Finally, when the productions DOWN-4 and DOWN-5 are inserted (and made stronger than DOWN-2), we have a partial model of Klahr and Siegler's stage 3.

To complete the model of this stage, the system must have some way of "muddling through" on conflict problems. Klahr and Siegler have made a useful distinction between three types of conflict problems. For conflict situations in which the side with greater weight descended, they used the term "conflict weight" problems. Similarly conflict problems in which the side with greater distance went down were labeled "conflict distance" problems, and conflicts that resulted in a balance were called "conflict balance" problems. This analysis suggests that we can model "muddling" behavior by the introduction of three additional rules:

DOWN-6
IF you have a balance with *side*,
  and *side* has the greater weight,
  and *side* has the lesser distance,
THEN predict *side* will go down.

DOWN-7
IF you have a balance with *side*,
  and *side* has the greater distance,
  and *side* has the lesser weight,
THEN predict *side* will go down.

Table 3.4
Revised model of behavior on the balance scale task

RANDOM STAGE	BALANCE-1 IF you have a balance with *side*, THEN predict the sides will balance.
	DOWN-1 IF you have a balance with *side*, THEN predict *side* will go down.
STAGE 1	BALANCE-2 IF you have a balance with *side*, and the weights are equal, THEN predict the sides will balance.
	DOWN-2 IF you have a balance with *side*, and *side* has the greater weight, THEN predict *side* will go down.
STAGE 2	BALANCE-3 IF you have a balance with *side*, and the weights are equal, and the distances are equal, THEN predict the sides will balance.
	DOWN-3 IF you have a balance with *side*, and the weights are equal, and *side* has the greater distance, THEN predict *side* will go down.
STAGE 3	DOWN-4 IF you have a balance with *side*, and *side* has the greater weight, and the distances are equal, THEN predict *side* will go down.
	DOWN-5 IF you have a balance with *side*, and *side* has the greater weight, and *side* has the greater distance, THEN predict *side* will go down.

BALANCE-4
IF you have a balance with *side*,
 and *side* has the greater weight,
 and *side* has the lesser distance,
THEN predict the sides will balance.

The condition sides of each of these rules are functionally equivalent, since they will each match on all three types of conflict problem. However, DOWN-6 will make correct predictions only on conflict weight problems and will make the wrong prediction in the other two situations. Similarly DOWN-7 will be correct only on conflict distance problems, and BALANCE-4 will be correct only on conflict balance tasks. If we assume that these three productions have equal strengths, then none will be preferred over another and one will be selected at random, giving "muddling-through" behavior. This explanation provides a more detailed account of the subjects' uncertainty on conflict problems than that given by Klahr and Siegler's single P4 rule with its "muddle-through" action.

It is worthwhile to examine the relations between these two sets of models. The productions included in both models of stage 1 are equivalent except for insignificant representational differences. However, Klahr and Siegler's model of stage 2 behavior requires the addition of only one production, while our version includes two rules. One of these rules, DOWN-3, is equivalent to P3, and fulfills a similar function in our model to that served by P3 in the other system. However, Klahr and Siegler's model of stage 2 requires no analog to our BALANCE-3, since P1 handles all situations in which the weights are the same (except for those covered by P3). Although our conflict resolution scheme relies on strength rather than specificity, we could make DOWN-3 stronger than BALANCE-2 to achieve a similar effect, but it will shortly become apparent why we have chosen to include the BALANCE-3 production. A similar relationship holds between Klahr and Siegler's P5 and our rules DOWN-4 and DOWN-5 for stage 3; as before, they managed to get by with one rule where we have used two, again through use of their specificity principle for conflict resolution. In this case P5 corresponds to DOWN-5, while situations matched by DOWN-4 are handled by P2. Finally, the "muddle-through" production P4 in the earlier model is replaced in our model by three rules with identical conditions but different actions; this is simply a more detailed way to describe the system's uncertainty on conflict problems.

At first glance one is tempted to judge Klahr and Siegler's approach as more elegant than ours, since their model of stage 3 contains only five productions and ours contains eleven. Even if we replace our three conflict rules with a single production analogous to P4, our final model would still consist of nine productions. However, our revised models have one characteristic that is lacking in Klahr and Siegler's set: *rules occurring in later stages are always discriminant versions of rules that have occurred in an earlier stage.* This feature lets us employ our theory of discrimination learning to account for the transition process from the random to the final stage shown in table 3.4, since this mechanism generates just such discriminant versions in its attempt to recover from errors. Although this feature held for some of Klahr and Siegler's rules (e.g., P5 is a variant on P2), it was by no means true of them all, and this is perhaps one reason why they never proposed a model of the transition process. Note that when we say that one rule is a "discriminant version" of another, we mean more than just the fact that the first rule has conditions that are a special case of the second; we also mean that the action sides of the two rules are the same. Thus P3 is a special case of P1 in the earlier model, but it is not a discriminant version of P1.[25]

A Model of the Transition Process

As we have noted, each of the rules in our revised stage model is a variant on one of the rules occurring at some earlier stage, and we have implemented an adaptive production system model of learning on the balance scale task that takes advantage of this insight.[26] The model begins with the rules BALANCE-1 and DOWN-1, which provide the initial behavior on which the learning is based. In addition the system contains a production for comparing the sides of the balance scale on dimensions like weight and distance, since the relative weights and distances must be present in memory if discrimination is to discover conditions referring to such relations. Finally, the model includes a production for noting when a correct prediction has been made and storing credit with the responsible rule, and a similar production for evoking the discrimination process when an incorrect prediction is made. Thus this learning program is nearly identical to the concept learning system we described in an earlier section. One difference is that the current model does not require a designating production to create new rules, since errors of omission never occur. Also no default rule is required to make negative predictions, since some sort of positive action is always appropriate.

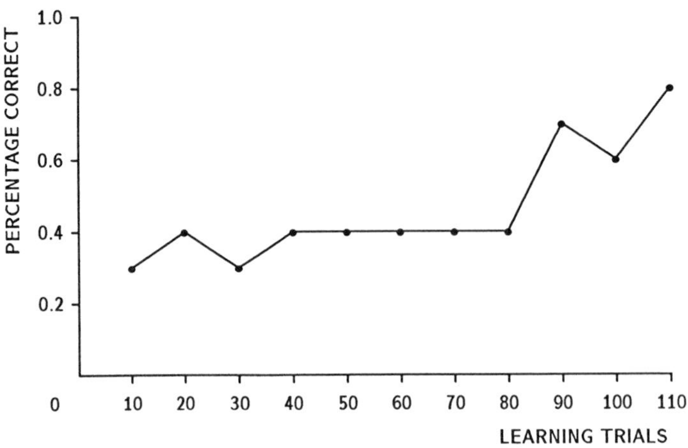

Figure 3.9
Learning curve for the balance scale task

The program was presented with problems selected randomly from seven basic problem types. These included problems in which only the weights differed, in which only the distances differed, in which both weights and distances were equal, in which the two cues agreed, and the three types of conflict problems discussed earlier. Figure 3.9 summarizes the model's errors as a function of time (in units of 10 trials). Since the system begins with the two random rules BALANCE-1 and DOWN-1, and since there are three basic predictions to choose from (left down, balance, and right down), one would expect 33 percent of the initial predictions to be correct, and this is approximately what we find.[27] By trial 100 the system has learned (and sufficiently strengthened) the stage 2 and stage 3 rules shown in table 3.4, so it makes correct predictions on all but the three conflict problems, giving a success rate of approximately 60 percent. In the case of conflict problems the model's representation of the environment (consisting only of information about relative weights and distances) is incapable of even *stating* the torque rule that would correctly predict results in a consistent manner. In other words, the program's representation of the problem is inherently incomplete. However, the discrimination process is sufficiently robust to learn useful rules despite this limitation, and the system arrives at a set of rules that make correct predictions much of the time, just as children do before they are taught the torque rule.

This brings another important feature of our theory to light: discrimination learning allows one to learn useful rules *even if one's representation is ultimately inadequate*. Since our system has no notion of torque, it can never fully understand the balance scale task, yet it does learn rules that lead to correct predictions in many cases. Since one can never guarantee that a representation is optimal, this is a powerful feature that would be advantageous to any learning system. This capability to learn useful rules despite incomplete representations is as fully important a characteristic of the discrimination process as its ability to learn in the presence of noise, and we are unaware of any other approach to learning that has this capability.

Let us trace the transition model's behavior on the troublesome conflict problems, since it reveals some interesting details about the discrimination process. The program begins by invoking either BALANCE-1 or DOWN-1 on these problems, sometimes predicting the correct outcome and sometimes making an error. When errors occur, the discrimination mechanism is called in an atttempt to determine the conditions under which the faulty prediction should be made. If the system bases its learning on a correct prediction made by DOWN-1 that was made on a conflict weight problem (in which the side with greater weight goes down), the discrimination process would construct as a variant the DOWN-2 rule shown in table 3.4 (though this is learned in other contexts as well). For correct applications of DOWN-1 on conflict distance problems, the system would create the variant DOWN-2.5 (shown below), and for conflict balance problems, it would construct a variant of BALANCE-1 that contained either a greater weight or a greater distance constraint in its condition side.

However, none of these variants will consistently be correct, and soon after they gain sufficient strength, these rules will lead to errors and generate variants of their own. The result will be the three productions included in our stage model—DOWN-6, DOWN-7, and BALANCE-4—each containing conditions that match when one side has greater weight and the other has greater distance but differing as to the predictions they make. One of these will always be correct on conflict weight problems, another on conflict distance problems, and the third on conflict balance problems, but none will be correct on all three. Thus they will continually be weakened and then strengthened, and the system's preference on conflict problems will oscillate between them. This effect is very similar to behavior that Klahr and Siegler observed in one of their subjects, who seemed to switch back and forth between weight and distance cues whenever the use of one led to an incorrect prediction on a conflict problem. However, their detailed model of the subject included a somewhat ad hoc mechanism for explaining this shift, while our model reacts in a similar fashion (though not in exactly the same manner) purely as a by-product of learning through discrimination. The long-term result is "muddle-through" behavior, in which different cues are used to make the decision at different times.

What is the exact relation between the stage model shown in table 3.4 and the transition model's learning path? Although the system creates all the variants given in the table in the specified order, it also learns other rules and so does not follow the exact stage sequence observed by the earlier researchers.[28] For example, at approximately the same time that it constructs DOWN-2, the model also creates the following production:

DOWN-2.5
IF you have a balance with *side*,
  and *side* has the greater distance,
THEN predict *side* will go down.

This rule is identical to DOWN-2 but includes a condition about greater distances instead of relying on greater weights. As it is implemented, there is no reason for the discrimination mechanism to prefer conditions about the weight to conditions about the distance. Unfortunately Klahr and Siegler found evidence for DOWN-2 (or P2, its equivalent), but no evidence for the above rule. Apparently children tend to focus more on weights than on distances, and our theory of discrimination learning has no way to account for such trends. One can imagine introducing preferences into the model to focus attention on some attributes in favor of others, but unless one can explain where these preferences originated, they would provide no more explanation than labeling one dimension as more "salient" than another. Thus our transition model does not account for the details of Klahr and Siegler's results, though it does provide a plausible initial explanation of the transition between the observed stages.

Two additional drawbacks of the model are closely intertwined. One of these is the speed with which the system achieves maximum predictive power. The problem arrives at stage 3 behavior with a hundred trials and using only 32 CPU seconds on a PDP-10 computer. In contrast, children take years to move from stage 1 to stage 3 behavior. A second difficulty is that by presenting the system only with information about weights and distances, we are telling it much about the space of rules it should search during the learning process. However, these two limitations tend to cancel each other out. Clearly the model learns so quickly precisely because we have presented it with so few alternatives to consider. Other idealizations of the task environment contribute further to the rapid learning. For example, the child is certain to be distracted by other events in his environment, but the model has no analogous attention stealers.

Idealizations of this type have a long and respectable history in science, dating from the time Galileo decided to ignore such annoying factors as air resistance. Thus the model can be viewed as a useful approximation of the actual situation, which we could complicate to achieve more accurate results if this were deemed worth the effort that would be involved. One might question whether the discrimination theory would still be useful in a more detailed model that had to deal with many irrelevant dimensions. However, we have seen in earlier sections that the discrimination process is very robust in the face of such irrelevant features. By including additional features to the representation of balance scale problems, we would slow down the system's progress but would not halt it, and this is precisely what we would desire in a more realistic model. In summary, though our model makes some important simplifications, it does provide an initial account of the transition process on the balance scale task, and it suggests that the discrimination learning theory may provide a useful framework for describing other aspects of cognitive development as well.

3.7 Evaluating the Theory

Now that we have examined the theory of discrimination learning, along with its applications to a number of domains, it is appropriate to attempt an initial evaluation. Scientific theories can be evaluated along a number of dimensions. One of these is *simplicity*, and the discrimination theory fares well on this criterion. Our implementation of the discrimination method required some six pages of LISP code, and the learning components of the systems discussed above ranged from 6 to 19 PRISM productions. Of course these measures ignore the much more complex implementations of LISP and PRISM, since our models exist within these more basic frameworks. However, it seems reasonable to assume that the usefulness of list processing and production system languages has already been proved in other domains. We are discussing here the simplicity of a learning theory that accounts for phenomena beyond the normal range of these more basic approaches to intelligence.

Another important criterion for any scientific theory concerns its *generality*. We have applied our theory of discrimination learning to the domains of concept attainment, strategy learning, language acquisition, and cognitive development, and we feel that this provides strong evidence for the generality of the theory. However, it is better still if one can predict new areas to which a theory can be applied. In this case the prediction process is straightforward: *the discrimination theory can be applied to any domain that involves the discovery of useful conditions on rules.* Thus one can imagine applications ranging from scientific discovery to motor learning. The current version of the theory is useful only in symbolic domains, but in principle it could be extended to numeric situations as well.

Another aspect of the generality dimension involves the types of rules that can be learned, and the conditions under which this is possible. We have seen that the discrimination theory can discover disjunctive rules, unlike most earlier condition-finding schemes. Moreover it can learn in noisy situations, recover from changes in its environment, and learn partially useful rules based on inadequate representations. Of course the method pays for this ability in searching a larger space than earlier approaches and tends to learn more slowly as a result. However, this is the traditional price one must pay with weak general methods that make few assumptions about the world in which they work. And from a psychological perspective this slowness is quite plausible, since humans are generally slow learners as well.

In addition to employing the discrimination technique, the four learning systems described in previous sections share a number of other general characteristics. One such feature is that each of the models contained a critic that was responsible for noting errors of commission and for invoking the discrimination mechanism. Second, all of the programs included a rule that noted correct predictions and stored the correct instantiation with the responsible production.[29] Finally, all of the systems represented information in very small chunks, such as (*move-1 before move-2*) and (*event-1 agent agent-1*). This was necessary to let the discrimination process discover and include relevant information to the exclusion of irrelevant knowledge.

Despite the similarities of SAGE, AMBER, and the other two learning systems, differences between the programs do exist. Given this situation, one may legitimately ask why a single, more general system could not be used for all of the domains. Now it is understandable that each domain would require its own performance rules, but why should there not be a common core of adaptive productions responsible for directing the learning process?

In fact this is precisely what we find with SAGE, a model of strategy acquisition that learns in three separate domains. One problem is that there are differences in the nature of the tasks that make some learning techniques inappropriate. For example, in concept attainment it is reasonable to start with a default production that says "no" whenever no stronger rule exists for saying "yes". This strategy leads to errors of omission, and a learning rule for dealing with such cases must be included. One could use an identical strategy for learning balance scale rules, except that a "no" response makes no sense in this context; the child either predicts that one side will go down or that the sides will balance. In this case it is more plausible to assume that down and balance rules already exist and that errors of omission never occur. Second, in some cases a concern with modeling psychological data prevented us from using completely general approaches. For example, since children never say "ing" after an agent, we felt it appropriate to have the designating production include the relevant semantic role when constructing a morpheme rule. Even though such a condition could be learned through discrimination, our concern with the data led us to introduce domain-specific knowledge into the learning process.

A final criterion for scientific theories is *fertility*, or the number of new and fruitful ideas that the theory generates. Our theory also fares well on this dimension, since it leads to two possible extensions that promise to deepen our understanding of learning and intelligence. The first of these concerns the formation of higher-level concepts that help to describe information succintly. Recall that in some cases the discrimination method is capable of discovering *sets* of conditions based on the comparison of a single good and bad instantiation. Suppose that in such cases, rather than including the set of conditions in a new variant, the routine instead created an entirely new production. This rule would contain the new set as its entire condition side and would have a new predicate in its action side (with arguments taken from the predicates in the condition) which acts as shorthand notation for the set of relations. Once it was sufficiently strong, this rule would fire whenever the combination of conditions was present, *rewriting this set of relations in a more compact form*. This restatement would have two advantages. First, in the future the discrimination process need only look for a single difference rather than a conjunction of differences so that its search process could be simplified considerably. Second, if the same set of conditions proved useful for other overly general rules, the speedup in discrimination would transfer to these cases as well. In fact what we are proposing is a way of *changing representations* so that they more compactly describe the world.

A second extension concerns the generality, and thus weakness, of the discrimination process. Proponents of the knowledge engineering approach to artificial intelligence would no doubt suggest that we alter the discrimination technique to let it draw on domain-specific knowledge to direct its search for conditions. We have no objection to such an extension, provided it can be accomplished in a general manner. However, we would prefer to address the more challenging problem of devising a system that begins with a very weak but general discrimination learning mechanism and *modifies* this method so that it is more efficient for the domain at hand. Such learning to learn has been proposed by a few researchers (Langley, Neches, Neves, and Anzai 1980; Lenat, Sutherland, and Gibbons 1982) and is clearly an order of magnitude more difficult than the work we have described to date. One clear prerequisite for such an approach, at least within the adaptive production systems framework, is the restatement of the learning theory as productions instead of LISP code. This will be necessary if the learning mechanisms are to change over time according to the same laws that the performance rules obey. This leads to the very tempting notion that the discrimination process can be applied to itself to generate more domain-specific and powerful versions *of* itself. Unfortunately our ideas on this approach remain vague, and we cannot yet construct any examples of such a magical bootstrapping process.

In this chapter we have described a theory of discrimination learning that is capable of discovering appropriate conditions on production rules. We compared this theory to the more traditional generalization-based approaches and found the discrimination method able to learn in situations where it was awkward or impossible for generalization to succeed. We examined implementations of the theory in four rather different domains and found that it led to robust learning in each case. The theory appears to be simple, general, and amenable to at least two promising extensions. Of course many other processes have an equally important role to play in learning and development, and we have seen examples of some of them in other chapters of this book. However, we hope to have convinced the reader that the discrimination method is an important approach to learning that deserves increased attention in future research efforts.

Notes

I would like to thank David Klahr for comments on an earlier version of this chapter. Stephanie Sage also provided useful comments, and carried out the experiments discussed in the section on concept learning.

1. Some of Bruner et al.'s subjects employed other strategies that did not rely on the "common features" approach. We have not discussed these strategies here because we are mainly concerned with the origin of ideas on generalization-based learning.

2. Thus, one can view Winston's system as relying on a simplistic version of discrimination to avoid overgeneralizations. However, since the system's learning method was centered around generalization, and since its version of discrimination could deal with neither far misses nor disjunctive rules, we have chosen to include the work in the present section.

3. Although this aspect of Mitchell's system bears some resemblance to the discrimination learning method, it differs in its continued reliance on finding features held in common by positive instances.

4. It is not clear whether this work should actually be included as an example of discrimination learning, since it differs considerably from the other methods that we will consider under that topic. However, the representation of concepts as discrimination nets, combined with the fact that common features were not exclusively required, has led us to include the work in this section. Quinlan (1983) has recently extended Hunt, Marin, and Stone's method to learning rules for chess and games, but we do not have the space to discuss his work in detail here.

5. In another paper Anderson, Kline, and Beasley (1980) describe a different version of the discrimination process in which a new condition was added to lessen the generality of the discriminant production. This approach is very similar to the one taken in the current chapter and not by coincidence, since we were involved in early discussions with Anderson and his coworkers about discrimination learning. In fact the initial version of Anderson's discrimination process generated variants whenever a rule was applied, taking only positive instances into account. Although this approach would in principle lead eventually to a rule including all the correct conditions, the search for these conditions would be very undirected and could take a very long time. Based on the condition-finding heuristic that was then being implemented in BACON.1, we suggested that the process instead construct variants based on differences between positive and negative instances, and this proposal was later incorporated into ACTF.

6. For those who dislike notions of strength, one may instead view this number as a measure of the rate of success for the rule, with bias being given to rules with a more successful history. Of course one might also delete overly general rules, but later we will discuss some reasons for retaining them.

7. Four additional rules would be created as well if we included negated conditions; these would include *not small*, *not thin*, *not red*, and *not square* as conditions.

8. In some cases their system also replaced variables with constants; however, this can be simulated by the addition of a new condition that restricts the symbols that a variable will match against.

9. As mentioned before, each rule has an associated *strength*. When an existing rule is reconstructed, its strength is incremented. However, until its strength exceeds that of the default rule, it will never be selected. Thus the default rule's strength effectively acts as a threshold which other rules must exceed before they are considered.

10. Note that a generalization-based learning system would predict exactly the opposite trend, since it starts with very specific rules and removes conditions as it progresses.

11. Occasionally more than one of the disjuncts is present during a positive instance; in such

cases variants containing each of the disjuncts are constructed following an error of commission.

12. A noise level of 1.0 would lead to complete regularity, though the system would learn the negation of the rule it was intended to learn.

13. SAGE has also learned useful heuristics for solving algebra problems in one variable, and for a seriation task in which blocks must be ordered according to their lengths. The system's behavior in these domains is discussed in Langley (1982, 1983); however, we will be using slide-jump as our main example in this discussion.

14. A more complex version of the task allows one to jump over coins of the same type. Although this results in a larger search space, such moves always lead to dead ends, and we will consider only the simpler version of the task.

15. Note that although this rule proposes *legal* moves, there is no guarantee that these will be *good* moves. As stated, the slide-1 rule will generate many bad moves, and learning must occur before only useful actions are suggested. Also note that the variable *coin* will match against the symbol *quarter* or *nickel* rather than against a particular coin.

16. One can imagine other means of determining good instances of a rule from bad instances, such as Anzai's (1978a, 1978b) loop move and shorter path heuristics, and these certainly have a role to play in domains where search alone is prohibitive. However, in the current version of SAGE we have chosen to focus on techniques that rely on knowledge of the complete solution path.

17. The slide-jump task has two optimal solution paths which are "mirror images" of each other; the particular path is determined entirely by the initial move. To ensure that SAGE made the same first move on every run, a special production was included that increased the activation of part of the problem description. This was sufficient to focus the system's attention on the relevant coin and to avoid the effort of trying to distinguish between two equally good moves.

18. Note that the variants slide-4 and slide-5 are *not* true on the slides required for the last half of the problem. For this reason it is essential that the original slide rule remain available and that the variants simply come to be preferred when competition occurs.

19. Altogether, SAGE generated some 18 variants on the initial slide rule, but only four of these can be considered useful; fortunately the strategy of giving variants low initial strengths and strengthening upon recreation was sufficient to focus attention on the more promising rules.

20. In spirit AMBER is very similar to Reeker's model, though they differ in many details. Historically PST had no impact on the development of AMBER. The initial plans for AMBER arose from discussions with John R. Anderson in the fall of 1979; we did not become aware of Reeker's work until the fall of 1980.

21. Asterisks represent pauses in the adult sentence. These cues are necessary for AMBER to decide that a morpheme like "is" is a prefix for "bounce" instead of a suffix for "Daddy." Although adults tend to speak slowly when addressing children, it is probably too much to assume that pause information is actually available to children learning their first language. Thus, AMBER's reliance on pauses must be viewed as a limitation of the current system that should be overcome in future versions.

22. Anderson's ALAS (1981) system uses a very similar process to recover from overly general morpheme rules. AMBER and ALAS have much in common, both having grown out of discussions between Anderson and the author. Although there is considerable overlap, ALAS generally accounts for later developments in children's speech than does AMBER.

23. Actually it is not clear that the second of these was necessary, since P2 would still make the correct prediction if P5 were absent.

24. Since both productions can match the variable *side* against either side, they will each

be selected half the time (on the average) during the random stage. Thus the system would predict that the left side would go down a quarter of the trials and would predict that the right side would descend the same fraction of the time.

25. The goal of stating all successive rules as discriminants of earlier rules was one of the reasons for including an initial random stage (in addition to its intrinsic plausibility). The productions BALANCE-3, DOWN-4, and DOWN-5 are all direct variants on the two rules from stage 1, but the DOWN-3 rule is not. In order to account for its origin, and for the origin of the stage 1 rules, a random stage had to be included.

26. The reason we have not attempted to model stage 4 behavior should now be apparent. The acquisition of a torque rule requires the introduction of an entirely new concept, while the discrimination process can only be used to find conditions on existing concepts. At least in its current form our discrimination theory cannot account for the manner in which the torque concept is acquired.

27. Actually, calculation of the initial probabilities is more complicated than this. One reason is that the system initially predicts a balance response 50 percent of the time, while it predicts right down and left down each 25 percent of the time. Another complication is that only two of the problem types lead to balanced scales, while five lead to one side or the other descending. However, the overall probabilities are close enough to 33 percent initially correct responses that we will not consider them further.

28. The reader may have noticed that the rules DOWN-3, DOWN-4, and DOWN-5 are all correct in the sense that they never lead to errors and are all variants of the original DOWN-1 production. Thus the balance scale task provides an example of another domain where the learning of disjunctive rules is required, and which our approach to discrimination learning can handle adequately.

29. The concept learner and AMBER also incorporated a rule that detected errors of omission and designated entirely new productions that would correct such errors in the future. This was not necessary in the strategy learning and balance scale tasks, though one can imagine variants in which it would be necessary.

References

Anderson, J. R., Kline, P. J., and Beasley, C. M. 1978. *A theory of the acquisition of cognitive skills*. Technical Report ONR 77-1. Yale University.

Anderson, J. R., and Kline, P. J. 1979. A learning system and its psychological implications. *Proceedings of the Sixth International Joint Conference on Artificial Intelligence*, pp. 16–21.

Anderson, J. R., Kline, P. J., and Beasley, C. M. 1980. Complex learning processes. In R.E. Snow, P. A. Federico, and W. E. Montague (eds.), *Aptitude, Learning, and Instruction: Cognitive Process Analyses*. Hillsdale, N.J.: Lawrence Erlbaum Associates.

Anderson, J. R. 1981. A theory of language acquisition based on general learning principles. *Proceedings of the Seventh International Joint Conference on Artificial Intelligence*, pp. 165–170.

Anzai, Y. 1978. Learning strategies by computer. *Proceedings of the Canadian Society for Computational Studies of Intelligence*, pp. 181–190.

Anzai, Y. 1978. How one learns strategies: Processes and representation of strategy acquisition. *Proceedings of the Third AISB/GI Conference*, pp. 1–14.

Baylor, G. W., Gascon, J., Lemoyne, G., and Pother, N. 1973. An information processing model of some seriation tasks. *Canadian Psychologist* 14, 167–196.

Brazdil, P. 1978. Experimental learning model. *Proceedings of the Third AISB/GI Conference*, pp. 46–50.

Brown, R. 1973. *A First Language: The Early Stages*. Cambridge, Mass.: Harvard University Press.

Bruner, J. S., Goodnow, J. J., and Austin, G. A. 1956. *A Study of Thinking*. New York: Wiley.

Feigenbaum, E. A. 1963. The simulation of verbal learning behavior. In E. A. Feigenbaum and J. Feldman (eds.), *Computers and Thought*. New York: McGraw-Hill.

Feigenbaum, E. A. Buchanan, B. G., and Lederberg, J. 1971. On generality and problem solving: A case study using the DENDRAL program. In *Machine Intelligence* 6. Edinburgh: Edinburgh University Press.

Forgy, C. L. 1979. *The OPS4 Reference Manual*. Technical Report. Department of Computer Science, Carnegie-Mellon University.

Hayes-Roth, F., and McDermott, J. 1976. Learning structured patterns from examples. *Proceedings of Third International Joint Conference on Pattern Recognition*, pp. 419–423.

Hedrick, C. 1976. Learning production systems from examples. *Artificial Intelligence* 7, 21–49.

Hunt, E. B., Marin, J., and Stone, P. J. 1966. *Experiments in Induction*. New York: Academic Press.

Iba, G. A. 1979. Learning disjunctive concepts from examples. Master's thesis. Massachusetts Institute of Technology.

Kelley, K. L. 1967. *Early syntactic acquisition*. Technical Report P-3719. The Rand Company.

Klahr, D., and Wallace, J. G. 1976. *Cognitive Development: An Information Processing Analysis*. Hillsdale, N.J.: Lawrence Erlbaum Associates.

Klahr, D., and Siegler, R. 1978. The representation of children's knowledge. In H. W. Reese and L. P. Lipsett (eds.), *Advances in Child Development*. New York: Academic Press.

Langley, P. 1978. BACON.1: A general discovery system. *Proceedings of the Second National Conference of the Canadian Society for Computational Studies of Intelligence*, pp. 173–180.

Langley, P. 1979. *Descriptive discovery processes: Experiments in Baconian science*. Dissertation. Carnegie-Mellon University.

Langley, P., Neches, R., Neves, D., and Anzai, Y. 1980. A domain-independent framework for learning procedures. *International Journal of Policy Analysis and Information Systems* 4, 163–197.

Langley, P. and Simon, H. A. 1981. The central role of learning in cognition. In J. R. Anderson (ed.), *Cognitive Skills and Their Acquisition*. Hillsdale, N. J.: Lawrence Erlbaum Associates.

Langley, P. 1982. Strategy acquisition governed by experimentation. *Proceedings of the European Conference on Artificial Intelligence*, pp. 171–176.

Langley, P. 1983. Learning search strategies through discrimination. *International Journal of Man-Machine Studies*, 18, 513–541.

Lenat, D. B., Sutherland, W. R., and Gibbons, J. 1982. Heuristic search for new microcircuit structures: An application of artificial intelligence. *AI Magazine* (Summer), 17–33.

Mitchell, T. M. 1977. Version spaces: A candidate elimination approach to rule learning. *Proceedings of the Fifth International Joint Conference on Artificial Intelligence*, pp. 305–310.

Mitchell, T. M. 1978. *Version spaces: An approach to concept learning*. Dissertation. Stanford University.

Mitchell, T. M. 1979. An analysis of generalization as a search problem. *Proceedings of the Sixth International Joint Conference on Artificial Intelligence*, pp. 577–582.

Mitchell, T. M., Utgoff, P., Nudel, B., and Banerji, R. B. 1981. Learning problem solving heuristics through practice. *Proceedings of the Seventh International Joint Conference on Artificial Intelligence*, pp. 127–134.

Mitchell, T. M., Utgoff, P., and Banerji, R. B. 1983. Learning problem solving heuristics by experimentation. In R. S. Michalski, J. G. Carbonell, and T. M. Mitchell (eds.), *Machine Learning: An Artificial Intelligence Approach*. Palo Alto, Calif.: Tioga Publishing.

Newell, A., Shaw, J. C., and Simon, H. A. 1960. Report on a general problem-solving program for a computer. *Information Processing: Proceedings of the International Conference on Information Processing*, pp. 256–264.

Piaget, J., and Inhelder, B. 1969. *The Psychology of the Child.* New York: Basic Books.

Pople, H. E. 1977. The formation of composite hypotheses in diagnostic problem solving: An exercise in synthetic reasoning. *Proceedings of the Fifth International Joint Conference on Artificial Intelligence*, pp. 1030–1037.

Quinlan, J. R. 1983. Learning efficient classification procedures and their application to chess end games. In R. S. Michalski, J. G. Carbonell, and T. M. Mitchell (eds.), *Machine Learning: An Artificial Intelligence Approach.* Palo Alto, Calif.: Tioga Publishing.

Reeker, L. H. 1976. The computational study of language acquisition. In M. Yovits and M. Rubinoff (eds.), *Advances in Computers.* New York: Academic Press.

Selfridge, M. 1981. A computer model of child language acquisition. *Proceedings of the Seventh International Joint Conference on Artificial Intelligence*, pp. 92–96.

Sleeman, D., Langley, P., and Mitchell, T. M. 1982. Learning from solution paths: An approach to the credit assignment problem. *AI Magazine* (Spring), 48–52.

Vere, S. A. 1975. Induction of concepts in the predicate calculus. *Proceedings of the Fourth International Joint Conference on Artificial Intelligence*, pp. 281–287.

Vere, S. A. 1977. Induction of relational productions in the presence of background information. *Proceedings of the Fifth International Joint Conference on Artificial Intelligence*, pp. 349–355.

Winston, P. H. 1970. *Learning structural descriptions from examples.* Technical Report AI-TR-231. Massachusetts Institute of Technology.

Young, R. M. 1976. *Seriation by Children: An Artificial Intelligence Analysis of a Piagetian Task.* Basel: Birkhauser.

4 Learning through Incremental Refinement of Procedures

Robert Neches

This chapter will discuss a model of learning through a process of inventing successively more refined procedures for performing a task. I will argue that this is related to the development of understanding of a procedure, as well as to improvements in the efficiency with which a goal can be achieved. In this introductory section, I will consider where a model of this sort fits in a theory of learning, give a brief account of the specific model and its empirical bases, and consider how that model applies to given an account of developments in children's addition procedures.

In the next section, I will discuss HPM (for Heuristic Procedure Modification), an operationalization of the general model as a computer program (Neches, 1981a). In that section. I will concentrate on the information processing demands of the system's learning mechanisms and consider how the system architecture was evolved to meet those demands.

After considering the structure of the system, a section of the paper will be dedicated to examining HPM's development of addition strategies. I will concentrate on showing how the information retained by the system about its past actions allows it to learn by using its set of current rules as a "parts kit" from which new rules can be assembled.

In the concluding section, after evaluating the strengths and weaknesses of the program in its current form, I will consider some implications of the approach represented by HPM. That concluding discussion will emphasize the importance of *meta-procedural knowledge,* that is, domain-independent knowledge about the general structure of procedures. It will concentrate on three points: learning without external feedback, the generation of interesting rule candidates, and the use of semantic knowledge in both learning and attention-focusing mechanisms.

4.1 The Importance of Invention to Theories of Learning

For many years, the dominant focus of research on learning was on the acquisition of facts; even today, in many psychology departments, learning and memory are viewed as virtually identical topics. More recently, though, more attention has been given to the development of strategies and algorithms. It has been argued (Langley, Neches, Neves, and Anzai 1980) that models of procedural learning must address two related issues: inducing *correct* rules for when to perform the various actions available to a system and developing *interesting* new actions to perform. Most of the computer simulations developed in recent years have concentrated on only one or the other of these issues.

Learning: Changing the Conditions for Performing an Action

Among the models concerned with the development of correct (or "appropriate") rules, there have been two major topics: *chunking* models have attempted to account for general phenomena of speed-up and automatization, while *concept formation* models have tried to explain changes in error patterns and the reduction of search. The notion of condition-action rules has been heavily used in both areas. The difference lies in the operations postulated to apply to existing rules in order to produce new rules.

Chunking models postulate the transformation of multistep operations into single-step operations through a process of "composition," in which a new rule is formed by taking the composite of two rules that had previously applied sequentially. Lewis (1978, chapter 7) has formally demonstrated the conditions under which rules constructed by composition can be assured of producing the same behavior as the initial set of rules. Neves and Anderson (1981) have shown how a composition-like mechanism could produce reductions in search and in reliance on external memory aids. Newell and Rosenbloom (1981) have shown that the learning curves predicted by composition are quite similar to those observable in a broad range of learning tasks.

Although chunking models seem to offer an account of some forms of learning, there are a range of errors for which they cannot account (e.g., the regularization of irregular verbs observed as a phase in language development). Several models have been developed to account for such observations. These models have been deeply influenced by AI research on rule induction, particularly that of Hayes-Roth and McDermott (1976), Vere (1977), Michalski (1977), and Mitchell (1977). This work has largely concentrated on *generalization,* in which a new rule is derived by making the conditions of some predecessor rule(s) less specific. The new rule will apply in all of the situations as did its predecessor(s), along with a number of additional situations in which it may or may not be appropriate. Thus, generalization techniques are error-prone, and depend on some auxiliary mechanism to catch and correct false generalizations. Generally, this is done either by giving rules confidence ratings that can be lowered in the event of negative feedback, or by a complementary process of *discrimina-*

tion. Discrimination requires the availability of information about both positive and negative examples; by seeking to find differences between the examples, the method generates additional conditions intended to make a rule applicable only in cases similar to the positive example.

Generalization and/or discrimination techniques have been used in programs modeling performance in concept-learning tasks (Anderson, Kline, and Beasley 1979), language comprehension and production at various age levels (Anderson 1981; Langley 1980), geometry theorem proving (Anderson, Greeno, Kline, and Neves 1981), and various puzzle-solving tasks (Langley, chapter 3). Sleeman, Langley, and Mitchell (1982) have suggested that these techniques represent a major mechanism for building procedures from weak heuristic search processes. According to their proposal, learning occurs when a second attempt at solving a problem permits comparison of the solution paths followed in the two attempts. In the second attempt operations will still be proposed by the same heuristic search methods as in the first attempt. However, since knowledge about the solution path is available, the learning system can begin to construct individual rules for proposing each kind of move. The cases where the proposed move was indeed on the solution path provide the basis for constructing the initial conditions for such rules, and for generalizing the rules. Moves that were proposed, but were not on the solution path, provide the basis for discrimination by standing as negative examples.

Learning: The Invention of New Actions

Although the mechanisms of composition, generalization, and discrimination have shown promise in explaining a range of learning phenomena, there is a set of evidence that indicates that they are not a sufficient basis for a complete computational model of procedural learning. The evidence consists of a number of recent studies that have tried to characterize differences between the strategies employed by experts and novices, some of which were reviewed in chapter 1. Lewis (1981), for example, has shown that expert-novice differences in strategies for solving algebra expressions could not have been produced by composition. The procedures produced by a composition process would not apply correctly in all cases, Lewis proved, and therefore additional rules would be required to ensure that the new procedure would work properly. These rules would have to be generated by some process other than composition.

Hunter's (1968) analysis of a subject with exceptional skills at mental arithmetic revealed aspects of the subject's performance that present difficulties for models of composition, generalization, and discrimination. For example, the subject's mastery of large mental multiplication problems depended on performing the component submultiplications in left-to-right order while keeping a running total of the intermediate products.[1] Development of the new procedure requires the introduction of wholly new components, e.g., keeping a running total of subproducts. The introduction of such new elements, and the control structure governing their sequence of execution, is clearly beyond the scope of mechanisms for composition, generalization, and discrimination.

Studies on expert/novice differences in physics (Simon and Simon 1978; Larkin 1981) provide another example. A general observation in those studies is that experts rely on working-forward strategies while novices are much more inclined to use means-ends analysis. Because these strategies involve very different actions, IT is much easier to understand the transition as stemming from a higher-level analysis of the semantics of the domain than as a rearrangement of actions.

The importance of learning mechanisms that can make use of domain-specific knowledge is also suggested by Neves' (1978) work on a program that learns to solve algebra equations by analyzing worked-out examples. The program's learning process requires synthesizing sequences of algebraic operations that would produce the differences observed between one line and the next in an example. Once such a sequence is found, it is taken to represent a larger operation, and the program examines the first line of the pair in an attempt to infer the appropriate conditions for applying the new macro-operator in the future. The rules produced by Neves' system could be passed on to generalization or discrimination processes, but they certainly could not initially be produced by those processes. Producing the rules requires the application of a means-ends analysis procedure that utilizes domain-specific knowledge about algebra. Without the provision for means-ends analysis to construct new actions, the system would be unable to produce meaningful new rules.

The Heuristic Procedure Modification Model

The preceding section illustrates some examples from a corpus of procedural inventions requiring explanation (see also Neches and Hayes 1978). Unfortunately, there are relatively little hard data on the psychological processes that produced those changes. From the studies that have been concerned with this, Neches (1981b) and Anzai and Simon (1979), it is possible to state only some very global properties of the strategy change process. To illustrate those points, let us consider some results reported by Neches (1981b) from an analysis of a subject's strategy changes while working at a computer graphics editing task:

Strategy changes are produced by fast, background processes. Although solution times decreased by 30 to 40 percent and the number of commands that were issued decreased by 20 to 30 percent, it was still the case that only 11.5 percent of the subject's protocol statements concerned strategy changes. Fully two-thirds of even those few statements were announcements of already-formulated changes rather than statements reflecting the formulation of a change.

Changes reflect local focus of attention. There were a number of cases—particularly involving error recovery strategies—where the subject made changes that used fewer operations to achieve a subgoal but later on forced him to use more operations to achieve his main goal. The subject seemed to have only very limited capacity to look ahead for inefficiencies; for example, in some cases actions were performed to test their feasibility, their results were deleted from the computer screen after being deemed satisfactory, and the same actions were then repeated.

Changes come about through a relatively undirected working-forward process. Over trials, many changes consisted of improvements to strategies produced by previous modifications. Approximately 40 percent of the protocol statements were classified as observations or evaluations, but there was no consistent relationship between these and strategy changes. That is, evaluations were often made without leading to changes, and changes were made that often were not preceded by evaluations.

All of the observations put together led to a view of strategy changes as being produced by a set of fast, opportunistic, heuristic processes. These processes seemed to operate in the background, and appear to be constrained by processing and memory limitations. These ideas are captured in a model with the following claims:

1. As operations in a procedure are planned and/or performed, an internal representation of them is formed in working memory.

2. A large number of pattern-driven heuristics act as demons, inspecting this internal representation and responding to situations that fit their

conditions by asserting a goal to make a specified type of change to a procedure.

3. Modification processes respond to the goals by seeking to construct a change of the specified type for that portion of the procedure which evoked the heuristic. These changes reflect only very limited understanding of the semantics of the procedure and might be likened to the patches that one programmer might make in trying to improve the efficiency of another programmer's code.

4. In many cases, the modification processes have become automatized and have merged, or "composed" (Lewis 1978), with the goal-setting process. Thus, changes may take place without explicit goal-setting being observed; procedure change will lead to observable problem-solving behavior only in relatively more complex cases.

5. The changes produced by these processes compete with the current form of the procedure, and are evaluated with respect to expectations about the improvement they will produce. Changes may either be reinforced (increased in strength until they mask the original procedure from ever being observed), or punished (decreased in strength until they become unlikely to appear).

6. As a modified procedure emerges, it is subject to the same learning processes as the initial procedure. Thus, drastically new strategies are produced through a sequence of small incremental refinements to an initial procedure, spread over a series of practice trials.

Pattern-driven heuristics are a key notion in this model. They are essential to accounting for the observation that human strategy changes seem to be produced with little conscious attention. The existence of patterns turns the change process into a specialized kind of recognition process, something that can proceed in parallel with other activities and demand relatively small resources. This, coupled with constraints on working memory size, also serves to explain the observations of local attention-focus and working-forward processing. Limitations on working memory mean that only relatively local information is available for pattern-matching, and this in turn necessitates a working-forward mode of processing.

An Example: Changes in Children's Addition Procedures

To give this discussion more substance, let us consider an example: changes in the procedures used by small children to perform simple addition.

Section 4.3 will discuss this topic in considerably more detail; I am introducing it here primarily to provide a context that will motivate the more technical sections that follow.

A number of researchers have shown that very young children add by a procedure similar to Cantor's axiomatization of arithmetic, sometimes known as the "SUM" or "counting-all" method (Carpenter and Moser 1979; Fuson and Richards 1979; Ginsburg 1977a, 1977b; Groen and Resnick 1977; Steffe and Thompson 1982). In this procedure separate sets of objects are counted out to represent each addend, these sets are combined into a single set, and that union set is then counted to determine its size. This method represents an understanding of addition in terms of set union.

Although there is still some debate about the form of adult addition processes (e.g., Ashcraft and Battaglia 1978), there is general agreement that children at the second-grade level commonly solve addition problems by a procedure somewhat more advanced than SUM. That procedure, known as "MIN" or "counting-on" (Groen and Parkman 1972; Ginsburg 1977a, 1977b; Svenson 1975; Svenson and Broquist 1975; Svenson, Hedenborg, and Lingman 1976), starts with the larger addend and increments it the number of times specified by the smaller addend. This procedure represents an implicit understanding of addition as repeated application of a successor function to an ordered sequence of numbers, which is essentially Peano's axiomatization.

The SUM and MIN procedures involve rather different actions and quite different underlying conceptualizations of arithmetic. Nevertheless, a sequence of changes evoked by pattern heuristics can transform SUM into MIN. There are actually a number of sequences that will lead from one to the other, producing a network of intermediate procedures (Neches 1981b). The intermediate procedures can be thought of as varying along a number of dimensions, such as degree of reliance on external memory aids. I will only be discussing variants of a single representative sequence of transitions leading from SUM to MIN in this chapter.[2]

Figure 4.1 shows three sample strategy transformation heuristics. To see how they can apply to the SUM procedure, let us consider the operations called for by that procedure. First, sets must be formed to represent each addend. This involves a separate counting-out process for each one: repeatedly fetching a new object and assigning it a number until an object gets a number-assignment that corresponds to the addend. After sets have been

- **Result still available:**
  An item of information has previously been computed, and is needed again.

  Modification: try to retrieve the item rather than recomputing it.

- **Untouched results:**
  A procedure produces an output, but no other procedure receives that result as input.

  Modification: try to eliminate computation of that item.

- **Effort Difference:**
  A difference in expended effort is observed when the same procedure is operating on the same input(s) at different times.

  Modification: try to use the method involving less effort.

Figure 4.1
Three sample strategy transformation heuristics

formed in this way for each addend, their union represents the sum. This union is then the object of a counting-up process: repeatedly fetching an object from the set and assigning it a number until all objects have gotten new number assignments. The size of the union set is then known.

Note that the intermediate results generated in the course of this procedure include (1) a set of objects with number assignments, known to correspond in size to the first addend, (2) a similar set for the second addend, (3) a set containing all of these same objects and their initial number assignments, but of unknown size because the objects have not yet been recounted, and, upon completion, (4) a set of known size, containing all the same objects with their new number assignments.

When this procedure is executed, there is a point in time where an instance can be observed of the kind of redundancy sought by the *result still available* heuristic. When counting up the union set, at the point where only the objects representing the first addend have been counted, the objects and number assignments resulting from counting up are no different from the result of counting out; they are simply being recounted. Eliminating the redundancy of recounting the objects representing the first addend produces a new procedure. In this procedure counting out is done to represent both addends, but the result for the first addend is used to initialize the count up of the union, so that the objects representing the second addend are then counted up starting from the value of the first addend (as opposed to counting up the objects for both addends starting from zero).

This new procedure is more efficient, because it eliminates some redundant counting. However, when it is executed, it becomes possible to note that the change has rendered unnecessary a previously-needed portion of the procedure. At the end of the new procedure, the objects used to represent the first addend have not been used—a condition for the *untouched results* heuristic. (Previously, these objects were used when they were recounted as part of the union set; now, the number representing the addend set is used, but not the objects themselves.) Since the number that represents the addend set is known in advance, it is not actually necessary to produce objects to represent that set if those objects are not going to be counted. Eliminating this inefficiency produces another new procedure. In this new procedure, objects are counted out to represent only the second addend. Those objects are then counted up, starting from the value of the first addend.

This new procedure is very close to the counting-on procedure embodied by MIN. The only difference is that it counts on from the first addend, rather than from the larger addend as done in the MIN procedure. However, when this procedure is applied to various problems, it is possible to note that for any pair of problems $a + b$ and $b + a$, the effort will be less for whichever one of the pair starts with the larger addend. The *effort difference* heuristic produces a final modification that will cause the larger addend to be treated as the first addend (if it is not already the first addend). This modification to the procedure of counting on from the first addend produces the full MIN procedure.

This analysis shows one of several ways by which successive refinement by strategy change heuristics could transform the SUM procedure into a MIN procedure that initially appeared to be quite different and totally unrelated.

There is a great deal of significance to the fact that these two procedures are related and that one can be derived from the other by equivalence-preserving transformations. Among their things, this tells us that there are multiple equivalent representations for the size of a set and therefore multiple representations for unions of sets (a beginning of a concept of multiple equivalent set partitionings). It also tells us that arithmetic can be expressed in terms of successor functions, as well as operations on sets (a concept necessary to understand more complex arithmetic operations that are not cleanly described in terms of sets). Thus, a transition from SUM to Min represents more than just a change in efficiency. It also represents a change in procedural, if not declarative, knowledge about fundamental mathematical concepts.

4.2 HPM: An Operationalization of the Heuristic Procedure Modification Model

The verbal model described in the preceding section is sufficient to permit task analyses that will suggest paths that the development of a procedure might follow. In attempting to validate the model, one course of action is to seek correspondences between those predictions and empirical observations. There are, however, considerable limitations on our ability to make use of empirical observations. Computer simulations, therefore, play a major role in the development of learning models such as this one.

This chapter is not the place for a detailed discussion of the role of computer simulation in general (but see Neches 1982). However, a few remarks are needed to clarify the expectations for a computer simulation in this particular case. Here, the attempt to operationalize the verbal model as a running program serves two related functions: it tests the sufficiency of the model by requiring a demonstration that it is adequate to perform the learning tasks required from it, and it forces a closer examination of the implications of the model by requiring specification of auxiliary mechanisms necessary to support the system's performance.

In addition to being intrinsically interesting, an understanding of the underlying mechanisms of the model is necessary to a detailed examination of its performance on learning tasks. Therefore, this section will consider the "architecture" of the HPM simulation; the section following will consider its application to the learning of addition procedures.

As will be seen in the section, the need to operationalize the verbal model as a program immediately raises two crucial questions:

What does it take to recognize that a strategy transformation heuristic is applicable?

What does it take to construct a change and insert it into a procedure?

The answers fall into two categories: representation of a *knowledge base* containing the kind of information needed by the system to detect and implement possible changes, and *attention focusing mechanisms* enabling the system to function in reasonable time by avoiding extended search through its knowledge base.

Representation of Knowledge about Procedures

Choosing to use a production-system model is itself a representational decision. The strategy transformation model, with its emphasis on pattern-driven heuristics, is quite naturally cast as a production system model. Although parsimony encourages one to use the same framework for the performance mechanisms as for the learning mechanisms, this is not the only reason for doing so. Production systems have many properties similar to those observed in human performance (Newell and Simon 1972, pp. 804–806). In addition, as Langley, Neches, Neves, and Anzai (1981) have pointed out, production system programs can be easier to modify than traditional programs. This is because the conditions associated with each action express the range of situations in which the actions are applicable; assuming that an appropriate language is available for specifying the conditions, actions that are not invalidated by a change should continue to have their conditions satisfied, actions necessitated by the change but not previously applicable should now have their conditions satisfied, and actions that are no longer required should no longer have their conditions satisfied. Thus, the side effects of a change are implemented without having to be explicitly propagated through the procedure.

So far, all that has been said is that production systems are a promising general representation, *if* the knowledge base that they operate upon is appropriate. There are several properties it must have in order to be appropriate. The two most important are that it must contain the kind of information needed to determine the applicability of learning heuristics, and it must allow for descriptions of its contents that are general enough to apply appropriately in many different situations.

Let us consider the issue of content first. What sort of information has to be retained about a procedure in order to detect an inefficiency and construct an appropriate change? One way to answer this question is to analyze the demands of the learning mechanisms we would like to have. Figure 4.2 presents a set of strategy transformation heuristics suggested by protocol and task analyses reported in Neches (1981b). If we examine these heuristics in terms of what must be known about a procedure in order to apply them, there are about a dozen categories of information. These are summarized in figure 4.3.

The key concept in HPM is the specification of a formalism for representing goals that is intended to capture the kind of information that figure 4.3 shows to be needed. If a suitable set of conventions is obeyed in the construction of this history so that it contains the kinds of information described in figure 4.3, then the strategy change heuristics shown in figure 4.2 can be restated formally as productions with conditions referring to propositions in the procedural trace. It should then be possible to carry out strategy transformations by having the actions of these productions construct new productions, which will change how a procedure is performed by masking or circumventing the behavior of the preexisting productions for that procedure. The sections following are each concerned with different parts of this underlying notion. The discussion that follows provides details of HPM's knowledge representation and then evaluates how well the goal and production traces do at providing the kind of information called for by figure 4.3. We will complete the picture by considering the use of the representation in actually making strategy transformation heuristics operational.

The Goal Trace and the Production Trace The data structures in HPM are determined by a set of conventions for describing procedures and information-passing between procedures. The formalism represents information as nodes in a semantic network that can stand for goals, data, and temporal markers. Procedures are represented as productions with conditions matching propositions in some goal structure, and with actions that add new propositions to the same goal structure. Thus, the process of executing a procedure entails building a goal structure, which is left behind afterwards as a *trace*, or, history, of the procedure's execution.

The goal structures left behind are hierarchical acyclic graphs, similar in many respects to Sacerdoti's (1977) planning nets but represented in a notation that combines features from Kintsch (1974) and Norman and Rumelhart (1975). Using the PRISM notion of trace data (Langley and Neshes 1981), HPM's knowledge base also contains nodes representing

REDUCTION TO RESULTS: *converting a computational process to a memory retrieval process.*

Frequent usage: *IF a procedure recurs frequently, and the set of different inputs to it seems small, THEN try to memorize it.* **(REQUIRES FREQ., P/G, I, EVENT INFORMATION.)**

Interesting subset: *IF a subset of inputs to a procedure share a common property, THEN try to memorize them.* **(REQUIRES P/G, I, DESCRI., EVENT INFORMATION.)**

REDUCTION TO A RULE: *replacing a procedure with an induced rule for generating its result.*

Correlation: *IF a procedure is observed for several inputs and their corresponding results, and whenever the input has some property, the result which is generated has some specific corresponding property, THEN set up a goal to use the input property to predict the result.* **(REQUIRES P/G, I, R, DESCRI., EVENT INFORMATION.)**

Effort difference: *IF a difference in expended effort is observed when the same goal is operating on the same input(s) at different times, THEN set up a goal to find a difference between methods used, and try to produce the circumstances which evoked the more efficient method.* **(REQUIRES EFF., P/G, I, EVENT, SUB INFORMATION.)**

Orderly succession: *IF a procedure is observed for a series of inputs, and each input is related to the previous one by being a successor in some known sequence, THEN try to use the successor function for that sequence and the result of the previous use of that procedure to predict the sequence of results.* **(REQUIRES P/G, I, EVENT, TIME, DESCRI. INFORMATION.)**

REPLACEMENT WITH ANOTHER METHOD: *substituting an equivalent procedure.*

Equivalent procedures: *IF a case is observed involving two different procedures, each of which operates on the same input and produces the same result, but one of which involves less effort, THEN try to substitute the more efficient method when the other method is called for.* **(REQUIRES P/G, I, R, EFF., EVENT, SUB INFORMATION.)**

Equivalent inputs: *IF the same procedure is observed to produce the same result for two* different *inputs, and the effort differs in the two cases, THEN try to substitute the easier input whenever the procedure is invoked with the harder one.* **(REQUIRES P/G, I, R, EFF., EVENT INFORMATION.)**

Side-costs: *IF the effort of* set-up *and* clean-up *operations are not small compared to costs of* mainstep *operations, THEN try to find the major factor dealt with by those operations, and look for a method in which that factor is not present.* **(REQUIRES P/G, SUB, EFF., DESCRI. INFORMATION.)**

Figure 4.2
Strategy transformation heuristics

UNIT BUILDING: *grouping operations into a set accessible as a single unit.*

Co-occuring procedures (composition): *IF a procedure, P_1, is frequently followed by another procedure, P_2, and the result of P_1 is used by P_2, THEN try the merger of the two as a new single procedure.* **(REQUIRES P/G, TIME, SUB INFORMATION.)**

Co-ocurring goals (planning): *IF a goal, G_1, is frequently followed by another goal, G_2, and the result of G_1 is used by G_2, THEN try planning to acheive the second goal whenever the first is asserted.* **(REQUIRES P/G, TIME, INFORMATION.)**

DELETION OF UNNECESSARY PARTS: *eliminating redundant or extraneous operations.*

Cancelling operations: *IF a sequence of connected procedures, $P_1, \ldots, P_n$, is observed for which the output of P_n is identical to the input of P_1, THEN try deleting the sequence.* **(REQUIRES P/G, I, R INFORMATION.)**

No influence: *IF some action contained in a procedure is observed to have* different *results at times when the procedure itself is observed to have the* same *inputs and results, try deleting the action.* **(REQUIRES P/G, I, R, SUB, EVENT INFORMATION.)**

Untouched results: *IF a procedure produces an output, but no other procedure receives that result as input, them try deleting the procedure.* **(REQUIRES P/G, I, R, EPISODE INFORMATION.)**

Constant outcome (dead branches): *IF a decision is made about what to do next on the basis of some action's result, but that action is observed to have a constant result, THEN try deleting the action.* **(REQUIRES P/G, I, R, EVENT, DESCRI., TIME INFORMATION.)**

Over-determined tests: *IF a procedure contains two tests as part of a decision, call them T_1 and T_2, and it is observed that the tests agree (i.e., T_1 is observed to succeed on several occasions, with T_2 also succeeding on all of those occasions, and is observed to fail on several other occasions, with T_2 also failing on all of those occasions), THEN try deleting one of the two tests.* **(REQUIRES P/G, EVENT, SUB, R, DESCRI. INFORMATION.)**

Figure 4.2 continued

SAVING PARTIAL RESULTS: *retaining intermediate results which would otherwise have to be recomputed later in a procedure.*

Result still available: *IF a procedure is about to be executed with a certain input, but the result of that procedure with the same input is recorded in working memory, THEN try to borrow that result now and in the future.* (REQUIRES P/G, I, R, TIME, PROC. INFORMATION.)

Result almost available: *IF a procedure is about to be executed with a certain input, and has previously been observed with the same input, but its result is not active in working memory, THEN try to retrieve that result and set up a goal to have that result kept available in the future.* (REQUIRES P/G, I, R, TIME, PROC. INFORMATION.)

Sub-part available: *IF an input to a procedure is divisible into parts, one of which has previously been observed as input to the same procedure, THEN set up a goal to try to borrow the result of the procedure for the part, and to try the procedure on the combination of that result with the remainder of the original input.* (REQUIRES P/G, I, R, TIME, DESCRI. INFORMATION.)

RE-ORDERING: *changing the sequence in which operations are performed.*

Crowding: *IF a large number of items are in working memory which have not been used, THEN set up a goal to change the sequence of operations.* (REQUIRES I, R, PROC. INFORMATION.)

Waiting: *IF a result is generated, but many operations intervene before any use of it is made, THEN set up a goal to change the sequence of operations so that the operation producing a result and the operation using it are performed closer in time.* (REQUIRES P/G, I, R, TIME INFORMATION.)

Non-optimal state utilization: *IF a state which appeared previously must be restored in order to satisfy the enabling conditions of a planned operation, THEN set up a goal to find the action which changed the state, and to place the planned operation ahead of that action.* (REQUIRES P/G, I, R, PROC., DESCRI. INFORMATION.)

Figure 4.2 continued

ABBREV.	DEFINITION
Descr.	Description or property associated with an object, e.g., *set-up, mainstep,* or *clean-up* as descriptions of subgoals.
Eff.	Effort.
Episode	The structure containing all goals that went into solving a single problem completely, e.g., solving the addition problem 2 + 3.
Event	Single instance of a goal with particular inputs.
Freq.	Frequency of occurrence.
I	Inputs of a goal instance.
Proc.	Processing information, such as presence in working memory, size of working memory, etc.
P/G	Procedure or goal.
R	Results of a goal instance.
Sub	Subgoals associated with a goal instance.
Time	Sequential or temporal ordering of events.

Figure 4.3
Categories of information implied by the heuristics

each cycle of the production system; these nodes are linked to nodes that represent individual production firings. The latter nodes have links to the specific propositions that triggered a particular instance of a production firing, as well as links to the propositions asserted by that instance. Thus, the node network representing an execution history can be viewed as either *goal-ordered* or *time-ordered*, depending on the perspective from which it is viewed. I will be referring to these two perspectives as the *goal trace* and the *production trace*, respectively.

For example, one of the first rules in a production system for addition by the SUM method is, *To add two numbers, generate sets corresponding to them and then count how many elements they contain.* Figure 4.4a gives the HPM production for this rule and gives an English paraphrase for its propositions, figure 4.4b shows the network representation after its execution, and figure 4.4c shows the trace data propositions corresponding to it.

Addition-plan	**IF**
((=a *goal* **ADD**)	there's an active *goal* to **ADD**,
(=a *status* (ACTIVE ! =))	
(=a *input* =i1)	which has two *inputs* to it
(=i1 *input-a* =a)	
(=a *input* =i2)	**THEN**
(=i2 *input-b* =a)	Assert a new *goal* to
==>	**GENERATE-SETS** as a *subgoal*
(=gs *goal* **GENERATE-SETS**)	of the **ADD** *goal*.
(=a *subgoal* =gs)	
	Make the new goal ACTIVE,
(=gs *status* (ACTIVE))	and give it the same two
(=gs *input* =i1)	*inputs*.
(=i1 *input-a* =gs)	
(=gs *input* =i2)	Create a node where the new
(=i2 *input-b* =gs)	goal's *result* can be found.
(=gs *result* =countable-set)	Assert that the new goal is to
	be followed by another goal.
(=gs *then* =cu)	
	This new goal is to **COUNT-UP**;
(=cu *goal* **COUNT-UP**)	it is also a *subgoal* of the **ADD**
(=a *subgoal* =cu)	goal, and is initially inactive.
(=cu *status* (SUSPENDED))	
(=cu *input* =countable-set)	It is to operate on the *result*
(=countable-set *input-a* =cu)	of the goal to **GENERATE-SETS**; a
(=cu *result* =set-size)	node is specified where its
	result can be found. (a)

Figure 4.4
The HPM representation of a production for addition, showing the production (a), the network structure after its execution (b), and the corresponding trace data propositions (c)

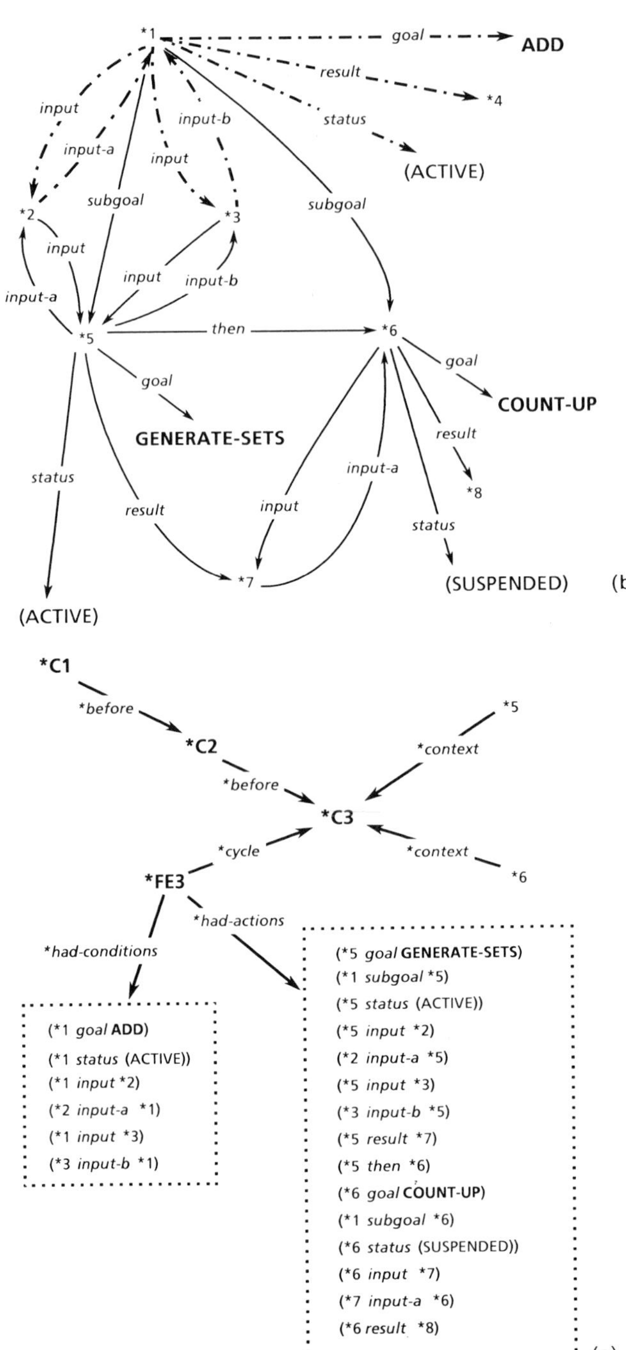

Figure 4.4 continued

The production responds to a goal to **ADD** by building structures in the network representing goals to **GENERATE-SETS** and **COUNT-UP**. These are linked by a *subgoal* relation from the initial goal, and a *then* relation from the first subgoal to the second. These establish the goal-subgoal hierarchy and the ordering of subgoals. *Input* and *result* relations from the goal nodes point to nodes describing operands of the goals. These are described in terms of various relations, with the most important being *value*, which indicates the concept instantiated by an operand. The *goal* and *value* relations are HPM's means of representing the type-token distinction discussed by Norman and Rumelhart (1975) and Woods (1975).

As figure 4.4 illustrates, a production must only specify the propositions relevant to its own processing; it need not indicate all relations from a node. Nevertheless, it is required to construct a goal-trace representation by using only a restricted set of propositions and obeying their semantics. The semantics of the goal-trace representation allow only the following types of nodes: (1) *GOAL* nodes, (2) *DATA* nodes, which instantiate concepts, (3) *SET* nodes, used for concepts that represent sets of *data nodes*, (4) *FIRING-EVENT* nodes, discussed previously, (5) *PREDICTION* nodes, discussed later in this section, and, (6) *EFFORT* nodes, which have a numeric value associated with them outside the semantic network that represents the estimated processing effort of a goal. An HPM production system for solving a task primarily consists of productions that add goals (such as was just illustrated), productions that set up data structures for goals requiring iteration by establishing *has-data* relations from the goals to *DATA* nodes, and productions that terminate processing of a goal by manipulating *result*, *value*, and *status* relations.

Effort Estimation It is very useful for a flexible system to have information about the effort involved in processing various goals. Information about the effort expended up to the current point facilitates implementation of bounded search strategies, a capability that can be extremely useful in problem solving. If information about effort is properly represented, it could be used in systems that would acquire knowledge enabling them to predict costs of proposed actions; such knowledge is crucial in weighted-move search strategies, another valuable planning and problem-solving; capability. Thus, there are a number of reasons why a representation of knowledge about effort is a desirable feature of an information-processing model. It is a particular concern in a system like HPM because the notion of effort can be a useful cue in directing attention toward useful strategy changes.

Effort estimation in HPM is handled by a set of system productions that can fire in parallel with the other productions in the system. Effort is treated as an attribute of goal nodes, with the effort of a process defined simply to be the size of goal structure underneath the goal node initiating that process.[3] The productions initialize the effort estimate of a goal to a unit amount when it is first asserted. Each time an immediate subgoal of that goal is completed, the effort estimate of the goal is increased by the effort expended on the subgoal. Under this mechanism, the effort of a goal cannot be known with complete accuracy until it is completed, although an estimate is always available. An interesting side effect of the mechanism is that the accuracy of the system's effort estimate for an active goal decreases with its distance from the goal currently being processed. That is, the deeper a task must be decomposed into subgoals, the less accurate the system's knowledge about how much effort has been expended toward achieving its higher-level goals. (David Klahr has facetiously called HPM's tendency to underestimate the effort for higher-level goals prior to their completion, "the graduate student effect.")

Satisfying the Information Requirements of Strategy Transformation Heuristics The data structures and processing mechanisms described above are intended to capture most of the information required to apply the strategy transformation heuristics described described in figure 4.2. As figure 4.3 showed, about a dozen different kinds of information are assumed by the heuristics. Let us consider how HPM's knowledge representation fares against this list:

1. *Descriptions* are not considered part of the trace itself; however the presence of goal nodes and data nodes provide points in the semantic structure where such descriptions could be attached.

2. *Effort* is explicitly represented by a **effort* relation to a special node. Estimates are maintained by system productions. The representation permits implementation of effort predictions as productions modifying effort nodes; thus HPM is amenable to modeling planning.

3. *Episodes*, or problem-solving contexts, are represented through the convention of starting processing with a production that has a *PROBLEM* proposition in its conditions and asserts a goal in its actions. Thus, segments of the goal trace can be defined as episodes by taking the string of *cycle* nodes in the production trace starting with that production and

ending with the production firing-event in which the goal asserted by that first production has its status changed to *DONE*.

4. *Events*, or instantiations of a particular combination of goal with operands, are represented at two levels. At one level, there are *goal* nodes with *input* relations to data nodes representing their operands. Clusters of these nodes can be compared via HPM's equivalent-structure-matching capabilities to find equivalent events. At a more detailed level, the production trace means that an event can be defined in terms of the context in which a particular goal instance occurred. That is, though the production trace, it is possible to refer to the conditions under which a goal instance was asserted, the goals asserted with it, or the conditions under which it was terminated.

5. *Frequency*, i.e., how often a goal, data object, or event recurs is not explicitly represented. HPM, in fact, provides no tools for acquiring information about frequency. This is a major deficiency in the current implementation, although it could perhaps be remedied through a scheme not unlike that now used for effort estimation. The major problem is that frequency, by definition, is a relative measure. When we talk about frequency, we are asking what proportion of some set of propositions is taken up be equivalent objects. It is difficult in this representation to determine what set(s) an object should be compared against and computationally expensive to use productions to do the comparisons.

6. *Inputs* to a goal are represented explicitly as data nodes related to goal nodes by the *input* relation. HPM's isomorphic-structure-matching facility permits recognition of equivalent instances.

7. *Processing information*, such as presence of an object in working memory, size of working memory, and "distance" (number of intervening operations) between events, is not represented in any usable form. Like the problems with frequency, it is a major deficiency in the current representation. The difficulty is one of opening up information about the production system architecture itself to the productions contained within in. I therefore do not foresee any computationally feasible solution in the near future. A theoretical solution would be to change the representation so that objects are not directly linked, as is done now, but rather are accessed by descriptions in the sense of Norman and Bobrow (1979). Descriptions would consist of lists of attributes, and most of the desired processing information could be maintained and retrieved as properties of individual objects.

8. *Procedure/goal* information is represented through the notion of *goal* nodes with *subgoal* relations to other goals. It is useful to distinguish between goals and the methods for achieving them. This distinction is captured in the goal trace, even though methods are not explicitly represented, because a method can be defined as the configuration of subgoals assigned to a given goal.

9. *Results* of goals are handled in much the same manner as inputs. There are some difficulties in representing results that are propositions rather than nodes, arising from the isomorphic structure matching algorithm not allowing for the recognition of equivalent propositions. These problems are not fundamental, however.

10. *Subgoals*, or more precisely, the hierarchical relationships between goal instances, are represented explicitly through the *subgoal* relation.

11. *Time*, or the sequential or temporal ordering of events is represented in two ways. The temporal ordering of subgoals under the same goal is represented explicitly by the *then* relation, when we are concerned with order of execution. The ordering of goals is represented by the **before* relation between cycle nodes in the production trace, when we are concerned with order of assertion. The nature of the production trace also makes it possible to distinguish between newly asserted propositions and those active due to associative retrieval or assertion on a prior cycle. With the temporal information that is explicitly represented, it is possible to compute the temporal relations between any two events. However, the representation produces the somewhat human property that the ease of doing so depends very much on the relatedness of the two events in question.

The representation offered in HPM is not quite sufficient to capture all of the required information. Nevertheless, it does capture many necessary aspects, so that a representation encoding at least the information that HPM encodes seems to be an unavoidable component of a learning system. As will be seen in the sections following, this entails storage of large amounts of information. Thus, the system is forced to deal with problem of finding appropriate objects of attention within the large mass of data available to it.

Processing Mechanisms for Controlling Information Explosion

HPM has a number of special features built into its architecture in order to process productions written in the goal trace formalism, along with its own productions for maintaining database consistency, collecting information, and making strategy changes. Among the most significant are the following:

1. *Goal-driven spreading activation.* **HPM** has a capacity for making the transmission of activation through the semantic network dependent on the nature of current processing. Activation is sent downward in the goal structure when a goal is initiated, but upwards and sideways when a goal is terminated.

2. *Conflict resolution by classes.* Productions in HPM are separated into a number of nonoverlapping classes, each of which represents a specialized information-processing function. The different classes operate in parallel, obeying separate conflict-resolution policies.

3. *Isomorphic structure matching.* HPM allows productions to find matches between network structures that are equivalent, but not identical, thus enabling learning mechanisms to find and compare instances of related events.

Spreading Activation Spreading activation can serve two somewhat related functions in a processing system: it can retrieve by association data of potential relevance to current processing goals, and it can be used to assign importance ratings to data. HPM's spreading activation scheme is largely oriented toward the first function.

Viewed in terms of the need for retrieval and importance-ranking mechanisms, spreading activation is an attractive notion. Collins and Loftus (1975) and Anderson (1976) have gone to some effort to establish its psychological plausibility. However, the notion is by no means well specified, and computational realizations of it have varied widely. These can roughly be divided into *general* spreading mechanisms like Anderson's and *context-sensitive* mechanisms like Thibadeau's (1981) CAPS system. In a general spreading mechanism, transmission of activation depends only on the activation level of a sending node and its link to other nodes. In a context-sensitive scheme, other factors determine whether or not activation is transmitted along each link from a sending node.

Technically, the spreading activation mechanism in HPM is a hybrid. Activation can be though of as stemming from "attention" given to a portion of the network by the firing of a production. A general spreading mechanism given some activation to all propositions immediately connected to the "attended" propositions. A context-sensitive mechanism controls activation of any propositions beyond the immediate connections. Since the latter mechanism plays a far more significant role in the system's overall performance, however, it makes more sense to describe HPM as employing a context-sensitive approach. The scheme employed by HPM is called *goal-driven activation spreading*.

To understand the necessity of a process like goal-driven activation spread, consider the structure shown in figure 4.4. Since the information represented there captures only the first of many steps required to completely perform the task, the structures needed to represent the entire solution process will be quite large.[4] Clearly, there is a rapid combinatorial explosion if we attempt to consider all of the indirect associates of even a single node. Nevertheless, the level of detail represented by these structures is needed to model both the performance processes underlying tasks like addition and the learning processes implied by strategy change heuristics. It seems unlikely that general spreading activation methods—based purely on elements shared by propositions without allowing for examination of those elements—can retrieve indirect associates and still remain sufficiently discriminating. Far too many uninteresting propositions would be activated. Furthermore, because general spreading models implicitly make an unsupported assumption that number of inter-node connections is somehow correlated with semantic importance, it is highly improbable that activation levels in a realistic semantic network would directly contribute to ranking nodes by importance.

HPM's goal-driven spreading scheme represents an alternative approach. It is of interest because it demonstrates how a system could have an associative retrieval process that embodies semantic knowledge without being domain-specific. The essential effect of the method is to enable retrieval of indirect associates most likely to be relevent to the system's immediate performance and learning goals, which avoiding the combinatorial explosion inherent in activating all indirect associates.

The context sensitivity of HPM's spreading activation policy comes from its handling of the propositions activated due to their direct connection with an attended proposition. The extent to which activation spreads beyond those propositions depends on the nature of the production that led to their activation. Activation is only sent further if the production is doing goal-related processing. In that case, the scheme tries to maximize the availability of information relevent to the kind of goal processing being done.

The basic dichotomy is between goal initiation and goal termination. When a new goal is asserted (or a suspended goal is reactivated), activation is spread further in the direction of propositions pertaining to the goal's type and inputs. For example, when the goal to **ADD** represented by***1** in figure 4.4 is asserted, the limited general spread of activation activates propositions involving the nodes immediately linked to ***1** and goal-driven activation spread extends the activation further to reach propositions involving nodes referenced by those propositions activated by ***2** and ***3** (the inputs), and **ADD** (the goal's type). This increases the likelihood that information pertaining to the specific operands of the goal, and methods for achieving the goal, will receive consideration. On the other hand, when a goal is terminated successfully, activation is spread further in the direction of porpositions involving superordinate goals, planned successor goals, and descriptions of the goal's result. For example, when the goal to GENERATE-SETS represented by ***5** in figure 4.4 is completed, goal-driven activation spread would reach associates of propositions activated by ***1** (the superordinate goal), ***6** (the planned successor), and ***7** (the goal's result). This increases the likelihood that information related to the continuation of problem-solving efforts will receive consideration.

By-class Conflict Resolution HPM is a parallel production system, or rather (to be more precise) simulates a parallel system. Productions are grouped into predefined classes, and there is a separate conflict resolution policy for each class. The instantiations fired are the union of the selections from the individual classes. A production may belong to only one class; membership is defined at the time the production is built.

The primary benefit of parallelism is not in speeding up processing but rather in reduction of active memory size. This is because of the assurance that productions can respond to data very quickly without having to wait for other productions to fire before them. In a parallel system, there is a reasonable assurance that if data are worth atttending to, they will be attended to promptly. Without such an assurance it would be necessary to keep data in active memory for long periods in order to ensure that productions matching to it have a fair chance to be selected for firing. With such an assurance, it becomes possible to minimize time in active memory without sacrificing processing capability.

Although these benefits arise because productions that do not interfere with each other can fire without delay, there is still the problem of preventing firing of productions that could interfere with each other. This problem makes unrestricted parallelism an unacceptable option. The notion of production classes in HPM is intended to respond to the interference problem. The production classes represent a division of the system's set of production rules into disjoint information-processing functions that may be performed concurrently.

Interference arises when two productions make redundant or conflicting assertions. This can only occur if they are performing the same functions. Therefore, productions in different classes can be presumed not to interfere with each other. The circumstances under which productions in the same class might interfere with each other vary according to the function being performed. HPM currently distinguishes six production classes:

1. *Goal-manipulation*—productions that operate on goal-trace structures. These are divided into three sub-categories: (a) goal-initiation productions, which assert new goals, (b) goal-execution productions, which act in response to goals without setting up subgoals, and (c) goal-termination productions, which end processing of goals. All applicable-goal-termination productions may fire; if none are present, an applicable goal-initiation or goal-execution production is selected.

2. *Data-bookkeeping*—productions that maintain the correctness of HPM's representation of complex data objects. For example, this class contains productions that update assertions about a set whenever a new member is added. Production instantiations selected for firing in this class are the union of selections for each different production. For a given production, the instantiations selected are those operating upon distinct data nodes, plus one from each set of instantiations operating on a common data node.

3. *Goal-bookkeeping*—productions that maintain correctness of goal structures. Included in this class are productions that ensure that the *status* relations of subgoals stay consistent with the goal that created them, productions which activate planned goals upon completion of preceding portions of the plan, and productions which manage information needed to control iterative processes. This class is parallel with no restrictions; the goal trace conventions make interferences impossible.

4. *Data-description*—productions which add information representing knowledge about properties of data objects. These give HPM the opportunity to make observations about the data it manipulates, e.g., recording

when one addend in an addition problem is smaller than the other. Only one production instantiation is allowed to fire.

5. *Strategy-change-noticing*—productions which detect or predict situations relevent to development of a strategy change. Since the results of these productions are intended to be used in constructing new methods for performing a task, an interference would be created if there were data pertaining to different possible changes asserted simultaneously. At the same time, opportunities to make changes are highly desirable. The selection policy for this class balances these two considerations by diving the instantiations into sets which matched the same object as their first condition. One instantiation from each such set is allowed to fire.

6. *Strategy-change-maker*—productions that perform actions in order to effect changes to a procedure, usually by building new productions. Changing a procedure is a drastic action, but its effects do not appear until the new production fires. Due to the comparatively strong nature of their actions, along with the danger of possible confusions if two incompatible changes are made, only a single production instantiation is selected. The risk that an interfering production could fire on a later cycle motivates the further restriction that competing instantiations are *permanently* blocked from firing if they had the same first element as the selected instantiation.

Isomorphic Structure Matching HPM's strong type-token distinction means that objects are represented in network structures of some potential complexity. If we were deeply concerned with modeling fuzzy concepts, there are circumstances where we might expect a system to have difficulty deciding if two pieces of data were members of the same category. However, even in those cases, we would not want it to have difficulty recognizing that two pieces of data represent instances of the same object.

Unfortunately, as Woods (1975) as observed, this is a common problem with semantic networks. HPM avoids this problem, without sacrificing the advantages of the type-token distinction, by a scheme of representing information about the network in structures outside of the network itself. Tags, called *formal-value* tags, are associated with nodes in the semantic network. These tags are constructed in a canonical fashion that causes nodes representing equivalent structures to have identical tags. This enables HPM to recognize equivalent objects by comparing their tags, regardless of the complexity of the network structures required to represent them.

The Symbiotic Relationship between Knowledge and Attention Focusing

At the beginning of this section, HPM was described as an attempt to answer two questions that arose in the course of formalizing a model of strategy changes: what does it take to recognize that a heuristic is applicable; and what does it take to construct a change and insert it in a procedure?

The immediate answers to these questions come in the form of the twin notions of *goal trace* and *production trace*. Information in the two overlapping traces provides the data against which conditions of strategy transformation heuristics can be tested. Information in the production trace provides information about the context in which assertions are made, allowing the system to determine the context in which the alternatives it develops should be followed. So far I have described the form of HPM's knowledge base; the use of that knowledge base will be illustrated when particular strategy transformation heuristics are discussed in section 4.3.

In examining the knowledge structures that seem to be necessary, it becomes clear that a large information base is an unavoidable property of a realistic model of performance and learning. This means that the demands of learning put a great stress on the attention-focusing mechanisms of an information-processing system. Since a learning system is forced to retain a large body of potentially extraneous information in order to avoid missing critical information, it becomes crucial that there be effective means for concentrating attention on important data and avoiding the distractions inherent in a large information space.

Answers to the question of how this can be done become essential to answering the original questions. It is useless to make available the prerequisite data for learning if it is not computationally feasibe to process that data. This was the topic of the preceding section.

The first part of the solution involves restricting the contents of active memory and using an associative retrieval mechanism to ensure that key information would be moved into active memory at appropriate times. The goal-driven activation spreading mechanism within HPM allows it to restrict its attention to a subset of the data available to it, with a reasonable degree of confidence that "interesting" data will be included in that subset.[5] Unfortunately, it turns out that it is essential that associative retrieval schemes err in the direction of over-retrieval. Absence of critical data from active memory is fatal, whereas presence of distracting data is merely dangerous.

A practical implication of this observation is that even goal-driven spreading must still leave active memory fairly large. Among the difficulties inherent in a large active memory is the increase in matches—many more productions are likely to find matching data, and many of those productions are likely to have more than one way to match against the data. This means that a learning system is strongly dependent on maintaining its focus of attention by appropriate selection of productions for firing, a problem familiar to production systems users as "conflict resolution."

Many of these problems are greatly simplified in a parallel system. Among other advantages, parallelism enables reducing the size of active memory by minimizing the time that elements remain active. A parallel system can assume that important data will have been attended to promptly upon its assertion, and therefore can safely eliminate data from active memory much earlier than a serial system. Reducing memory size reduces the number of potential uninteresting matches, thereby easing the conflict resolution problem.

If it is adaptive for a learning system to be parallel, why then have such as Newell and Simon (1972) been led to claim that humans are serial processors? For one thing, it is not strictly true that the entire human information-processing system is serial, a point illustrated by the familiar "cocktail party effect" (Norman 1976). What is really meant is that the mind is *serial with respect to certain functions*, primarily the processing of goals. This should be (and is) also true of HPM, which is forced to behave serially for production classes like goal-manipulation where interfering assertions could result from allowing multiple production firings.

4.3 The HPM Simulation

This section is concerned with showing how the HPM goal trace formalism applies to the simulation of cognitive processes. First, I will discuss how a simulation of a primitive addition procedure is implemented. The purpose of this discussion is both to illustrate the application of the formalism and to introduce an initial procedure. The second part of this section will be concerned with heuristics for optimizing procedures, how those heuristics are implemented in HPM, and an overview of their role in optimizing the initial addition strategy. The final parts of this section will consider some examples of this process in more detail.

The SUM Strategy for Addition

Psychological researchers from a number of different paradigms have shown that very young children commonly solve addition problems by a procedure that has been dubbed the SUM or "counting-all" method (Carpenter and Moser 1979; Fuson and Richards 1979; Ginsburg 1977a, 1977b; Groen and Resnick 1977; Steffe and Thompson 1982). The essential properties of this method are that external objects (e.g., fingers or blocks) are counted out to represent each addend, and that these sets of objects are then merged and the combined set counted in order to produce the sum. Figure 4.5 presents an HPM production system for the SUM method, paraphrased into English for understandability.

The ADD.HPM Production System for the SUM Method Briefly, the **ADD.HPM** production system solves addition problems as follows. When a problem is encountered, the first production builds a goal to **ADD**. The *Addition-plan* production responds by building subgoals to **GENERATE-SETS** of countable objects, and to **COUNT-UP** those sets. The *Goal-to-generate-sets* production responds to the former goal by building subgoals to **MAKE-A-SET** separately for each addend. An HPM goal-bookkeeping production intervenes to order the two goals, and then productions respond to the first. A production called *Make-a-set-of-fingers* proposes satisfying the **MAKE-A-SET** goal by counting out fingers; it sets up a *DATA* node attached by a *has-data* relation which will be used to keep track of the counting. This enables a set of productions which realize a counting procedure that generates objects until the number of objects corresponds to the number desired.

The leader of these productions asserts a goal to **CORRESPOND-ELEMENTS** that operates on the *has-data* node. It builds a bookkeeping production which will append the goal's result to the set represented by the data node and update the numerosity of the set. The production that responds to that goal builds a pair of subgoals: one to **GET-NEXT** (i.e., the successor) for the last object contained in the set and another to **GET-NEXT** for the number of the set. These are primitive goals in HPM, given that the type of object is known, and can therefore be immediately satisfied. Since the set started out empty, these goals produce the first finger and the number **ONE**. A production defining completion of the **CORRESPOND-ELEMENTS** goal asserts a proposition associating the finger with the number and marks the goal as **DONE**. The data-

Goal-to-add:
IF there is a problem involving a plus-sign and two numbers,
THEN set up a goal to **ADD** with instances of the numbers as its inputs, and mark the goal as ACTIVE.

Addition-plan:
IF there is an ACTIVE goal to **ADD** with two inputs,
THEN assert an ACTIVE new goal to **GENERATE-SETS** as a *subgoal* of the addition goal, and give it the same two *inputs*; assert that it is to be followed by a goal to **COUNT-UP**, which is initially SUSPENDED, that this goal is also a *subgoal* of **ADD**, and that its *input* is the *result* of the new **GENERATE-SETS** goal.

Finished-adding:
IF there is an ACTIVE goal to **ADD**, and it has a *subgoal* to **COUNT-UP** that is DONE,
THEN the goal to **ADD** is DONE, and its *result* is the *result* of the **COUNT-UP** goal.

Goal-to-generate-sets:
IF there is an ACTIVE goal to **GENERATE-SETS** with two *inputs*,
THEN assert an ACTIVE new goal to **MAKE-A-SET** as a *subgoal* with the first *input* as its *input*; make another such *subgoal* with the second *input* as its *input*.

Sets-have-been-generated:
IF there is an ACTIVE goal to **GENERATE-SETS** with two *subgoals* to **MAKE-A-SET**, and both *subgoals* are DONE,
THEN the goal to **GENERATE-SETS** is DONE, and its *result* is a set which has as subsets the *result* of the first **MAKE-A-SET** goal and the *result* of the second.

Make-a-set-of-fingers:
IF there is an goal to **MAKE-A-SET**, its *input* is a number, and the goal is ACTIVE,
THEN create a node representing an empty set, assert that the set contains fingers, assert that the set *has-number* ZERO, and link the goal to the node with the *has-data* relation.

Goal-to-correspond-elements:
IF there is an ACTIVE goal to **MAKE-A-SET**, and it *has-data* consisting of a set with a (possibly null) *current-member*, and the set has a number associated with it,
THEN set up an ACTIVE *subgoal* to **CORRESPOND-ELEMENT** with the set as its *input*, and build a data-bookkeeping production to act as a demon for that sub-goal's completion: "When the subgoal is DONE, attach its *result* to the set as its *current-member*, find a number assigned to that *result*, and make that number the numeric value associated with the set."

Figure 4.5
Paraphrases of productions in the ADD.HPM simulation of the SUM method

Have-a-set:

IF there is an ACTIVE **MAKE-A-SET** goal that *has-data* in the form of a set having a number associated with it, the *input* of the goal is also a number, and the number of that set is equivalent to the *input*,

THEN the goal is DONE and its *result* is the set.

Make-an-element:

IF there is a goal to **CORRESPOND-ELEMENT**, its *input* is a set with a*current-member*, and that set has a number associated with it,

THEN create two **GET-NEXT** goals as *subgoals*, where the *input* of the first is the *element* which is the set's *current-member*, and the *input* of the second is the number associated with the set; make the first *subgoal* ACTIVE, make the second SUSPENDED until the first is complete.

Have-an-element:

IF there is an ACTIVE goal to **CORRESPOND-ELEMENT**, which has a pair of *subgoals* to **GET-NEXT** that both are DONE, and the *result* of the second subgoal is a number,

THEN the goal to **CORRESPOND-ELEMENT** is DONE; associate the number found by the second *subgoal* with the *element* found by the first *subgoal*, and make the result of the goal be the *result* of the first *subgoal*.

Start-counting-up:

IF there is an ACTIVE goal to **COUNT-UP**, its *input* is a set, and there is no set associated with the goal by a *has-data* relation,

THEN create an empty set and assert that its members are to be drawn from the *input* set; associate the node for the new set with the goal via a *has-data* relation.

Count-element:

IF there is an ACTIVE goal to **COUNT-UP** which *has-data* in the form of a set that has a *current-member* and a number associated with it,

THEN set up an ACTIVE subgoal to **CORRESPOND-ELEMENT** with that set as its *input*, and build a bookkeeping production to act as a demon for the subgoal's completion: "When the *subgoal* is DONE, make its *result* an *element* of its *input* set and specify that it is the *current-member*, find a number assigned to that *result* and make that number the numeric value associated with the set."

Finished-counting-up:

IF there is an ACTIVE goal to **COUNT-UP**, the goal *has-data* in the form of a set that has a *current-member* and a number associated with it, the set is equivalent to the goal's input (i.e., contains exactly the same elements), and the number associated with the set comes from the same source as a number associated with its *current-member*,

THEN the goal to **COUNT-UP** is DONE, its *result* is the number associated with the *has-data* set; assert that number

Figure 4.5 continued

bookkeeping demon built when the goal was asserted now fires, adding the finger to the set and assigning its associated number as the size of the set. Since the resulting set is not yet the same size as the addend, the lead production fires again, asserting another **CORRESPOND-ELEMENTS** goal. This process repeats until the set that is being constructed is the same size as an addend.

At that point a production fires that marks the first **MAKE-A-SET** goal as complete and the newly constructed set as its result. An HPM goal-bookkeeping production notices that another goal had been planned to follow this one and so resets the *status* of the second **MAKE-A-SET** goal to **ACTIVE**. That goal is handled exactly as the first was. Thus, both goals finish with their result expressed as a set of fingers, where each finger has a number assigned to it, where the size of each set is the number assigned to the last finger in the set, and where that number corresponds to an addend.

A production that recognizes that goals with such results satisfy the goal to **GENERATE-SETS** fires next, marking that goal as *DONE* and specifying its result to be a set representing the merger of the subgoals' results. Several HPM data-bookkeeping productions fire to construct a complete representation of that set, while simultaneously one of its goal-bookkeeping productions notices the **COUNT-UP** goal (which had been planned to follow this one) and resets that goal's *status* to **ACTIVE**. At this point, the goal to **ADD** can be achieved by the subgoal to **COUNT-UP** the combined set of fingers.

The productions that handle that subgoal are close analogues of the productions that respond to **MAKE-A-SET** goals. The primary difference is that the iterative assertion of **CORRESPOND-ELEMENT** goals is stopped not when a desired number is reached (since that number is unknown), but rather when the set of objects is exhausted. Thus, the **COUNT-UP** goal completes with a set of objects which have been counted, where each object has a number assigned to it, where the number of the set is the number of the last object in the set, *and* where the set contains all of the objects in the input set. Finally, the *Finished-adding* production recognizes that completion of such a goal satisfies the original **ADD** goal, and that the result of the **ADD** goal is given by the number of the set produced by the **COUNT-UP** goal.

Some Psychological Notes on ADD.HPM The production system described above solves addition problems entirely by counting methods. Although HPM's ability to modify this procedure is of intrinsic interest as a work of artificial intelligence, it would be nice if there was some psychological validity to its efforts as well. This section is concerned with considering the psychological implications of the **ADD.HPM** simulation. I will concentrate on two points: the extent to which the simulation agrees with notions of counting principles, and the assumptions made about external memory.

Two notes should be made on the psychology of this production system's embedded model of counting. First, it should be noted that its run-time characteristics are consistent with a number of reaction-time studies that suggest that (regardless of method employed for addition) children count objects at a rate averaging somewhat under 1 per second (Groen and Parkman 1972; Groen and Resnick 1977; Svenson 1975). The simulation takes seven cycles to count an object; the plausible assumption that one production cycle corresponds to 50 to 100 msecs. of human processing yields the appropriate counting speed. Second, it should be noted that the counting rate reflected in the simulation is a side effect of the goals necessary within the constraints of the HPM formalism to obey counting principles shown to be understood by small children (Gelman and Gallistel 1978; Greeno, Riley, and Gelman 1981).

Gelman and Gallistel (1978) have argued that there are five principles inherent in the "understanding" of counting and presented evidence for the belief that preschoolers can indeed apply these principles appropriately:

1. *Stable ordering* Number names must be generated in a fixed sequence.
2. *One-one correspondence* Every object counted must have its own number name assigned to it, and every number name used must be assigned to an object.
3. *Cardinality* The number of a set is given by the number name assigned to the very last object to be counted.
4. *Abstraction* Objects to not need to be of the same type in order to be counted.
5. *Indifference to order* The size of a set remains the same regardless of the order in which its elements are counted.

Let us see the extent to which the simulation presented earlier reflects these principles.

Stable Ordering Like Greeno, Riley, and Gelman's (1981) SC simulation, **ADD.HPM** implements an ordering on the number names by chaining them via a "next" relation. In **ADD.HPM**, objects are counted by repeatedly asserting **CORRESPOND-ELEMENT** goals, which take the object last counted, find the number assigned to that object, and use the successor of that number for assignment to the next object. Because both counting out a new set of objects and counting up a preexisting set are accomplished by higher goals that invoke **CORRESPOND-ELEMENT** goals, the principle of stable ordering is obeyed in all phases of counting.[6]

One-One Correspondence The procedure embedded in the productions responding to **CORRESPOND-ELEMENT** goals ensures that exactly one number will be generated for each element counted. Therefore one-one correspondence will be maintained as long as all elements are counted and each element is counted only once.

When counting out a new set of object, these conditions are satisfied by the *Make-a-set-of-fingers* production. This creates a *has-data* node to control iteration of **CORRESPOND-ELEMENT** goals in the context of a **MAKE-A-SET** goal. The node is set up in a way that ensures that an entirely new object must be constructed each time a **CORRESPOND-ELEMENT** goal is applied to the set of objects counted thus far.

When counting up a preexisting set, correspondance is maintained by the interaction between the **CORRESPOND-ELEMENT** goal and HPM's conventions for representing sets. These conventions require that objects within the same set be ordered; if no ordering is imposed, then time of entrance to the set is used. Thus, the requirements of counting each element exactly once are met if the elements are in the same basic set.

If the elements of a set are contained in two separate subsets, then the requirements are met as long as it is ensured that a given subset can only be counted once. Meeting this requirement is more complicated; HPM satisfies it only through the interaction of several rules. First, a set is only allowed to be directly divided into two subsets (although those subsets may themselves be divided into subsets). Second, the *Retrieve-next-across-subsets* production implements the notion that the successor of the last element in a subset of a set is the first element of any other subset of the same set.

Cardinality This is represented in **ADD.HPM** by productions that change the number assignment on a set of objects-that-have-been-counted each time another object is added to such a set. These productions are built by the productions that assert **CORRESPOND-ELEMENT** goals, *Goal-to-correspond-elements* and *Count-element*.

Abstraction When counting up a predefined set,the productions in **ADD.HPM** are utterly insensitive to the contents of the set. The productions that obtain successive elements from the set being counted, *Retrieve-the-next* and *Retrieve-next-across-subsets*, look only at the relations between elements and not at the elements themselves. When creating a new set, ADD.HPM is biased toward making all members of the set belong to common category because the only production given to it for performing 'this function, *Make-the-next*, is designed to create a new set consisting of instantiations of objects drawn from a specified set (e.g., the set of FINGERS). However, this is a feature of convenience and not a fundamental property of the production system. It could easily be modified without affecting other aspects of the system; therefore, it seems reasonable to allow ADD.HPM to pass the abstraction test despite this deficiency.

Indifference to Order ADD.HPM fares worst on this test; the rigid requirement that all sets be represented as ordered means that the production system must count objects within a set in a fixed order. Although this is in violation of the principle, it is also the case that the simulation does not display this flaw when counting objects in different subsets.[7] That is, the *Retrieve-next-across-subsets* production allows it to count subsets in any order even though the objects within a subset must be counted in fixed order. Thus, in principle, ADD.HPM could be modified to show greater indifference to ordering by representing each counted object as a subset rather than as an element. I have chosen not to do so because it would unnecessarily complicate the productions for retrieving elements from sets, by requiring machinery for keeping track of which subsets have been accessed.

In summary, although weak on one of the principles of counting, ADD.HPM is basically consistent with those principles. Its weakness on the one principle is a result of having simplified the implementation on a point that is not directly related to the main thrust of the research.

HPM's representation of sets, again in the interests of simplifying the implementation, introduces another psychological implausibility. There is no bound on the size of a set; thus HPM can represent a set of any size in working memory. These considerations must be taken into account in transferring results from the simulations back into psychological domains, but they are not fundamental flaws in the system.

Strategy Transformations in HPM

The purpose of the goal trace formalism is to enable writing of domain-independent heuristics for modifying procedures. Previous sections have presented the formalism itself along with arguments for its range of expressiveness, processing rules supporting the formalism, and an example of a procedure stated in the formalism. Here, we will discuss how HPM modifies procedures in terms of its alterations to the SUM procedure just presented.

Figure 4.2 has shown the informal specifications of a number of strategy transformation heuristics, such as the three shown in figure 4.1: *result still available, untouched results,* and *effort difference.*

Although many other heuristics could also be given, these are sufficient for modeling the transition from a SUM procedure to a MIN procedure. Therefore the discussion will be restricted to these three. It is easy to see how heuristics such as these would improve a procedure; no sophisticated justification is required for them. The questions of interest lie in their operationalization and application. This section discusses their application in modifying the SUM strategy.

HPM gets from SUM to MIN through a series of incremental refinements. The first involves eliminating redundancies in counting up the combined set of objects representing the two addends. Since counting consists of creating a set of objects in which numbers have been assigned sequentially to each object in the set, there is a point where the counting-up process creates a set of objects and number assignments equivalent to that created when building a set to represent one of the addends. After that point, the process continues adding to the set by taking objects corresponding to the other addend, which makes the unique. At this intermediate point, however, it is possible to recognize that the counting-out for one addend (i.e., the *result* of a **MAKE-A-SET** goal) can also serve as part of the counting-up process (i.e., as an intermediate result in processing the **COUNT-UP** goal). When a production is built that implements the change, the resulting procedure differs in that the **COUNT-UP** goal starts its iteration of **CORRESPOND-ELEMENT** subgoals with a *has-data* relation to a set containing the elements produced by one of the **MAKE-A-SET** goals, rather than starting with an empty set. This causes processing to pick up with the result of the other **MAKE-A-SET** goal. Rather than counting all of the objects in the combined set, the new procedure therefore counts only the objects representing one of the addends, but counts them starting from the number given by the other addend instead of starting from 1.

Now, when double-counting of the one addend is eliminated in this fashion, an inefficiency is introduced which can be detected through the *untouched results* heuristic. When the objects produced under a **MAKE-A-SET** goal are no longer counted under **COUNT-UP** goal, they are not really used at all. That is, there is no point in creating these objects if they aren't going to be counted. The only function that they still serve is to give the starting number for counting up the objects representing the other addend. That information can be gotten elsewhere, however, since the size of the set representing an addend is (of course) given by the addend itself. This change is realized by building a production which responds to whichever **MAKE-A-SET** goal is used to speed up the **COUNT-UP** goal. The production asserts that the **MAKE-A-SET** goal has assigned an object the number given by the addend that was input to the goal. This satisfies its termination conditions, causing the goal to complete with a single element set as its result. That single element has the correct number assignment for initializing counting of the objects representing the other addend. Note that this new production would give an erroneous result if it fired to all instances of **MAKE-A-SET** goals. However, the conditions of the new production are constructed from the production trace. Therefore, the conditions describe the context for asserting the particular goal-instance that is used in the first shortcut, and the new production will not fire in the general case. The result of this second change is a procedure that counts out objects corresponding to one of the addends and then counts up those objects starting from the number after the other addend.

When one or both of these changes are made, the opportunity is created for HPM to discover effort differences between different trials with the same problems. This is because the effort involved depends on whether the addend treated specially is the larger or smaller of the two. Effort is minimized in the case where objects are generated to represent the smaller addend and their counting is initialized by the larger addend. The result is a procedure in which, for problems where the other shortcuts would treat the smaller addend specially, the problems are transformed into an equivalent form where the larger addend is taken as special. Problems in which the shortcuts would initially be applied to the larger addend are left as they are. This new procedure has the properties of the MIN procedure: effort is now proportional only to the size of the smaller addend.

Operationalizing the "Results Still Available" Heuristic

We have seen that very straightforward heuristics can be used to account for transitions between procedures. Operationalizing these heuristics in HPM requires dealing with the following set of problems: (1) detecting instances of situations described in the heuristics' conditions, (2) determining the precursors of those situations (i.e., learning to predict them), (3) constructing appropriate new actions for productions which implement strategy changes, and (4) discovering the range of application for a new production. This chapter is primarily concerned with the first three, where the goal-trace conventions permit making assumptions that greatly simplify the problems.

Determining Applicability of the Heuristic The approach taken in HPM to operationalizing conditions for heuristics basically consists of reexpressing the conditions as patterns in sets of goal-trace propositions. It is not essential that all of these patterns coexist in time, because of the production trace. It is not essential that they consist of a fixed group of propositions because alternative groups can be captured by different productions which assert the same higher-level proposition in the manner of trend detectors in Langley's (1979) BACON system.

In the *result still available* heuristic, the stated condition is that a previously computed item is needed again. However, this explicit condition really consists of several implicit conditions that go into deciding that an item is "needed again." In HPM, the first step begins when the system notices that the input for a goal is something that has been used before. This post hoc discovery comes too late for HPM to change its course of action on that trial; HPM cannot tell that it *will* reuse a computed value, only that it *just has* reused one. Since inputs can come to a goal either as the *result* of another goal or through a *has-data* relation from a higher-level goal, two versions are needed of the production which makes this discovery. Figure 4.6 illustrates the production that applies when the current source of a goal's input is a *has-data* node. This is the production that initiates the first strategy transformation in the development from SUM to MIN.

The conditions for the production can be put into three groups: conditions governing when it fires (ensuring that it will fire as early as possible), main conditions checking that criteria for firing the production are met (in this case, that the goal's input has a potential alternative source), and conditions that pick up data needed on the action side of the production (by

Consider-keep-partials-for-data-node:

IF a goal has just been asserted with a particular data node as input,

there is a different data node with an equivalent value,

the goal was established in response to a *has-data* relation between the input and a higher goal,

and trace-data is available for the production asserting the goal and for the actions of the production that terminated the goal which had the other data node as its result,

THEN build a production to predict that this relationship will recur:

"**IF** another instance of this goal is asserted with this input under the equivalent conditions, and another instance of the other goal terminated in the same way as observed this time,

THEN predict that the result of that other goal will be equivalent to the input of the new goal-instance."

Figure 4.6
A prediction production for initiating strategy transformations based on the *result still available* heuristic

inspecting the production trace to find the context in which the earlier source completed and the current source was asserted).

Finding Conditions for the New Production The action of the first production builds a new production that essentially predicts that the same situation, if observed again, would produce the same relationships between goal-trace propositions. That is, the prediction is that any goal terminating with equivalent assertions to the observed earlier source will have its result equivalent to the input of any goal asserted under conditions equivalent to those for the observed current goal.

The major function of the prediction production is to facilitate generalizing the scope of strategy change productions. As mentioned earlier, once a change is made, it is impossible to compare its effects against what would have happened otherwise. The use of predictions allows HPM to refine conditions of its productions before changes are made; when building strategy change productions, HPM can draw information from the production traces for successful predictions.

Since a new prediction production is only built when the prediction is known to be true for the current case, HPM behaves as if the prediction had been made and tested for that case. This causes a strategy transformation production to fire and build a second production which will change the strategy. The strategy transformation production is shown in figure 4.7

As before, there are several versions of the production in order to allow for each of the alternative information-passing methods that can be used in the goal-trace formalism. The one shown is the version that applies in making the first strategy change. Its first conditions require that a successful prediction has been made. Like the noticing production, it also contains conditions that identify the context in which the new source goal was terminated. In addition, it contains conditions that identify the circumstances under which the to-be-replaced goal was asserted. Finally, it has conditions specialized for *has-data* data nodes that represent sets; these conditions test whether the current goal makes use of any propositions allowed in describing sets (e.g., the *current-member* relation) or other data objects. Related to those conditions are others that seek to find or construct the analogous propositions for the result of the potential new source goal.

When the production shown in figure 4.7 actually builds the production for the strategy change, the conditions of that production are derived from the conditions just described. First, they borrow the conditions that led to assertion of the data's current source. This ensures that the new production can fire at time the source would have been asserted, thus enabling it to override the production that would do so. Second, they borrow the terminating conditions of the goal that first produced the data. This ensures that the value is available to be copied, and that the new production has the ability to do so. Third, they borrow the initiating conditions of the first goal, expressed in terms of the production trace since they may no longer be true at the critical point in time. These conditions increase the likelihood that the new production will fire only in situations closely equivalent to the current situation. Finally, the new production is given the conditions needed to specify auxilary propositions such as *current-member* relations. Figure 4.8 provides an example of a new production resulting from this process. This new production, which implements the first shortcut for the

Keep - partial - set - for - data:

IF a goal has just been asserted with a particular data node as input,

there is a different data node with an equivalent value,

the goal was established in response to a *has-data* relation between the input and a higher goal,

trace-data is available for the production asserting the goal and for the actions of the production that terminated the goal which had the other data node as its result,

a prediction has been asserted and confirmed that the goal's input and the other data node would match,

the input is a set with an element as current member,

and the other data node has some relation associating it with an element equivalent to that current member,

THEN construct a production to avoid recomputation of the set by copying the prior data node over:

"**IF** the evoking conditions are present for the production which asserted the *has-data* relationship between the higher goal and the current input of the current goal, and an instantiation of the goal which produced the alternative source has both been asserted and completed under the same circumstances as this occasion, and that goal's result has relations that correspond to those needed to predict the current member,

THEN assert that the higher goal *has-data* to a node which has the set represented by the alternative source as its subset; assert a current-member for this new set, along with any other relations used in the conditions of the goal of interest."

Figure 4.7
A strategy transformation production for the *result still available* heuristic

IF a set containing a left-thumb, a left-index-finger, a right-thumb, a right-index-finger, and a right-middle-finger is input to an active COUNT-UP goal,

that goal has no *has-data* node,

a MAKE-A-SET goal that produced a left-thumb and a left-index-finger is done,

that goal was asserted as a subgoal of a GENERATE-SETS goal,

the set produced by the MAKE-A-SET goal has a left-thumb as its first element and a left-index-finger as its last element,

and the set is of size two,

THEN assert that the COUNT-UP goal *has-data* to a node which has the MAKE-A-SET goal's result as a subset, the left-thumb as its first member, the left-index-finger as its current and last member, and the number two as its size.

Figure 4.8
A sample production modifying the SUM strategy for the problem 2 + 3

problem 2 + 3, will compete with the *Start-counting-up* production illustrated in figure 4.4.

Determining Appropriate Actions for New Productions The actions of the new production are almost entirely determined by the constraints of the goal trace formalism. This is exactly the point of having such a formalism; the amount of reasoning that the system must do in order to construct a change is minimized. In this case, the actions are completely determind by the intent to borrow a previously generated set in order to avoid reconstructing it. Having found that the set was constructed as a *has-data* node attached to a higher-level goal, the first thing to do is to replace that node with one representing the previously computed set. However, it is only necessary to set up the new linkages, since the production's conditions ensure that it fires in place of the productions which would have added the old linkages. Since the constraints of the formalism say that elements may be added to a set while an active goal has a *has-data* link to it, the production asserts propositions creating a new set that has the previously computed set as a subset. This maintains the correctness of the goal trace if additional members are added to the set, as is the case here, because the additional members are represented as belonging to the "copy" of the set rather than the original set. The goal-trace formalisms for sets, and the HPM system productions that maintain them, guarantee that the original and the copy are treated identically when their values are accessed but are distinguished when querying the source of those values.

The other actions of the new production are also determined by the constraints of the formalism. When a data node representing a set is being made available to subgoals by a *has-data* relation, there is a restricted set of possible propositions that might be accessed by those subgoals. The remaining actions of the productions assert propositions that duplicate those which appeared in the set being copied.

Other Applications The *result still available* heuristic applied in the case just discussed because the set produced by a counting-up process was equivalent to a set produced by a counting-out process. Since there are two counting-out processes in the SUM procedure, one for each addend, it is useful to ask how HPM compares the sets produced by those two processes. In particular, what happens when the second addend is counted out?

There are three cases to consider. When the larger addend is counted out first, the set of objects generated for the second addend never becomes equivalent to it, and so the heuristic never applies. When the smaller addend is counted out first, a subset of the objects counted out for the second addend is equivalent, and the heuristic applies. When the addends are the same—that is, there is a "tie problem"—then the sets are equivalent at completion and the heuristic can be gotten to apply if we allow one change to the SUM simulation. This leaves us with two cases where a change could occur.

In the first case, HPM can discover the possibility of a change but cannot construct a working modification because it is unable to keep track of the items to be counted twice. This discovery essentially amounts to representing the problem as a tie problem (*min* + *min*) plus incrementing from *min* to *max*. Although HPM cannot immediately capitalize upon the discovery, there is a later point at which it would be useful. Once tie problems are mastered and no longer require counting, the discovery would permit a new strategy that uses the fast procedure for the tie problem part, followed by counting for the remaining part.[8]

In the second case tie problems, HPM requires some minor modifications to be able to discover and use the shortcut. The problem is that the heuristic as now specified responds to a goal taking as input something that was computed twice. The set corresponding to the second addend meets only half of this requirement. It was computed twice, since it is equivalent to the set already generated for the first addend. However, the set for the second addend never becomes the input of a goal in the current form of the simulation. This is because it is merged into a set representing the combined addends; that set is passed on for further processing.

However, it is a trivial modification to the SUM simulation to require that the merger of the two addend sets be accomplished by a primitive goal, rather than by the production that terminates the *GENERATE-SETS* goal. This modification is fairly plausible psychologically, and would have no effect on other processing. Given that modification, HPM would discover the repetition of computation when it merged the sets for the two addends. It would then construct the change. One set would be used to represent both addends, but there would be separate nodes pointing to that set for each addend. Because there would be separate nodes, the system would remember to count twice. Because the sets are identical, there would be no confusion about which objects to count—even if they were represented as a undifferentiated set of objects in a visual display.

These points are important because they provide the beginnings of an explanation for the well-known "tie problem" effect reported by every researcher since Groen and Parkman (1972). Most explanations of this effect have claimed that tie problems are faster than others because of direct memory retrieval. This, it has been claimed, comes about either because the repetition of the addend makes the problems easier to store and retrieve, or because it makes them more salient and therefore more likely to be practiced. The preceding discussion suggests an expansion upon the saliency theme. Tie problems may become salient because there is a strategy change that will work only for them, and for no other type of problem.[9] This could make them a subject for attention from the "interesting subset" heuristic for reduction to results proposed in figure 4.2.

Furthermore, another factor appears because of the independence of this strategy change from the change that deletes a portion of the total count. Since they are independent, they could be discovered simultaneously, which means that a highly advanced strategy for tie problems would come into effect much earlier than for other problems. This, in turn, means that the efficient strategy could be practiced much longer. Thus, it seems as if there might be multiple factors facilitating performance on doubles problems.

Operationalizing the "Effort Difference" Heuristic

The effort difference heuristic, informally specified, said that if two instances of the same goal differed in effort, it was worthwhile to try to duplicate the circumstances in which the effort was less. There are a number of possible causes why the effort could differ, the main ones having to do with circumstances that cause a more efficient method to be applied towards satisfying the initial goal.

Thus, this heuristic becomes applicable as soon as prior strategy changes produce alternative methods for solving a problem, as can be seen by by considering what goal trees and effort estimates would look like for the original SUM strategy, the modified strategy when double-counting of the smaller addend is avoided.

Applicability of the Heuristic's Conditions HPM's automatic effort-estimation productions, which can be analogized to Langley's (1979) data-collection productions, provide the basic information needed to compare efforts. The isomorphic structure matching capabilities provide the ability to compare inputs. The first half of the condition for this heuristic can therefore be formally restated as wanting two nonidentical instances of the same goal, with equivalent but nonidentical input(s), where one goal-instance involved greater effort (i.e., had a larger subgoal tree) than the other. Unfortunately, life is not so easy that such a simple production would suffice. In order for the heuristic to have any applicability, it is necessary to have some hypothesis about *when* the effort difference will occur.

The second half of the initial production's conditions are concerned with generating an initial hypothesis. Generally, they seek a point where the processing paths diverged for the two cases; the hypothesis will be that the circumstances leading to that divergence predict the effort difference. Specifically, the conditions first test for production-firing events in the fast and slow cases where the conditions in both events referenced the goal-instances. Next, they seek conditions that otherwise were nonequivalent. Finally, they require that the actions in a preceding firing-event were equivalent. These factors, taken together, formalize the notion of divergence.

The assumption is that, if there is such a point where processing was equivalent beforehand and differed thereafter, the effort difference must be due to processing occurring after that point. Under this assumption, observing that point will therefore pinpoint the cause of the effort difference. Note that this assumption is by no means infallible; one could easily construct cases in which it would fail miserably. However, it is valuable as an heuristic that should work in many cases and serves to begin the strategy change process even in those cases where it does not work.

Finding Conditions of the New Production When the strategy-change-noticing production fires, it builds a prediction production and *post hoc* constructs structures equivalent to having successfully predicted the case it has just observed. As before, the purpose of the prediction production is to give the system a means of refining the conditions for expecting an effort difference. The presence of a successful prediction triggers a strategy-change-making production.

This production builds a rule that notices when the slower method has been asserted, and simply cancels it. This clears the way for firing the production that asserts the plan for the faster method. Why do it that way? Why not simply have the production take the conditions under which the slower method was planned and assert the plan for the faster method? The answer is that this approach buys greater efficiency over the long run by simplifying the learning process, even though giving up some efficiency in the short run by making a less-than-optimal change.

By allowing the less-efficient plan to be asserted and canceled, HPM defers the problem of finding the conditions under which the plan is asserted. This problem can be nontrivial if there are several different productions that assert the same plan. Since the inefficient plan can be immediately recognized and canceled, HPM can make the change in all cases, even if it has not yet determined all the conditions under which the plan might appear. Furthermore, the task of finding those conditions is simplified because it can now be left to other strategy change mechanisms such as the composition rule for unit building. (The production for asserting the efficient plan and canceling the inefficient plan would dependably fire immediately after any production asserting that plan. It therefore would become a candidate for composition, producing a new production with the desired effect of using the conditions of the old plan to assert the new plan.) Thus, this scheme allows the system to arrive at a general form of the strategy change more quickly, at the cost of having that form be less than optimal. Combining that change with other strange mechanisms provides some promise that the system could still arrive at an optimal form of the change later on.

Therefore, the conditions of the new production first look for instances of the goal with the appropriate input(s). Then, the conditions seek to check if an inefficient plan has been asserted in connection with that goal. There are two ways in which this could happen: either a *has-data* relation has been established to an inappropriate node, or a *sub-goal* relation has been established to an inappropriate goal. These possibilities cannot be handled within a single production. HPM handles the problem by having two versions of the strategy change making production. Each inspects the action part of the production firing-event where processing diverged between the efficient and inefficient instances. Both consider the firing-event for the less efficient instance; one inspects it for assertion of a *has-data* relation, while the other looks for assertion of a *subgoal* relation. Whichever of the two versions fires determines the conditions in the new production that are supposed to detect the assertion of the inefficient plan, as well as the actions required for canceling it.

In the case of the addition simulation, the effort difference results from the starting point for counting. As has been pointed out at several points in the discussion, there are two points in the development of the MIN strategy where effort differences can be detected. The first point comes when the rules for skipping a portion of the total count have been developed. As we have seen, HPM discovers one such rule for each addend in a problem; both rules skip the unnecessary total count by asserting a *has-data* node produced when an addend was originally counted out. The second point arises when HPM discovers that these first shortcuts both leave untouched the set counted for their addend. Once again, a rule can be built for each added, which asserts only the subgoal necessary to produce a single object with a number assignment to that addend.

Comparison of problems solved by the two rules found at the first point invokes the version of the effort-difference rule that looks for *has-data* relations. Comparison of problems solved by the two rules found at the second point invokes the version that looks for *subgoal* relations. Because the second point has only been hand simulated, I will consider only the application of the *has-data* version of this strategy change.

Let us imagine that both strategy changes for eliminating a portion of the total count are competing for the opportunity to fire, and that on one occasion the production fired that causes counting up from 2, while on another occasion the production fired that causes counting up from 3. There is an effort difference for the two instances, which HPM can now consider.[10] The effort difference shows up at the topmost level, in the two goal instances for **ADD.** At that level, there is no apparent cause for the effort difference—both instances assert the same subgoals and have no *has-data* relations. Therefore, no response is made to the effort difference in the **ADD** goals.

However, one level down, there is a divergence to be found between the two **COUNT-UP** goal instances, and they also display an effort difference. The divergence occurs at the production immediately following assertion of the goal. In both instances, the goal is asserted under identical circumstances (by the *Addition-plan* production) and activated under the same circumstances (by the *Continue-planned-subgoal* production after completion of the **GENERATE-SETS** goal). Immediately following activation of the goal, one of the two new productions fires. In the more efficient case, the production initializing the total count at **3** fires, adding a *has-data* relation to a set with the addend count for **3** as a subset. In the less efficient case, the production for **2** fires, and the simulation is forced to count one more element (a process receiving an effort estimate of 5 units). This configuration of information triggers the strategy change making production for effort-differences, which builds a new production that has as its conditions the assertion of a goal to **COUNT-UP**, with inputs **2** and **3** and a *has-data* relation to a set consisting wholly of a subset representing the addend **2**.

Constructing the Actions of the New Production The actions of the new production are quite simply determined by the constraints of the goal-trace formalism. In the case of an inappropriate *has-data* relation, the relation should simply be deleted and a production built that will set the *status* of any goal responding to the *has-data* node to *FAILED*. In the case of an inappropriate *subgoal* relation, the subgoal should have its *status* changed to *FAILED*; any processing which began in response to that goal will be cut off by HPM's built in productions for propagating goal *statuses*.

In the example we're considering, this means that the actions of the new production cancel the *has-data* node with subset 2. This has the effect of setting the situation back to where things were when the **COUNT-UP** goal was first activated. This situation satisfies the conditions of the alternative production, which fires and asserts a *has-data* relation to a set with subset 3. The simulation can then continue, following this more efficient alternative.[11]

This causes the system to take an extra cycle to process *2* + *3* problems, as opposed to *3* + *2* problems. There is some converging evidence in the psychological literature indicating that humans display a similar order effect. Svensson (1975) has found a small reaction-time effect for *Max* + *Min* problems being solved slightly faster than the corresponding *Min* + *Max* problems. Svensson, Hedenborg, and Lingman (1976), analyzing verbal protocols, found that an average of 93.6 percent of problems presented as *Min* + *Max* were transposed by their subjects into *Max* + *Min*. The lowest percentage of such transpositions for any of their subjects was 85 percent. Finally, a reanalysis of Knight and Behrens' (1928) ranking of the difficulty of single-digit addition problems shows that a much larger preponderance of *Max* + *Min* are ranked as easy than would be expected by chance alone.

4.4 Conclusion

HPM is a processing environment implemented within the PRISM production-system framework. It is intended to model cognitive processes in the development of improved strategies. The model is similar in many respects to the psychological theory offered by Anzai and Simon (1979) but differs from the computational model accompanying that theory (Anzai 1978) in a number of respects.

In order to manage its multiple tasks of performance and learning, the HPM system embodies a number of special architectural features. Three features are especially important. The ability to match quickly structures of arbitrary size and complexity in order to find equivalences or isomorphisms enables HPM to represent subtle type-token and event-instantiation distinctions without losing the ability to detect higher-level identities between the objects represented. The ability to use processing context to direct the spread of activation through its semantic network enables HPM to ameliorate problems of large working memory size while still ensuring that potentially relevent data will be brought into active memory. Finally, the ability to maintain parallel tracks of productions through its mechanisms for separate conflict-resolution with each class of productions enables HPM to construct new productions with fewer concerns about introducing unintended conflicts or database inconsistencies.

The most important aspect of HPM is the notion of a goal-trace formalism. These conventions for specifying procedures and actions in the system cause those procedures to leave a history of their execution behind them. This history is a hierarchical semantic network representation of the process that preserves information about relations between goals and data. The parallel notion of a production trace preserves information about both the time ordering of events and the context in which goals were initiated and terminated. The existence of the formalism greatly simplifies the implementation of heuristics for improving procedures by proving a formalism for specifying the heuristics and by imposing constraints that limit the reasoning power required to construct appropriate modifications. Furthermore, the domain-independent conventions move the system closer to the goal of being able to demonstrate domain-independent learning capabilities.

Weaknesses

There are a number of psychological issues not directly addressed by the model developed in this chapter and several computational defiencies in the HPM implementation of that model.

Two particular psychological issues concern me most:

1. *Accessibility.* The model assumes the relative accessibility of extremely detailed information about both on-going processes and related past experiences. How can this be reconciled with known limitation on the ability to report this information (Nisbett and Wilson 1977; Ericsson and Simon 1980)?
2. *Time course.* The model deals in great detail with what happens when a change is made to some procedure. However, it is considerably less specific in explaining why some changes take time to discover.

There are two possible explanations for why the detailed information inherent in the goal trace might be usable without being reportable. One would fall back on the classic distinction between recognition and recall. Strategy transformation heuristics, this argument would say, are built-in schemas that match themselves to trace data through a pattern recognition process. Other processes, such as would be required to produce, say, a detailed verbal report, would have to retrieve propositions through some sort of search process involved in recall.

The second argument about accessibility would come from a possible method for better focusing attention. HPM's current goal-driven spreading activation policy, although considerably more selective than alternative schemes, still activates an fairly large set of propositions. One way to reduce that set, thereby aiding focus of attention, would involve activating propositions probabilistically. That is, certain propositions likely to be irrelevent for performance, but of possible interest for learning, might have some probability of being activated on a given occasion. Thus, on any particular occasion, active memory would be smaller because some of the propositions that could have received activation failed to do so at that particular time.

This second proposal could also provide an explanation of why some changes take time. If the prerequisite information has only some probability of being in memory, then naturally some number of trials may be needed before all of the information required to discover a strategy change was activated in memory simultaneously. If this were the case, then the system would be making a not-implausible trade, accepting a slower learning rate in order to reduce resource demands.

Strengths

Langley and Simon (1981) have argued that learning cannot take place without feedback, but it has long been a question of great interest how humans could perform learning tasks without apparent feedback from the environment. HPM shows how a system can learn entirely from its own performance without need for external feedback.

The reason why the system is not reliant on external feedback is interesting in its own right. Strategy transformations, and the pattern heuristics that guide them, represent metaknowledge about interesting properties of procedures. This metaknowledge is independent of any particular knowledge domain in which those procedures might operate. It guides a system in its learning efforts by focusing attention on possibilities for the construction of *interesting* new rules. The strategy transformation model places a much greater emphasis on this process of hypothesizing interesting rules than a number of other learning models.

One outcome of the model is the ability to offer theory-driven analyses of developmental sequences in procedures. The need for such analyses has been recognized for some time (Resnick 1976). Although *post hoc* stage models have been offered to describe the development of procedures in a number of task domains (e.g., Klahr and Wallace 1970; Baylor and Gascon 1974; Ohlsson 1977), only one such study has offered a theory of the processes producing the intermediate procedures. That study (Anzai and Simon 1979) offered a theory that bears many resemblances to this one. However, the HPM model has the capability to *generate* developmental sequences of procedures, whereas Anzai and Simon stopped after showing only that their model could explain a particular developmental sequence.

The development of the goal-trace formalism as a domain-independent means of expressing strategy transformation rules is another strength of the model. Anzai and Simon implemented a learning system specific to the Tower of Hanoi puzzle, discussed how their heuristics might be generalized, but did not address the problems inherent in actually doing so. This model does make at least a step further in this direction.

One motivation for seeking greater generality in the computer implementation is that it forces one to face a major issue that is too easily avoided in a task-specific simulation: the problem of extraneous information. In task-specific programs, it is possible to get the program to run by holding back information that would confuse it. That is, if the program is task-specific, the programmer has the option of deciding what information is relevent to performing the task. Presenting a program with only the information it really needs can greatly simplify its decision processes, thereby enhancing its performance. Intelligent systems, however, have to be able to make relevence decisions for themselves. HPM is a step toward a learning system that can do just that.

HPM's ability to focus attention through the large mass of procedural data that it keeps is partly due to the notion of strategy transformation heuristics. It is also due to a number of architectural features of the production system, notably its goal-driven spreading activation method and its "by class" production conflict resolution procedure. The design of HPM as a production system architecture is of interest for two reasons. First, it demonstrates an important point: the information-processing demands of learning have implications for the structure of an entire information-processing system. This is because of the ubiquitous attention-focusing problem created by the need to maintain the trace data upon which learning is based. Second, the architecture demonstrates some interesting approaches to resolving those problems. These approaches bring metaknowledge to bear in forcing processing decisions to reflect semantic rather than syntactic criteria. This is, if anything, the unifying concept of this chapter: an examination of the ways in which intelligent systems can employ meta-knowledge about procedures to guide themselves through learning tasks.

Notes

This research was sponsored by the Learning Research and Development Center, supported in part by funds from the National Institute of Education (NIE), United States Department of Education. The opinions expressed herein are solely those of the author, and do not necessarily reflect the positions of policies of any government agency.

1. This contrasts with the traditional pencil-and-paper algorithm in which columns are multiplied from right to left, with subproducts recorded and later totaled to compute the product.

2. The others differ primarily in the order in which heuristics apply, and a single sequence is sufficient to make the points of primary interest. Still it is worth noting that a strategy transformation analysis shows a number of different learning paths that could be taken from one procedure to another, a point of interest both for instructional task analyses (Neches 1979, 1981b) and theories of individual differences (Resnick and Neches 1983).

3. Although more sophisticated definitions could no doubt be provided, the one given seems a useful first approximation and is certainly adequate for the purposes at hand. A more sophisticated definition might take account of the amount of planning required for a task, say by making the measure sensitive to the number of production firings required to build the goal structure instead of depending only on the size of the goal structure.

4. For example, the structure representing the complete solution for an addition problem by the SUM method typically contains about 200 nodes, with each node linked to between 5 and 10 others. Even if we take the lower bound, 5 direct associates means 25 indirect associates within two links, 125 within three links, and so on.

5. By "interesting data", I mean propositions likely to trigger productions that will contribute to the system's progress at either performance or learning.

6. Counting out and counting up, as implemented in **ADD.HPM**, differ only in how the system obtains the objects to which numbers will be assigned.

7. In defense of the system, it should also be noted that its failing only extends to *performing* counting. The isomorphic structure matching functions would allow the system to *recognize* the equivalence of two different counting orders for the same set.

8. This strategy has been reported as one commonly observed in older children by Svenson. Hedenborg, and Lingman (1976).

9. A more intelligent system than HPM might be able to make the strategy change work for non-tie problems by adding actions to the procedure that modified the visual display so as to make the set/subset relationships apparent. However, even so, tie problems would still be distinguished, partly because no extra actions would be required, and partly because further strategy changes can be made to the tie-problem routine but not to the unequal-addends routine.

10. Actually, rather than allowing productions to compete, the simulation covered only the critical points by taking two runs, one in which HPM was forced to choose the first production and one in which it was forced to choose the second.

11. Note that the methods of canceling the less efficient method have the effect that they are not included in the effort estimate, regardless of the number of production firings required to assert and then abort them. This is consistent with repeated observations in the protocols that subjects will abandon a method for a more efficient one despite the costs of switching after the less efficient method has been started.

References

Anderson, J. R. 1976. *Language, Memory, and Thought.* Hillsdale, N.J.: Lawrence Erlbaum Associates.

Anderson, J. R. 1981. A theory of language acquisition based on general learning principles. *Proceedings of the Seventh International Joint Conference on Artificial Intelligence,* pp. 97–103.

Anderson, J. R., Greeno, J. G., Kline, P. J., and Neves, D. M. 1981. Acquisition of problem-solving skill. In J. R. Anderson (ed.), *Cognitive Skills and Their Acquisition.* Hillsdale, N.J.: Lawrence Erlbaum Associates.

Anderson, J. R., Kline, P. J., and Beasley, C. M. 1979. Complex learning processes. In R. E. Snow, P. A. Federico, and W. E. Montague (eds.), *Aptitude, Learning and Instruction: Cognitive Process Analyses.* Hillsdale, N.J.: Lawrence Erlbaum Associates.

Anzai, Y. 1978. Learning strategies by computer. *Proceedings of the Second National Meeting of the Canadian Society for Computational Studies of Intelligence,* Toronto, Canada.

Anzai, Y., and Simon, H. A. 1979. The theory of learning by doing. *Psychological Review* 86(2), 124–140.

Ashcraft, M. H., and Battaglia, J. 1978. Cognitive arithmetic: evidence for retrieval and decision processes in mental addition. *Journal of Experimental Psychology: Human Learning and Memory* 4(5),527–538.

Baylor, G. W., and Gascon, J. 1974. An information processing theory of aspects of the development of weight seriation in children. *Cognitive Psychology* 6, 1–40.

Carpenter, T. P., and Moser, J. M. 1979. *An investigation of learning of addition and subtraction.* Theoretical Paper No. 79. Wisconsin Research and Development Center for Individualized Schooling.

Collins, A. M. and Loftus, E. F. 1975. A spreading activation theory of semantic processing. *Psychological Review* 82, 407–428.

Ericsson, K. A., and Simon, H. A. 1980. Verbal reports as data. *Psychological Review* 87(3),215–251.

Fuson, K. C., and Richards, J. 1979. Children's construction of the counting numbers: From a spew to a bidirectional chain. *Advance Papers of the Wingspread Conference.*

Gelman, R., and Gallistel, C. R. 1978. *The child's understanding of number.* Cambridge, Mass. Harvard University Press.

Ginsburg. H. 1977a. *Children's Arithmetic: The Learning Process.* New York: Van Nostrand.

Ginsburg, H. 1977b. The psychology of arithmetic thinking. *Journal of Children's Mathematical Behavior* 1 (4), 1–89.

Greeno, J. G., Riley, M. S., and Gelman, R. 1981. *Young children's counting and understanding of principles.* Unpublished manuscript.

Groen, G. J., and Parkman, J. M. 1972. A chronometric analysis of simple addition. *Psychological Review* 79, 329–343.

Groen, G. J., and Resnick, L. B. 1977. Can preschool children invent addition algorithms? *Journal of Educational Psychology* 69, 654–652.

Hayes-Roth, F., and McDermott, J. 1976. Learning structured patterns from examples. *Proceedings of the Third International Joint Conference on Pattern Recognition,* pp. 419–423.

Hunter, I. M. L. 1968. Mental calculation. In P. C. Wason and P. N. Johnson-Laird (eds.), *Thinking and Reasoning.* Baltimore: Penguin Books.

Kintsch, W. 1974. *The representation of meaning in memory*. Hillsdale, N.J.: Lawrence Erlbaum Associates.

Klahr, D., and Wallace, J. G. 1970. The development of serial completion strategies: An information processing analysis. *British Journal of Psychology* 61, 243–257.

Knight, F. B., and Behrens, M. S. 1928. *The learning of the 100 addition combinations and the 100 subtraction combinations*. New York: Longmans, Green.

Langley, P. W. 1980. A production system model of first language acquisition. *Proceedings of the 8th International Conference on Computational Linguistics*, pp. 183–189.

Langley, P. W. 1979. Re-discovering physics with BACON.3. *Proceedings of the Sixth International Joint Conference on Artificial Intelligence*, pp. 505–508.

Langley, P., and Neches, R. 1981. PRISM User's Manual. Technical Report. Department of Psychology, Carnegie-Mellon University.

Langley, P., Neches, R., Neves, D., and Anzai, Y. 1981. A domain-independent framework for procedure learning. *Policy Analysis and Information Systems*, Special Issue on Knowledge Acquisition and Induction 4(2),163–197.

Langley, P., and Simon, H. A. 1981. The central role of learning in cognition. In J. R. Anderson (ed.), *Cognitive Skills and Their Acquisition*. Hillsdale, N.J.: Lawrence Erlbaum Associates.

Larkin, J. H. 1981. Enriching formal knowledge: A model for learning to solve textbook physics problems. In J. R. Anderson (ed.), *Cognitive Skills and Their Acquisition*. Hillsdale, N.J.: Lawrence Erlbaum Associates, pp. 311–334.

Lewis, C. H. 1978. *Production system models of practice effects*. Dissertation. Department of Psychology, University of Michigan at Ann Arbor.

Michalski, R. S. 1977. Towards computer-aided induction. Report No. 874. Department of Computer Science, University of Illinois at Urbana-Champaign.

Mitchell, T. M. 1977. Version space: A candidate elimination approach to rule learning. In *Proceedings of the Fifth International Joint Conference on Artificial Intelligence*, pp. 305–310.

Neches, R. 1979. *Promoting self-discovery of improved strategies*. Paper presented at the annual conference of the American Educational Research Association, San Francisco, Calif.

Neches, R. 1981a. HPM: a computational formalism for heuristic procedure modification. In *Proceedings of the Seventh International Joint Conference on Artificial Intelligence*, pp. 283–288.

Neches, R. 1981b. *Models of heuristic procedure modification*. Dissertation. Psychology Department, Carnegie-Mellon University.

Neches, R. 1982. Simulation systems for cognitive psychology. *Behavior Research Methods and Instrumentation* 14(2),77–91.

Neches, R., and Hayes, J. R. 1978. Progress towards a taxonomy of strategy transformations. In A. M. Lesgold, J. W. Pellegrino, S. Fokkema, and R. Glaser (eds.), *Cognitive Psychology and Instruction*. New York: Plenum.

Neves, D. M. 1978. A computer program that learns algebraic procedures by examining examples and by working test problems in a textbook. *Proceedings of the Second Annual Conference of the Canadian Society for Computational Studies of Intelligence*, Toronto, Canada.

Neves, D. M. and Anderson, J. R. 1981. Knowledge compilation: mechanisms for the automatization of cognitive skills. In J. R. Anderson (ed.), *Cognitive Skills and Their Acquisition*. Hillsdale, N.J.: Lawrence Erlbaum Associates.

Newell, A., and Rosenbloom, P. S. 1981. Mechanisms of skill acquisition and the law of practice. In J. R. Anderson (ed.), *Cognitive Skills and Their Acquisition.* Hillsdale, N.J.: Lawrence Erlbaum Associates, pp. 1–55.

Newell, A., and Simon, H. A. 1972. *Human Problem Solving.* Englewood Cliffs, N.J.: Prentice-Hall.

Nisbett, R. E., and Wilson, T. D. 1977. Telling more than we can know: Verbal reports on mental processes. *Psychological Review* 84, 231–259.

Norman, D. A. 1976. *Memory and Attention* 2nd ed. New York: Wiley.

Norman, D. A., and Bobrow, D. G. 1979. Descriptions: an intermediate stage in memory retrieval. *Cognitive Psychology* 11(1),107–123.

Norman, D. A., Rumelhart, D. E., and LNR Research Group. 1975. *Explorations in Cognition.* San Francisco: Freeman.

Ohlsson, S. 1977. *Production system reconstructions of theories for the solving of three-term series tasks.* Department of Psychology, University of Umea, Umea, Sweden.

Resnick, L. B. 1976. Task analysis in instruction. In D. Klahr (ed.), *Cognition and Instruction.* Hillsdale, N.J.: Lawrence Erlbaum Associates.

Resnick, L. B., and Neches, R. 1983. Factors affecting individual differences in learning ability. In R. J. Sternberg (ed.), *Advances in the Psychology of Human Intelligence* Vol. 2. Hillsdale, N.J.: Lawrence Erlbaum Associates.

Sacerdoti, E. D. 1977. *A Structure for Plans and Behavior.* New York: American Elsevier.

Simon, D. P., and Simon H. A. 1978. Individual differences in solving physics problems. In R. Siegler (ed.), *Children's Thinking: What Develops?* Hillsdale, N.J.: Lawrence Erlbaum Associates.

Sleeman, D., Langley, P., and Mitchell, T. 1982. Learning from solution paths: an approach to the credit assignment problem. *AI Magazine* (Spring) 48–52.

Steffe, L. P., and Thompson, P. W. 1982. Children's counting in arithmetical problem solving. In T. P. Carpenter, J. Moser, and T. A. Romberg (eds.), *Addition and Subtraction: A Cognitive Perspective.* Hillsdale, N.J.: Lawrence Erlbaum Associates.

Svenson, O. 1975. Analysis of time required by children for simple additions. *Acta Psychologica* 39, 289–302.

Svenson, O., and Broquist, S. 1975. Strategies for solving simple addition problems. *Scandanavian Journal of Psychology* 16,143–151.

Svenson, O., Hedenborg, M. L., and Lingman, L. 1976. On children's heuristics for solving simple additions. *Scandanavian Journal of Educational Research* 20,161–173.

Thibadeau, R. 1981. *The CAPS production system.* Department of Psychology, Carnegie-Mellon University.

Vere, S. A. 1977. Induction of relational productions in the presence of background information. *Proceedings of the Fifth International Joint Conference on Artificial Intelligence,* pp. 349–355.

Woods, W. A. 1975. What's in a link: foundations for semantic networks. In D. G. Bobrow and A. Collins (eds.), *Representation and Understanding.* San Francisco: Academic Press, pp. 35–82.

5 Learning by Chunking: A Production System Model of Practice

Paul Rosenbloom and Allen Newell

Performance improves with practice. More precisely, the time to perform a task decreases as a power-law function of the number of times the task has been performed. This basic law—known as the *power law of practice* or the *log-log linear learning law*—has been known since Snoddy (1926).[1] While this law was originally recognized in the domain of motor skills, it has recently become clear that it holds over the full range of human tasks (Newell and Rosenbloom 1981). This includes both purely perceptual tasks such as target detection (Neisser, Novick, and Lazar 1963) and purely cognitive tasks such as supplying justifications for geometric proofs (Neves and Anderson 1981) or playing a game of solitaire (Newell and Rosenbloom 1981).

The ubiquity of the power law of practice argues for the presence of a single common underlying mechanism. The *chunking theory of learning* (Newell and Rosenbloom 1981) proposes that *chunking* (Miller 1956) is this common mechanism—a concept already implicated in many aspects of human behavior (Bower and Winzenz 1969; Johnson 1972; DeGroot 1975; Chase and Simon 1973). Newell and Rosenbloom (1981) established the plausibility of the theory by showing that a model based on chunking is capable of producing log-log linear practice curves.[2] In its present form, the chunking theory of learning is a macro theory: it postulates the outline of a learning mechanism and predicts the global improvements in task performance.

This chapter reports on recent work on the chunking theory and its interaction with production-system architectures (Newell 1973).[3] Our goals are fourfold: (1) fill out the details of the chunking theory; (2) show that it can form the basis of a production-system learning mechanism; (3) show that the full model produces power-law practice curves; and (4) understand the implications of the theory for production-system architectures. The approach we take is to implement and analyze a production-system model of the chunking theory in the context of a specific task—a 1,023-choice reaction-time task (Seibel 1963). The choice of task should not be critical because the chunking theory claims that the *same* mechanism underlies improvements on *all* tasks. Thus, the model, as implemented for this task, carries with it an implicit claim to generality, although the issue of generality will not be addressed.

In the remainder of this chapter we describe and analyze the task and the model. In section 5.1 we lay the groundwork by briefly reviewing the highlights of the power law of practice and the chunking theory of learning. In section 5.2 the task is described. We concentrate our efforts on investigating the control structure of task performance through the analysis of an informal experiment. In section 5.3 we derive some constraints on the form of the model. Sections 5.4, 5.5, and 5.6 describe the three components of the model: (1) the *Xaps2* production-system architecture; (2) the initial performance model for the task; and (3) the chunking mechanism. Section 5.7 gives some results generated by running the complete model on a sample sequence of experimental trials. The model is too costly to run on long sequences of trials, so in addition to the simulation model, we present results from an extensive simulation of the simulation (a meta-simulation). We pay particular attention to establishing that the model does produce power-law practice curves. Finally, section 5.8 contains some concluding remarks.

5.1 Previous Work

The groundwork for this research was laid in Newell and Rosenbloom (1981). That paper primarily contains an analysis and evaluation of the empirical power law of practice, analyses of existing models of practice, and a presentation of the chunking theory of learning. Three components of that work are crucial for the remainder of this chapter and are summarized in this section. Included in this summary are some recent minor elaborations on that work.

The Structure of Task Environments

In experiments on practice subjects are monitored as they progress through a (long) sequence of trials. On each trial the subject is presented with a single *task* to be performed. In some experiments the task is ostensibly identical on all trials; for example, Moran (1980) had subjects repeatedly perform the same set of edits on a single sentence with a computer text editor. In other experiments the task varies across trials; for example, Seibel (1963) had subjects respond to different combinations of lights on different trials. In either case the *task environment* is defined to be the ensemble of tasks with which the subject must deal.

Typical task environments have a *combinatorial* structure (though other task structures are possible); they can be thought of as being composed from a set of elements that can vary with respect to attributes, locations, relations to other elements, and so forth. Each distinct task corresponds to one possible assignment of values to the elements. This structure plays an important role in determining the nature of the practice curves produced by the chunking theory.

The Power Law of Practice

Practice curves are generated by plotting task performance against trial number. This cannot be done without assuming some specific *measure* of performance. There are many possibilities for such a measure, including such things as quantity produced per unit time and number of errors per trial. The power law of practice is defined in terms of the time to perform the task on a trial. It states that the time to perform the task (T) is a power-law function of the trial number (N):

$$T = BN^{-\alpha}. \tag{5.1}$$

If this equation is transformed by taking the logarithm of both sides, it becomes clear why power-law functions plot as straight lines on log-log paper:

$$\log(T) = \log(B) + (-\alpha)\log(N). \tag{5.2}$$

Figure 5.1 shows a practice curve from a 1,023-choice reaction-time task (Seibel 1963), plotted on log-log paper. Each data point represents the mean reaction time over a block of 1,023 trials. The curve is linear over much of its range but has deviations at its two ends. These deviations can be removed by using a four-parameter *generalized* power-law function. One of the two new parameters (A) takes into account that the asymptote of learning is unlikely to be zero. In general, there is a nonzero minimum bound on performance time—determined by basic physiological and/or device limitations—if, for example, the subject must operate a machine. The other added parameter (E) is required because power laws are not translation invariant. Practice occurring before the official beginning of the experiment—even if it consists only of transfer of training from everyday experience—will alter the shape of the curve, unless the effect is explicitly allowed for by the inclusion of this parameter. Augmenting the power-law function by these two parameters yields the following generalized function:

$$T = A + B(N + E)^{-\alpha}. \tag{5.3}$$

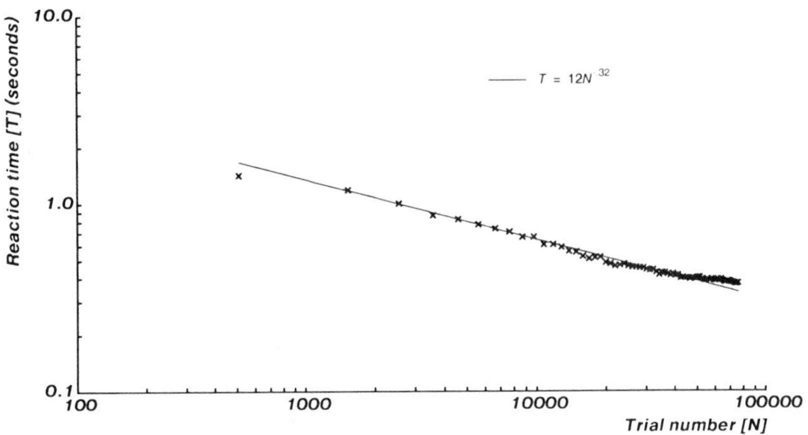

Figure 5.1
Learning in a ten-finger, 1,023 choice task (log-log coordinates). Plotted from the original data for subject JK (Seibel 1963)

A generalized power law plots as a straight line on log-log paper once the effects of the asymptote (A) are removed from the time (T), and the effective number of trials prior to the experiment (E) are added to those performed during the experiment (N):

$$\log(T - A) = \log(B) + (-\alpha)\log(N + E). \tag{5.4}$$

Figure 5.2 shows the Seibel data as it is fit by a generalized power-law function. It is now linear over the whole range of trials. Similar fits are found across all dimensions of human performance; whether the task involves perception, motor behavior, perceptual-motor skills, elementary decisions, memory, complex routines, or problem solving. Though these fits are impressive, it must be stressed that the power law of practice is only an *empirical* law. The true underlying law must resemble a power law, but it may have a different analytical form.

The Chunking Theory of Learning

The chunking theory of learning proposes that practice improves performance via the acquisition of knowledge about patterns in the task environment. Implicit in this theory is a model of task of performance based on this pattern knowledge. These patterns are called *chunks* (Miller 1956). The theory thus starts from the *chunking hypothesis*:

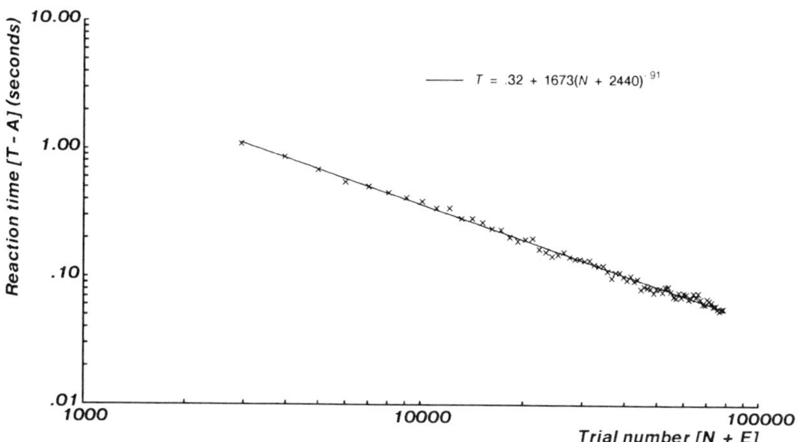

Figure 5.2
Optimal general power law fit to the Seibel data (log-log coordinates)

THE CHUNKING HYPOTHESIS A human acquires and organizes knowledge of the environment by forming and storing expressions, called *chunks*, which are structured collections of the chunks existing at the time of learning.

The existence of chunks implies that memory is hierarchically structured as a lattice (tangled hierarchy, acyclic directed graph, etc.) rooted in a set of *primitives*. A given chunk can be accessed in a top-down fashion, by *decoding* a chunk of which it is a part, or in a bottom-up fashion, by *encoding* from the parts of the chunk. Encoding is a recognition or parsing process.

This hypothesis is converted into a performance model by adding an assumption relating the presence of chunks to task performance:

PERFORMANCE ASSUMPTION The performance program of the system is coded in terms of high-level chunks, with the time to process a chunk being less than the time to process its constituent chunks.

One possible instantiation of this assumption is that performance consists of serially processing a set of chunks, with the components of each chunk being processed in parallel. Performance is thus improved by the acquisition of higher-level chunks. A second assumption is needed to tie down this acquisition process:

LEARNING ASSUMPTION Chunks are learned at a constant rate on average from the relevant patterns of stimuli and responses that occur in the specific environments experienced.

This assumption tells us the rate at which chunks are acquired, but it says nothing about the effectiveness of the newly acquired chunks. Do all chunks improve task performance to the same extent, or does their effectiveness vary? The answer to this question can be found by examining the structure of the task environment. If patterns in the task environment vary in their frequency of occurrence, then the effectiveness of the chunks for those patterns will also vary. The more frequently a pattern occurs, the more the chunk gains. The final assumption made by the theory is that the task environment does vary in this fashion:

TASK STRUCTURE ASSUMPTION The probability of recurrence of an environmental pattern decreases as the pattern size increases.

This assumption is trivially true for combinatorial task environments. As the pattern size grows (in terms of the number of elements specified), the number of possibilities grows exponentially. Any particular large pattern will therefore be experienced less often than any particular small pattern.

There is one notable case where the task structure assumption is violated—when the task environment consists of just one task. This lack of variability means that the subject is presented with the identical experimental situation on every trial. One way to look at this situation is as a combinatorial task environment in which each element can take exactly one value. Now, as the size of the pattern grows, the number of patterns of that size *decreases* rather than increases. As we shall see shortly, this violation does not result in a markedly different prediction for the form of the practice curve.

The chunking curve Starting with the three assumptions, and with a little further specification, an approximate functional form can be derived for the practice curves predicted by the chunking theory:

1. *Performance.* Assume that performance time is proportional to the number of chunks that are processed, with P (the number of elements in the task environment) chunks required initially.

2. *Learning.* Let λ be the constant rate of acquisition of new chunks.

3. *Task structure.* Let $C(s)$ be the number of chunks needed to cover all patterns of s elements or less in the task environment.

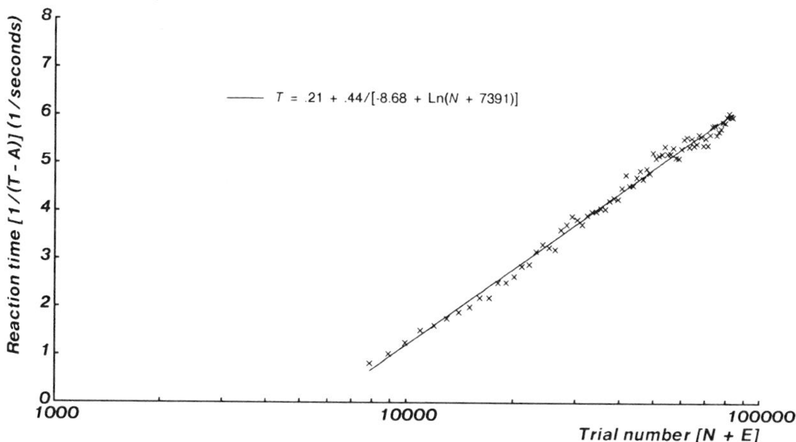

Figure 5.3
Best fit of the Seibel data by the combinatorial chunking function (X-axis log scaled)

Given these additional specifications, the chunking theory of learning predicts a learning curve of the form:

$$\frac{dT}{dN} = -\frac{\lambda}{P}\left(\frac{dC}{ds}\right)^{-1} T^3. \qquad (5.5)$$

This equation depends on the structure of the task environment, as described by $C(s)$. It is a power law when $C(s)$ is a power law. For a combinatorial task environment, dC/ds is given by $(P/s)b^s$, where b is the number of values that each element can take. For $b > 1$ (a standard combinatorial environment) the chunking theory predicts the following learning curve (for arbitrary constants A, B, D, and E):

$$T = A + \frac{B}{D + \log(N + E)}. \qquad (5.6)$$

Figure 5.3 shows the Seibel data plotted in coordinates in which practice curves predicted by the combinatorial chunking model are straight lines. The linearity of this plot is as good as that for the general power law (figure 5.2), and the r^2 values are comparable: 0.993 for the power law versus 0.991 for the chunking model. This function and the power law can mimic each other to a remarkable extent. Figure 5.4 contains two curves; one of them is the combinatorial chunking law fit to the Seibel data (figure 5.3), and the

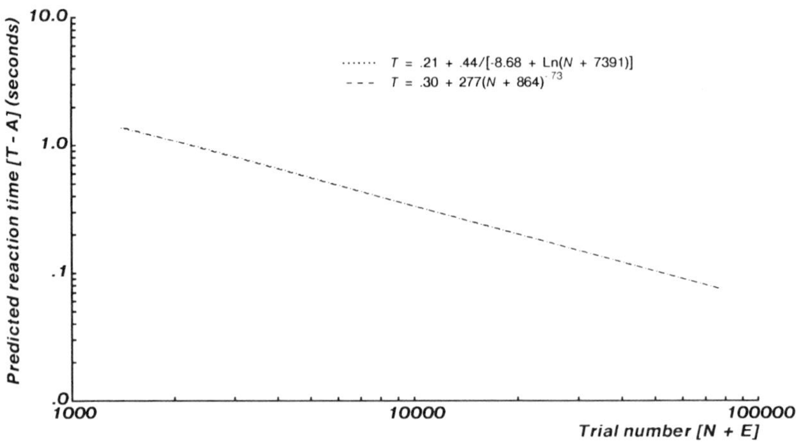

Figure 5.4
A practice curve generated by the chunking theory of learning (log-log coordinates). Its optimal power-law fit is also shown.

other is the best power law approximation to that curve. The curves are indistinguishable (r^2 of 1.000).

For $b = 1$ (only one task in the task environment) dC/ds becomes simply P/s. Plugging this expression into equation (5.5) yields a hyperbolic curve of the form (for arbitrary constants A, B, and E):

$$T = A + \frac{B}{N + E}. \tag{5.7}$$

Since a hyperbolic function is just a special case of the power law (with $\alpha = 1$), this function is trivially well fit by a power law.

5.2 The Task

It is difficult, if not impossible, to produce and evaluate a theory of learning without doing so in the context of some concrete task to be learned. The first characteristic required of such a task is that it be understood how the learning mechanism can be applied to it. For our purposes this corresponds to understanding what aspects of the task can be chunked. The second characteristic required of the chosen task is that the control structure of initial task performance be understood. Discovering such a performance model is well within the domain of a learning system, but practice is the subclass of learning that deals only with improving performance on a task that can already be successfully performed. Thus our models will always start with some method, no matter how inefficient, for performing the chosen task.

The task that we shall employ is a 1,023-choice reaction-time task (Seibel 1963). This is a perceptual-motor task in which the task environment consists of a stimulus array of ten lights, and a response array of ten buttons in a highly compatible one-one correspondence with the lights. On each trial some of the lights are *On*, and some are *Off*. The subject's task is to respond by pressing the buttons corresponding to the lights that are *On*. Ten lights, with two possible states for each light, yields 2^{10} or 1,024 possibilities. The configuration with no lights on is not used, leaving 1,023 choices.

This task easily meets the first criterion; in fact the macro structure of chunking in this task has already been analyzed (Newell and Rosenbloom 1981). The task has an easily recognizable combinatorial structure. The lights and buttons are the elements of the task environment. Each element has one attribute with two possible values: *On* and *Off* for the lights, *Press* and *NoPress* for the buttons. These lights and buttons will form the primitives for the chunking process.

One auxiliary benefit of selecting this task is that it fits in with a large body of experimental literature, allowing exploration of the theory's implications to a large range of nearby phenomena. The literature on perceptual-motor reaction time is a rich source of data on human performance. For this particular task, practice curves already exist out to more than seventy thousand trials (Seibel 1963). Figures 5.1, 5.2, and 5.3 are plotted from the data for one subject in that experiment.

Unfortunately the existing practice curves present highly aggregated data (by 1023-trial blocks), leaving us with little evidence from which to deduce the within-trial structure of performance (the second required characteristic). In order to gain some insight into this structure, an informal investigation into the performance of human subjects in this task was performed. A version of the experiment was programmed on an *Alto* personal computer (Thacker, McCreight, Lampson, Sproull, and Boggs 1982). The bit-map screen (8.5 × 11 in. at 72 points to the inch) was used for the presentation of the stimulus lights. The screen was dark, allowing

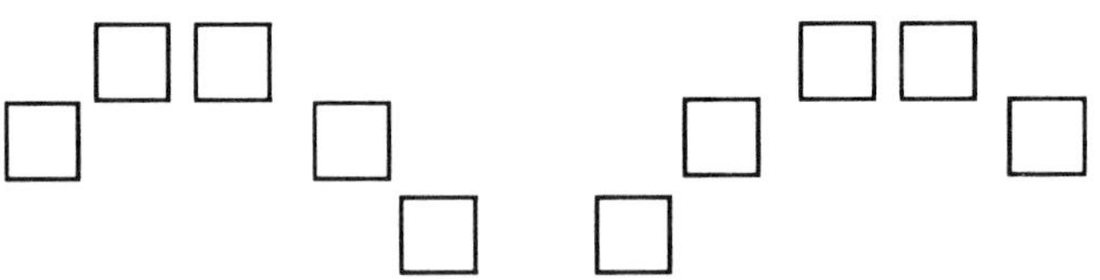

Figure 5.5
The stimulus array of ten lights

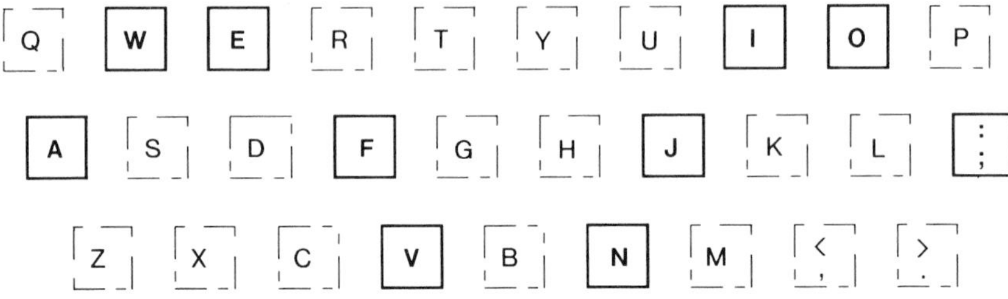

Figure 5.6
The response array (a portion of *Alto* the keyboard) with the ten keys highlighted

On-lights to be represented as solid white squares (0.85 cm on a side), while *Off*-lights were dark with a white rim. The lights all fit into a rectangle 12 × 2.8 cm (figure 5.5). At an approximate distance of 43 cm, the display covers 16° of visual arc.

The *Alto* keyboard allows the sensing of multiple simultaneous key-presses, so ten keys were selected and used as buttons. The keys (a, w, e, f, v, n, j, i, o, ;) were chosen so as to make the mapping between stimulus and response as compatible as possible. The keys all fit into a rectangle 18.3 × 4.9 cm (figure 5.6).

Each trial began with the presentation of a fixation point between the center two lights. After 333 msec the fixation point was replaced by the ten lights. A clock was started at this point (accurate to within one jiffy, or about 17 msec), and the time was recorded for each button that was pressed. The trial continued until the subject had pressed the button corresponding to each *On*-light, even if wrong buttons had been pressed along the way. It was not necessary to hold down the buttons; once they had been pressed they could be released. After all of the required buttons had been pressed, the screen was cleared. With this setup, the fastest way to complete a trial was to press all ten buttons as soon as the lights appeared. To rule out this possibility, the subject received, via the screen, feedback about the correctness of the response, and his cumulative percent correct over the previous 20 trials. Subjects were instructed to respond as quickly as possible while maintaining a low error percentage. Following error feedback, the screen went blank until the start of the next trial—approximately 2 sec.

Four male graduate students in their twenties were run informally in a somewhat noisy environment (a terminal room). A trial sequence was generated from a random permutation of the 1,023 possibilities. This fixed sequence was divided into 102-trial blocks (except for the last block) and used for all subjects. Subject 1 completed 2 blocks of trials (or 204 trials), subject 2 completed 1 block, subject 3 completed 4 blocks, and subject 4 completed 1 block. Any trial in which a bad key (one corresponding to an *Off*-light) was pressed was considered to be an error of *commission*, and any trial that took longer than 5 sec was considered to be an error of *omission*. These error trials—12 percent of the total trials—were removed from the main analysis.

All four subjects improved during the course of the experiment, but the data are somewhat ragged due to the small number of trials. All of the data for any of these subjects fit within one data point of the graphs of Seibel's subjects. Figure 5.7 shows the longest of these curves (subject 3: 408 trials).

The learning curve verifies the power-law nature of learning in this task, but we are primarily interested in the micro structure of within-trial performance. Figure 5.8 shows the within-trial structure of some typical correct trials. The ten short, wide bars represent the lights, separated into the two hands. A solid outline signifies an *On*-light, while a dotted outline marks an *Off*-light. The narrow bars record the amount of time between the start of the trial and when the button corresponding to that light was pressed.

Most of the trials show a similar pattern: groups of buttons are pressed nearly simultaneously, with gaps between these compound responses. These compound responses are termed *response groups*. The numbers above the bars denote the response group to which each keypress belongs. The response groups primarily fall into four classes: (1) a single *On*-light, (2) a group of adjacent *On*-lights, (3) all of the *On*-lights in a single hand, and (4) all of the *On*-lights.

For subjects 1 and 2, response groups were computed by forcing any two responses within 100 msec of each other to be in the same response group.

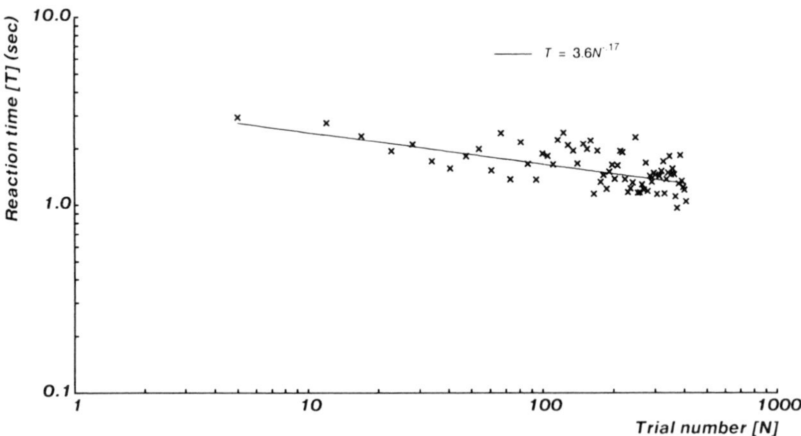

Figure 5.7
Subject 3's learning curve (log-log coordinates). The data are aggregated by groups of five trials.

This algorithm works because the distribution of interbutton response times is bimodal, with a break at about 100 msec. The distributions for subjects 3 and 4 are unimodal, so the concept of a response group is more difficult to define and thus less useful for them. This difficulty is partly due to the high degree to which both subjects responded to all lights at once, resulting in a paucity of intergroup times.

For all four subjects the response groups *increased* in size with practice. This is exactly what we would expect if chunking were operating. Unfortunately it is not possible to conclude that either the presence or growth of response groups is evidence for chunking. The size of response groups can be artificially increased by sequentially preparing a number of fingers (poising them above the appropriate keys), and then pressing all of the prepared fingers simultaneously (and some subjects behaved this way). It is not possible to fully disentangle the effects of these consciously selected strategies, and changes in strategy, from the effects of chunking.

Though the experiment provides no clear evidence for chunking, it does provide some guidance for the construction of a model of the task. The following facts are true of the data:

1. There is no single *right* control structure for the task. The subjects employed qualitatively different strategies.

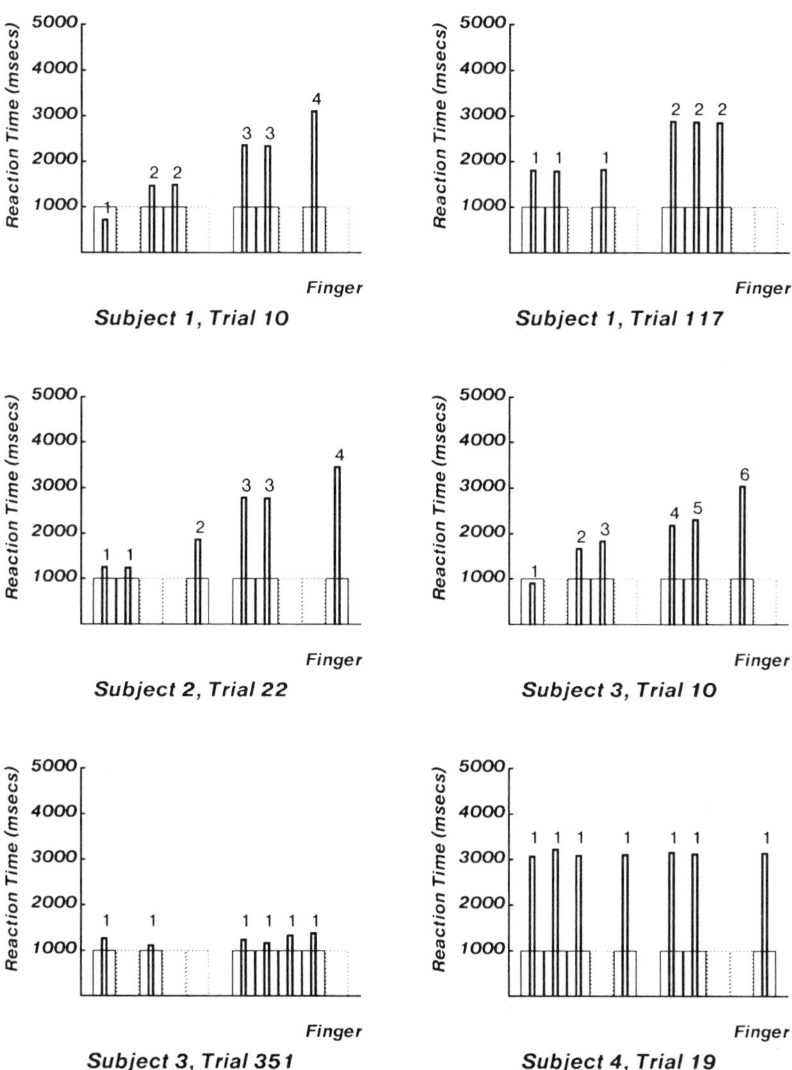

Figure 5.8
Six typical trials

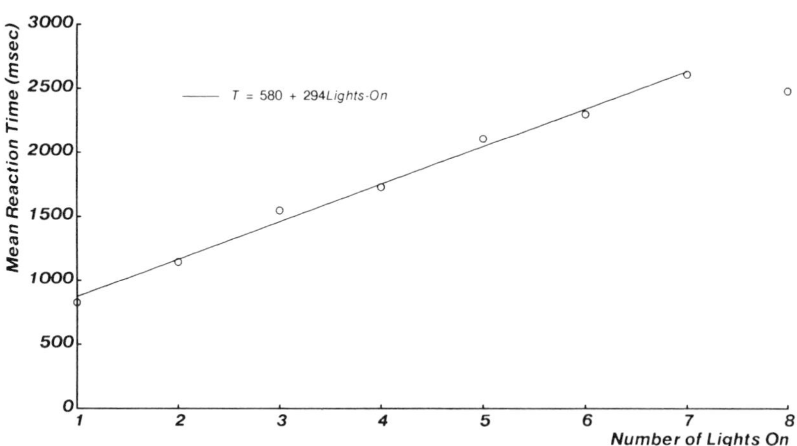

Figure 5.9
Reaction times versus member of *On*-lights. The data are averaged over all trials of the four subjects, except those with five *On*-lights on one hand.

2. Each subject used predominantly one strategy.
3. The lights were processed in a predominantly left-to-right fashion.
4. The number of *On*-lights is a significant component of the reaction time. Ignoring those trials in which all five lights on a hand were on, figure 5.9 plots reaction time versus the number of *On*-lights.[4] The figure reveals the strong linear trend of this data; all but the final point (one *Off*-light per hand) fall close to the regression line. Subjects may be employing a different strategy for those trials, such as preparing to press all of the keys and then removing the finger from the key corresponding to the *Off*-light.

Taking these facts into consideration, a reasonable control structure for this task can be based on a simple iterative algorithm:

Focus a point to the left of the leftmost light.
While there is an *On*-light to the right of the focal point **Do**
  Locate the *On*-light.
  Map the light location into the location of the button under it.
  Press the button.
  Focus the right edge of the light.

The model of practice for this task starts with this simple model of initial task performance and a chunking mechanism. As experimental trials are processed, chunks are built out of the stimulus and response patterns that are experienced. These chunks reduce the response time on later trials by allowing the subject to process a group of lights on each iteration, rather than just a single light.

We will return to describe the implementation of the initial performance model in section 5.5 after the architecture of the production system in which it is implemented has been laid out.

5.3 Constraints on the Model

A useful initial step in the development of the model is the derivation of *constraints*—codifications of fundamental limitations—on the form of the model. Any particular implementation of the model is going to be wrong, at least along some dimensions. By delineating boundaries on the set of *all* legitimate models, constraints provide a means by which knowledge can be transferred to later more "correct" models of the task and to models in other task domains. Constraints can be formulated in terms of either the *behavior* of the model or its *structure*. Behavioral constraints are the weakest and are provided in profusion by the results of psychological experiments. The power law of practice is an example, one we are using heavily. In essence, behavioral constraints circumscribe the input-output pairs of the model, leaving the model itself as a black box with any number of possible internal structures.

Structural constraints are much stronger; they limit the space of structures that may be inside the box. At their most powerful, structural constraints are capable of ruling out large classes of architectures. Though the rewards can be substantial, formulating and proving the correctness of such constraints is difficult. For each proposed constraint, proofs of four properties are required:

1. *Universality.* The limitation must be a universal property of the performance of the system.

2. *Architecturality.* The universality of the limitation must be a reflection of an architectural restriction, not just a regularity of the task environment.

3. *Minimality.* The constraint must describe the minimum architectural restriction capable of producing the limitation.

4. *Uniqueness.* The constraint must be the only valid implementation of the architectural restriction.

Ignoring these properties can lead to overly restrictive, or simply incorrect, constraints. However, these properties are difficult to establish, and we have not succeeded in formally proving them for the constraints we propose. Minimality is a particularly hard concept to work with because it requires an ordering on the space of constraints, an ordering that is not always clearly defined. For some of the constraints we will not even attempt to evaluate this property. For the remaining three properties we have resorted to informal arguments in their favor. Though this is a serious shortcoming, we still feel that these constraints are reasonable and interesting.

Once we have outlined the constraints, we can proceed to a discussion of one model that sits within the design space bounded by the constraints. Wherever possible, design decisions are justified on the basis of these constraints. But, as long as the constraints leave room for variation, these justifications can extend only as far as showing that a mechanism is *sufficient* to meet a constraint. *Necessity* can only come from a more constrained design space.

Many sources of knowledge can be employed to generate constraints on the model. For example, a number of computational and psychological considerations have led to the choice of a production-system architecture as the basis for the performance system (Newell and Simon 1972; Newell 1973). Other psychological constraints have lead to further refinement in the class of production-system architectures that is explored (e.g. see Anderson 1976; Newell 1980; and Thibadeau, Just, and Carpenter 1986). In this section we focus on those constraints derivable from the chunking theory.

The five strongest constraints have significant impact on the nature of the production-system architecture used as the basis of the model. These five constraints are described here, leaving other weaker constraints to be discussed as they arise in the model. The theoretical constraints take the form:

If the chunking theory is correct,
then any architecture that implements it must meet some condition.

An example of this kind of argument in another domain is:

If the theory of evolution is correct,
then any model of reproduction must allow for the inheritability of mutations.

The form of argument is similar in spirit to that made by VanLehn (1981) concerning the implications of *repair theory*.

It is possible to make general arguments that all constraints derivable from the chunking theory must be universal and are almost certainly architectural. Universality follows directly from the assumed universality of the chunking theory of learning. If the model is universal, and some limitation is necessary wherever the model applies, then the limitation must also be universal. Architecturality is more difficult to establish conclusively, so we resort to a simpler plausibility argument. We start by noticing that if the limitations are universal, then either the restriction is architectural or all task environments must reflect the limitation. Since the former choice is the simpler assumption of the two, we feel safe in assuming it until proven incorrect.

The first major constraint is a direct consequence of the performance assumption: chunks improve performance because the time to process a chunk is less than the time required to execute the constituent chunks. This assumption rules out one of the more obvious schemes for processing chunks: decode the chunk into a set of subchunks, and then serially process the subchunks. Such a scheme is reasonable if chunks are thought of as nothing more than a space-efficient code for information, but it results in the time to process a chunk being the sum of the times to process the constituent chunks, plus some overhead for decoding. This consideration leads us to the following constraint:

THE PARALLEL CONSTRAINT The model must contain some form of parallel processing—it cannot have a control structure that is totally serial.

This constraint is definitely not unique. One alternative is that subchunks are processed by a second, faster, serial process. It is difficult to distinguish a parallel process from an arbitrarily fast serial process, so the result must be left open to this extent.

The simplest control structure meeting the parallel constraint is one that processes chunks (and everything else) in parallel. However, such an architecture would also violate the performance assumption. If any set of chunks can be processed in parallel, packaging them into a higher-level chunk will not improve performance. At the extreme all of the light-button pairs in Seibel's task could be processed simultaneously, achieving an optimal algorithm. A second constraint is required if the chunking process is to produce performance improvements:

THE BOTTLENECK CONSTRAINT The parallel capability of the control structure must be restricted so that a bottleneck exists. This can be a serial bottleneck or, more generally, some form of capacity limitation.

Chunking thus improves performance by alleviating the flow through a bottleneck. As with the parallel constraint, the bottleneck constraint is not the unique response to the required limitation. One alternative is that the problem stems from a limitation on the learning system (another part of the architecture) rather than on the performance system. That is, the performance system is capable of executing any set of productions that can be acquired by the subject, but the learning system is only capable of acquiring knowledge in terms of chunks. Without a principled reason for choosing this alternative, we believe that the bottleneck constraint should be preferred because of the existing evidence for capacity limitations in humans (e.g., Miller 1956).

From the first two constraints we get the picture of a parallel system with at least one bottleneck. We can constrain this architecture even further by bounding the location of the bottleneck:

THE ENCODING CONSTRAINT The bottleneck occurs after the process of chunk encoding has completed.

THE DECODING CONSTRAINT The bottleneck occurs before the final process of chunk decoding has begun.

If either of these constraints did not hold, then chunking would not fulfill its function of reducing the flow through the bottleneck. These constraints appear to be minimal and unique.

With the addition of these two constraints, the architecture has been limited to one that is parallel at its extremes, with a limited capacity in between. However, it is a mistake to think that this implies a serial cognitive system with parallel sensory and motor components. Practice improves performance on the full range of human tasks, specifically including purely cognitive tasks. The processing of cognitive chunks therefore requires parallel computation just as do sensory and motor chunks. The last theoretical constraint—a minimal and unique one—is thus:

THE COGNITIVE-PARALLELISM CONSTRAINT The locus of parallelism in the system cannot be constrained to the sensory and motor portions of the system.

5.4 The Xaps2 Production-System Architecture

The *Xaps* architecture (Rosenbloom 1979) was designed to investigate merging the concepts from (1) symbolic production systems (specifically, the *Ops2* language; see Forgy 1977), (2) activation models of short-term memory (e.g., Anderson 1976; Shiffrin and Schneider 1977), and (3) linear associative memories (see Anderson and Hinton 1981 for a good review of this work). From 1 *Xaps* got its production-system control structure and list-based representation, from 2 came the activation values attached to working memory elements (modeling recency, priming effects, importance, focus of attention, etc.), and from 3 came the parallel firing of productions. The resulting design bore many resemblances to *Hpsa77* (Newell 1980) and *Act* (Anderson 1976).

The main function of *Xaps* was as a test-bed for assumptions about the decay of working-memory elements (e.g., item decay, time decay, and fixed total activation), the combination of activation values in the match, and the use of productions as conduits of activation. Its development was actively driven by work in the LNR group at UCSD on the modeling of motor skills, such as finger tapping and typing (Rumelhart and Norman 1982), recognition networks (McClelland and Rumelhart 1981; Rumelhart and McClelland 1982), and slips of the mind (Norman 1981).

The *Xaps2* architecture is a direct descendant of *Xaps*. Like *Xaps*, it is a parallel, symbolic, activation-based production system.[5] *Xaps2* differs in having an object-oriented representation (rather than a list one), and in its control and activation assumptions.[6] The changes have been driven by the needs and constraints of the current research. While the justifications for the design decisions in *Xaps2* will often be given in terms of the task at hand, we must stress that there are very few features in the language particular to this task. *Xaps2* is a general purpose production-system architecture.

The following sections describe the primary nonlearning components of the *Xaps2* architecture: working memory, production memory, and the cycle of execution. The chunking mechanism is properly a part of this architecture (as it is implemented by *Lisp* code, not productions), but it is described later (section 5.6) because its implementation is dependent on the form of the initial performance model (section 5.5).[7]

Working Memory

Most modern production systems concur in defining working memory to be the active set of data to which productions attend. They diverge on the choice of a representation for the individual data elements that compose this working-memory set. In *Xaps2* the basic working memory data structure is the *object*. In the model of Seibel's task individual objects are used to represent instances of goals, patterns of perceived stimuli, and patterns of responses to be executed.

Objects are tokens, in the sense of the classical type-token distinction; they are defined by the combination of a *type* and an *identifier*. This style of representation allows more than one instance of a type to be active and kept distinct simultaneously, a facility required for representing the goal structure of Seibel's task and for chunking stimulus and response patterns. As an example, the following object represents an instance of the goal to perform one trial of the task:[8]

(**OneTrial** Object134)

The type encodes the name of the goal, while the identifier is a unique symbol encoding the goal instance. Identifiers tend to be arbitrary symbols because they are created on the fly during execution of the model.

In addition to its two defining symbols, each object optionally has a set of *attributes*. These attributes provide a description of the object containing them. For example, the description of a goal includes a statement of its current STATUS—should we *Start* fulfilling the goal, or is it already *Done*. When the relevant attributes, and their values, are added to the above goal instance, the object looks like

(**OneTrial** Object134 [INITIAL-LOCATION *0.99*] [STATUS *Done*])

The object has two attributes: INITIAL-LOCATION, which tells us to start looking for stimulus patterns at location *0.99*, and STATUS, which tells us that this particular goal instance is *Done*. The type and identifier are *definitional* characteristics of an object in that changing either of them creates a new object. In contrast, the values of attributes can be changed as needed, such as when the STATUS of a goal changes, without affecting the identity of the object.

An important (and unusual) aspect of the *Xaps2* working memory representation is that an attribute may in fact have more than one value represented for it at the same time. Each reflects a *proposed* value for the attribute. Parallel execution of productions often results in two productions simultaneously asserting different values for the same attribute of an object. This conflict is resolved by allowing both (or all) of the proposed values to be placed in working memory. The final selection of which value to employ is made on the basis of accumulated evidence about the choices.

Augmenting the previous example with the appropriate additional values yields the full symbolic representation of the object:

(**OneTrail** Object134
[INITIAL-LOCATION *0.99 None 0.0 0.36*]
[STATUS *Done Initialize Object138 Object144 OnePattern Start*])

Up to this point working memory has been described as a totally symbolic structure consisting of a set of objects. What has been ignored is the active *competition* for attention that occurs among these symbols. Attention is modeled by associating an *activation* value with each type, identifier, and value. This is simply a real number in the range $[-1, 1]$. A positive value indicates active presence in working memory, a negative value indicates *inhibition* of the item, and a zero value is equivalent to absence from working memory. Activation values in the range $[-0.0001, 0.0001]$ are subthreshold and assumed to be zero.

Although types, identifiers, and values all have activation levels, they do not directly compete with each other. Instead, each competes within a limited scope: the types compete with each other, the identifiers compete with each other within each type, and the values compete with each other within each attribute of each object. The rule is that competition occurs between two symbols if and only if a process of selection is possible between them.

Competition clearly occurs among the alternative values within an attribute. If we want to know the STATUS of a goal, we need to select the *best* value from the set of proposed ones. Competition also occurs between instances of the same type; for example, the model of Seibel's task must repeatedly choose one light to attend to out of all of the stimuli that make up the model's visual input. Competition between types generally involves a choice between different goals. The utility of this is currently unclear.

One place where competition is not appropriate is among attributes within an object. Attributes contain information about orthogonal dimensions of an object, so competition is not only not required, but it is actually a hindrance. An early version of *Xaps2* did include competition between attributes, but it was abandoned because of the ensuing difficulty of simultaneously maintaining the independent pieces of knowledge about an object.

Within the scope of each competition, the activation values are kept normalized by forcing the absolute values of the activations to sum to 1. The absolute values of the activations are used because of the presence of negative activations (inhibition). This concept of normalizing working memory is derived from work on associative memories (Anderson 1977). It is employed in *Xaps2* to ensure that the levels of activation in the system remain bounded. The normalization process has a number of implications for the maintenance of activation in *Xaps2*:

1. It produces a set of independent capacity limitations—one for each scope of competition. These are not fixed limits on the number of items; instead, they are limits on the amount of activation available to keep items in working memory. They impose variable limits on the number of active items.
2. It implements a form of mutual inhibition between the competing items. Which items are inhibited, and by how much, is determined dynamically as a function of the competing items.
3. It defines a saturation level (ceiling) of 1 for the activation of any item.

With activation values included (in angle brackets), the example working memory object becomes:

(**OneTrial**⟨0.1606⟩ Object134⟨1.0⟩
[INITIAL-LOCATION *0.99*⟨0.75⟩ *None*⟨0.1406⟩
0.0⟨0.0156⟩ *0.36*⟨0.0938⟩]
[STATUS *Done*⟨0.5⟩ *Initialize*⟨0.0078⟩
Object138⟨0.0313⟩ *Object144*⟨0.125⟩
OnePattern⟨0.3281⟩ *Start*⟨0.0078⟩])

For convenience we will refer to that value of an attribute that has the highest activation level as the *dominant* value of that attribute. In this object the values *0.99* and *Done* are the dominant values for the INITIAL-LOCATION and STATUS attributes, respectively.

Production Memory

Productions in *Xaps2* contain the standard components: a set of conditions which are partial specifications of objects in working memory, and a set of actions that result in changes to working memory. In addition each production has an *execution type*: **Always**, **Once**, or **Decay**. These have implications for conflict resolution and action execution and are therefore discussed in those sections. Here is the definition of a typical production along with a rough english-like paraphrase of what it does:[9]

```
(DefProd AfterOneStimulusPattern Always
  ((OnePattern =GoalIdentifier [STATUS =SubGoalIdentifier])
   (OneStimulusPattern =SubGoalIdentifier [STATUS Done]))
  →
  ((OnePattern =GoalIdentifier [STATUS MapOnePattern])))
```

If there is an instance of the **OnePattern** goal
    that is suspended while a subgoal is being pursued
  and that subgoal is an instance of the **OneStimulusPattern** goal
    that has completed (the STATUS is *Done*),
then establish a new subgoal for the **OnePattern** goal
    that is an instance of the **MapOnePattern** goal.

This production, called AfterOneStimulusPattern, is an **Always** production with two conditions and one action. Notice that conditions and actions do *not* specify activation values (or weights). The activation values in working memory are used in the production-system cycle, but productions themselves are totally symbolic. The details of the conditions and actions are discussed in the following section on the production system cycle.

The Production-System Cycle

The recognize/act production-system cycle is mapped onto a four stage cycle in *Xaps2*. Recognition consists of (1) the match, and (2) conflict resolution. Actions are performed by (3) executing the production instantiations, and (4) updating working memory. The match starts with the productions and working memory, and returns a set of legal production *instantiations* (productions with all free parameters bound). Conflict resolution takes this set of instantiations and determines which ones should be executed on the current cycle. These production instantiations are then executed, with the results being accumulated into a *preupdate* structure. This structure is then merged with working memory in the final stage, to yield the working memory for the next cycle. The following sections treat these four topics in more detail.

The Match The match is responsible for computing a candidate set of executable productions and parameters for those productions. This is accomplished by matching production conditions to objects in working memory. The conditions of all of the productions are simultaneously matched against working memory, providing one source of the parallelism required by the parallel constraint. Each condition partially specifies an object as a pattern built out of constant symbols, variables, and real-number comparison functions. The components of an object (type, identifier, attributes, and values) differ in the kinds of patterns that can be created for them.

1. **Type.** Types are specified by constant symbols only, signifying that an exact match is required. In general, variables are required only when the correct value is not known a priori, that is, when a run-time selection must be made among competing alternatives. Since types compete for attention, but dynamic selection among them is not required, variables are not needed.

2. Identifier. Identifiers are specified primarily by variables but occasionally by constant symbols. A variable can match any identifier, as long as multiple instances of the same variable match the same thing, within a single production. Identifiers are usually created dynamically by the system—as in the creation of a new goal instance—and are thus not available to existing productions. Run-time selection among identifiers is the rule. Specification of the type, and a description in terms of the object's attributes, yields the identifier of the object as the binding of a variable.

3. ATTRIBUTES. Every attribute that is specified in the condition must successfully match against the object in working memory, but the reverse is not true. There may be attributes in the object that are not specified in the condition. This allows conditions to partially specify objects by describing only known attributes. When an attribute is specified, it is always a constant symbol. Variables are not allowed because, as with types, attribute names are known when productions are created. Searching for a value when the attribute is unknown is thus disallowed in the match.

4. *Values.* Values are specified by constant symbols, variables, and real-number comparison functions. The specification is matched only against the dominant value of the attribute. Many values can be proposed for each attribute, but the match can see an object in only one way at a time (according to its dominant values). This mechanism enables productions

to perform a selection of the "best" value for each attribute. If the pattern for a value is *negated*, the match succeeds only if *no* successful match is found for the pattern. Again, only the dominant values are involved in the determination.

The process of matching the condition side of a production to working memory produces *instantiations* of the production. An instantiation consists of all of the information required to execute the actions of a production: the production name, bindings for all of the variables in the production, and an activation value. More than one instantiation can be generated for a production through different combinations of bindings to the variables. For an instantiation to be generated, each condition must be successfully matched to some positively activated object in working memory. As with values of attributes, whole conditions can be negated, signifying that the match succeeds only if no successful match is found for the condition.

The function of the first two components of an instantiation—the production name and variable bindings—should be obvious; they determine which actions to execute, and what values will be passed as parameters to those actions. The functions of the activation value are less obvious: it establishes an ordering on the instantiations of a single production (used in conflict resolution), and it provides activation values for the results of the production's action. The value is computed by first calculating an activation value for the match of each condition and then combining them into a single value. The combination function has been tuned so that it gives preference to large condition sides with well-matched conditions (highly activated condition matches). Favoring large condition sides is analogous to the special-case conflict resolution strategy in the *Ops* languages. The computation is the sum of the condition activations divided by the square root of the number of conditions. This computation is half way between summing the activations, emphasizing the number of conditions, and taking the average, emphasizing the activation of the condition matches. Negated conditions have no effect on this computation.

The activation of a condition match is computed from (1) the working-memory activation of the object matched by the condition and (2) the *goodness-of-fit* of the object's description (in terms of its attributes) to the partial description specified by the condition. The first component, the activation of the working-memory object, is defined to be the product of the activations of its type and its identifier. The choice of multiplicative combination (as opposed to additive or some other scheme) is somewhat ad hoc. It was chosen because it causes the sum of the activations of all of the objects in a type to equal the activation of the type. Object134 has an activation of 0.1606 ($= 0.1606 \times 1.0$).

The goodness-of-fit of the match is determined by how well the values of the object's attributes are fit by the patterns in the condition. When the values of an attribute are defined on a *nominal* scale (i.e., they are symbolic), the match must be all-or-none, so a successful match is a perfect match (assigned a value of 1.0). When the values are defined on a *ratio* scale (i.e, a real number), a more sophisticated partial match is possible (this is the real-number match alluded to earlier). The pattern for such a value specifies the *expected* value, and an *interval* around the expected value in which the match is considered to have succeeded. The goodness-of-fit is perfect (1.0) for the expected value and decreases monotonically to threshold (0.0001) at the edge of the interval:

$$Activation = e^{-9.21[(value - expected)/interval]^2}. \tag{5.8}$$

This partial match can be symmetric, with the match interval defined on both sides of the expected value, or one sided (just greater than or just less than). Though this partial matching mechanism was added to *Xaps2* to model the topological space in which Seibel's task is defined, its utility is definitely not limited to just this task.

The total goodness-of-fit measure is the product of the measures for each of the attributes in the condition. The activation of the condition match can then be defined as the product of this measure and the activation of the working-memory object. No deep justification will be attempted for this scheme; it is enough that it is one possible mechanism and that it has proven more tractable in practice than the alternatives that have been tried.

To make this whole mechanism more concrete, consider as an example the match of the following condition to Object134:

If there is an instance of the **OneTrial** goal
  that has an INITIAL-LOCATION > 0.7 (within 1.0).

In this condition the type is specified by the constant symbol **OneTrial**, and the identifier is specified as a variable (signified by an equals sign before the name of the variable) named Identifier. These both match successfully, so the activation of the object is 0.1606 (as computed before). There is only one attribute specified, so its goodness-of-fit is simply multiplied by 0.1606 to get the activation of the condition. The value is specified by the condition as a one-sided (greater-than) real-number comparison with the interval for a successful match set to 1.0. The expected value (0.7) is compared with the dominant value of the INITIAL-LOCATION attribute (0.99), yielding a goodness of fit of 0.4609 (from equation 5.8). The activation for this match is thus 0.0740 ($= 0.1606 \times 0.4609$).

Conflict Resolution Conflict resolution selects which of the instantiations generated by the match should be fired on a cycle. This is done by using rules to eliminate unwanted instantiations. The first rule performs a thresholding operation:

- Eliminate any instantiation with an activation value lower than 0.0001.

The second rule is based on the hypothesis that productions are a limited resource:

- Eliminate all but the most highly activated instantiation for each production.

This rule is similar to the special case and working-memory recency rules in the *Ops* languages. It allows the selection of the most focussed (activated) object from a set of alternatives. Following the execution of these conflict-resolution rules, there is at most one instantiation remaining for each production. While this eliminates within-production parallelism, between-production parallelism has not been restricted. It is possible for one instantiation of every production to be simultaneously executing. This provides a second locus of the parallelism required by the parallel constraint.

What happens next depends on the execution types of the productions that generated the instantiations:

1. Instantiations of **Always** productions are always fired.

2. Instantiations of **Decay** productions are always fired, but the activation of the instantiation is cut in half each time the identical instantiation fires on successive cycles. A change in the instantiation occurs when one of the variable bindings is altered. This causes the activation to be immediately restored to its full value.

3. Instantiations of **Once** productions are fired only on the first cycle in which the instantiation would otherwise be eligible. This is a form of refractory inhibition.

Standard *Xaps2* productions are of execution type **Always**, and nearly all of the productions in the model are of this type. **Decay** productions have found limited use as a resettable clock, while no productions of execution type **Once** have been employed.

Production Execution Following conflict resolution, all of the instantiations still eligible are fired in parallel, resulting in the execution of the productions' actions. Each production may execute one or more actions, providing a third type of parallelism in the architecture. The actions look like conditions; they are partial specifications of working-memory objects. Execution of an action results in the creation of a fully specified version of the object. Variables in the action are replaced by the values bound to those variables during the match, and new symbols are created as requested by the action.

Unlike the *Ops* languages, actions only cause modifications to working memory; they are *not* a means by which the model can communicate with the outside world. Communication is an explicit part of the task model. Actions modify working memory in an indirect fashion. The effects of all of the actions on one cycle are accumulated into a single data structure representing the updates to be made to working memory. The actual updating occurs in the next (and final) stage of the production system cycle (described in the following section).

The first step in creating the pre-update structure is to assign activation levels to the components of the objects asserted by the production actions. The identifier of the objects, and all of the values asserted for attributes, are assigned an activation level equal to the activation of the production instantiation asserting them. This allows activation to flow through the system under the direction of productions—like *Hpsa77* (Newell 1980) and *Caps* (Thibadeau, Just, and Carpenter 1982)—as opposed to the undirected flow employed by spreading-activation models (Anderson 1976). No good scheme has been developed for assigning activation to the type; currently, it is just given a fixed activation of 1.0. The activation levels can be made negative by inhibiting either the whole object, or a specific value. This is analogous to the negation of conditions (and values) during the match.

If the same object is asserted by more than one action, the effects are accumulated into a single representation of the object: the type activation is set to the same fixed constant of 1.0, the identifier activations are summed and assigned as the identifier activation, and all of the activations of the same value (of the same attribute) are summed and assigned as the activation of that value. This aggregation solves the problem of synchronizing simultaneous modifications of working memory. Activation and inhibition are commutative, allowing the actions to be executed in any order without changing the result. The same is not true of the operations of insertion and deletion, as used in the *Ops* languages.

After the actions have been aggregated, any external stimuli to the system are added into this structure. External stimuli are objects that come from outside of the production system, such as the lights in Seibel's task. These stimuli are inserted into the preupdate structure just as if they were the results of production actions. An activation value of 0.01 is used for them. This level is high enough for the stimuli to affect the system and low enough for internally generated objects to be able to dominate them.

Following the inclusion of stimuli, the preupdate structure is normalized (just as if it were the working memory) and used to update the current working-memory state. Normalization of the preupdate structure allows for the control of the relative weights of the new information (the preupdate structure) and the old information (working memory).

Updating of Working Memory The updates to working memory could be used simply as a replacement for the old working memory (as in Joshi 1978), but that would result in working memory being peculiarly memoryless. By combining the preupdate structure with the current working memory, we get a system that is sensitive to new information, but remembers the past, for at least a short time. Many combination rules (e.g., adding the two structures together) are possible, and many were experimented with in *Xaps*. In *Xaps2* the two are simply averaged together. This particular choice was made because it interacts most easily with the lack of refractoriness in production firing. The updates can be thought of as specifying some *desired* state to which the productions are trying to drive working memory. Repetitive firing of the same set of production instantiations results in working memory asymptotically approaching the desired state. Any weighted sum of the new and the old (with the weights summing to 1) would yield similar results, with change being either slower or faster. Averaging (equal weights of 0.5) was chosen because it is a reasonable null assumption.

Anything that is in one of the states being combined but not the other is assumed to be there with an activation value of 0.0. Thus, ignoring normalization, items not currently being asserted by productions (i.e., not in the preupdate structure) exponentially decay to zero, while asserted items exponentially approach their asserted activation levels. This applies to inhibited as well as activated items—inhibition decays to zero if it is not continually reasserted.

Averaging the two working-memory states preserves the total activation, modulo small threshold effects, so the effects of normalization are minimal when it is employed with this combination rule. It has a noticeable effect only when no item within the scope of the normalization is being asserted by a production. Without normalization, all of the items would decay to zero. With normalization this decay is reversed so that the activations of the items once again sum to 1. The result is that the activations of the items remain unchanged. Basically, items stick around as long as they have no active competition. Old items that have competition from new items will decay away.

One consequence of the gradual updating of working memory is that it often takes more than one cycle to achieve a desired effect. This typically happens when the dominant value of an attribute is being changed. Addition of new attributes can always be accomplished in one cycle, but modifying old ones may take longer. It is essential that knowledge of the desired change remain available until the change has actually been made. In fact some form of test production is frequently required to detect when the change has been completed, before allowing processing to continue.

5.5 The Initial Performance Model

The chunking theory has been applied to Seibel's task, yielding a model that improves its performance with practice. Not covered by this model is the initial learning of a correct method for the task. Our future plans include extending the chunking theory to the domain of method acquisition, but until then, the model must be initialized with a correct method for performing the task. We consider only a single method, based on the algorithm at the end of section 5.2, though subjects exhibit a range of methods. This method is straightforward but slow—efficiency comes from chunking.

The algorithm is implemented as a hierarchy of five goals (figure 5.10). Each goal is a working-memory type, and each goal instance is an object of the relevant type. In addition to the goal-types there are two types representing the model's interfaces with the outside world, one at the stimulus end and the other at the response end. We will start with a description of these interfaces and then plunge into the details of the model's internal goal hierarchy.

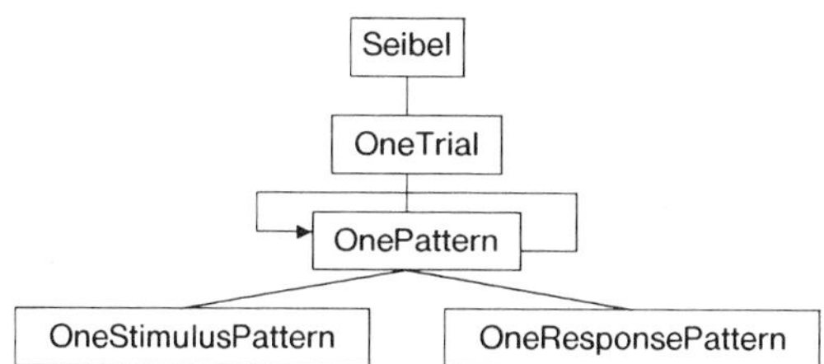

Figure 5.10
The model's goal hierarchy for Seibel's task

Interfacing with the Outside World

The model interacts with the outside world through two two-dimensional Euclidean spaces. These spaces are defined in terms of object-centered coordinates. One space, the *stimulus* space, represents the information received by the model as to the location of the lights within the stimulus array. The other space, the *response* space, represents the information that the model transmits to the motor system.

The locations of objects within these spaces are specified by relative x, y coordinates. The exact coordinate system used is not critical, but this particular one has proved to be convenient. The use of rectangular coordinates allows left-to-right traversal across the lights to be accomplished by just increasing x. With relative coordinates, the left (top) edge of the space is 0.0, and the right (bottom) edge is 1.0. Since the buttons and lights in the task have been arranged so as to maximize the compatibility of their locations, using the same set of relative coordinates for the two spaces makes trivial the job of mapping stimulus locations into response locations.

The Stimulus Space

The stimulus space is a rectangle just bounding the total array of lights. To the model this array appears as a set of objects representing the lights (both *On* and *Off*). A typical *On*-light looks like (ignoring activations):

(**External-Stimulus** Object0012 [COMPONENT-PATTERN *On*]
[SPATIAL-PATTERN *One*]
[MINIMUM-X *0.21*] [MAXIMUM-X *0.36*]
[MINIMUM-Y *0.00*] [MAXIMUM-Y *0.30*])

All stimuli have the same type (**External-Stimulus**), but the identifier is unique to this light on this trial. Productions must match the object by a description of it, rather than by its name.

A total of six attributes are used to describe the stimulus object. Two of the attributes (COMPONENT-PATTERN and SPATIAL-PATTERN) specify the pattern represented by the object. The particular stimulus object shown here represents just a single *On*-light, but stimulus objects can represent patterns of arbitrary complexity (e.g., an arrangement of multiple lights). The attribute COMPONENT-PATTERN specifies what kind of objects make up the pattern—limited to *On* and *Off* (lights) for this task. The other attribute, SPATIAL-PATTERN, specifies the spatial arrangement of those components. The value *One* given in object Object0012 signifies that the object consists of one *On*-light and nothing else. This single value suffices for the initial performance model, but others are created when new chunks are built.

The remaining four attributes (MINIMUM-X, MAXIMUM-X, MINIMUM-Y, and MAXIMUM-Y) define the *bounding box* of the stimulus pattern. The bounding box is a rectangle just large enough to enclose the stimulus. It is specified by its minimum and maximum x and y coordinates. For example, object Object0012 is flush against the top of the stimulus space and a little left of center.

We make the simplifying assumption that the entire array of lights is constantly within the model's "visual field." This cannot be literally true for our subjects because of the large visual angle subtended by the display (16°) but was more true for Seibel's subjects who worked with a display covering 7° of arc. Because the model is assumed to be staring at the lights at all times during performance of the task, the stimulus objects are inserted into working memory on every cycle of the production system (see the previous section for how this is done).

The Response Space The response space is constructed analogously to the stimulus space; it is a rectangle just bounding the array of buttons. This is a response space (as opposed to a stimulus space) because the objects in it represent patterns of modifications to be made to the environment, rather than patterns of stimuli perceived in the environment. Objects in this space represent locations at which the model is going to press (or not press) the buttons. The fingers are not explicitly modeled; it is assumed that some other portion of the organism enables finger movement according to the combination of location and action.

Response objects look much like stimulus objects. For example, the response object corresponding to stimulus object Object0012 might look like:

(**External-Response** Object0141 [COMPONENT-PATTERN *Press*]
[SPATIAL-PATTERN *One*]
[MINIMUM-X *0.3*] [MAXIMUM-X *0.36*]
[MINIMUM-Y *0.0*] [MAXIMUM-Y *0.2*]

The only differences are the type (**External-Response**), the identifier, which is unique to this instance of this response, and the value of COMPONENT-PATTERN, which is *Press* rather than *On*.

Response objects are created dynamically by the model as they are needed. Once they are created, response objects hang around in working memory until competition from newer ones causes them to drop out.

The Control Structure: A Goal Hierarchy

The control structure imposed on the *Xaps2* architecture is that of a goal hierarchy. This control structure is totally serial at the level of the goal. Information about proposed subgoals and suspended supergoals can coexist with the processing of a goal instance, but only one such instance can be actively pursued at a time. The choice of this tightly controlled structure is not forced by the nature of the architecture. Instead, it came from the following three motivations:

1. The control structure provides the bottleneck required by the bottleneck constraint. Though this satisfies the constraint, it does so only in a weak sense because it is not an architectural limitation. This contrasts with *Hpsa77* (Newell 1980), in which the mechanism of variable binding creates a structural bottleneck in the architecture.

2. The bottleneck is only across goals, not within goals. During the processing of goal instances, productions are free to execute in parallel. The parallel constraint is therefore still met. In addition the cognitive-parallelism constraint is met; goals are employed all through the performance system, so the locus of parallelism is not limited to just the sensory and motor components.

3. Complicated execution paths (e.g., iterative loops) are difficult to construct in loosely controlled systems. While such systems may be logically adequate, covincing activation-based control schemes to loop, solely on the basis of activation values, has proved difficult to accomplish.

The first requirement of a system that employs a goal hierarchy is a representation for the goals. As stated earlier, each goal is represented as an object type, and a goal instance is represented as an object with a unique identifier. Object134 represents a typical goal instance—the goal name is **OneTrial**, and the identifier is Object134. Because goals can be distinguished by their types, and multiple instances of the same goal can be distinguished by their identifiers, it is possible to maintain information about a number of goal instances simultaneously.

The goal hierarchy is processed in a depth-first fashion, so the second requirement is a *stack* in which the current state of execution can be represented. In *Xaps2* working memory does not behave as a stack; more recent objects will tend to be more highly activated, but this is not sufficient for the implementation of a goal hierarchy. The primary difficulty involves simultaneously keeping the goals in the stack active and maintaining the proper ordering among them. If the stack is just left alone, subgoal activity causes the objects in the stack to decay. The oldest objects may very well decay right out of working memory. If the stack is continually refreshed by reassertion of its elements into working memory, then the ordering, which depends on activation levels, will be disturbed. Some variation on this scheme may still work, but we have instead pursued a more symbolic representation of the goal stack.

Each goal instance has a STATUS attribute. Together, the STATUS attributes (i.e., the dominant value of the STATUS attributes) of the active goal instances completely determine the control state of the model. Three common STATUS values are *Start*, *Started*, and *Done*. *Start* means that the goal is being initialized; *Started* signifies that initialization is complete and that the goal is being pursued; and *Done* signifies that the goal has completed. The stack is implemented by pointing to the current subgoal of a suspended supergoal via the STATUS attribute of the supergoal. Notice that any goal instance whose STATUS is the identifier of some other goal instance must be suspended by definition because its STATUS is no longer *Started*. A goal can therefore be interrupted at any time by a production that changes its STATUS from *Started* to some other value. Execution of the goal resumes when the STATUS is changed back to *Started*.

Activating a subgoal of a currently active goal is a multistep operation. The first step is for the goal to signify that it wants to activate a subgoal of a particular type. This is accomplished by changing the STATUS of the goal to the type of the subgoal that should be started. This enables the productions that create the new subgoal instance. Four tasks must be performed whenever a new subgoal is started:

1. The current goal instance must be blocked from further execution until the subgoal is completed.

2. A new instance of the subgoal must be created. This is a new object with its own unique identifier.

3. The parameters, if any, must be passed from the current goal instance to the subgoal instance.

4. A link, implementing the stack, must be created between the current goal instance and the new subgoal instance.

As noted earlier, the supergoal is suspended as soon as the desire for the subgoal is expressed (task 1). Changing the STATUS of the current goal instance effectively blocks further effort on the goal. The other three tasks are performed by a set of three productions. Because the type of an object (in this case the name of the goal) cannot be matched by a variable, a distinct set of productions is required for each combination of goal and subgoal. One benefit of this restriction is that the goal-instance creation productions can perform parameter passing from goal to subgoal as part of the creation of the new instance. The first production of the three performs precisely these two tasks: (2) subgoal creation and (3) parameter passing. Schematically, these productions take the following form:

Production schema Start⟨Goal name⟩:
If the current goal instance has a subgoal name as its STATUS,
then generate a new instance of the subgoal with STATUS *Start*
(parameters to the subgoal are passed as other attributes).

When such a production executes, it generates a new symbol to be used as the identifier of the object representing the goal instance. The second production builds a stack link from a goal to its subgoal (task 4), by copying this new identifier into the STATUS attribute of the current goal instance. This must be done after the first production fires, because this production must examine the newly created object to determine the identifier of the new goal instance:

Production schema CreateStackLink⟨Goal name⟩:
If the current goal instance has a subgoal name as its STATUS
and there is an active object of that type with STATUS *Start*,
then replace the goal's STATUS with the subgoal's identifier.

The third production checks that all four tasks have been correctly performed before enabling work on the subgoal:

Production schema Started⟨Goal name⟩:
If the current goal instance has a subgoal identifier as its STATUS
and that subgoal has STATUS *Start*,
then change the STATUS of the subgoal to *Started.*

At first glance it would appear that the action of this third production could just be added to the second production. In most production systems this would work fine, but in *Xaps2* it doesn't. One production would be changing the values of two attributes at once. Since there is no guarantee that both alterations would happen in one cycle, a race condition would ensue. If the subgoal is *Started* before the stack link is created, the link will never be created. Generally, in *Xaps2* separate productions are required to make a modification and test that the modification has been performed.

It generally takes one cycle of the production system to express the desire for a subgoal and three cycles to activate the subgoal (one cycle for each of the three productions), for a total of four cycles of overhead for each new subgoal. This number may be slightly larger when any of the modifications requires more than one cycle to be completed.

Goals are terminated by *test* productions that sense appropriate conditions and change the STATUS of the goal instance to *Done*. If the subgoal is to return a result, then an intermediate STATUS of *Result* is generated by the test productions, and additional productions are employed to return the result to the parent goal and change the STATUS of the subgoal instance to *Done*, once it has checked that the result has actually been returned. The standard way of returning a result in *Xaps2* is to assert it as the new value for some attribute of the parent goal instance. It may take several cycles before it becomes the dominant value, so the production that changes the STATUS to *Done* waits until the result has become the dominant value before firing. Terminating a goal instance generally requires one cycle, plus between zero and four cycles to return a result.

The parent goal senses that the subgoal has completed by looking for an object of the subgoal type whose identifier is identical to the parent's STATUS, and whose own STATUS is *Done*. Once this condition is detected, the parent goal is free to request the next subgoal or to continue in any way that it sees fit.

The mechanism described so far solves the problem of maintaining the order of stacked goal instances. However, it does not prevent the objects representing these instances from decaying out of working memory. This is resolved by an additional production for each goal-subgoal combination that passes activation from the goal type to the subgoal type. The topmost goal type passes activation to itself and downwards to the next level. All of the other goal types simply pass activation to their subgoal types. These productions fire on every cycle.

Keeping the types (goals) active ensures that at least one instance of each goal can be retained on the stack. Multiple instances of the same goal, such as would be generated by recursion, would result in lossage of instances through competition. In order for recursion to work, either the architecture would have to be changed to fire all instantiations of a production (one goal instance per instantiation) instead of only the "best," or a separate production would be required for each instance (which must be created dynamically, as are the goal instances). The five goal types are discussed in the following sections.

*The **Seibel** Goal* Seibel is the top level goal type for the task. It enters the working memory as a stimulus from the outside world (see the previous section for a discussion of stimuli), corresponding to a request to perform the task. The Seibel goal type is used solely to keep the **OneTrial** goal active.

*The **OneTrial** Goal* A desire for a new instance of the **OneTrial** goal is generated exogenously each time the stimulus array is changed, that is, once each trial. Both this desire, and the new stimulus array are inserted into working memory as stimuli. The Seibel goal could have detected the presence of a new stimulus array and generated the **OneTrial** goal directly, but we have taken this simpler approach for the time being because we wanted to focus our attention on within-trial processing.

The **OneTrial** goal implements the following aspects of the performance algorithm (section 5.2):

Focus a point to the left of the leftmost light.
While there is an *On*-light to the right of the focal point **Do**
⟨Goal **OnePattern**⟩

The point of focus is modeled as the value of an attribute (INITIAL-LOCATION) of the **OneTrial** goal instance. This should be thought of as the focus of attention within the visual field, rather than as the locus of eye fixation. Setting the initial focus takes two cycles. First the goal's STATUS is changed to *Initialize*, and then a production that triggers off of that STATUS sets the value of the INITIAL-LOCATION to *0.0* (the left edge of the stimulus space).

The entire body of the **While** loop has been moved inside of a single goal (**OnePattern**), so the loop is implemented by repeatedly starting up **OnePattern** goal instances. The first instance is created when a test production has determined that the INITIAL-LOCATION has been set. Subsequent instances are established whenever the active **OnePattern** instance has completed. The focal point gets updated between iterations because the **OnePattern** goal returns as its result the right edge of the light pattern that it processed. This result is assigned to the INITIAL-LOCATION attribute.

What we have described so far is an infinite loop; new instances of the OnePattern goal are generated endlessly. This is converted into a **While** loop with the addition of a single production of the following form:

Production DoneOneTrial:
If there is a **OneTrial** goal with STATUS **OnePattern**
and there is no *On*-light to the right of its INITIAL-LOCATION,
then the **OneTrial** goal is *Done*.

The test for an *On*-light to the right of the INITIAL-LOCATION is performed by a one-sided (greater-than) real-number match to the MINIMUM-X values of the stimulus objects. The expected value is the INITIAL-LOCATION, and the interval is 1.0. The match will succeed if there is another light to the right, and fail otherwise. The preceding production therefore has this test negated.

The reaction time for the model on Seibel's task is computed from the total number of cycles required to complete (STATUS of *Done*) one instance of the **OneTrial** goal. Experimentally this has been determined to be a fixed overhead of approximately 13 cycles per trial, plus approximately 31 cycles for each *On*-light—an instance of the **OnePattern** goal (see section 5.7). These numbers, and those for the following goals, are from the full performance model, which is the initial performance model with some additional overhead for the integration of chunking into the control structure (section 5.6).

*The **OnePattern** Goal* The **OnePattern** goals control the four steps inside the **While** loop of the performance strategy:

Locate the *On*-light.
Map the light location into the location of the button under it.
Press the button.
Focus the right edge of the light.

Two of these steps (**Map** and **Focus**) are performed directly by the goal instance, and two (**Locate** and **Press**) are performed by subgoals (**OneStimulusPattern** and **OneResponsePattern**).

At the start a typical instance of the **OnePattern** goal looks like[10]

(**OnePattern** Object45 [INITIAL-LOCATION *0.0*])

The first step is to locate the next stimulus pattern to process. This is accomplished by a subgoal, **OneStimulusPattern**, which receives as a parameter the INITIAL-LOCATION and returns the attributes of the first *On*-light to the right of the INITIAL-LOCATION. These attributes are added to the **OnePattern** instance, to yield an object like:

(**OnePattern** Object45
[INITIAL-LOCATION *0.0*]
[STIMULUS-COMPONENT-PATTERN *On*]
[STIMULUS-SPATIAL-PATTERN *One*]
[STIMULUS-MINIMUM-X *0.21*] [STIMULUS-MAXIMUM-X *0.36*]
[STIMULUS-MINIMUM-Y *0.00*] [STIMULUS-MAXIMUM-Y *0.30*])

The mapping between stimulus and response is currently wired directly into the performance algorithm. This is sufficient but not essential for the current model. In some follow-up work we are investigating the relationship between this model and stimulus-response compatibility. In these systems the mapping is performed in a separate subgoal. This provides flexibility, and the ability to perform a considerable amount of processing during the mapping.

The mapping employed in the current model is a minimal one; all that is required is turning the stimulus attributes into response attributes and changing the COMPONENT-PATTERN from *On* to *Press*. This mapping is performed by a single production to yield an object of the following form:

(**OnePattern** Object45
[INITIAL-LOCATION *0.0*]
[STIMULUS-COMPONENT-PATTERN *On*]
[STIMULUS-SPATIAL-PATTERN *One*]

[STIMULUS-MINIMUM-X *0.21*] [STIMULUS-MAXIMUM-X *0.36*]
[STIMULUS-MINIMUM-Y *0.00*] [STIMULUS-MAXIMUM-Y *0.30*])
[RESPONSE-COMPONENT-PATTERN *Press*]
[RESPONSE-SPATIAL-PATTERN *One*]
[RESPONSE-MINIMUM-X *0.21*] [RESPONSE-MAXIMUM-X *0.36*]
[RESPONSE-MINIMUM-Y *0.00*] [RESPONSE-MAXIMUM-Y *0.30*])

These response parameters are passed to a subgoal, **OneResponse Pattern**, that converts them into a new response object. Following completion of this subgoal, the **OnePattern** goal terminates, passing the coordinate of the right edge of the selected stimulus pattern as its result (to be used as the focal point for the next search).

Not counting the time to perform its two subgoals, a typical instance of this goal requires 12 cycles of the production system, including the overhead involved in starting and finishing the goal.

*The **OneStimulusPattern** Goal* The **OneStimulusPattern** goal is responsible for finding the next *On*-light to the right of the INITIAL-LOCATION, which it receives as a parameter from its parent **OnePattern** goal. This selection is made by a single production employing the same type of one-sided real-number match used to determine when the trial has completed. It looks for an *On*-light to the right of the INITIAL-LOCATION for which there are no other *On*-lights between it and the INITIAL-LOCATION. (Recall that *Off*-lights are ignored in this algorithm.) As long as there is some *On*-light to the right of the INITIAL-LOCATION, it will be found. If there is more than one, the closest one to the INITIAL-LOCATION is selected. On completion, the goal instance returns the values of the six attributes describing the selected stimulus pattern to the parent **OnePattern** goal. A typical instance of this goal requires nine cycles of the production system, including the overhead involved in starting and finishing the goal, though it may be higher.

*The **OneResponsePattern** Goal* Conceptually the **OneResponsePattern** goal is the mirror image of the **OneStimulusPattern** goal. Given the parameters of a response object, its task is to create a new response object with those values. We assume that the motor system automatically latches on to response objects as they are created, so creation of the object is the last step actually simulated in the model. A typical instance of this goal requires ten cycles of the production system, including the overhead involved in starting and finishing the goal, though it may be higher.

5.6 The Chunking Process

The initial performance model executes an instance of the **OnePattern** goal for each *On*-light in the stimulus array. Patterns consisting of a single *On*-light are *primitive* patterns for the model; they are at the smallest grain at which the perceptual system is being modeled. Larger, or *higher-level*, patterns can be built out of combinations of these primitive patterns. For example, a single higher-level pattern could represent the fact that four particular lights are all *On*. The same holds true for response patterns, where the primitive patterns are single key presses. Higher-level response patterns that specify a combination of key presses can be built out of these primitive response patterns.

According to the chunking theory of learning, chunks represent patterns experienced in the task environment. They improve performance because it is more efficient to deal with a single large pattern than a set of smaller patterns. The remainder of this section describes the design of this chunking process—how chunks represent environmental patterns and how they are acquired from task performance. As currently constituted, this is an error-free design; chunks are always acquired and used correctly. Rather than model errors directly by a bug-laden final model, the problem of errors is tackled by discussing the types of errors simple versions of the model naturally make, and the mechanisms implemented to ensure that these errors do not occur.

The Representation of Chunks

We propose that a chunk consists of three components: (1) a stimulus pattern, (2) a response pattern, and (3) a connection between the two. In contrast to systems that treat chunks as static data structures, we consider a chunk to be an active structure. A chunk is the productions that process it. The obvious implementation of this proposal involves the creation of one production per chunk. The production would have one condition for each primitive component of the stimulus pattern and one action for each primitive component of the response pattern. The connection is implemented directly by the production's condition-action link. This implementation is straightforward enough, but it is inadequate for the following reasons:

1. These productions violate the control structure of the model by linking stimuli to responses directly, without passing through the intervening

bottleneck. If such productions could be created, then it should also be possible to create the optimal algorithm of ten parallel productions, one for each light-button combination.

2. The chunking mechanism implied by these productions is nonhierarchical; a chunk is always defined directly in terms of the set of primitive patterns that it covers.

3. The direct connection of stimulus to response implies that it is impossible for the cognitive system to intervene. The mapping of stimulus to response is wired in and unchangeable.

These problems can all be solved by implementing each chunk as three productions, one for each component. The first production *encodes* a set of stimulus patterns into a higher-level stimulus pattern, the second production *decodes* a higher-level response pattern into a set of smaller response patterns, and the third production indirectly *connects* the higher-level stimulus pattern to the higher-level response pattern.

For the acquisition of a chunk to improve the performance of the model, these productions must help overcome the bottleneck caused by the model's inability to process more than one pattern at a time. This bottleneck can be precisely located within the **OnePattern** goal—between the termination of the **OneStimulusPattern** goal and the beginning of the **OneResponsePattern** goal. According to the encoding constraint, encoding must occur before the bottleneck, that is, before the **OneStimulusPattern** goal completes and selects the pattern to use. Likewise the decoding constraint implies that decoding must occur after the bottleneck, that is, after the start of the **OneResponsePattern** goal. The connection production must appear somewhere in between.

The model must execute an instance of the **OnePattern** goal for each pattern processed—approximately 31 production-system cycles. If there are four *On*-lights in the stimulus, then the initial performance model requires four iterations, or about 124 cycles. If one pattern can cover all four *On*-lights, only one iteration is required, cutting the time down to 31 cycles. If instead we had two patterns of two *On*-lights each, it would take two iterations, or about 62 cycles. Just as the chunking theory of learning proposes, performance can be improved through the acquisition of patterns experienced during task performance.

For simplicity, the current system works only with chunks that are built out of exactly two subchunks. This is not a limitation on the theory; it is merely the simplest assumption that still lets us investigate most of the interesting phenomena. The remainder of this section describes how the three components of a chunk are represented and how they are integrated into the model's control structure. We delay until the following section the description of how a chunk is built.

The Encoding Component The initial performance model perceives the world only in terms of primitive stimulus patterns consisting of either a single *On*-light or a single *Off*-light. The encoding component of a chunk examines the currently perceived patterns, as reflected by the contents of working memory, and, based on what it sees, may assert a new higher-level stimulus pattern. When this new object appears in working memory, it can form the basis for the recognition of even higher-level patterns. The entire set of encoding productions thus performs a hierarchical parsing process on the stimuli.

Encoding is a goal-free data-driven process in which productions fire whenever they perceive their pattern. This process is asynchronous with the goal-directed computations that make up most of the system. This works because the perceived patterns interact with the rest of the system through a filter of goal-directed selection productions. As an example, the selection production in the previous section chooses one pattern from the stimulus space based on its location and COMPONENT-PATTERN. In essence we are proposing that the traditional distinction between parallel data-driven *perception* and serial goal-directed cognition be modified to be a distinction between parallel data-driven *chunk encoding* and serial goal-directed cognition. In the remainder of this section we describe the details of this chunk-encoding process.

Representation of Higher-Level Stimulus Patterns All stimulus patterns, be they primitive or higher-level, are represented as working-memory objects of type **External-Stimulus**. For purposes of comparison, here are some objects representing a primitive pattern, and a higher-level pattern:

(**External-Stimulus** Primitive-Example
[COMPONENT-PATTERN *On*]
[SPATIAL-PATTERN *One*]
[MINIMUM-X *0.21*][MAXIMUM-X *0.36*]
[MINIMUM-Y *0.00*][MAXIMUM-Y *0.30*])

(**External-Stimulus** Higher-Level-Example
[COMPONENT-PATTERN *On*]
[SPATIAL-PATTERN *Spatial-Pattern-0145*]
[MINIMUM-X *0.21*][MAXIMUM-X *0.78*]
[MINIMUM-Y *0.00*][MAXIMUM-Y *0.64*])

They are almost identical; what differs is the values of some attributes. The four attributes defining the bounding box are interpreted in the same fashion for all patterns. They always define the rectangle just bounding the pattern. For primitive chunks, this is a rectangle just large enough to contain the light. For higher-level chunks, it is the smallest rectangle that contains all of the lights in the pattern.

The COMPONENT-PATTERN of primitive patterns is always *On* or *Off*, signifying the type of light contained in the pattern. For higher-level patterns a value of *On* is interpreted to mean that all of the lights contained in the pattern are *On*. Other values are possible for higher-level patterns, but in the current task we only deal with patterns composed solely of *On*-lights. This means that the *Off*-lights are dealt with by ignoring them—not that the *Off*-lights can't be there.

The primary difference between primitive and higher-level patterns is in the value of the SPATIAL-PATTERN attribute. For primitive patterns it always has the value *One*, signifying that the entire bounding box contains just a single light. For higher-level patterns the value must indicate how many *On*-lights there are within the box and what their positions are. One alternative for representing this information is to store it explicitly in the object in terms of a pattern language. The pattern language amounts to a strong constraint on the variety of patterns that can be perceived. This is the tactic employed in most concept formation programs (e.g., Evans 1968; Mitchell, Utgoff, Nudel, and Banerji 1981). It is a powerful technique within the domain of the pattern language, but useless outside of it.

We have taken the less-constrained approach pioneered by Uhr and Vossler (1963) in which there is little to no precommitment as to the nature of the patterns to be learned. A unique symbol is created to represent each newly perceived pattern. This symbol is stored as the value of the SPATIAL-PATTERN attribute—*Spatial-Pattern-0145* in the preceding example. Instead of the meaning being determined in terms of a hard-wired pattern language, it is determined by the productions that act on the symbol. The encoding production knows to create an object with this symbol when it perceives the appropriate lower-level patterns. Likewise the connection production knows how to create the appropriate response object for this symbol. With this scheme any pattern can be represented, but other operations on patterns, such as generalization, become difficult.

Integration of the Encoding Component into the Model When the concept of chunking is added to the initial performance model, changes in the control structure are needed for the model to make use of the newly generated higher-level patterns. The initial performance model iterates through the lights by repeatedly selecting the first *On*-light to the right of the focal point and then shifting the focal point to the right of the selected light. When there are higher-level patterns, this algorithm must be modified to select the *largest* pattern that starts with the first *On*-light to the right of the focal point, while shifting the focal point to the right of the pattern's bounding box. Accomplishing this involves simply changing the selection production so that it does not care about the SPATIAL-PATTERN of the object that it selects. It then selects the most highly activated stimulus object consisting of only *On*-lights, with no other such object between it and the INITIAL-LOCATION. The largest pattern is selected because a higher-level pattern containing n components will be more highly activated than its components. If a production has n equally activated conditions, call the activation a, then its actions will be asserted with an activation level of $(\sqrt{n}) \cdot a$ (derived from $n \cdot a/\sqrt{n}$).

Originally it was intended that this selection be based solely on the match activation of the competing instantiations. The effect of size was added (via the combination of activation) to the effect of nearness to the INITIAL-LOCATION (via a real-number match). This often worked, but it did lead to omission errors in which a large pattern was preferred to a near pattern, skipping over intermediate *On*-lights without processing them. To avoid these errors, the more explicit location comparison process described in section 5.5 is currently employed.

Selection now works correctly, that is, if the encoding process has completed by the time the selection is made. Since encoding is an asynchronous, logarithmic process, determining the time of its completion is problematic. This problem is partly solved by the data-driven nature of the encoding productions. Encoding starts as soon as the stimuli become available, not just after the **OneStimulusPattern** goal has started. This head start allows encoding usually to finish in time.

For the cases when this is insufficient, a pseudoclock is implemented by the combination of an **Always** production and a **Decay** production. Encoding takes an amount of time dependent on the height of the chunk hierarchy, so waiting a fixed amount of time does not work. Instead, the clock keeps track of the time between successive assertions of new stimulus patterns by encoding productions. If it has been too long since the last new one, encoding is assumed to be done. The clock is based on the relative activation levels of two particular values of an attribute. One value remains at a moderate level; the other value is reset to a high level on cycles in which a new pattern is perceived, and decays during the remainder. When the activation of this value decays below the other value, because no new encoding productions have fired, encoding is considered to be done. This mechanism is clumsy but adequate.

The Encoding Productions Encoding productions all have the same structure, consisting of three conditions and one action. The three conditions look for the two stimulus patterns that make up the new pattern, and the absence of other *On* patterns between the two desired ones. The action creates a new object in working memory representing the appropriate higher-level pattern.

At first glance only the first two conditions would seem to be necessary, but absence of the third condition can lead to errors of omission. Suppose that an encoding production is created for a pattern consisting of a pair of *On*-lights separated by an *Off*-light. If the middle light is *Off* the next time the two lights are *On*, there is no problem. The problem occurs when all three lights are *On*. Without the third condition, the production would match and the higher-level pattern would be recognized. If that pattern is then used by the performance system, it would press the buttons corresponding to the two outer lights, and then move the focal point past the right edge of the pattern's bounding box. The middle *On*-light would never be processed, resulting in a missing key press. By adding the third condition, the pattern is not recognized unless there is no *On*-light embedded between the two subpatterns. These errors are therefore ruled out.

Let's look at a couple of concrete examples. In this first example we encode two primitive patterns (*On*-lights) separated by an *Off*-light. The relevant portion of working memory is:

(**External-Stimulus** Object0141 [COMPONENT-PATTERN *On*]
[SPATIAL-PATTERN *One*]
[MINIMUM-X *0.21*] [MAXIMUM-X *0.36*]
[MINIMUM-Y *0.00*] [MAXIMUM-Y *0.30*])
(**External-Stimulus** Object0142 [COMPONENT-PATTERN *Off*]
[SPATIAL-PATTERN *One*]
[MINIMUM-X *0.42*] [MAXIMUM-X *0.57*]
[MINIMUM-Y *0.00*] [MAXIMUM-Y *0.30*])
(**External-Stimulus** Object0143 [COMPONENT-PATTERN *On*]
[SPATIAL-PATTERN *One*]
[MINIMUM-X *0.63*] [MAXIMUM-X *0.78*]
[MINIMUM-Y *0.34*] [MAXIMUM-Y *0.64*])

Encoding the two *On*-lights yields a new higher-level stimulus pattern with a bounding box just big enough to contain the two *On*-lights; the *Off*-light is simply ignored. The COMPONENT-PATTERN remains *On*, and a new symbol is created to represent the SPATIAL-PATTERN. The object representing the pattern looks like:

(**External-Simulus** Object0144 [COMPONENT-PATTERN *On*]
[SPATIAL-PATTERN *Spatial-Pattern-0145*]
[MINIMUM-X *0.21*] [MAXIMUM-X *0.78*]
[MINIMUM-Y *0.00*] [MAXIMUM-Y *0.64*])

The production that performs this encoding operation has the form:

Production Encode1:
If there is an **External-Stimulus** object
consisting of just one *On*-light,
whose left edge is 0.21 (within 0.15), right edge is 0.36 (within 0.15),
top edge is 0.00 (within 0.30), bottom edge is 0.30 (within 0.30),
and there is an **External-Stimulus** object
consisting of just one *On*-Light,
whose left edge is 0.63 (within 0.15), right edge is 0.78 (within 0.15),
top edge is 0.34 (within 0.30), bottom edge is 0.64 (within 0.30),
and there is *No* **External-Stimulus** object
consisting of *On*-lights in any spatial pattern,
whose left edge is left of 0.63 (within 0.27),

then create a new **External-Stimulus** object
consisting of *On*-lights in configuration *Spatial-Pattern-0145*,
whose left edge is 0.21, right edge is 0.78,
top edge is 0.0, bottom edge is 0.64.

The first condition looks for an *On*-light bounded by [0.21, 0.36] horizontally, and [0.00, 0.30] vertically. The bounding box is matched by four two-sided real-number condition patterns. The lights may not always be positioned exactly as they were when the production was created, so the match is set up to succeed over a range of values (the interval of the real-number match). The sizes of the intervals are based on the notion that the accuracy required is proportional to the size of the pattern. The horizontal intervals are therefore set to the width of the pattern (0.36 − 0.21 = 0.15), and the vertical intervals are set to the height of the pattern (0.30 − 0.00 = 0.30).

The second condition works identically to the first, with only the location of the light changed. The third condition ensures that there are no intervening *On*-lights. This last condition is actually testing that no *On* pattern starts between the right edge of the first subpattern and the left edge of the second subpattern. That this works depends on the fact that the lights are being processed horizontally and that there is no horizontal overlap between adjacent lights. Currently this knowledge is built directly into the chunking mechanism, a situation that is tolerable when only one task is being explored but intolerable in a more general mechanism.

The preceding example chunked two primitive patterns together to yield a higher-level pattern, but the same technique works if the subpatterns are higher-level patterns themselves, or even if there is a mixture. In the following example a higher-level pattern is combined with a primitive pattern. Suppose the situation is the same as in the previous example, plus there is an additional *On*-light to the right. After the encoding production fires, working memory consists of the four objects mentioned earlier (three primitive ones and one higher-level one), plus the following object for the extra light:

(**External-Stimulus** Object0146 [COMPONENT-PATTERN *On*]
[SPATIAL-PATTERN *One*]
[MINIMUM-X *0.84*] [MAXIMUM-X *0.99*]
[MINIMUM-Y *0.68*] [MAXIMUM-Y *0.98*])

A higher-level pattern can be generated from this pattern and

Object0144. The new pattern covers the entire bounding box of the four lights. The encoding production for this is:

Production Encode2:
If there is an External-Stimulus object
consisting of *On*-lights in configuration *Spatial-Pattern-0145*,
whose left edge is 0.21 (within 0.57), right edge is 0.78 (within 0.57),
top edge is 0.00 (within 0.64), bottom edge is 0.64 (within 0.64),
and there is an External-Stimulus object
consisting of just one *On*-Light,
whose left edge is 0.84 (within 0.15), right edge is 0.99 (within 0.15),
top edge is 0.68 (within 0.30), bottom edge is 0.98 (within 0.30),
and there is *No* External-Stimulus object
consisting of *On*-lights in any spatial pattern,
whose left edge is left of 0.84 (within 0.06),
then create a new External-Stimulus object
consisting of *On*-lights in configuration *Spatial-Pattern-0147*,
whose left edge is 0.21, right edge is 0.99,
top edge is 0.0, bottom edge is 0.98.

As should be clear, this production is basically the same as production Encode1. The bounding boxes are appropriately changed, and the SPATIAL-PATTERN of one of the subpatterns is *Spatial-Pattern-0145*, the name for the higher-level pattern generated by production Encode1, and not *One* (signified in the productions by the phrase "consisting of just one *On*-light"). When production Encode2 fires, it creates a stimulus object of the following form:

(**External-Stimulus** Object0148 [COMPONENT-PATTERN *On*]
[SPATIAL-PATTERN *Spatial-pattern-0147*]
[MINIMUM-X *0.21*] [MAXIMUM-Y *0.99*]
[MINIMUM-Y *0.00*] [MAXIMUM-Y *0.98*])

The Decoding Component Decoding productions perform the inverse operation of encoding productions. When one matches to a higher-level pattern, it generates that pattern's two subpatterns. Because decoding must occur after the start of the **OneResponsePattern** Goal (after the bottleneck), it is defined on response patterns, rather than stimulus patterns. We assume that decoding occurs because the motor system only responds to primitive **External-Response** objects. When the response is specified by a higher-level pattern, it must be decoded down to its component primitives before the response can occur.

The entire set of decoding productions acts as a hierarchical decoding network for higher-level response patterns. Unlike encoding, decoding is initiated under goal-directed control. The **OneResponsePattern** goal's parameters describe a response pattern that is to be executed. From this description the goal builds the appropriate **External-Response** object, and decoding begins. Decoding can't begin until the goal has built this object, but once it has begun, it continues to completion without further need of direction from the goal. Integrating the decoding component into the performance model is thus trivial; whenever an object representing a higher-level response pattern is generated, the appropriate decoding productions will fire. The one complication is that, as with encoding, decoding requires a variable number of cycles to complete. The problem of determining when decoding is done is solved by the use of a second pseudoclock. In fact this mechanism is inadequate for this purpose, but the problem does not affect the execution of the remainder of the model, so the current scheme is being employed until a better alternative is devised.

The following decoding production is the analogue of production Encode2. It has one condition that matches the higher-level response pattern corresponding to the stimulus pattern generated by production Encode2, and it has two actions which generate response patterns corresponding to the two stimulus subpatterns of production Encode2. One of the sub-patterns is primitive, while the other is a higher-level pattern that must be decoded further by another production:

Production Decode2:
If there is an **External-Response** object
  consisting of *Press*-keys in configuration *Spatial-Pattern-0151*,
  whose left edge is 0.21 (within 0.78), right edge is 0.99 (within 0.78),
    top edge is 0.0 (within 0.98), bottom edge is 0.98 (within 0.98),
then create a new **External-Response** object
  consisting of *Press*-keys in configuration *Spatial-Pattern-0150*,
  whose left edge is 0.21, right edge is 0.78,
    top edge is 0.00, bottom edge is 0.64,
and create a new **External-Response** object
  consisting of just one *Press*-key,
  whose left edge is 0.84, right edge is 0.99,
    top edge is 0.68, bottom edge is 0.98.

The Connection Component A connection production links a higher-level stimulus pattern with its appropriate higher-level response pattern. The entire set of connection productions defines the *stimulus-response mapping* for the task. This mapping must occur under goal direction so that the type of mapping can vary according to the task being performed. It would not be a very adaptive model if it were locked into always responding the same way to the same stimulus.

The connection productions need to be located before the encoding component and after the decoding component—between the end of the **OneStimulusPattern** goal and the start of the **OneResponsePattern** goal. They are situated in, and under the control of, the **OnePattern** goal. This goal already contains a general mechanism for mapping the description of a primitive stimulus pattern to the description of the appropriate primitive response pattern. These descriptions are local to the **OnePattern** goal and are stored as attributes of the object representing the goal.

The connection productions extend this existing mechanism so that higher-level patterns can also be mapped. Whether a connection production fires, or the initial mechanism executes, is completely determined by the SPATIAL-PATTERN of the stimulus pattern. If it is *One*, the initial mechanism is used; otherwise, a connection production is required. Integration of the connection productions into the performance model is therefore straightforward. The following production connects a higher-level stimulus pattern with SPATIAL-PATTERN *Spatial-Pattern-0147* to the corresponding higher-level response pattern:

Production Map-Spatial-Pattern-0147:
If there is a **OnePattern** goal whose STATUS is *MapOnePattern*
  containing the description of a stimulus pattern
    of *On*-lights in configuration *Spatial-pattern-0147*,
  whose left edge is 0.21 (within 0.78), right edge is 0.99 (within 0.78),
      top edge is 0.0 (within 0.98), bottom edge is 0.98 (with 0.98),
then add the description of a response pattern
  consisting of *Press*-keys in configuration *Spatial-Pattern-0151*,
  whose left edge is 0.21, right edge is 0.99,
      top edge is 0.00, bottom edge is 0.98.

The key to making the proper connection is that the production matches to the unique SPATIAL-PATTERN specified by the stimulus pattern (*Spatial-Pattern-0147*), and generates the unique SPATIAL-PATTERN for the response pattern (*Spatial-Pattern-0151*). As an example, suppose working memory contains an object of the form:

(**OnePattern** Object131 [STATUS *MapOnePattern*]
[STIMULUS-COMPONENT-PATTERN *On*]
[STIMULUS-SPATIAL-PATTERN *Spatial-Pattern-0147*]
[STIMULUS-MINIMUM-X *0.21*] [STIMULUS-MAXIMUM-X *0.99*]
[STIMULUS-MINIMUM-Y *0.00*] [STIMULUS-MAXIMUM-Y *0.98*])

The connection production would modify this element by adding the description of the corresponding response pattern. The object would then have the form:

(**OnePattern** Object131 [STATUS *MapOnePattern*]
[STIMULUS-COMPONENT-PATTERN *On*]
[STIMULUS-SPATIAL-PATTERN *Spatial-Pattern-147*]
[STIMULUS-MINIMUM-X *0.21*] [STIMULUS-MAXIMUM-X *0.99*]
[STIMULUS-MINIMUM-Y *0.00*] [STIMULUS-MAXIMUM-Y *0.98*]
[RESPONSE-COMPONENT-PATTERN *Press*]
[RESPONSE-SPATIAL-PATTERN *Spatial-Pattern-151*]
[RESPONSE-MINIMUM-X *0.21*] [RESPONSE-MAXIMUM-X *0.99*]
[RESPONSE-MINIMUM-Y *0.00*] [RESPONSE-MAXIMUM-Y *0.98*])

The Acquisition of Chunks

Chunk acquisition is a task-independent, primitive capability of the architecture. The acquisition mechanism is therefore implemented as *Lisp* code, rather than as a set of productions within the architecture. The mechanism continually monitors the execution of the performance model and acquires new chunks from the objects appearing in working memory. It accomplishes this by building productions for the three component of the chunk. There are two principal structural alternatives for this mechanism: (1) the components can be created all at once, or (2) they can created independently. There are clear trade-offs involved.

With the all-at-once alternative the components of a chunk are all created at the same time. The primary advantage of this approach is simplicity in creating the connection component. In order to create a correct connection production, the corresponding stimulus and response SPATIAL-PATTERNS must be known. With the all-at-once alternative the SPATIAL-PATTERNS are directly available because the connection production is created concurrently with the encoding and decoding productions. With the independent alternative, making this connection is more difficult. The connection production must determine the appropriate SPATIAL-PATTERNS, even though they are denoted by distinct symbols and may not be in working memory at the time. This is difficult, but if possible, it does lead to two advantages over the all-at-once approach. First, it places only a small demand on the capacity of working memory. When the stimulus information is around, the encoding component can be created, and likewise with the decoding component. All of the information does not have to be active at once. Second, transfer of training is possible at a smaller grain size. With the all-at-once alternative transfer of training occurs only when the entire chunk is usable in another task. With the independent alternative individual encoding and decoding components can be shared, because a new connection production can be created during the transfer task that makes use of stimulus and response patterns from the training task.

Implementing the independent alternative looked hard enough that the all-at-once alternative was chosen for this initial attempt at building a chunking mechanism. Creating all of the components at once eliminates the problems of the independent alternative by forcing all of the information to be in working memory at the same time. This information exists within the instances of the **OnePattern** goal. Each instance describes a stimulus pattern and its associated response pattern. Given two of these instances, we have all of the information required to create a chunk. Built into the current chunking mechanism is the knowledge that chunks are based on the data in these goal instances and how patterns are encoded as attributes of the **OnePattern** objects.

Basing the acquisition of chunks on the information in **OnePattern** goal instances, rather than on the raw stimuli and responses, has the consequence of limiting chunk acquisition to only those patterns that are actually employed by the model during performance of the task. The potentially explosive number of possibilities for chunking is thus constrained to the relatively small set of patterns to which the subject actually attends. Many incidental patterns may be perceived in the process, but practice only improves performance on those components of the task actually performed.

Chunks are built out of the two most highly activated instances of the **OnePattern** goal in working memory, assuming that there are at least two present. These instances represent the two most recently processed patterns. Two of the architectural choices made in *Xaps2* were motivated by the need to have two instances of this goal simultaneously active:

1. Competition among objects is limited to within types so that pursuance of other goals would not cause old instances of the **OnePattern** goal to disappear from working memory.

2. The working-memory threshold is set at 0.0001 so that competition from the current instance of the **OnePattern** goal does not wipe out the previous instance before there is a chance to chunk them together. This is adequate for the current model but will not be for cases where the patterns take longer to process. This limitation amounts to a reasonable restriction on the length of time over which the chunking process can combine two patterns.

In order to ensure that the two most highly activated **OnePattern** instances are both from the same trial—we don't want cross-trial chunks—working memory is flushed between trials. This is a kludge intended to simulate the effects of intertrial activity.

Once a chunk has been created, we want the model to use it when appropriate, but not to recreate it. If the model were continually recreating the same chunks, production memory would quickly fill up with useless information. This problem breaks down into two subproblems: within-trial duplications, and across-trial duplications. First, consider the problem of within-trial duplication. Suppose a chunk was just created from the two most highly activated **OnePattern** objects; what is to stop the system from continually recreating the same chunk as long as those two objects are the most activated? To avoid this, the chunking mechanism keeps track of the identifiers of the last two instances that it chunked together. It only creates a new chunk if the identifiers of the two most highly activated instances differ from the stored identifiers. This also is an ad hoc solution necessary until we understand better what the true constraint should be.

Across-trial duplications occur when a chunk is created during one trial and then recreated when similar circumstances arise on a later trial. As currently constructed the model will never produce a duplicate of this type. If a chunk already exists that combines two patterns into a higher-level pattern, then the encoding component of the chunk ensures that whenever those two patterns are perceived, the higher-level pattern will also be perceived. The higher-level pattern will be selected for processing instead of the two smaller ones, so there is no possibility of them ever again being the two most recently used (most highly activated) patterns. This does assume error-free performance by the model, a condition that we have taken pains to ensure holds.

Trial	Type	Chunks Used			Chunks Acquired		Cycles
1	○●●○●	-●---	--●--	----●	-●●--	--●○●	106
2	●○●○●	●----	--●○●		●○●○●		75
3	●●○○○	●----	-●---		●●---		72
4	●●●○●	●●---	--●○●		●●●○●		74
5	●○●○●	●○●○●					44
6	●○○●●	●----	---●-	----●	●○○●-	---●●	105
7	●○○●●	●○○●-	----●		●○○●●		74
8	●○○●●	●○○●●					44
9	●●○●●	●●---	---●●		●●○●●		75

Figure 5.11
The nine-trial sequence simulated by the model: ● is *On*, ○ is *Off*, and – is *don't care*

5.7 The Results

In this section we present and analyze results from simulations of the complete model, consisting of the production-system architecture, the performance model, and the chunking mechanism. These simulations demonstrate that the model works: the chunking theory can form the basis of a practice mechanism for production-system architectures. In addition these simulations provide a detailed look at the acquisition and use of chunks and verify that the model does produce power-law practice curves. In section 5.1 we showed that the chunking equation—an approximation of the full model—produces curves that are well matched by a power law. Now we can demonstrate it directly, though not analytically, for the exact model of one task.

The Results of a Simulation

The complete model has been run successfully on a specially selected sequence of nine trials for the left hand (five lights only). This sequence was devised especially to illustrate important aspects of the model. For each trial in this sequence, figure 5.11 shows the task to be performed, the chunks used, the chunks acquired, and the reaction time in number of production system cycles. Figure 5.12 presents an alternative organization of the chunks acquired during this sequence of trials—the chunk hierarchy. Each node in this hierarchy represents one chunk that was acquired. The node's children represent the two subchunks from which that chunk was created.

At the most global level these results demonstrate directly that the task

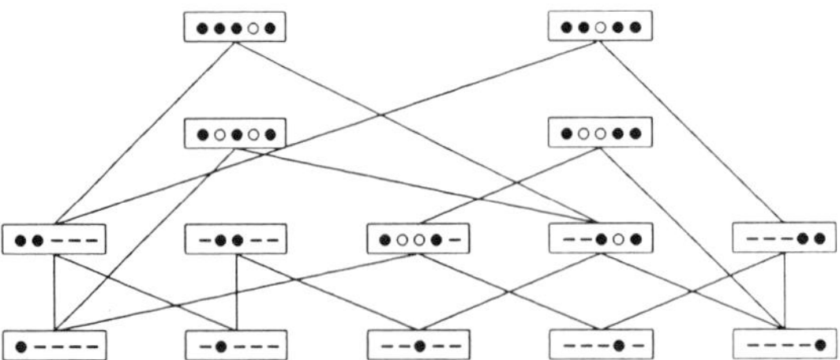

Figure 5.12
The tree of chunks created during the nine-trial simulation

was performed successfully, chunks were acquired, and they did improve the model's performance. Looking in more detail, first examine the relationship between the last column in figure 5.11, the number of cycles per trial, and the third column, the chunks used. We can see that the time to perform a trial is approximately given by

$$NumberOfCycles = 13 + (31 \times NumberOfPatternsProcessed). \qquad (5.9)$$

A three-pattern trial takes about 106 cycles (105–106 in the data), a two-pattern trial takes about 75 cycles (72–75 in the data), and a one-pattern trial takes 44 cycles (44 in the data).

A chunk is acquired for the first and second patterns used, the second and third patterns used, and so forth, up to the number of patterns in the trial. The number of chunks acquired on a trial is therefore given by

$$NumberOfChunksAcquired = NumberOfPatternsProcessed - 1. \qquad (5.10)$$

The rate of acquisition of chunks is one every 31 cycles, once the constant overhead of 44 cycles per trial (13 plus the time to process the first pattern on the trial) has been removed, satisfying the learning assumption (section 5.2).

This learning is demonstrably too fast. For the ten-light task environment, the entire task environment can be learned within $\log_2(10)$, between three and four, iterations through the task environment (at 1,023 trials per iteration). This could be remedied in one of two ways. The first possibility is to propose that there are actually more chunks to be learned than we have described. For example, the level at which primitive patterns are defined could be too high, or there may be other features of the environment that we are not capturing. The second alternative is that chunks are not learned at every opportunity. Gilmartin (1974) computed a rate of chunk acquisition of about one every eight to nine seconds—less than one chunk per trial in this task. Without speculating as to the cause of this slow down, we could model it by adding a parameter for the probability (<1) that a chunk is learned when the opportunity exists. We do not know which alternative is correct but would not be surprised to find both of them implicated in the final solution.

One point clearly illustrated by this sequence of trials is that chunking is hierarchical, without having a strong notion of *level*. Chunks can be based on primitive patterns, higher-level patterns, or a mixture. The sequence illustrates the following combinations: (1) the creation of chunks from primitive patterns (trials 1, 3, and 6), (2) the creation of chunks from higher-level patterns (trials 4 and 9), (3) the creation of chunks from one primitive pattern and one higher-level pattern (trials 2 and 7), and (4) the creation of no chunks (trials 5 and 8). The *Off*-lights in the chunks represent the regions in which no *On*-light should appear (section 5.6).

Also illustrated is how the chunks created on one trial can be used on later trials. As one example, look at trials 6 through 8 in figure 5.11. All three trials employ the identical task, containing three *On*-lights. On trial 6 the three *On*-lights are processed serially (105 cycles), and two chunks are acquired for the two combinations of two successive *On*-lights. Notice that the two chunks share the middle *On*-light as a subpattern. On the following trial, trial 7, the first chunk created on trial 6 is used, taking care of the first two *On*-lights. All that is left is the third *On*-light, which is a primitive pattern. The time for trial 7 is 74 cycles, a savings of 31 over trial 6. During trial 7 a chunk is created that covers all three *On*-lights by combining the two patterns employed during the trial. On trial 8 only one pattern is required, and the trial takes only 44 cycles.

Chunks not only improve performance on trials that are exact repetitions of earlier trials; they can also be transferred to trials that merely share a subpattern. Thorndike first described transfer along these lines: "A change in one function alters any other only in so far as the two functions have as factor identical elements." (Thorndike 1913). Trials 1 and 2 illustrate this variety of transfer of training. Both trials have the third and fifth lights *On* and the fourth light *Off* but differ in the first two lights. Nevertheless, the chunk created in the first trial is used to speed up the performance of the second trial. The same chunk is also reused in trial 4.

The complete model has also been run successfully on a sequence of 20 ten-light trials, with results comparable to those for the five-light sequence.

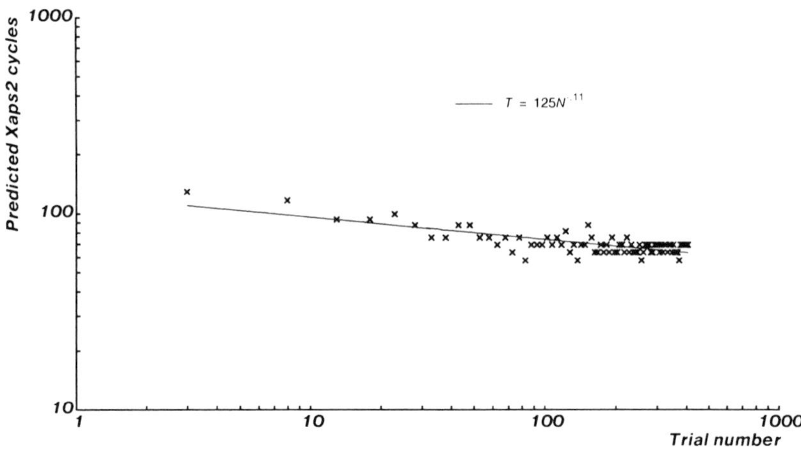

Figure 5.13
Practice curve predicted by the metasimulation (log-log coordinates). The 408-trial sequence performed by subject 3 (aggregated by five trials).

Simulated Practice Curves

The model is too costly computationally to run the long trial sequences required for the generation of practice curves. The execution time varies with the number of productions in the system—slowing down as chunks are added—but in the middle of the 20 trial sequence, the model took an average of 22 CPU minutes to process each pattern (approximately 31 production system cycles) on a *DecSystem 2060*. This deficiency is overcome through the use of a metasimulation—a more abstract simulation of the simulation. The metasimulation is faster than the simulation because it ignores the details of the performance system. If merely keeps track of the chunks that would be created by the model and the patterns that would be used during performance. From this information, and equation (5.9), it estimates the number of cycles that the production-system model would execute.

Via this metasimulation, extensive practice curves have been generated. As a start, figure 5.13 shows the practice curve generated by the metasimulation for the 408 trial sequence used for subject 3 (section 5.2). Comparing this curve with the curve for the human subject (figure 5.7), we see a basic similarity, though the human's curve is steeper and has more variability.

Seibel ran his subjects for 75 blocks of 1,023 trials each (Seibel, 1963). To

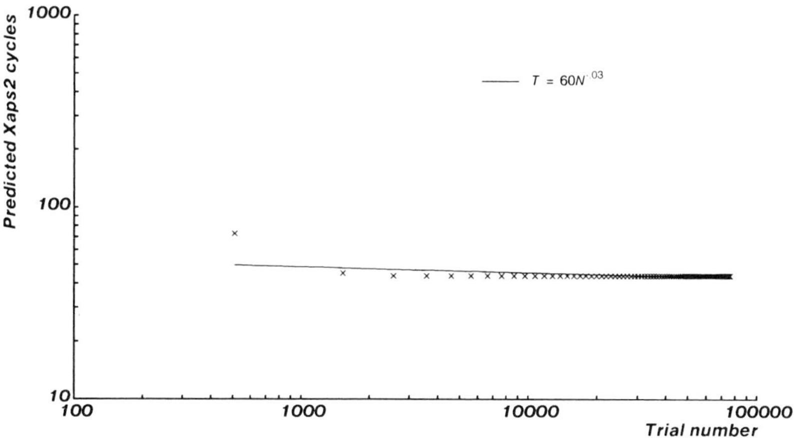

Figure 5.14
Practice curve predicted by the metasimulation (log-log coordinates). Seventy-five data points, each averaged over a block of 1,023 trials.

compare the model with this extensive data, the metasimulator was run for the same number of trials. A single random permutation of the 1,023 trials was processed 75 times by the metasimulation. Figure 5.14 shows the practice curve generated by the metasimulation for this sequence of trials. It is clear from this curve that creating a chunk at every opportunity leads to perfect performance much too rapidly—by the third block of trials.

A much better curve can be obtained by slowing down the rate of chunk acquisition, per the second suggestion made earlier in this section. We can make a quick, back-of-the-envelope calculation to find a reasonable value for the probability of acquiring a chunk, given the opportunity. To do this, we will make three assumptions:

1. Assume that the model has the opportunity to acquire a chunk each time a pattern is processed and that there is no overhead time.
2. Assume that the time to process a pattern is in the range of times for a *simple reaction time*—100 to 400 msec (Card, Moran, and Newell 1984).
3. Assume that it takes 8 to 9 sec to acquire a chunk (Gilmartin 1974).

The probability (p) of acquiring a chunk is essentially the rate of chunking, as measured in chunks per pattern. This rate can be computed by dividing the time per pattern (0.1 to 0.4 sec) by the time per chunk (8.0 to 9.0 sec). Using the extreme values for the two parameters, we find that the proba-

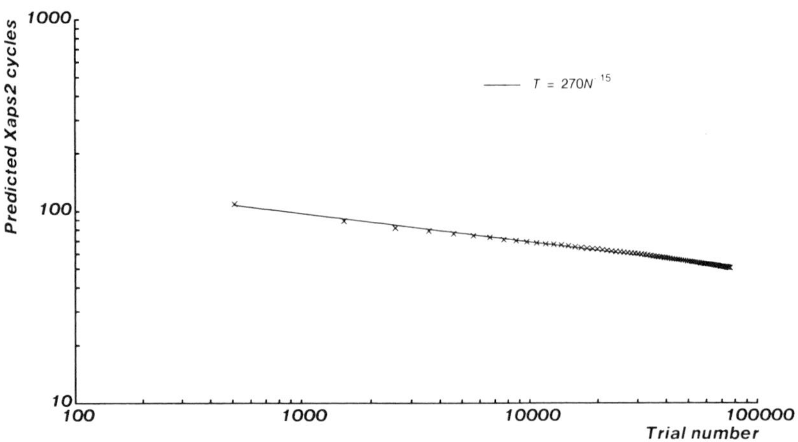

Figure 5.15
Practice curve predicted by the metasimulation (log-log coordinates). Seventy-five data points, each averaged over a block of 1,023 trials. The probability of creating a chunk, when there is an opportunity, is 0.02.

bility should be in the interval [0.01, 0.05]. We have chosen to use one value in this interval, $p = 0.02$.

Figure 5.15 shows the results of a metasimulation in which chunk acquisition is slowed down by this factor. This curve is linear in log-log coordinates over the entire range of trials ($r^2 = 0.993$). A slight wave in the points is still detectable, but the linearity is not significantly improved by resorting to the generalized power law (r^2 is still 0.993). We currently have no explanation for this phenomenon. We can only comment that the deviations are indeed small and that similar waves appear to exist in the general power law fit to Seibel's data (figure 5.2), though they are somewhat obscured by noise.

If a low probability of chunk acquisition is required in order to model adequately highly aggregated long sequences of trials (figure 5.15), and a high probability is required for an adequate fit to less aggregated, short trial sequences (figure 5.13), then there would be a major problem with the model. Fortunately the one value of 0.02 is sufficient for both cases. Figure 5.16 shows the same 408 trial sequence as figure 5.13, with the only difference being the reduced probability of chunk acquisition. Thus, given a reasonable value for p, the chunking model produces good power-law curves over both small and large trial ranges.

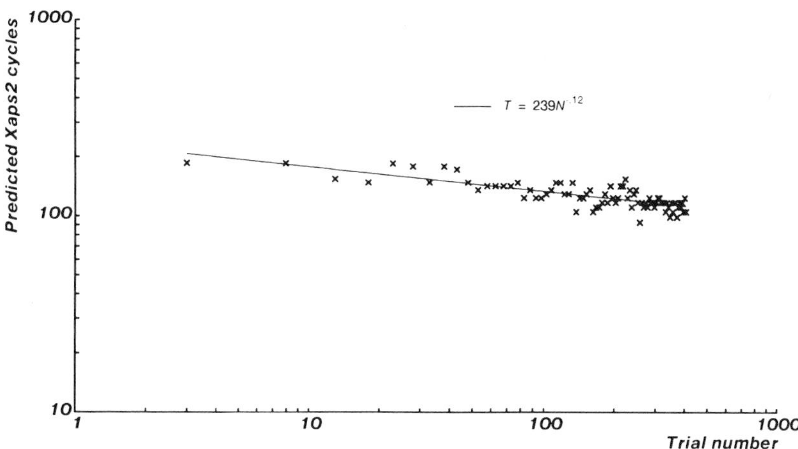

Figure 5.16
Practice curve predicted by the metasimulation (log-log coordinates). The 408-trial sequence performed by subject 3 (aggregated by five trials). The probability of creating a chunk, when there is an opportunity, is 0.02.

The most important way in which figure 5.15 differs from the human data (figure 5.1) is that the power (α) of the power-law fit is lower for the metasimulation—0.15 for the metasimulation versus 0.32 for the central linear portion of the subject's curve. One approach to resolving this discrepancy is to examine the metasimulation for parameters that can be modified to produce larger powers. Modification of p, the one parameter mentioned so far, can cause small perturbations in α but is incapable of causing the large increase required. When p was varied over [0.001, 1.0], α only varied over the range [0.03, 0.15].[11]

One parameter that can effect α is the number of lights (and buttons) in the task environment. Increasing this number can significantly raise α. With 20 lights and buttons, the metasimulation produced a practice curve with an α of 0.26.[12] For the shorter 408 trial sequence, an α of 0.16 was generated, compared with 0.17 for subject 3 (figure 5.7). While this manipulation yields good results, it is still true that those ten extra lights and buttons don't actually exist in the task environment. An alternative interpretation is required in which these ten virtual lights and buttons are thought of as modeling unspecified other features of the task environment.

Given the simulation results in this section, a rough estimate of the cycle time of the *Xaps2* production-system architecture can be computed. One method is to compute the mean response time for the human data; remove some portion of it, say half, as an estimate of the task time outside the scope of the model; and divide the remainder by the mean number of cycles per trial. The value varies with the number of lights used in the simulation (10 or 20) and whether a long simulation is being compared with the Seibel data (figure 5.1) or a short simulation is being compared to subject 3 (figure 5.7), but all four computations yield a value between 3 and 6 msec. The average value is 4 msec.

One cycle every 4 msecs is a very fast rate. The accepted value for production-system architectures is generally thought to be on the order of the *cognitive cycle time*—between 25 and 170 msec (Card, Moran, and Newell 1984). Note, however, that the model simulates the cognitive system at a smaller grain size than is normally done. The cognitive cycle is more appropriately identified with the complete processing of one pattern (one iteration through the **OnePattern** goal). If we ignore the implementation of the model's goal structure as productions and just look at this level of goal-directed processing, the architecture looks remarkably like a conventional serial production system. During each cycle of this higher-level "production system" (a **OnePattern** goal), we *recognize* a single pattern (a **OneStimulusPattern** goal) and *act* accordingly (a **OneResponsePattern** goal)—approximately 31 cycles. The *Xaps2* cycle time of 3 to 6 msec per cycle yields a time estimate for this higher-level cycle of between 93 and 186 msec, with a mean of 124 msec. These times are well within the accepted range for the cognitive cycle time.

5.8 Conclusion

This chapter has reported on an investigation into the implementation of the chunking theory of learning as a model of practice within a production-system architecture. Starting from the outlines of a theory, a working model capable of producing power-law practice curves has been produced. This model has been successfully simulated for one task—a 1,023-choice reaction-time task.

During this research we have developed a novel highly parallel production-system architecture—*Xaps2*—combining both symbolic and activation notions of processing. The design of this architecture was driven by the needs of this work, but the resulting system is a fully general production-system architecture. Most important, it meets a set of constraints derived from an analysis of the chunking theory. These constraints must be met by any other architecture in which the chunking theory is embedded.

A performance model for the reaction-time task has been implemented as a set of productions within this architecture. Though the architecture provides parallel execution of productions, the control structure of the model is a serially processed goal hierarchy, yielding a blend of serial and parallel processing. The goal hierarchy controls a loop through three tasks: (1) select a stimulus pattern to process, (2) map the stimulus pattern into an appropriate response pattern, and (3) execute the response pattern. Two of these tasks, 1 and 3, require the model to communicate with the outside world. The required stimulus and response interfaces are modeled as two-dimensional Euclidean spaces of patterns. The model perceives patterns in the stimulus space and produces patterns in the response space. As with the production-system architecture, the design of the control structure and interfaces have been driven by the needs of this work. A second look shows that there is very little actual task dependence in these designs. The control structure, or a slightly more general variant, works for a large class of reaction-time tasks.

To this model is added the chunking mechanism. Chunks are acquired from pairs of patterns dealt with by the performance model. Each chunk is composed of a triple of productions: (1) an encoding production that combines a pair of stimulus patterns into a more complex pattern, (2) a decoding production that decomposes a complex response pattern into its simpler components, and (3) a connection production that links the complex stimulus pattern with the complex response pattern. Chunks improve the model's performance by reducing the number of times the system must execute the control loop. Both simulations and metasimulations (simulations of the simulations) of the model have been run. The result is that chunking can improve performance, and it does so according to a power-law function of the number of trials.

The results of this investigation have been promising, but there is much work still to be done. One open question is whether these results will hold up for other tasks. As long as the task can be modeled within the control structure described in this article, power-law learning by chunking is to be expected. For radically different tasks, the answer is less certain. To investigate this, the scope of the model needs to be extended to a wider class of tasks.

A number of aspects of the model need improvement as well. The production-system architecture needs to be better understood, especially in relation to the chunking theory and the task models. Oversimplifications in the implementation of the chunking theory—such as allowing only pair-wise chunking—need to be replaced by more general assumptions. In addition a number of ad hoc decisions and mechanisms need to be replaced by more well-reasoned and supported alternatives.

Notes

This research was sponsored by the Defense Advanced Research Projects Agency (DOD), ARPA Order No. 3597, monitored by the Air Force Avionics Laboratory under Contract F33615-78-C-1551. We would like to thank John Anderson, Pat Langley, Arnold Rosenbloom, and Richard Young for their helpful comments on drafts of this chapter.

Since this work was completed, a task-independent version of chunking has been developed (Rosenbloom and Newell 1986) and integrated into a general problem-solving architecture (Laird, Rosenbloom, and Newell 1986).

1. Power-law curves plot as straight lines on log-log paper.

2. For a summary of alternative models of the power law of practice, see Newell and Rosenbloom (1981). Additional proposals can be found in Anderson (1982) and Welford (1981).

3. A brief summary of this work can be found in Rosenbloom and Newell (1982).

4. When all of the lights on one hand are on, it can be treated as a single response of the whole hand, rather than as five individual responses. In fact the reaction times for these trials are much faster than would be expected if the five lights were being processed separately.

5. *Xaps2* is implemented in *MacLisp* running on a DecSystem 2060.

6. The assumptions in *Xaps2* bear a strong family resemblance to those in the *Caps* architecture (Thibadeau, Just, and Carpenter, 1982).

7. Our ultimate goal is to develop a task independent implementation of chunking, but until that is possible, we must live with this unsatisfactory but necessary dependence.

8. In this and following examples, the notation has been modified for clarity of presentation. Some of the names have been expanded or modified. In addition types have been made bold, identifiers are in the normal roman font, attributes are in SMALL CAPITALS, and values are *italicized.*

9. The syntax of this production has been modified slightly for presentation purposes. Symbols beginning with "=" are *variables*. This is the only example of the internal form of a production to appear; in the remainder of this chapter we use the paraphrase form.

10. For simplicity of presentation, an additional STATUS attribute in the following three examples is not shown.

11. The range was sampled at 0.001, 0.01, 0.02, 0.1, and 1.0.

12. Each ten-light trial, in a single random permutation of the 1,023 trials, had an additional ten random lights appended to it, to yield 1,023 twenty-light trials. This block of trials was then repeated 75 times.

References

Anderson, J. R. 1976. *Language, Memory, and Thought*. Hillsdale, N.J.: Lawrence Erlbaum Associates.

Anderson, J. A. 1977. Neural models with cognitive implications. In D. LaBerge and S. J. Samuels (eds.), *Basic Processes in Reading*. Hillsdale, N.J.: Lawrence Erlbaum Associates.

Anderson, J. R. 1982. Acquisition of cognitive skill. *Psychological Review* 89, 369–406.

Anderson, J. A., and Hinton, G. E. 1981. Models of information processing in the brain. In G. E. Hinton and J. A. Anderson (eds.), *Parallel Models of Associative Memory*. Hillsdale, N.J.: Lawrence Erlbaum Associates.

Bower, G. H., and Winzenz, D. 1969. Group structure, coding, and memory for digit series. *Experimental Psychology Mongraph* 80, 1–17.

Card, S. K., Moran, T. P. and Newell, A. 1984. *The Psychology of Human-Computer Interaction*. Hillsdale, N.J.: Lawrence Erlbaum Associates, in press.

Chase, W. G., and Simon, H. A. 1973. Perception in chess. *Cognitive Psychology* 4, 55–81.

DeGroot, A. D. 1965. *Thought and Choice in Chess*. The Hague: Mouton.

Evans, T. G. 1968. A program for the solution of geometric-analogy intelligence test questions. In M. Minsky (ed.), *Semantic Information Processing*. Cambridge, Mass.: The MIT Press.

Forgy, C., and McDermott, J. 1977. *The Ops2 Reference Manual*. IPS Note No. 77–50. Department of Computer Science, Carnegie-Mellon University.

Gilmartin, K. J. 1974. *An information processing model of short-term memory*. Dissertation. Carnegie-Mellon University.

Johnson, N. F. 1972. Organization and the concept of a memory code. In A. W. Melton and E. Martin, (eds.), *Coding Processes in Human Memory*. Washington, D.C.: Winston.

Joshi, A. K. 1978. Some extensions of a system for inference on partial information. In D. A. Waterman and F. Hayes-Roth (eds.), *Pattern-Directed Inference Systems*. New York: Academic Press.

Laird, J. E., Rosenbloom, P. S., and Newell, A. 1986. Chunking in Soar: The anatomy of a general learning mechanism. *Machine Learning* 1, 11–46.

McClelland, J. L., and Rumelhart, D. E. 1981. An interactive activation model of context effects in letter perception: Part 1. An account of basic findings. *Psychological Review* 88(5), 375–407.

Miller, G. A. 1956. The magic number seven plus or minus two: Some limits on our capacity for processing information. *Psychological Review* 63, 81–97.

Mitchell, T. M., Utgoff, P. E., Nudel, B., and Banerji, R. 1981. Learning problem-solving heuristics through practice. *Proceedings of the Seventh International Joint Conference on Artificial Intelligence*. Los Altos, Calif.: Morgan-Kaufmann.

Moran, T. P. 1980. *Compiling cognitive skill*. AIP Memo 150. Xerox PARC.

Neisser, U., Novick, R., and Lazar, R. 1963. Searching for ten targets simultaneously. *Perceptual and Motor Skills* 17, 427–432.

Neves, D. M., and Anderson, J. R. 1981. Knowledge compilation: Mechanisms for the automatization of cognitive skills. In J. R. Anderson (ed.), *Cognitive Skills and their Acquisition*. Hillsdale, N.J.: Lawrence Erlbaum Associates.

Newell, A. 1973. Production systems: Models of control structures. In W. G. Chase (ed.), *Visual Information Processing*. New York: Academic Press.

Newell, A. 1980. Harpy, production systems and human cognition. In R. Cole (ed.), *Perception and Production of Fluent Speech*. Hillsdale, N.J.: Lawrence Erlbaum Associates (also available as CMU CSD Technical Report, Sep 1978).

Newell, A., and Rosenbloom, P. S. 1981. Mechanisms of skill acquisition and the law of practice. In J. R. Anderson (ed.), *Cognitive Skills and Their Acquisition*. Hillsdale, N.J.: Lawrence Erlbaum Associates.

Newell, A., and Simon, H. A. 1972. *Human Problem Solving*. Englewood Cliffs, N.J.: Prentice-Hall.

Norman, D. A. 1981. Categorization of action slips. *Psychological Review* 88, 1–15.

Rosenbloom, P. S. 1979. The XAPS Reference Manual.

Rosenbloom, P. S., and Newell, A. 1982. Learning by chunking: Summary of a task and a model. *Proceedings of the Second National Conference on Artificial Intelligence*. Los Altos, Calif.: Morgan-Kaufmann.

Rosenbloom, P. S., and Newell, A. 1986. The chunking of goal hierarchies: A generalized model of practice. In R. S. Michalski, J. G. Carbonell, and T. M. Mitchell (eds.), *Machine Learning: An Artificial Intelligence Approach*, Vol. 2. Los Altos, Calif.: Morgan-Kaufmann.

Rumelhart, D. E., and McClelland, J. L. 1982. An interactive activation model of context effects in letter perception: Part 2. The contextual enhancement effect and some tests and extensions of the model. *Psychological Review* 89, 60–94.

Rumelhart, D. E., and Norman, D. A. 1982. Simulating a skilled typist: A study of skilled cognitive-motor performance. *Cognitive Science* 6, 1–36.

Seibel, R. 1963. Discrimination reaction time for a 1,023-alternative task. *Journal of Experimental Psychology* 66(3), 215–226.

Shiffrin, R. M., and Schneider, W. 1977. Controlled and automatic human information processing: II. Perceptual learning, automatic attending, and a general theory. *Psychological Review* 84, 127–190.

Snoddy, G. S. 1926. Learning and stability. *Journal of Applied Psychology* 10, 1–36.

Thacker, C. P., McCreight, E. M., Lampson, B. W., Sproull, R. F., and Boggs, D. R. 1982. Alto: a personal computer. In D. P. Sieworek, C. G. Bell, and A. Newell (eds.), *Computer Structures: Principles and Examples*. New York: McGraw-Hill.

Thibadeau, R., Just, M. A., and Carpenter, P. A. 1982. A model of the time course and content of reading. *Cognitive Science* 6, 157–203.

Thorndike, E. L. 1913. *Educational Psychology. II: The Psychology of Learning*. Bureau of Publications, Teachers College, Columbia University.

Uhr, L., and Vossler, C. 1963. A pattern-recognition program that generates, evaluates, and adjusts its own operators. In E. Feigenbaum and J. Feldman (eds.), *Computers and Thought*. New York: McGraw-Hill.

VanLehn, K. 1981. *On the representation of procedures in repair theory*. Technical Report No. CIS-16. Xerox PARC.

Welford, A. T. 1981. Learning curves for sensory-motor performance. *Proceedings of the Human Factors Society, 25th Annual Meeting*.

6 Truth Versus Appropriateness: Relating Declarative to Procedural Knowledge

Stellan Ohlsson

Man has always been of two minds with respect to his own knowledge processes. Some thinkers, like Locke, Russel, and Carnap, have seen knowledge as arriving from without, from the world itself, through the process of observation. Others, like Plato, Descartes, and Kant, while not denying that thinking needs observation as a source of particular facts, have argued that knowledge grows from within, through a process of deliberation.

Psychology in general, and the psychology of learning in particular, has agreed more with the empiricists than with the rationalists. Concepts like trial-and-error, contiguity, reinforcement, and frequency are intended to help explain how experience shapes behavior. The theme of recent work on procedural learning (see Anderson, Kline, and Beasley 1980; Anzai and Simon 1979; Langley 1982; Neches 1981; Neches and Hayes 1978; Ohlsson 1983) could be called *internal experience*. Humans are assumed to store in memory an information-rich trace of their own cognitive processing. Familiar items from the empiricist's tool-kit—observation, abstraction, induction—are then applied to this trace (rather than to a sequence of real-world events).

The importance and psychological reality of experience-oriented learning methods cannot be doubted. But we may ask whether they exhaust the repertoire of change mechanisms in human cognition. Consider the task of dividing, say, 137 by five. If a person has to perform such calculations without aids, he is likely to find out that $x/5$ can beneficially be reconceived as $2X/10$. It seems obvious that this shortcut is discovered with the help of the knowledge that $1/5 = 2/10$, rather than through a trace of calculating activities. Also cognitive psychology cannot ignore situations in which people are demonstrably incapable of learning from experience (Brehmer 1980), nor learning results that seem quite insolated from empirical experience (Smedslund 1961).

The purpose of this chapter is to explore the following *Rational Learning Thesis*:

PART A Significant improvements in a problem-solving procedure can be computed from declarative knowledge related to the corresponding task, without reference to a trace of the workings of that procedure.

PART B Mechanisms that perform such computations are important in human learning.

Part A belongs to the study of intelligence in general, human or artificial. The phrase "knowledge related to the ... task" should be conceived broadly to include both knowledge of the subject matter of the task, and knowledge about the task itself. Part B is a conjecture of psychology. It might turn out that A is true, while B is false, in which case there are learning methods available to computers which are beyond humans.

The thesis asserts the importance of one type of learning method; it should not be misunderstood as saying that experience-oriented methods are less important. Indeed, looking at the example given previously, we see that even if the possibility of substituting $2x/10$ for $x/5$ is discovered through thinking about number facts, the point of making the substitution must be that to compute $2x/10$ involves less cognitive strain than to compute $x/5$. This relation between the two operations is most easily discovered by comparing traces of their execution. Rational and empirical learning methods interact in producing cognitive change.

After the preliminaries in the immediately following section, a theory of rational learning is presented, implemented, and applied to an example.

6.1 Implications and Productions

Logical analyses of reasoning have sought arguments that guarantee the truth of their conclusions. Ordinary logic, sometimes called theoretical logic, has therefore developed a sophisticated language for dealing with truth, based on propositions, implications, inference rules, and proofs.

A side-tradition in logic developed instead from the type of argument that Aristotle called the practical syllogism. The aim of a practical argument is to establish the appropriateness of an action. Philosophers and logicians have had a harder time reaching consensus about practical than about theoretical logic (see Aune 1977; Raz 1978). One reason for this might be the lack of a language of appropriateness as powerful as the traditional logical language of truth. However, a production-system language can be conceived as just such a language. Its basic unit is the production, a rule which says that under conditions $C_1, \ldots, C_n$, some action A is appropriate.

One of the strong advantages of the traditional logical language is that it has a well-developed semantics. No general semantics for production-system languages has been put forward (although Anderson 1976 has provided a set-theoretic semantics for the propositional network of the ACT system). The present section represents a first step toward such a semantics. Its purpose in this context is to help highlight the differences between implications and productions. The distinction between them is central to the approach to learning presented in the following section.

An implication is a proposition, and thus has a truth-value. The formula.

$$P_1, \ldots, P_n \gg Q$$

can be read "It is true that $P_1, \ldots, P_n$ imply Q." A production, on the other hand, is an exhortation. The formula

$$C_1, \ldots, C_n \Rightarrow A$$

is to be read: "When $C_1, \ldots, C_n$, then do A!" A production is not true or false but more or less useful, more or less appropriate. Notice in particular that the imperative character of productions does not disappear when the action consists in the drawing of a conclusion ("When $C_1, \ldots, C_n$, then infer Q!").

A second difference is that the antecedents of an implication are always propositions, while the conditions of a production can include goals, questions, and evaluations, entities that do not have truth-values and so are not propositional in the sense that they can enter meaningfully into truth-functional relationships (e.g., implication).

But the left-hand sides also differ in the following way. In the implication

P implies Q

the left-hand side, taken out of context, asserts P. For instance, if the implication is "If I am happy, I laugh," the left-hand side, taken by itself, asserts that I am happy. But the left-hand side in the production

$$P \Rightarrow Q$$

does not, taken by itself, assert P. A production system interpreter does not test the truth of the propositions that appear in conditions; it tests for the existence of the corresponding expressions in working memory. A reading which would make this explicit would be

When there exists an x,

such that x equals P

and x is a member of working memory

$\Rightarrow$,

then infer Q!

In terms of a familiar logical distinction (Suppes 1957), the difference is that in the implication, P is *used*, while in the production, it is *mentioned.* The relation between P being in working memory and P being true is, of course, equivocal; the system could have made a mistake, somebody might have lied to it, P might have been true once but has ceased to be so, and so forth.

The consequent of an implication is a proposition. But the right-hand side of a production specifies an action to be executed. It is equivalent to mathematical expressions like $f(x)$, which obviously lack truth-values. Their imperative nature can be emphasized by the reading "apply f to x!" Since productions that perform inferences must write their results in working memory, most productions discussed throughout this chapter will have action sides of the form "write x!"

In summary, we have two different representations: the language of implications created for discussions of truth and the language of productions intended for the expression of appropriateness. The problem of relating knowledge to action can then be stated in terms of relations between these two languages.

6.2 A Theory of Rational Strategy Change

Consider a system with a set of beliefs expressed as implications and a set of productions for performing some task. The problem of how knowledge can influence action is the problem of how the beliefs can affect additions to the production set. A belief relevant to a particular task may entail a shortcut or some other improvement in the current strategy for doing the task. For example, the information that it is not possible to reserve seats on trains in Switzerland has several effects on one's procedure for getting around in that country. An intelligent system needs methods for identifying the revisions of its strategies which are called for by its beliefs.

A Space of Rational Learning Methods

One straightforward method of relating declarative knowledge to procedures has recently been proposed. It can be outlined as follows:

Method *O*: Proceduralization

If it is known that

A implies *B*,

then create

When $A \Rightarrow$ write *B*!

The new production performs the inference from *A* to *B* whenever possible. A detailed theory of how this method might be implemented in humans has been presented by Neves and Anderson (1981) in the context of a simulation model of problem solving in geometry.

Taken as a general learning mechanism, proceduralization is too weak. It is obviously true that only valid inferences can be useful. But the converse does not hold. Indeed, it is a basic difficulty of inference problems that not all valid inferences are useful or appropriate in all situations. For instance, the inference from *P* to not-not-*P* is always valid, but putting double negations in front of every available proposition may not be the best policy for solving your current problem. The creation of production rules must be selective. Summarizing in slogan form, we state:

PRINCIPLE 1 Appropriateness is a subset of truth.

The principle implies that we should look on the set of beliefs as a pool of suggestions about which new strategic rules to create. Each true implication represents a possible procedure. But principle 1 also implies that we must find constraints on which of those procedures should be implemented.

The sources of beliefs relevant to a certain task are very varied. General world knowledge is probably the most important. The statement of the task is another source. Beliefs about a task can also be received from a teacher, a parent, or an experimenter. The activity of trying to solve a problem can lead to discoveries about it. Finally propositional reasoning from beliefs generated in any of the preceding ways can provide yet further declarative insights. We summarize these points in the next principle:

PRINCIPLE 2 Implicational truths about a task come from diverse sources, but regardless of source, each such truth constitutes an opportunity for strategy change.

But which implications should be allowed to give rise to procedures? A new production must, if it is to be useful, work together with the already existing productions. For instance, the implication "If *P*, then *Q*" is only interesting if *Q* is ever needed in the solution to the relevant problem. If not, the corresponding production would only slow down processing (assuming seriality) and should not be created. Generalizing this simple observation, we state the main conjecture of this chapter:

PRINCIPLE 3 The current strategy for a particular task is the main source of constraints on additions to that strategy.

The outcome of these deliberations is the following formulation of rational learning methods:

METHOD SCHEMA Given

1. a set of implications I^*,
2. a set of productions P^*,
3. a set of T^* of tests $T_1, T_2, \ldots, T_n$, on either one or both of I^* and P^*, and
4. a function F that maps the pair I^* and P^* onto productions,

then, if all the tests are true (i.e., if $T_1(I^*, P^*) = \text{true}$, $T_2(I^*, P^*) = \text{true}$, $\ldots$, $T_n(I^*, P^*) = \text{true}$), and $F(I^*, P^*) = PD$, add PD to the set I^*.

Propositional knowledge is here represented by I^*, and procedural skill by P^*. A method conforming to this schema relates knowledge to action through the set of tests T^*. Each test can be seen as establishing that a particular relation holds between the (current) set of implications and the (current) set of productions. When all tests are satisfied, F is computed in order to generate the new production to be added to P^*. This framework defines a space of rational learning methods, different members of the space being constructed by specifying T^* and F*; each such member can be applied to different (I^*, P^*) pairs. For instance, in proceduralization there is single test, namely that there is an implication not yet proceduralized. The F consists in letting the antecedent of the implication become the condition of the production and letting the consequent become the action. The previous argument against proceduralization as a general learning mechanism can now be rephrased as saying that in that method, T^* does not take P^* into account. Four other specific learning methods from this space will be considered next.

Selecting Relevant Implications

The first learning method to be considered here embodies a fairly general criterion for relevance of an implication to a set of productions:

METHOD 1 Rule of relevance:

If (test 1) there is an implication

A_1 A_2 imply B

and (test 2) there is a production with B in its action side and some goal G in its condition side, that is,

$\ldots(\text{GOAL} = G)\ldots \Rightarrow$ write B!

and (test 3) there is a second production with (say) A_1 in its condition side,

$\ldots A_1 \ldots \Rightarrow \ldots$

then create the two new productions

$(\text{GOAL} = G)\ A_1 \Rightarrow$ write $(\text{GOAL} = (\text{GET}\ A_2))$!

and

$(\text{GOAL} = G)\ A_1\ A_2 \Rightarrow$ write B!

The rationale for the rule of relevance is as follows: The second test—that some production creates B—ensures that B is relevant for the task at hand. Similarly the third test—that some production looks for A_1—anchors the condition side of the new production in pertinent data. If neither A_1 nor A_2 were ever produced, the new production might be irrelevant. But if at least one of them appears, it might be worthwhile to try to derive the other. If it can be found quickly enough, there might be an overall saving in the amount of computation needed to get B. The new productions are restricted by the goal G to the context in which B is usually created. The implementation of this method to be discussed later is symmetric with respect to A_1 and A_2 and handles an arbitrary number of antecedents.

The rule of relevance is a learning heuristic; it is not guaranteed to produce a strategy improvement every time it applies, but sometimes it will do so. It can achieve effects similar to those of composition (Lewis 1978). In terms of Neches' (1981) typology of transformation types, the effects of the rule of relevance belong to either "unit building" or "replacement with a different method," depending on the circumstances under which it applies.

Variants of the method can easily be spawned. For instance, one could delete the third test, since any new way of computing B might be useful. Going in the opposite direction, one could add a fourth test, checking the occurrence of A_2 in some production. If A_2 is very hard to come by, the first of the two new productions in the rule of relevance may send the system off on a wild goose chase; better test for both A_1 and A_2. However, the mechanism actually implemented corresponds closely to the rule as stated here.

As an illustration, suppose that the system's task is to diagnose heart trouble (G). Its diagnostic procedure includes observing whether the patient is cyanotic or not. The possible diagnoses include various congential heart diseases, such as the endocardinal cushion defect (ECD). Suppose further that the system's current diagnostic procedure only concludes ECD after having eliminated all other alternatives. Through a textbook (or some such source) it is learned that lack of cyanosis (A_1) in conjunction with a so-called left-axis deviation (A_2) in the EKG implies that the disease is ECD (B). Relating this new knowledge to the existing diagnostic procedure, the rule of relevance finds that lack of cyanosis is a datum used by some productions in the current procedure and that the diagnosis ECD is sometimes concluded. It will then create the two new rules: "If the goal is to diagnose heart trouble and if the patient shows a lack of cyanosis, then look for a left-axis deviation" and "If the patient shows a lack of cyanosis and has a left-axis deviation, then conclude that the disease is ECD."

Differentiating Useful Consequents

One problem with inference systems is that a single proposition may give rise to several different conclusions. It may not be obvious which conclusion is most useful with respect to a particular problem, or in a particular context. The next learning method adresses this problem:

METHOD 2 Rule of differentiation:
If (test 1) there are two implications

A implies B_1

A implies B_2

and (test 2) there is a production

$C\ D_1 \Rightarrow$ write B_1!

and (test 3) there is a second production

$C\ D_2 \Rightarrow$ write B_2!,

then create the three new productions

$A \Rightarrow$ write (GOAL = (GET D_1) or (GET D_2))!,

$A\ D_1 \Rightarrow$ write B_1!,

and

$A\ D_2 \Rightarrow$ write B_2!

The proposition A can give rise to two different conclusions. Tests on the already existing productions reveal that both conclusions are relevant, but under different conditions. The discriminating conditions D_1 and D_2 (possibly including goals) are incorporated into the new productions (while the shared condition C is ignored). The implementation of this method to be discussed later handles an arbitrary number $C_1, \ldots, C_n$ of shared conditions.

For instance, while learning to drive I may acquire a procedure to look in the rearview mirror to check that there is no car close behind (D_1) before I decrease speed (B_1). Also I may learn that if I am in the left lane (D_2) when a faster car is coming up behind, I should switch to the right lane (B_2). Venturing up on the freeway for the first time, I quickly realize that preparing a right-hand turn (A) implies both decreasing speed and switching to the right lane. Using the differentiating conditions, the rule of differentiation would turn this insight into the two rules: "If you are preparing a right-hand turn, and no car is close behind, then decrease speed" and "If you are preparing a right-hand turn and you are in the left lane, then switch to the right lane." Both rules can apply on the same occasion, of course.

Using Metaknowledge to Discriminate

In order to state the third method, the concept of a metaproposition must be introduced. Take "(Bigger-than A_1 Bob)" as an example of an ordinary, object-level, proposition. It refers to objects in the world and its truth must be ascertained through investigations of those objects. But a proposition, or the formula it is expressed in, can itself be the subject of some other proposition. An example would be "(Mentions (Bigger-than A_1 Bob) Bob)" which refers to the first proposition and asserts that Bob is one of its arguments. Such a proposition will be called a *metaproposition*, and its predicate a metapredicate. Metapropositions refer to expressions, so their truth or falsity is investigated by inspection of those expressions. The next learning method shows one way of using metacognitions in strategy improvement:

METHOD 3 Rule of specification:
If (test 1) there is an implication

$A\ M(x)$ imply C,

where A is an object-level proposition and $M(x)$ is a metaproposition referring to expression x,

and (test 2) there is a production

$\ldots A \ldots \Rightarrow \ldots$

and (test 3) there is a second production

(GOAL $= G$) $\ldots \Rightarrow$ write C!

and (test 4) there is an expression E such that $M(E)$ is true,

then create the new production

(GOAL $= G$) $A\ E \Rightarrow$ write C!

The rationale for this method is similar to that for the rule of relevance: two of the tests ascertain that C and A are relevant to the existing procedure. But $M(x)$ has taken the role of A_2. The new twist is that E can replace $M(x)$ since the last test checks that $M(x)$ is true when E is present; hence the validity of the new production. Notice that the expression E is more specific than $M(x)$, since it is one out of the possibly large number of expressions all of which make $M(x)$ true. Thus this method is a form of discrimination. The substitution of E for $M(x)$ in the new production is similar to existential specification in standard first-order logic (Suppes 1957), hence the name of this method. The implementation of this method to be discussed later handles an arbitrary number of antecedents, but will only consider the first specification E and $M(x)$ that it finds.

As an example, while learning to solve simple systems of two equations, you may learn a procedure that takes, say, an equation like $aX + bY + c = 0$ and transforms it in some way. You may also learn various conditions for when a system is unsolvable, for instance, when the number of unknowns is greater than the number of equations. Next your teacher tells you that if the parameters of the second equation are the same as those of the first, then the system is unsolvable. With this principle in mind, you encounter the system $2X + 4Y - 4 = 0$ and $2X = 4 - 4Y$, which, as you find out, gives the same parameters for X and Y. The rule of specification then creates the heuristic that an equation system of the form $aX + bY + c = 0; aX = c - bY$ is unsolvable.

Using Implicational Knowledge to Generalize

The rule of specification can be contrasted with the following method, which works in the opposite direction:

METHOD 4 Rule of generalization:
If (test 1) there is an implication

A_1 implies A_2

and (test 2) there is a production

$(\text{GOAL} = G)\ldots A_1 \ldots \Rightarrow$ write $C!$,

then create the new production

$(\text{GOAL} = G)\ldots A_2 \ldots \Rightarrow$ write $C!$

Since the proposition A_2 is true in a wider set of situations than A_1—which it must be if the implication is to hold—then substituting A_2 for A_1 in the production creating C makes the latter fire in more situations than before; that is, it amounts to a generalization of that production. This method is not implemented as yet and is not involved in the computer runs to be discussed later.

Different methods could have been discussed, or other versions of the same methods. The rules of relevance, differentiation, and specification correspond closely to the learning mechanisms actually implemented in the program to be described in the next section. Discussion of the properties of these learning methods and of the learning effects they generate will be postponed until the details of their current implementation have been presented.

6.3 Implementing the Theory

System Architecture

The learning methods just described have been implemented in PSS3, a production-system language constructed by the author (Ohlsson 1979). PSS3 allows the user to structure production memory. Groups of productions can be collected into production sets. During a cycle one and only one production set is active. Its productions have priority over all other productions. Within production sets, conflicts are resolved through a linear priority ordering. Only a single instantiation of a production is computed during matching, namely the one maximizing the recency of the match. The working memory elements are considered in order of recency during a match, and the condition elements are considered in order from left to right. Production sets can activate each other in arbitrary patterns.

PSS3 also features ranged variables, in addition to the commonly used unrestricted variables. A ranged variable will only match against the members of a specified list of expressions. A member of a range can be a complex expression which contains other variables. Finally, PSS3 can handle sequence variables which match against any string of expressions, including the null string. Sequence variables are not restricted to the tail end of expressions as they are in some other production-system languages.

Elements in working memory may contain variables. Facilities exist that allow a PSS3 production to test whether one working memory element is an instance of another working memory element. For example, a production can identify that (OLD *A*) is an instance of (OLD *X*) while both reside in working memory.

There is a single working memory shared by all procedures. Working memory is a list of expressions, ordered by recency. It has a fixed capacity, set by the user. The capacity remains the same thoughout a run. To complete the runs in the present chapter, a memory capacity of about 75 elements was needed. Each memory element is unique; that is, multiple copies of the same expression are not allowed. There is no decay of working memory elements.

Productions can also match against a visual buffer memory. This memory is a read-only memory; that is, expressions in it can be read, but not altered. Actions executed by a production matching against the buffer memory (e.g., the creation of a new expression) operate on working memory, not on the buffer memory. Information can only enter the buffer memory through the perceptual system. The buffer has no capacity limit.

Performance Organization

The learning methods operate in the context of a task-independent performance program that conforms to the theory of problem solving (Newell and Simon 1972). It begins a solution attempt by reinstating a problem space and a strategy (problem space hypothesis; see Newell 1980). This is done by retrieving from permanent memory an expression containing a description of the initial knowledge state, pointers to the operators, a description of the goal state, and a pointer to the relevant strategy. The initial representation in the space is a mental model of the problem situation, which is then manipulated through the operators (assumption about mental modeling; see Johnson-Laird 1980). The system is capable of propositional reasoning as well as model manipulation (assumption of dual mechanisms).

Procedural skills are not encoded in a single homogeneous set of productions. Instead, production memory is organized in terms of nodes corresponding to procedures or routines for performing particular tasks or subtasks (assumption about active network). Thus each node functions as a program for performing a particular task. A strategy is a node and so is an operator. The structure of each node is a PSS3 production set. A node is responsible for solving a particular task. It does so either by making inferences (or other information processing steps) or by calling on other nodes. All the (task-specific) productions in a node may be of the call-on-others variety; we would naturally call such a node a strategy, since it directs the work of other nodes. On the other hand, a node may consist solely of inference productions; we would tend to call such a node an operator, since it does "real" work (rather than just control work). However, these are ideal cases. Most nodes can be expected to contain a mixture of inference productions and strategic productions. Thus the distinction between strategies and nodes has no structural basis in this system but is only a question of what role a particular node plays in a certain process. A node that serves as a strategy for the moment may appear as an operator at another time. Nodes can call on each other in arbitrary patterns; for instance, a node can call on itself recursively.

For example, consider the arithmetical skill of long division. The operation of division would be a node in the system, containing those productions that are relevant to the task of performing division and are currently known to the system. When solving a division problem, that node would become reinstated as the current top node; that is, it would serve as strategy for that task. The procedures for adding, subtracting, and multiplying numbers would likewise be implemented as nodes. The node for division will occasionally fire a production that calls on one of those other nodes; thus, they would serve as operators. However, while solving a multiplication problem, the multiplication node would serve as the strategy node.

The node for division would also contain productions that know directly the answer to basic division problems like $x/2$. Thus the division node would typically contain both strategic productions and inference productions. These productions would have been added one by one to the node by various learning mechanisms. Thus, the node becomes progressively better "stocked" with methods for performing its task. The strategic productions and the inference productions constitute the task-specific kernel of each node. However, they do not exhaust the productions that belong to a node.

Over and above the task-specific productions, there are task-independent productions for such functions as popping and pushing the goal stack, recognizing that goals are satisfied, for testing the applicability of operators, for backward chaining as well as forward search. They represent the general intelligence of the system. In principle, the program could solve at least simple search problems using nothing but its task-independent productions and the relevant operators.

The general and the task-dependent productions are interfaced by storing pointers to all general productions at each node (assumption about distributed general intelligence). Since the number of task-independent productions must be small (less than a hundred in the present case), this amounts to a minor addition to each node. The skeleton of a node is thus a list of the general productions, plus a slot for task-specific ones. There can be zero, one, or any number of productions in the slot.

This organization ensures smooth interaction between task-specific heuristics and inferences, on the one hand, and the general skills on the other. For each subtask, the system will use its task-specific productions if they have anything to say about the current situation and fall back on its general productions otherwise.

The system is entirely goal-driven (assumption about goal dependence). An operator is always executed because there is a goal to apply it. There is no other way to make it go. This does not mean that the system always works backward. Apply-type goals (i.e., goals to apply certain operators) can be set in a working forward manner. The system can also handle Get-type goals (i.e., goals to achieve a certain expression).

Activation of nodes is handled solely by task-independent productions. The mechanism is simple: whenever the currently active goal is to apply an operator, activate the corresponding node. Thus a production activates a node by setting a goal that is relevant to that node. In this way the control structure of the system is instantaneously responsive to the structure of the task. For any task the control structure is the goal tree for that task (assumption about flexible control structure).

There is no special mechanism for passing arguments from one node to another. The specification of an Apply-type goal may contain a specification of the arguments to which the operator is to be applied (e.g., "apply Add to 1 and 3"). Task-independent productions then check whether those arguments are currently available in working memory and set up the appropriate Get goals if they are not. If now arguments are specified in the Apply goal, other task-independent productions will search working memory for suitable arguments, and return the first set of arguments found.

Perceptual System

PSS3 has a perceptual interface suitable for small texts of the type presented in psychological experiments on simple reasoning tasks. A problem is presented to the program in natural language format. The text is stored in a two-dimensional Lisp array, one word to a cell.

The array can only be accessed through a structure called the EYE. The EYE always "focuses" on a single cell in the array. It has a "visual field" spanning the cell in focus plus the four adjacent cells in the array. When the EYE "looks," information about the contents of the five cells in its visual field "streams through" the EYE and becomes stored in the perceptual buffer memory. The EYE can only accept a single type of input, namely an instruction about size and direction of the next "saccade." Thus, it can only execute ballistic saccades. After having executed a saccade, it always looks at its destination and prints out a picture of the current content of its visual field. The EYE is implemented as a Lisp function.

The EYE is controlled by a set of productions—a node—called the visual system. From the point of view of the visual system, the EYE is a primitive action that can appear in the right-hand side of productions. The visual system translates intentions to look at certain objects in the array into EYE movements. It also reads the visual buffer memory, and puts (low-level) encodings of its contents into working memory. The EYE and the visual system together constitute the perceptual system.

The main (but not the only) employer of the perceptual system is the READ operator, which translates conceptual goals like "read the question" into stimulus-oriented instructions like "look at the first word of the third line," which become goals for the visual system. The READ operator also knows how to make (higher-level) encodings (e.g., propositions) out of the outputs from the perceptual system.

The parsing rules currently employed in the perceptual system are quite ad hoc. The main purpose of the perceptual system is to allow the tracing of strategy transformations through changes in how the problem text is accessed.

Learning Mechanisms

Three learning mechanisms have been implemented that correspond closely to the rules of relevance, differentiation, and specification.

Implementation of these methods required a number of design decisions. First, how should the temporal relation between learning and problem solving be conceived? The learning mechanisms could, in principle, work during intertrial intervals, or even during sleep. However, since humans appear to learn while doing, it seemed more plausible to postulate that they work during (perhaps in parellel with) task-oriented activity.

Second, since the methods perform tests on productions, the issue of inspectability of procedural memory must be faced. The learning methods considered here perform tests on productions. Therefore the system must be able to inspect its procedural memory. However, it is a cognitive commonplace that people have very limited access to their own procedural knowledge, the stock examples being our lack of awareness of how we parse natural language and how we keep our balance on a bicycle (Polanyi 1958). To make the implementation plausible, some limitations on the ability of the learning mechanisms to inspect procedural memory must be formulated.

The learning methods have been implemented as productions. All productions match against working memory (or against the perceptual buffer, which is not relevant in this context). If tests are to be performed on productions, the latter must be represented in working memory. This representation is governed by the following rules. When a production fires, it projects an image of itself into working memory. Only a single production image is present in working memory at any one time; when a new production projects, the previous image is deleted. Furthermore only task-specific productions project in this way; neither the general productions nor the productions making up the learning mechanisms do. Thus the task-specific productions "pass through" working memory, "showing themselves" to the learning productions. But at any one time working memory contains only the last task-specific production to fire. It is the only part of procedural memory that can be inspected.

A third issue concerns the distinction between productions and instantiations. Should a production project an image of itself into working memory or an image of its current instantiation? Since people seem more aware of what inferences they make than of how they make them (i.e., by what rules they are made), it is more plausible to postulate that people can inspect instantiations. In accordance with this, the image projected into working memory is instantiated.

Each method corresponds to a single designating production, that is, a production which can build other productions (Anderson and Kline 1979). Designating productions are task independent, so they belong to the general intelligence of the system; they are represented at each node.

Each designating production looks for a learning opportunity, signaled by the presence of an implication in working memory. For instance, the mechanism corresponding to the rule of relevance waits for an implication of the form "A_1 and A_2 imply C," and the mechanism corresponding to the rule of differentiation looks for a pair of implications "A implies B_1" and "A implies B_2." When a learning opportunity is noticed, the designating production fires, creating a small set of opportunity-specific productions.

The latter are of two kinds. The first type embodies the tests that belong to the method (i.e., in terms of the method schema given in the first section, they constitute T^*). For instance, the designating production corresponding to the rule of relevance creates one test production that looks for the presence of B in the action side of some production and another that looks for A_1 in the condition side of some production, and so forth. For each test in the method, the designating production creates a corresponding test production.

When a test production fires, it leaves a proposition in working memory, signaling that the test it embodies has been found to be satisfied. The second type of opportunity-specific production will be called a *mapping* production. Such productions react to the presence of signals from the test productions. When all the tests have been found to be satisfied, the mapping production fires. It is itself a designating production, which creates the new task-specific productions. In terms of the method schema (see section 6.1), the mapping production computes F; that is, it maps the outputs of the tests onto the new productions. In principle, there is a single mapping production for each learning opportunity.

The main reasons why the learning methods are implemented to work in this stepwise fashion is that all the tests connected with a particular method may not be satisfied at the same time (e.g., during the same production cycle). One test may be satisfied during one cycle, but, due to the changing content of working memory, it may have ceased to be satisfied before the other tests have become true. Indeed, there is no guarantee that all tests will be satisfied during the same problem-solving trial, as we shall see later. Therefore, the tests have to be represented in a way that allow them to be satisfied at different points in time, independently of each other.

The opportunity-specific productions are added to each node. They fire only once; like some insects that die after completing their job of reproduction, these rules do not fire again, once they have generated their offspring.

In summary, a single learning method corresponds to a single designating production. When an opportunity for it to fire arises, it creates one opportunity-specific test production for each test in the method, plus one opportunity-specific mapping production. When all test productions belonging to an opportunity have fired, the mapping production belonging to the same opportunity fires, creating the new task-specific productions.

In a system with a structured production memory, there must be some rule for the placement of new productions. In which node should they go? In the present implementation, all new task-specific productions are added to the node that is serving as strategy—the current "top" node. As a consequence the goal incorporated into new task-specific productions is always the top goal.

One consequence of the foregoing assumptions is that a task-oriented production can only serve as input to a learning process if it fires. Productions that do not fire are never seen by the learning productions. Thus learning builds only on relevant procedures.

A second consequence is that the learning of a single new production can be spread out over several problem solving trials. Depending on the exact sequence of problems encountered, there can be any number of trials before all the test productions connected with a particular learning opportunity have fired.

To what extent does this implementation reintroduce trace data into the learning process? The fact that the program can inspect instantiations of productions may appear to undermine the claim that procedural learning is possible without trace data. However, the decision to use instantiations was not made because the learning mechanisms need the trace information potentially present in them but because of psychogical plausibility. In fact the learning mechanisms do not extract the trace information in the production instantiations. For instance, they never compare the left and right sides of the same production, nor do they ever relate constants in the instantiations to expressions in working memory. Similarly, the fact that productions show themselves in working memory in the order in which they fire also implies that some trace information is available. Again the decision to limit inspectability of procedural memory in this way was not made on the basis of the learning mechanisms but from psychological plausibility. This type of trace information is also ignored by the learning mechanisms: the mapping productions have no way of knowing in which order the test productions have fired, nor has a particular test production any way of knowing which of its fellow tests have fired at any one time. The general question of the relation between these learning mechanism and inductive learning mechanisms will be taken up again in the discussion section.

A fourth learning mechanism was added to the system. It is a backward-to-forward converter; that is, it converts a backward search to a working forward sequence by creating productions that anticipate the results of the backward search. It is an empirical learning method, making use of trace information. With respect to its effects, the method bears a family resemblance to both the action sequence identifier in Anzai and Simon (1979) and the particular application of the composition method described by Neves and Anderson (1981), but it achieves the effect by inspection of the goal tree. This method cannot introduce new problem-solving steps, only change the order of those already existing; it cannot discover a new strategy, but it can make a strategy run faster.

This concludes the description of the theory of rational learning. The next section describes the task domain to which the theory is to applied.

6.4 The Three-Term Series Problem

The ability to reason is central to intelligent behavior. Psychologists have tried to assess this ability through a variety of simple inference problems. A three-term series problem assigns relative positions to three objects along some linear dimension through two binary relational statements. The question is which of the three objects is at the end of one or the other directions of that dimension. For example, "*Al* is bigger than Bob. Bob is

⟨state⟩ ::= ⟨element⟩ | ⟨element⟩ ⟨state⟩
⟨element⟩ ::= ⟨proposition⟩ | ⟨model⟩
⟨model⟩ ::= (⟨endl⟩ ⟨object-sequence⟩ ⟨end2⟩)
⟨end⟩ ::= BIG | SMALL | . . .
⟨object-sequence⟩ ::= ⟨object⟩ | ⟨object⟩ ⟨object-sequence⟩
⟨object⟩ ::= AL | BOB | CARL | . . .
⟨proposition⟩ ::= ⟨assertion⟩ | ⟨question⟩
⟨assertion⟩ ::= (⟨predicate⟩ ⟨object-sequence⟩)
⟨predicate⟩ ::= Bigger-than | Biggest-of | Answer | Candidate
⟨question⟩ ::= (⟨predicate⟩ ? ⟨object-sequence⟩)

ANSWER(X) —answers question X with the help of already available propositions; the answer is said and the solution attempt terminated

ASK(X) —asks question X of the current model, i.e., compares the question with the model in order to read off a new proposition from it

INTEGRATE(X) —integrates the proposition X into the current model

PLACE(X) —places object X in the (empty) model

READ(X) —reads the item X from the problem text

CONVERT(X) —converts proposition X into its opposite

Figure 6.1
Problem space and operators for the basic model-building strategy

bigger than Carl. Who is smallest?" Several theories of how people solve such problems have been proposed (see Hunter 1957; DeSoto, London, and Handel 1965; Huttenlocher 1968; Clark 1969; Noordman 1977; Sternberg 1980), but all of them except the work by Quinton and Fellows (1975) have ignored learning effects.

The three-term series problem is a natural testing ground for the theory presented in the previous two sections. Of course, it is simple enough to be computationally tractable. But, more important, there are many declarative truths about linear dimensions and about the task domain as such that could form starting points for rational learning processes. Examples will be given in the next section.

Figures 6.1 and 6.2 represent the initial strategy of most adult humans on this task. This strategy is a member of the general class of strategies defined by Ohlsson (1980a), although the notation has been changed for readability. It will here be called the "initial" or "model-building" strategy. Figure 6.1 contains assumptions about representation. People think both

When there is a question (⟨predicate⟩ ?)
and there is a proposition (⟨predicate⟩ ⟨object⟩),
then apply ANSWER to (⟨predicate⟩ ?) !

When the model is (⟨end1⟩ ⟨object1⟩ ⟨object2⟩ ⟨object3⟩ ⟨end2⟩)
and there is a ⟨question⟩,
then apply ASK to ⟨question⟩ !

When the model is (⟨end1⟩ ⟨object1⟩ ⟨object2⟩ ⟨object3⟩ ⟨end2⟩),
then apply READ to the question !

When the model is (⟨end1⟩ ⟨object1⟩ ⟨object2⟩ ⟨end2⟩)
and there is a most recent ⟨proposition⟩
and an effort to apply INTEGRATE to ⟨proposition⟩ has failed,
then apply CONVERT to ⟨proposition⟩ !

When the model is (⟨end1⟩ ⟨object1⟩ ⟨object2⟩ ⟨end2⟩)
and there is a most recent ⟨proposition⟩,
then apply INTEGRATE to ⟨proposition⟩ !

When the model is (⟨end1⟩ ⟨object1⟩ ⟨object2⟩ ⟨end2⟩),
then apply READ to the second premise !

When the model is (⟨end1⟩ ⟨object1⟩ ⟨end2⟩)
and the most recent proposition is (⟨predicate⟩ ⟨object2⟩ ⟨object1⟩),
then apply INTEGRATE to (⟨predicate⟩ ⟨object2⟩ ⟨object1⟩) !

When the model is (⟨end1⟩ ⟨end2⟩)
and the most recent proposition is (⟨predicate⟩ ⟨object1⟩ ⟨object2⟩),
then apply PLACE to ⟨object2⟩ !

When at the beginning of the solution attempt,
then apply READ to the first premise !

Figure 6.2
The basic model-building strategy

with propositions and with mental models. The operators read in propositional information from the problem text, translate it into a mental model, and then read off the answer from the model. Figure 6.2 shows heuristics by which the space in figure 6.1 can be searched. The basic assumption is that people initially process the two propositions and the question in the order in which they appear in the problem text. This strategy can be interpreted as a simple carry-over of normal reading habits.

The strategy contains the following four further assumptions. First, the mental model depends on the predicate in the first premise with respect to its orientation in cognitive space. Second, the translation of the first premise into a model proceeds in two steps. The second argument of the premise is placed in the model, and then the premise as a whole is integrated. Third, integration of a premise with two arguments x_1 and x_2 succeeds only when x_2 is already part of the current model, and constitutes one of its end objects. Fourth, if integration of a premise fails, a propositional inference is made to convert it; the integration operation is then applied to the new proposition.

This strategy has the following characteristics: (1) Structurally different problems necessitate different amounts of computation; in other words, it has a jagged difficulty profile over problems. (2) At the end of a solution attempt, any question about the series (e.g., "Who is in the middle?") can be answered. (3) It can easily be extended to handle unorthodox problems with three terms, as well as many n-term series problems. (4) It uses a double representation, namely both a mental model and propositions.

Quinton and Fellows (1975) have found empirically that adults after working through a hundred problems sometimes discover the following perceptual or expert strategy, which is also shown in figure 6.3: if the relational terms in the first premise and the question are the same, look at the first argument of the first premise; if not, look at its second argument. The argument you have looked at is the candidate for the answer. If the candidate does not recur in the second premise, it is the answer to the problem. If it does, the other argument in the second premise is the answer. This strategy will here be called the "final," "expert," or "perceptual pattern" strategy.

This strategy has the following characteristics: (1) All problems are solved with the same amount of computation; that is, its difficulty profile is flat. (2) No other question about the series can be answered except the one stated in the problem text (without further processing of the text). (3) It is

When there is a proposition (Candidate ⟨object1⟩)
and there is an ⟨object2⟩ different from ⟨object1⟩
and there is an ⟨object3⟩ different from ⟨object1⟩,
then write (Answer ⟨object1⟩) !

When there is a proposition (Candidate ⟨object1⟩)
and there is an ⟨object2⟩ which is equal to ⟨object1⟩
and there is an ⟨object3⟩ different from ⟨object1⟩,
then write (Answer ⟨object3⟩) !

When there is an ⟨object⟩,
then write (Candidate ⟨object⟩)
and look at the first term of the second premise
and look at the second term of the second premise !

When there is a ⟨predicate1⟩
and there is a ⟨predicate2⟩
and they are different,
then look at the second term of the first premise !

When there is a ⟨predicate1⟩
and there is a ⟨predicate2⟩
and they are equal,
then look at the first term of the first premise !

When at the beginning of the solution attempt,
then look at the predicate of the first premise
and look at the predicate of the question !

Figure 6.3
The perceptual or expert strategy discovered by Quinton and Fellows (1975)

essentially dependent on the problem format described in the first paragraph in this section. Any change in the problem (e.g., introduction of true/false question like "Is Al bigger than Bob?") makes it inapplicable. (4) It does not make use of any mental model of the situation mentioned in the problem text.

6.5 Applying the Theory

The initial strategy for three-term series problems shown in figures 6.1 and 6.2 was implemented according to the performance organization discussed earlier. The strategy was implemented as a node, and each of the operators ANSWER, INTEGRATE, PLACE, and so forth, were also implemented as nodes. Various implicational statements were then "fed" to the program, allowing the rational learning mechanisms described previously to work.

The learning model passed through three major phases: the model-building phase, the propositional phase, and the perceptual phase. In the first phase the program builds a mental model of the situation described in the problem text, or some part thereof. After some learning has occurred, this part of the strategy is eliminated, and the program proceeds entirely on the basis of the meaning of the statements in the problem text, without building any mental model of the problem situation. This propositional strategy is in turn replaced by a strategy that works entirely on the basis of certain similarity judgments between lexical items in the text itself; in other words, the final stage is identical with the expert strategy described in the last section.

This learning sequence was produced by "hand-feeding" implicational truths to the program. The program did not create its declarative knowledge. Several sources of declarative truths about a task were specified in an earlier section. How a system comes to believe in various implications is a separate issue, to be dealt with by a different theory.

It is difficult to construct a learning curve for the present system. Its rate of learning depends on the rate of acquisition of relevant implications. Since these were fed to the program by hand, it would have been possible to produce learning curves with varying slopes simply by varying the rate at which the implications were fed to the program. In short, it is unclear what should be used as the ordinate in a learning curve for the present system. The quantitative analysis of the system's behavior will therefore be carried out in terms of the three major stages, the model-building stage, the propositional stage, and the perceptual pattern stage. For each of these strategies, a set of 16 assessment runs were made, covering all the variants of the basic form of the three-term series problem. In an assessment run the learning mechanisms are switched off, so that no learning can occur. The program then works with whatever strategy it has learned up to that point.

The program was fed a total of 15 implications, and transformed them into 41 different productions, which were successively added to the top node. The main phenomenon to be shown here is that as learning proceeds, the computational work performed by the program is shifted from one category of productions to another. In particular, there is a shift from "central processing" (i.e., work being done in the top-node) to "peripheral processing" (i.e., work being done by the visual system). The productions

Table 6.1
Number of production-system cycles to solution for the initial (model-building) strategy, the propositional strategy, and the perceptual pattern strategy on a typical three-term series problem

	Strategy		
Locus of activity	Initial	Propositional	Perceptual
Top node	15 (0.10)	28 (0.28)	5 (0.11)
Strategic	11	9	1
Inferential	4	5	4
General	0	14	0
Subnode	91 (0.60)	26 (0.26)	7 (0.15)
Strategic	0	0	0
Inferential	22	14	1
General	69	12	6
Visual system	46 (0.30)	46 (0.46)	34 (0.74)
Sum	152	100	46

Note: Productions that initialize a run, adjust the goal-stack, or transfer control from one node to another are not included.

firing in each run were classified into the following categories: (1) strategic productions, which are task-specific productions that set goals (since the current goal controls which node is active, setting goals is a way to organize the work of other nodes), (2) inferential productions, which are all task-specific productions that insert knowledge-elements in working memory other than goals, and (3) general productions, which are task-independent productions that belong to the general intelligence of the system. The breakdown of the cycles to solution into these three categories is done separately for "top-node activity" (i.e., cycles occurring under the control of the strategy for the current task) and for "subnode activity" (i.e., cycles occurring in the nodes called by the strategy node, which includes the model-building operators plus TALK and READ; see table 6.1). The productions firing in the visual system and productions that control the visual system by instructing it what to look at constitute the category "visual" in table 6.1. Productions that initialize a run are ignored, because they are the same for every run, regardless of problem and level of learning; human subjects would presumably fire some sort of initialization routine at the beginning of an experiment but hardly at the beginning of every trial. Furthermore productions that push and pop the goal stack are ignored because they should be considered part of the system architecture; likewise the (single) production that transfers control from one node to another is disregarded. The results of this analysis can be seen in the table.

There are several effects in table 6.1. First, there is drop in the number of cycles to solution, from 152 for the initial strategy to 46 for the perceptual pattern strategy. This is a substantial drop, but it is not as big as one would expect from a consideration of data. What little empirical evidence there is indicates that the model-building strategy takes about ten seconds to execute, while the perceptual pattern strategy can be carried out in less than two seconds (Ohlsson 1980b), a speedup with a factor of five rather than a factor of three. However, the overall speedup is accompanied by a substantial shift in processing from the strategy and its operators to the visual system. The category "visual" grows from 30 to 74 percent due to the strategy transformations. Since this category is intended to represent preattentive, peripheral processing that is both fast and may occur in parallel with higher processing, the model actually predicts a bigger speedup than by a factor of three. A third major effect in table 6.1 is the successively decreasing role of the problem-solving operators. In the beginning almost all inferential work was being done by them. The perceptual pattern strategy does not call up any subnode, except the TALK node that has to be called on to say the answer. Thus the goal structure for the task has been "flattened out"; the expert strategy does not call on any other nodes than input-output nodes (i.e., the visual system and the TALK node). Connected with this is the changing role of the top node. In the initial strategy, the top node is truly a strategy node. Its main work is to set goals that call other nodes into action in a particular sequence. In the propositional strategy the top node has acquired inferential productions so that it can now perform most of the inferential work by itself, without calling on other nodes. The activity in the top node is then more extensive than before. In the final transformation to the perceptual pattern strategy, the character of the work done by the top-node changes again, as the visual system takes over almost all the work of adapting to the particular task at hand. The work done by the top node then dwindles once more. In short, the analysis in table 6.1 shows an orderly and interpretable set of trends as we move from left to right in the table.

The successive changes in the strategy can also be traced by looking at the pattern of eye movements executed by the program (the perceptual system of the program was described in a previous section). In figure 6.4 we see the successive fixation points of the program at each of the three levels

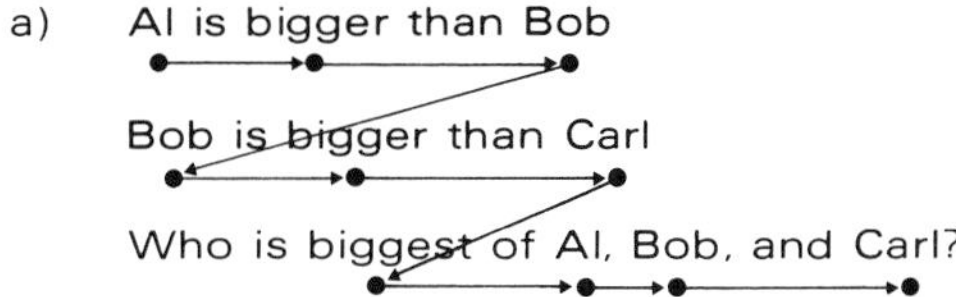

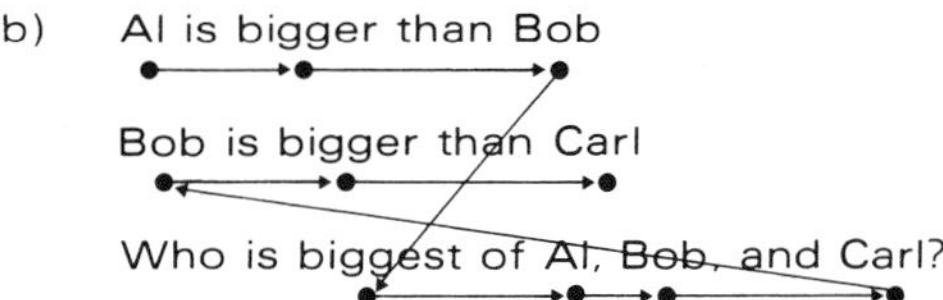

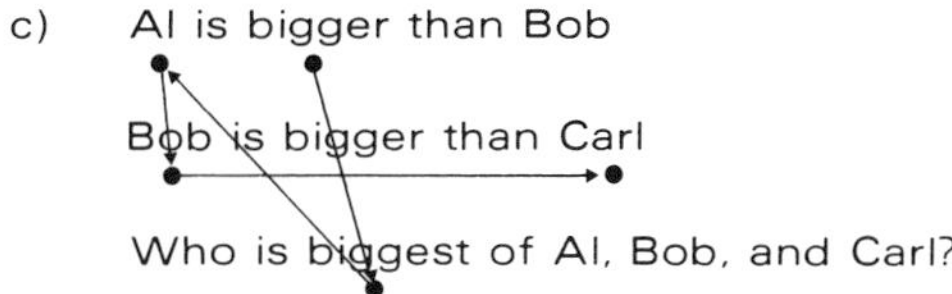

Figure 6.4
Eye movements across the stimulus display by the program at each of three levels of learning

of learning. Initially, it reads the sentences in the problem text in the order in which they are stated; the eye "sweeps" over the three sentences one at a time, stopping at the content words. The second part of figure 6.4 shows that the only change in the use of the problem text associated with the transition from the model-building to the propositional strategy is to read the question before the second premise. Finally, in the bottom part of figure 6.4 the dramatic change in the pattern of visual attention that accompanies the transition from the propositional to the perceptual strategy can be seen. The eye now looks at the predicate in the first premise, the predicate in the question, then at the first term in the first premise, and, finally, at both terms in the second premise. No statement in the text is read; only certain words are focused on.

Let us now consider some details about how this process came about. The first transformation was to eliminate the integration of the second premise into the mental model derived from the basis of the first premise. This transformation involves two substeps, the first one being triggered by the following implication:

If x is biggest of the set M, and if y is bigger than x, then y is biggest of the union of M and y.

This implicational statement is generally valid, and of the type one would expect most people in our culture to have in their world knowledge. Applied to the three-term series problem, this statement says that if x is the biggest object in the two-object model built from the first premise, and if the second premise says that y is bigger than x, then y is biggest of all three objects mentioned in the problem. So, if the question asks which object is biggest, y is the answer.

This implication is seized by the rule of relevance. It builds a set of opportunity-specific test productions in the way described previously, which finds that the proposition "x is biggest of x, y, and z" occurs in the right-hand side of a production (i.e., one of the inference productions in the ASK operator) and that the proposition "y is bigger than x" occurs in the condition side of some production (e.g., in the condition sides of the inference productions in the INTEGRATE operator).

The opportunity-specific mapping-production then creates the two rules:

When "x is biggest of x and y," and "z is bigger than x,"
then write that "z is biggest of z, x, and y!"

and

When "z is bigger than x," see whether "x is biggest of x and y!"

Thus two productions are created at this point, one inference production (the first one) and one strategic production (the second).

On the runs following the creation of these productions, as soon as the second premise has been read (but before it has been integrated into the model), the program tries to recode the information in the two-object model into the form "x is biggest of x and y." Naturally there are no heuristics for how to do this, since it is a step that has not so far been part of this procedure. There is no production in the node that knows how to do this. The general problem-solving procedures then take over and find out through backward search through the operators that a statement of this form can be produced by the ASK operator. However, the ASK operator is a question-answering process, so it needs a question as input. Therefore the question is read in from the problem text. Notice that the question is now read at the same time as before (i.e., after the second premise) but for a different reason. Having read the question, it is applied to the two-object model, and a statement of the form required by the new inference production is derived. That production then fires, and a statement of the form "x is biggest of x, y, and z" is derived, without completing the model of the internal order of the three objects.

This step thus eliminates an operation that has been found to be redundant—the integration of the second premise—at the price of having to figure out how to produce a proposition of the form "x is biggest of x and y." This requires more processing than the eliminated step. However, as soon as a means of producing the wanted proposition has been found, it can be encoded by some empirical or experience-oriented learning mechanism. (This is the task of the backward-to-forward converter briefly mentioned at the end of section 6.2.) Thus the pattern predicted by the present theory is one in which the solution time temporarily becomes longer as an improvement in a procedure is introduced but which then falls below its previous value once the new procedure has been "smoothed out."

Next, let us see what happens when the proposition "x is biggest of x and y" has been derived from the two-object model, but the second premise turns out to be "y is bigger than z." The new inference production cannot fire; it does not cover this case. Thus the new procedure cannot work, and the program falls back on its previous procedure, integrating the second premise into the mental model and reading off the answer from it.

Further thinking about the definition of the basic form of the three-term series problem may lead to the following insight:

If x is biggest of x and y, and the second premise relates z to y, then x is biggest of x, y, and z.

This is so because the only way that z could be stated to be bigger than x is through either of the two statements "x is smaller than z," and "z is bigger than x," both of which relate z to x. If the second premise instead relates z to y, none of those statements can be true, so x is biggest.

In contrast to the previous truth given to the program, this implication cannot be expected to reside in most persons' world knowledge. Its validity is confined to the basic form of the three-term series problem and could therefore only be contemplated after thinking about the structure of the problem.

Given this new declarative insight, the rule of specification gets something to work on. It, or more precisely, the test productions it creates to deal with this learning opportunity, observes that the statement "*x* is biggest of *x*, *y*, and *z*" occurs in an action side and that the statement "*x* is biggest of *x* and *y*" appears in a condition side (i.e., in the condition of the inference production created in the previous step). It then looks for some expression that would make the metapredicate "second premise that relates *z* to *y*" true. Finding "*y* is bigger than *z*," the new inference production is created:

When "*x* is biggest of *x* and *y*," and "*y* is bigger than *z*,"
then write that "*x* is biggest of *x*, *y*, and *z*!"

This new inference production extends the elimination of the integration of the second premise to new cases. When these two learning steps have been repeated for those cases in which "smaller" replaces "bigger," this elimination is complete. For all three-term series problems, the strategy node then contains productions that know how to derive the answer, given only the two-object model and the second premise.

The order in which the two learning steps described so far occur is not dependent on the order in which the implicational truths that trigger them arrive in working memory. The step described first must be completed first, because the second step tests for the existence of some production that employs a proposition of the form "*x* is biggest of *x* and *y*." No production does, until the first step has been completed. Thus the first step is a prerequisite for the second step.

It is also notworthy that the second step cannot, by the nature of the case, be completed during a single trial. The tests created in connection with that learning opportunity cannot be satisfied, unless the program encounters one problem in which the inference production created in the first step fires (otherwise test 2 is not satisfied) and also a problem in which it does not (otherwise test 1 is not satisfied). Thus this step cannot be completed in less than two trials; if the problem sequence encountered is random, the number of trials needed can obviously be larger.

The two learning steps described so far corresponds fairly closely to the tactics described by Quinton and Fellows (1975) as the second premise strategy, parts 1 and 2.

Having completed the foregoing transformation, the program solves problems by recoding the first premise twice: from "*x* is bigger than *y*" to "(BIG *x y* SMALL)" to "*x* is biggest of *x* and *y*." Since the model is not going to be used for the integration of the second premise, the operation of translating the first premise into model format has now become redundant. This is so because the following implication obviously holds:

If *x* is bigger than *y*, then *x* is biggest of *x* and *y*.

Thus the wanted expression can be derived from the first premise, without going through the model-building operation.

However, the proposition "*x* is biggest of *x* and *y*" also serves as antecedent in the following implication:

If *x* is bigger than *y*, then *y* is smallest of *y* and *x*.

Which conclusion should be derived from the first premise? Obviously this depends on what the question is: if the question asks which object is biggest of the lot, then the statement about which is biggest of the two mentioned in the first premise is of interest, and vice versa.

Given the two implications, the rule of differentiation looks for the conditions that differentiate the situations in which one consequent is produced from those in which the other is produced. Finding that they are, indeed, the presence of a question of one or the other form, it creates the following three new productions, one strategic and two inferential:

When "*x* is bigger than *y*,"
then get either "Which is biggest of *x*, *y*, and *z*?"
 or "Which is smallest of *x*, *y*, and *z*?"

When "*x* is bigger than *y*," and "Which is biggest of *x*, *y*, and *z*?"
then write that "*x* is biggest of *x* and *y*!"

When "*x* is bigger than *y*," and "Which is smallest of *x*, *y*, and *z*?"
then write that "*y* is smallest of *y* and *x*!"

This step has the effect of moving up the reading of the question so that it occurs immediately after reading the first premise, rather than after reading the second premise. This produces the eye-movement patterns seen in the middle part of figure 6.4. This step corresponds closely to what Quinton and Fellows (1975) call the first premise strategy. Its effect, when it has been completed for all cases, is to eliminate the translation of the first premise into a mental model.

Again, this step cannot, by the nature of the case, be completed in a single trial. The two differentiating conditions (i.e., the two types of question) simply do not occur in one and the same problem and thus cannot both be observed by the test productions in one and the same trial.

Looking at the dependencies, it is clear that this step cannot be performed unless at least the first of the previous steps have been completed. Thus the learning steps are partially ordered.

When these two transformations have been completed, the program works in the following way: Read the first premise; read the question. Derive which object is the best answer, given only the two objects mentioned in the first premise; call it x. Read the second premise; see whether it puts the third object—call it z—even further along the relevant dimension than x or not; if so, answer with z, otherwise with x. This is a propositional strategy; there is no mental model involved. The sentences in the problem text are read, and inferences performed on the basis of their meaning. One can describe the main effect of these transformations as having changed the procedure from working in terms of the referent of the problem text, that is, from working in terms of (a model of) the situation described in the problem text, to working with the sense of the problem text. These steps have made the program abstract away from the referent and solve the problem exclusively in terms of sense.

The next phase in the learning—from a propositional to a perceptual procedure—is brought about through repeated applications of the rule of relevance. Since no new learning method is involved, it will be described in less detail.

The implications that trigger the last learning steps relate the outcomes of the propositional inferences to the form of the problem text. For instance, if the predicates of the first premise and of the question denote the same dimension, then the outcome of the propositional inference from the first premise will always be identical to the first term of the first premise. This insight is expressed in the implication:

If x_1 is the predicate of the first premise, x_2 is the predicate of the question, x_1 is equal to x_2, and x_3 is the grammatical subject of the first premise,
then x_3 is the answer candidate from the first premise.

On the other hand, if the two predicates of the first premise and the question denote different dimensions, then it is instead the second term of the first premise that is the candidate answer from the first premise.

The rule of relevance applied to these insights creates productions that eliminate the need for reading the first premise at all; they arrive at the right candidate by comparing predicates, and then focusing on the right term. For instance, the foregoing implications gives rise to, among others, the following productions:

When "x_1 is the predicate of the first premise,"
then get "x_2 is the predicate of the question" (i.e., look at the predicate of the question)!

When "x_1 is the predicate of the first premise"
and "x_2 is the predicate of the question" and "x_1 is equal to x_2,"
then get "x_3 is the first term of the first premise" (i.e., look at the first term of the first premise)!

These productions have the effect that the first premise need no longer be read and comprehended. One of its objects is picked up and carried along to the processing of the second premise, and that is all.

Similarly, the outcome of the propositional inferences from the second premise can be anticipated by realizing that if x is the candidate from the first premise, and x is not identical to either of the two terms of the second premise, then x must be the answer; if it is identical to one of them, it is the other term that is the answer. The rule of relevance then creates productions which eliminate the need for reading and comprehending the second premise. The term carried along from the first premise is compared to the two terms in the second premise, and then the answer is known, as in the following production:

When "x_1 is the candidate" and "x_2 is the first term of the second premise,"
"x_3 is the second term of the second premise," and "x_1 is equal to x_3,"
then write "x_2 is the answer!"

At the end of this transformation the strategy used by the program is a version of the strategy described in figure 6.3. Three-term series problems are then solved with the help of three successive judgments on pairs of lexical items: the predicates in first premise and question, the candidate and first argument in second premise, the candidate and second argument in second premise. This strategy generates the eye movement pattern in the lower part of figure 6.4. This strategy is perceptual because most of its information processing takes the form of perceptual judgments on stimulus items. It works with the form of the problem text.

One way of summarizing this learning process is to say that it is a process of successively emptying the task of its content. The initial strategy works three-term series problems by imagining the referent of the problem text; most humans would experience this mental model as a visual image. The first learning process eliminates the mental model, thus emptying the task of its sensory content. The result is a method that works with the sense of the problem text, making inferences on the basis of the meaning of the premises. In the final sequence of transformations, the task is also emptied of its conceptual content, in that the program now disregards the meaning of the problem text and attends only to its form. This sequence captures well the intuitive notion that extended drill on such simple problems results in a "mechanical" activity.

Accompanying this change is a shift in the balance between thinking and perceiving. For the initial strategy several information processing steps intervene between the reading of the sentences in the problem text. Thus the time to solution is longer than the time needed simply to read the text. For the propositional strategy the time to work the problem is almost the same as the time to read the three sentences because the inferential steps are fewer and simpler. For the perceptual strategy, however, no thinking is needed. This strategy only utilizes the structure that is inherent in the stimulus display. It solves the problems in less time than it takes to read the sentences. Thus the locus of the information process has been pushed toward the periphery.

6.6 Discussion

The chapter began with the thesis that people are capable of rational as well as empirical learning. A space of rational learning methods was defined, and three of its members specified and implemented. When combined with general problem-solving methods and an initial performance strategy for a simple domain, these learning heuristics produced strategy transformations that led to a more efficient performance strategy.

How general are these learning mechanisms? The actual implementation of them is domain independent in the sense that it does not presuppose anything about the types of objects or operators that are going to be used in solving a problem. Nor does it assume anything about the strategy that is to be improved. The mechanisms only know about productions and implications, and their syntax. The expressions that appear as components of the productions and the implications are treated as units, and their internal structure is ignored. Thus the mechanisms are applicable to any production system and any set of implications. However, whether they will produce useful strategy transformations on a particular task is a different question. It can only be answered by actually running the system.

A related question is whether these learning mechanisms produce any dysfunctional rules or not. First, notice that no rules are created unless there are implications available. The nature of the rules created will to a large extend depend on the implications fed into the system. False implications (e.g., "if *x* is smaller than *y*, then *x* is bigger than *y*") will obviously lead to destructive production rules. Second, the learning mechanisms do not turn implications into productions unless they relate to existing productions in certain ways. The very purpose of those tests is to establish that the new productions are relevant to those that already exist. Therefore they strongly cut down on the possibility to create harmful rules. They might create useless rules, but it is difficult to think of circumstances under which they will create harmful rules. Third, in the simulation exercise, no weird rules were in fact created, although some rules were created repeatedly.

It is now time to consider some of the broader implications of the theory. Two basic facts about procedural learning are that it is gradual and that it is dependent upon learner activity. Theories must be evaluated with respect to how they handle these two facts.

Why then is learning not instantaneous according to the present theory? The most basic answer is that new productions themselves constitute the raw material for further learning. Thus some learning steps are dependent on other steps. Generalizing over the examples in the previous section, we can say that such dependencies arise in the following way: Suppose that in a particular learning opportunity a production Pd_1 will be created if test T becomes satisfied. As it happens, none of the productions in the current procedure satisfy T. But as problem-solving activity continues, another learning opportunity arises, giving birth to a production Pd_2, which does satisfy T. Thus Pd_1 can be created, but it had to "wait" for some other learning to occur. Such dependencies impose a partial ordering on the strategy transformations.

A second cause of gradual learning is that all tests associated with a particular learning opportunity cannot be carried out at once. This in turn depends on the limited inspectability of procedural memory. If a learning method has set up three tests to be performed, it has to look at three different productions. Since only a single production can be represented in working memory at any one time, the learning mechanism has to "wait" for the right productions to fire in order to satisfy the tests. As we saw in the preceeding section, the relevant productions may not all fire during the same trial; thus the learning of a single production can be spread out over several problem solving trials.

In summary, learning is gradual partly because of the inherent properties of the learning methods and partly because of the limited inspectability of procedural memory. This should be compared to the explanations offered in systems like ACT (Anderson, Kline, and Beasley 1979) and SAGE (Langley 1982), in which learning is gradual partly because new productions are postulated to accumulate strength gradually.

Why, according to the present theory, is it necessary to learn by doing? Why cannot the learner simply sit and think about the problem? The answer is again based on the limited inspectability of procedural memory. Productions can only be inspected when they are represented in working memory, and in order to be represented there, they have to fire. In other words, activity is necessary in procedural learning because procedures can only be accessed as data while they are being executed.

A new interpretation can now be given of situations in which you must execute a skill—using, say, the stick shift of a car—in order to instruct someone else in it. One explanation of this phenomenon is that you observe your own motor behavior as you execute the skill and then describe it to the learner. This interpretation is peculiar because the external behavior could be observed by the learner as well—but why does he need the subsequent description? According to the present theory, what you do as you execute the skill is that you introspect your procedure for it and you then try to communicate that procedure. Execution is a way of retrieving the procedure.

Given that learning is gradual, what determines its rate? According to the present theory a major factor is the availability of declarative knowledge about the task. If the learner can describe the properties of the task domain to himself, then there is something for the rational learning methods to work on. Thus the theory predicts that rational learning will be ineffective when regularities across problems are difficult to describe. The domain of matchstick problems may be taken as an example (Brooke 1973). On the other hand, rational learning will be effective when regularities across problems are easy to state, as in the three-term series problem. Also the theory predicts that rational learning will be more effective when the properties of the task domain are stated explicitly by a teacher than when they have to be discovered by the learner. In short, the theory captures at least one aspect of the commonsense idea that the better you understand a task, the faster you will figure out how to solve it.

Nothing has been said here about how a person arrives at declarative truths about problems, how powerful a propositional reasoning system must be presupposed, and how propositional reasoning about a problem interacts with other efforts to solve the problem. However, the psychology of propositional reasoning is a research problem in its own right which cannot be adequately treated within the confines of the present chapter.

How different are the methods proposed here from inductive learning methods? Do they constitute a separate class of methods, or should they be construed as variations on some well-known method? When contemplating this question, it is important to attend to the various types of information that is ignored by these methods. First, they are insensitive to the temporal order between events. The new productions that are created are in no way a function of which information-processing operation occurs before or after which other one. Second, the methods are equally impervious to the distance in time between separate events. Tests are carried out, but it does not matter for the outcome whether all become satisfied at one and the same time, or whether there is a considerable lapse of time between the satisfaction of one and the satisfaction of the others (unless the result of a test is displayed from working memory in the meantime). Third, the methods take no notice of the frequency of events. Every learning opportunity is noticed and acted upon once, regardless of frequency. Fourth, the methods disregard feedback. The outcome of the learning processes is not dependent upon the success or failure of the various operations of the performance program. For instance, a learning opportunity that arises in connection with some application of an operator Q is not ignored or discarded, even if it turns out that Q fails to achieve its goal. Unless the concept of induction is to be twisted out of recognition, it must be concluded that the present learning methods are noninductive in nature.

It is interesting in this regard to compare the present theory with the theory of advice taking presented by Hayes-Roth, Klahr, and Mostow (1981). Working in Lisp (or a Lisp-like system), they have exploited the dual nature of functional expressions like (Avoid taking-points me) as both a proposition with "Avoid" as its predicate, and as an executable call to the procedure "Avoid." An advice of the form "Avoid taking points!" (during a cardgame) is first mapped onto a functional expression as a representation of its meaning. When it is found that this declarative expression cannot be executed (because the system does not yet know how to proceed in order to avoid taking points), a process begins to make it executable. This involves finding the relations between the expression and other, already executable expressions. Many different types of operations are needed for this: successive specification of the procedure, expansion of definitions, and so forth. The advice taker is thus a rational learner: it relates advice to definitions of procedures rather than to traces of their execution. The process of establishing relationships between the advice and the existing procedures is similar to the present effort of letting implications give rise to productions only if they can be anchored in some sensible way in already existing productions.

However, the advice taker starts with advice, that is, information that is already procedural in nature, while the rational learner presented here makes use of purely declarative statements. Second, the advice taker does not seem to be selective with respect to the advice given to it and so is subject to the same criticism as proceduralization. How to provide selectivity in the creation of new procedures is one of the major concerns of the present research. A third difference is that the advice taker does not seem to be embedded in a theory of how its activity is related to task-oriented activities; nor does it appear to be supplemented with any hypotheses about limitations on the inspectability of procedural memory. The last comment is not a criticism of the advice taker, since no psychological claims have been made for it.

Hayes-Roth, Klahr, and Mostow (1981) state that the advice taker comprises 200 rules. This seems rather overwhelming in view of the three rules used in the present work. Such a comparison would be premature, however, since the advice taker has been applied to more complex task domains and has also proved its generality by being applied to more than one domain.

What will be the fate of the present theory? It would be surprising if the specific learning methods would not need revision when confronted with further analyses and observations. But the space of methods that perform tests jointly on current implicational beliefs and current procedures, and then constructs new procedures out of them, may fare better. Its consequences, particularly when combined with limitations on the inspectability of procedural memory, are varied and interesting.

The space of learning methods was in turn derived from the rational learning thesis that was stated at the start of this chapter. The first part of this thesis states that significant improvements in a problem-solving strategy can be computed from knowledge about a task without reference to a trace of the workings of that procedure. The simulation exercise presented in this chapter provides evidence for this statement. Although the task domain is simple, the strategy transformations produced by the learning mechanisms are radical; the final strategy has virtually nothing in common with the initial one. The second part of the thesis states that rational learning mechanisms are important in human learning. The evidence provided here is indirect and weaker. There is empirical evidence for the initial and final strategies as formalized in figures 6.1, 6.2, and 6.3 but very little evidence with respect to the learning sequence that connects them. Detailed comparison between the predictions of the present theory and data from humans must await empirical studies of learning effects in the three-term series problem.

In the present author's opinion, the thesis that declarative truths may lead to improvements in a procedure even in the absence of a trace of that procedure is one of the facts about mental life that cognitive psychology has to come to grips with, one way or the other.

Notes

1. This statement is complicated by the concept of perceptual productions (Simon 1975), which do seem to make tests on reality rather than on working memory, but this complication will be ignored here.

2. Or deletions; or revisions; or reorganizations; etc. But in this paper I only consider additions.

3. This contrasts with so-called logic programming, as in PROLOG and related systems, in which all implications become procedures; indeed, writing implications is the only way to define procedures (see Tarnlund 1981).

4. The medical details of this example have been taken from Johnson, Duran, Hassebroch, Moller, Prietula, Feltovich, and Swanson (1981). They should not be held responsible for the fantasies their article has inspired in the present author.

5. The system could, in principle, try several different problem spaces for one and the same problem, or search a certain space with the help of several different strategies. No program making use of these options has been written yet, however.

6. By "mental model" is meant a symbol structure that represents an object by being structurally isomorphic to it, rather than describing it, as a proposition does.

7. This type of network resembles the active structural networks discussed by Rumelhart and Norman (1975), though they are not identical. Rumelhart and Norman (1975) stress that the type of nodes they consider are both data and process; this is only true of the present nodes in a very limited sense, as we shall see.

8. A human eye does not move smoothly over the visual field. Instead, it moves in small jumps from one fixation point to another. These jumps occur several times a second, and are called *saccades*.

9. The rule of relevance actually creates two mapping productions, because it is symmetric with respect to A_1 and A_2. Only one of them fires on any one learning opportunity, however.

10. It may seem faintly amusing to speak of expertise with respect to such a miniscule task domain, but the term is used here as a convenient way of referring to a strategy that is very much faster than the initial strategy.

References

Anderson, J. R. 1976. *Language, Memory, and Thought*. Hillsdale, N.J.: Lawrence Erlbaum Associates.

Anderson, J. R., and Kline, P. J. 1979. A General Learning Theory and Its Application to Schema Abstraction. In G. H. Bower (ed.), *The Psychology of Learning and Motivation*, Vol. 13. New York: Academic Press.

Anderson, J. R., Kline, P. J., and Beasley, C. M. 1980. Complex Learning Processes. In R. E. Snow, P.-A. Federico, and W. E. Montague (eds.), *Aptitude, Learning, and Instruction*, Vol. 2. Hillsdale, N.J.: Lawrence Erlbaum Associates.

Anzai, Y., and Simon, H. A. 1979. The theory of learning by doing. *Psychological Review* 86, 124–140.

Aune, B. 1977. *Reason and Action*. Boston: Reidel.

Brehmer, B. 1980. In one word: Not from experience. *Acta Psychologica* 45, 223–241.

Brooke, M. 1973. *Tricks, Games and Puzzles with Matches*. New York: Dover.

Clark, H. H. 1969. Influence of language on solving three-term series problem. *Journal of Experimental Psychology* 82, 205–215.

DeSoto, C. B., London, M., and Handel, S. 1965. Social reasoning and spatial paralogic. *Journal of Personality and Social Psychology* 2, 513–521.

Hayes-Roth, F., Klahr, P., and Mostow, D. J. 1981. Advice taking and knowledge refinement: An iterative view of skill acquisition. In J. R. Anderson (ed.), *Cognitive Skills and Their Acquisition*. Hillsdale, N.J.: Lawrence Erlbaum Associates.

Hunter, I. M. L. 1957. The solving of three-term series problems. *British Journal of Psychology* 48, 268–298.

Huttenlocher, J. 1968. Constructing spatial images: A strategy in reasoning. *Psychological Review* 75, 550–560.

Johnson, P. E., Duran, A. S., Hassebrock, F., Moller, J., Prietula, M., Feltovich, P. J., and Swanson, D. B. 1981. Expertise and error in diagnostic reasoning. *Cognitive Science* 5, 235–283.

Johnson-Laird, P. N. 1980. Mental models in cognitive science. *Cognitive Science* 4, 71–115.

Langley, P. 1982. Strategy acquisition governed by experimentation. *Proceedings of the European Conference* on Artificial Intelligence, pp. 171–176.

Lewis, C. H. 1978. *Production system models of practice effects*. Dissertation. University of Michigan.

Neches, R. 1981. *Models of heuristic procedure modification*. Dissertation. Carnegie-Mellon University.

Neches, R., and Hayes, J. R. 1978. Progress towards a taxonomy of strategy transformations. In A. M. Lesgold, J. W. Pellegrino, S. D. Fokkema, and R. Glaser (eds.), *Cognitive Psychology and Instruction*. New York: Plenum Press.

Neves, D. M., and Anderson, J. R. 1981. Knowledge compilation: Mechanisms for the automatization of cognitive skills. In J. R. Anderson (ed.), *Cognitive Skills and their Acquisition*. Hillsdale, N.J.: Lawrence Erlbaum Associates.

Newell, A. 1980. *Reasoning, problem solving and decision processes: The problem space hypothesis*. In R. Nickerson (ed.), *Attention and Performance VIII*. Hillsdale, N.J.: Lawrence Erlbaum Associates.

Newell, A., and Simon, H. A. 1972. *Human Problem Solving*. Englewood Cliffs, N.J.: Prentice-Hall.

Noordman, L. G. M. 1977. *Inferring from language*. Dissertation. Rijksuniversiteit to Groningen.

Ohlsson, S. 1979. *PSS3 reference manual*. Working Paper No. 4. Cognitive Seminar, Department of Psychology, University of Stockholm.

Ohlsson, S. 1980a. Strategy grammars. An approach to generality in simulation of human reasoning. *Proceedings of the AISB-80*, Amsterdam.

Ohlsson, S. 1980b. *A possible path to expertise in the three-term series problem*. Working Paper. Cognitive Seminar, Department of Psychology, University of Stockholm.

Ohlsson, S. 1983. On the automated learning of problem solving rules. *Proceedings of the Sixth European Meeting on Cybernetics and Systems Research*. Amsterdam: North-Holland.

Polanyi, M. 1958. *Personal Knowledge*. London: Routledge and Kegan Paul.

Quinton, G., and Fellows, B. J. 1975. "Perceptual" strategies in the solving of three-term series problems. *British Journal of Psychology* 66, 69–78.

Raz, J. (ed.). 1978. *Practical Reasoning*. Oxford: Oxford University Press.

Rumelhart, D. E., and Norman, D. A. 1975. The active structural network. In D. A. Norman, D. E. Rumelhart, and LNR Research Group (eds.), *Exploration in Cognition*. San Francisco: Freeman.

Simon, H. A. 1975. The functional equivalence of problem solving skills. *Cognitive Psychology* 7, 268–288.

Smedslund, J. 1961. The acquisition of conservation of substance and weight in children: III. Extinction of conservation of weight acquired "normally" and by means of empirical controls on a balance. *Scandinavian Journal of Psychology* 2, 85–87.

Sternberg, R. J., Guyote, M. J., and Turner, M. E. 1980. Deductive reasoning. In R. E. Snow, P.-A. Federico, and W. E. Montague (eds.), *Aptitude, Learning, and Instruction*, Vol. 1. Hillsdale, N.J.: Lawrence Erlbaum Associates.

Suppes, P. 1957. *Introduction to Logic*. Princeton, N.J.: Van Nostrand.

Tarnlund, Stenäke. 1981. *A programming language based on a natural deduction system*. Technical Report No. 6. Computing Science Department, Uppsala University, Box 2059, S-750 02 Uppsala. UPMAIL.

7 Composition of Productions

Clayton Lewis

When a task is performed repeatedly, the character of its execution changes in a number of ways. It gets faster, and its logic seems to change. Decisions that were made haltingly when the task was first performed seem hardly to be made at all. Distinct steps in the process may seem to blur together into smooth sequences.

Productions give a framework for thinking concretely about how such changes in the execution of a procedure might occur. If one considers a production to represent a distinct step in execution, one is led to the idea that as a procedure is exercised its productions are *combined* in some way, forming new productions that do the same work but with fewer distinct steps.

This chapter describes one way of combining productions, called "composition," that captures these intuitive notions and provides a possible model for them. Besides describing this mechanism, the chapter aims to give a formal analysis of what the mechanism can and cannot do when it is used in a model of learning.

The analysis centers on the notion of *safety* of operations: a learning mechanism is safe if it affects the way a task is performed but not the outcome of the task. Safe mechanisms have some advantages for modeling learning, since they can be employed freely without fear that they will disrupt the basic functioning of the system on which they operate. But there are cases where learning does change the outcome of tasks, so a learning model that employs only safe operations cannot capture the whole range of learning phenomena.

If unsafe operations are needed, how can their disruptive effects be constrained? How can the changes of task outcome be limited to inessentials? Composition is a *syntactic* operation, in that it uses only an analysis of the form of the productions on which it acts. It doesn't perform any analysis of the goals of a system on which it acts or make any observation of what the system is doing as it works. It incorporates no knowledge of tasks or heuristics to be used to streamline them. It appears that without this *semantic* dimension to its analysis composition cannot steer a course between the unacceptable limits of strict safety on the one hand and unacceptable disruption of task outcomes on the other.

The body of the chapter is organized into three sections, bracketed by this introduction and a closing discussion. The first section gives an informal description of composition and some of the learning phenomena it can model. The second presents a formal analysis: definitions of composition and its workings that are used to show when composition is a safe operation and when it is not. The third section considers two situations where safe operations are not adequate to model learning and where the control of the needed unsafe operations seems to call for some new ideas.

7.1 Background

The intuitive idea of composition

Consider these two productions:

*p*1: *If* Lucy has the fish, *then* give the fish to Fred.

*p*2: *If* Fred has the fish, *then* give the fish to Ethel.

Starting in the state

Lucy has the fish

the first production will fire, passing the fish to Fred. But now the condition of the second production is satisfied, so the fish gets passed to Ethel.

Effort can obviously be saved by replacing these productions with just one:

If Lucy has the fish, *then* give the fish to Ethel.

This single production will pass the fish along to its final destination in just one step. Composition of productions is just a way of formalizing the derivation of this sort of combined production and dealing with some more complex situations that may arise in the general case.

Complications Suppose we elaborate the second production:

*p*2′: *If* Fred has the fish *and* Lucy's husband is not home, *then* give the fish to Ethel.

Is there still a suitable combined production? Yes, it is

If Lucy has the fish *and* Lucy's husband is not home, *then* give the fish to Ethel.

As can be seen, the part of the condition of the second production that is taken care of by the action of the first production can be dropped, but other conditions have to be kept.

Suppose the first production is changed to

*p*1′: *If* Lucy has the fish, *then* make Lucy divorce Ricky and marry John Wayne *and* give the fish to Fred.

Now the combination is tricky. If we take just

If Lucy has the fish *and* Lucy's husband is not home, *then* make Lucy divorce Ricky and marry John Wayne *and* give the fish to Ethel,

then things can go astray. How? Well, suppose Lucy is married to Ricky, who is at home, but John Wayne is *not* home, and Lucy has the fish. Then *p*1′ will fire, and Lucy will marry John Wayne. Since John Wayne is not home, the fish will be passed to Ethel by *p*2′. But the putative combined production does something different. In the initial state Lucy's husband is Ricky, who *is* at home. So the production won't fire, and the fish doesn't get passed.

The solution is to restate the conditions carried over from the second production to reflect any changes that the action of the first production will make. In this case the correct combined production is

*p*1′2′: *If* Lucy has the fish *and* John Wayne is not home, *then* make Lucy divorce Ricky and marry John Wayne *and* give the fish to Ethel.

Actually, similar adjustments to the statement of *actions* carried along from the second production may also be needed. But at about this point the *formal* development to be given later becomes clearer and easier to follow than informal examples.

Housekeeping Although the combined production in the example will do the right thing if it applies, what if it doesn't? Suppose Lucy has the fish, but John Wayne is at home. The original productions won't pass the fish to Ethel, but they will pass it to Fred, and they will make Lucy remarry. The combined production won't apply at all. Clearly then the combined production isn't a *replacement* for the original productions. It can just be thrown in together with the original productions, but there is then a potential conflict in that the original first production will always be applicable when the combined production is and there are then two different actions to sort out.

Most production systems have ways of selecting between two different applicable productions, but the problem can be avoided in any system as follows. Add the combined production to the original set, but *modify the condition of the first production* so that it will not apply unless the combined production does *not* apply.

In the example, one then ends up with three productions:

*p*1′: *If* Lucy has the fish *and* John Wayne is at home, *then* give Fred the fish *and* make Lucy divorce Ricky and marry John Wayne.

*p*2′: *If* Fred has the fish *and* Lucy's husband is not at home, *then* give the fish to Ethel.

*p*1′2′: *If* Lucy has the fish *and* John Wayne is not at home, *then* make Lucy divorce Ricky and marry John Wayne *and* give the fish to Ethel.

The reader can eheck that this new set of productions will always do just the same thing as the original set, but, when conditions are right, it will get the fish into Ethel's hands in just one step.

Applications

Speed Even the preceding example shows that combining productions can save steps in carrying out a procedure. It is easy to see that if the initial set of productions were much larger, so that the fish was passed through scores of hands before coming to rest, it would still be possible to form a single composite production that would move the fish in just one step.

To use this mechanism as part of a theory of speedup during practice, one can propose that each time a production is applied following another, the composite of these two productions is formed (with some probability, perhaps) and incorporated into the production set. Over time, frequently occuring sequences of productions will be superseded by single productions that do the same work in a single step. The scheme has the attractive feature that it allocates these new productions to areas of function that are commonly used, without the need for complex analysis or record keeping. Simulations of simple linear cases, like extended fish passing, show roughly exponential speedup; however, real practice generally gives power law (see Newell and Rosenbloom 1981 and Chapter 5, this volume). It is not known what the performance of the procedure is in more complex cases.

Conversion of Serial to Parallel Logic When tests that are stated originally in the conditions of separate productions are merged into a composite

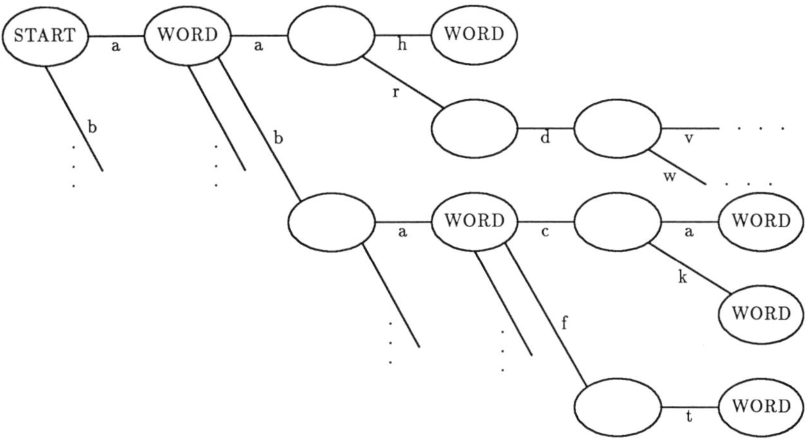

IF the current space is blank and the node pointed to is marked WORD,
THEN announce WORD!

IF the current space is blank and the node pointed to is not marked WORD,
THEN announce NOT A WORD!

IF the current space has an A in it and the node pointed to has an A link,
THEN move the pointer along the A link and move to the next space.

IF the current space has an A in it and the node pointed to has no A link,
THEN announce NOT A WORD!

(Similar productions exist for letters B through Z.)

Figure 7.1
Data structure and productions for identifying words.

production, it is then possible to evaluate them *in parallel*, whereas previously they could only be evaluated serially as the separate productions were applied. Figure 7.1 shows a production system designed to illustrate this possibility.

The structure at the top of the figure is a lexicon: it represents all the words of English in graph form. The productions are designed to scan a string of letters presented in a row of spaces and determine whether they form a word that is in the lexicon. Figure 7.2 traces the productions in recognizing the word ABA.

Now suppose that the scheme just discussed of forming composites of productions applied in sequence is installed and operated on this production system and that AB is a commonly encountered sequence of letters. Then the following composite production will eventually be formed:

Pointer set to START node. The string of spaces to be processed contains ABA and a blank to mark the end of the string. The current space is the first one, containing A.

The current space has an A in it. Since there is an A link from the current node, the first A production fires. The pointer is moved along the A link, to the right. The next space, containing B, becomes the current space.

There is a B link, so the first B production applies. The pointer is moved along the B link. The next space, containing A, becomes current.

The current space contains A, and there is an A link, so the first A production applies. The pointer is moved along the A link to the right, and the next space, which contains a blank, becomes current.

The current space is blank, and the node now pointed to is marked WORD, so the first production applies. The system announces WORD!

Figure 7.2
Trace of productions in figure 7.1 in determining that ABA is a word.

If the current space has an A *and* the node pointed to has an A link *and* the next space has a B *and* the node along the A link has a B link, *then* move two spaces *and* move the pointer along the A and then the B link.

If ABA is commonly presented, this production will form in time:

If the current space has an A *and* the node pointed to has an A link *and* the next space has a B *and* the node along the B link has an A link *and* the space two over has an A *and* the space three over has a blank *and* the node reached by following the A, B, A links is marked WORD, *then* move over three spaces *and* move the pointer along the A, B, A links *and* announce WORD!

ABA can now be recognized in just one application, and the serial tests for the three letters can now be done all at once.

This simple mechanism will tailor the performance of the production system so that frequently encountered words will be recognized more frequently than rare ones. In fact any string whose *parts* are frequent should be classified more quickly than others.

Einstellung Another effect of practice is the tendency for a well-practiced procedure to become inflexible, so that even advantageous variations in it may not be made. In Luchins' famous water-jar experiments (Luchins 1945) subjects who solved a number of problems using one algorithm failed to find a shortcut solution to a later problem that unpracticed subjects usually found. As will be seen, composition can be used to model this phenomenon, but only by making some new assumptions about the way productions are applied.

One can imagine modeling the process of "mechanization" of a procedure by the amalgamation of separate productions into large units that *skip over* chances to take shortcuts. For example, consider this set of productions:

If A has the fish, *then* give it to B *and* announce "passing fish to B."

If B has the fish, *then* give it to C *and* announce "passing fish to C."

If C has the fish, *then* give it to D *and* announce "passing fish to D."

If D has the fish, *then* announce "success!" *and* stop.

If B has the fish *and* the fish is a herring, *then* give it to D.

Suppose this system is run many times, starting with A having a trout, and composite productions are formed from productions that apply consecutively. Eventually this production will be formed:

If A has the fish, give it to D *and* announce "passing fish to B" *and* announce "passing fish to C" *and* announce "passing fish to D" *and* announce "success!" *and* stop.

If we now start with a herring at A, the big production can pass the fish directly to D, announcing the steps to B and C along the way. If this happens, there is no opportunity for the shortcut production for herring to apply, because the fish never reaches B!

Is this a model of *Einstellung*? On the surface it may appear to be. Before practice, the herring shortcut is applicable. After practice in which the herring shortcut cannot be used, the shortcut is blocked. But some critical details are glossed over in this account.

First, is the herring shortcut really blocked after practice? If the original first production is left in place, then in some production systems it might apply instead of the composite, allowing the shortcut to be used. If this is a problem, the original first production can simply be dropped. The composite production has no condition beyond that of the original first production; therefore there is no case where the composite production cannot apply but the original production can. If the first production is dropped, the herring shortcut is blocked after practice.

There is another point not so easily dealt with. Would the shortcut have been used *before* practice? As the original productions are stated, when B has a herring, there are two productions that could apply, one of which is the shortcut. Nothing has been said that ensures that the shortcut production would be the one to apply before practice, as *Einstellung* requires.

To remedy this problem, consider modifying the original productions so that the shortcut is guaranteed to apply when a herring is used. The original production

If B has the fish, *then* give it to C *and* announce "passing fish to C"

can be changed to

If B has the fish *and* it is not a herring, *then* give it to C *and* announce "passing fish to C."

That seems to do the trick. Unfortunately this change destroys the *Einstellung* effect! If the composite production discussed earlier is restated to reflect the change to the second production, it becomes

If A has the fish *and* it is not a herring, *then* give it to D *and* announce "passing fish to B" *and* announce "passing fish to C" *and* announce "passing fish to D" *and* announce "success!" *and* stop.

The modified version of the original first production becomes

If A has the fish *and* not (it is not a herring), *then* give it to B *and* announce "passing fish to B."

Clearly the shortcut production will still be used, even after the composite production has formed.

Can the example be salvaged? Going back to the original set of productions, consider another way of ensuring that the shortcut production will be used before practice. Instead of modifying the production that competes with the shortcut, adopt as a rule of *conflict resolution* that when two productions are applicable, the one whose condition is more specific will apply. This discipline will guarantee that the shortcut is used before practice if a herring is presented. Since the form of the composite is unchanged, the shortcut production will be blocked as before, and the *Einstellung* demonstration is complete.

The point of this discussion is that *Einstellung* can be modeled using composition but not without considering what will be called the *application discipline* of the production system. In the example the rules of conflict resolution had to be adjusted; simply changing the conditions of the productions to ensure that the shortcut would be used before practice meant that the composite production would not block the shortcut after practice.

Safe and Unsafe Operations

The general facts underlying the *Einstellung* example will be developed in the formal analysis. In outline, under many circumstances composition is what is called a *safe* operation, in the parlance of program optimization (Cocke and Schwartz 1970). That is, it does not change the *result* of a computation but only the way in which the result is obtained. In particular, for any system of productions with mutually exclusive productions, composites can be freely formed without disturbing the results of computations. When conditions are not mutually exclusive, the rules of conflict resolution, and other aspects of the way productions are applied, become critical, and in some cases composition becomes *unsafe*: results of computation can be affected. Whereas speedup and the change from serial to parallel operation can be modeled by safe operations, *Einstellung* in general cannot, since taking or not taking the shortcut produces different results. For example, the announcements made in the fish-passing example are different before and after practice, if the shortcut is used before and not after. This change in results cannot be accomplished by a safe operation on the productions.

7.2 Formal Analysis

Basic Definitions

This section develops a framework in which composition of productions can be precisely defined and the conditions under which it is and is not a safe operation. The framework is intended to accommodate a very wide range of different notions of production systems that operate on different forms of data, have different rules of conflict resolution, and so on. Accordingly the reader is asked to be patient with a certain amount of new terminology.

Many of the ideas presented here are drawn from Vere (1977) and Lewis (1978).

A *production system* consists of a data base, a set P of productions and an *application discipline* (D). The data base might be a semantic network, a string of symbols, or any other convenient object. All that is crucial here is that it have a set of possible *states* (S). Each production has a *condition* and an *action*.

A condition is a predicate on the set of states S. That is, it is a mapping on S that yields the value TRUE or FALSE for any state.

An action is a partial mapping from S to nonempty subsets of S: applied to any state for which the condition of the production is TRUE, it gives a set of possible new states. Usually an action will give just one new state when it is applied, so it can be thought of just as a mapping from state to state. But in some systems the use of variables allows the same action to map a given state into more than one new state, depending on the binding chosen for the variables.

If p is a production with condition c and action f, and s and s' are states, p will be said to *map* s to s' if c is TRUE for s and s' is a member of $f(s)$, the set of states obtained by applying f to s.

When the production system operates, the data base begins in some state. The productions are examined to discover whether the condition of any of them has the value TRUE for this state. If no condition is satisfied, the system halts. If a production is found whose condition is satisfied, its action is applied, giving some possible new states. The application discipline has the job of selecting from among the possible new states the one or ones that will be taken. A *deterministic* application discipline will always choose just one next state, and a *nondeterministic* one may permit several possibilities corresponding to different computations that might proceed from a given state.

This last point needs some explanation. Suppose a production system has reached state s, and the application discipline chooses s' as the next state. If the application discipline is deterministic, then it will always pick s' when it comes to the state s: the choice is fixed. But if the application discipline is nondeterministic, the choice can vary: if s is reached another time some state other than s' might be picked as the next state. Thus to describe what a nondeterministic system will do one has to specify a *set* of possible next states for s, since the choice can vary.

The application discipline also deals with a possibility that has been passed over so far. Suppose there are two or more productions whose conditions are satisfied by a given state. What action or actions should be applied? This question has many possible answers, corresponding to different application disciplines. In some systems productions are ordered, establishing a priority. If several productions are applicable, in that their conditions are TRUE, only the action of the production with the highest priority is actually applied. In other systems a random selection is made from among the applicable productions. These possibilities, and others, are covered by the following definition.

An *application discipline* (D) is given a state and a set of productions and yields a set of states. In operation, the set of productions (P) is just the set of productions whose conditions are satisfied by the current state, s, and $D(s, P)$ is the set of permissable next states. Remember that although only one next state will occur in any given computation, the definitions allow for nondeterministic application disciplines that have a range of possible next states to choose among.

An application discipline must meet two conditions if P is a set of productions and s is any state:

1. If P is empty, then $D(s, P)$ is empty.
2. If P contains just one production, then any state in $D(s, P)$ must be a member of $f(s)$, where f is the action of the production in P.

Condition 1 says that if no productions are applicable, there is no next state: the system halts. Condition 2 says that if only one production is applicable, then its action is taken. D will be called *nonblocking* if it has the further property that

3. $D(s, P)$ is empty only when P is empty.

A nonblocking production system cannot halt if there is any production whose condition is satisfied.

The application discipline captures what is usually called conflict resolution, in that it may determine which of several applicable productions will actually be used. But it also represents other aspects of the regime of operation. For example, if an action can be applied in more than one way to a given state, the application discipline selects which are permitted.

In doing its work an application discipline may need information that is not contained in either the state of the data base or the set of productions, such as an indication of how recently a production has applied. For simplicity this information has not been explicitly called out in the definition. The interested reader can either modify the exposition to carry along an extra argument to D, or simply add a section to the data base to hold this information.

It may be desired that the actions of several applicable productions all be applied, instead of a choice being made. This is permitted in the definition: there is no restriction on the application discipline when more than one production is applicable. An application discipline can be called *parallel* if $D(s, P)$ contains states arrived at by *functional compositions* of the actions of productions in P. If the order of application of the actions is important, D might select only one order on some basis, or might permit several orders and thus be nondeterministic.

A production system will be called *serial* if only one production is applied at a time, that is, if $D(s, P)$ only contains states produced by applying actions of single productions in P, whenever P is a set of productions whose conditions are satisfied by s. This can happen because of the rules used by D or because only one production has its condition satisfied at a time. A production system whose conditions are mutually exclusive will be serial no matter what its application discipline is.

With these definitions in hand, the operation of a production system can be described more precisely. If s is any state in S, let $A(s)$ be the set of applicable productions: the productions whose conditions are TRUE for s. Then the *immediate successors* of s are given by $D(s, A(s))$. If D is deterministic, $D(s, A(s))$ will have at most one member, and so s has at most one immediate successor. A state with no immediate successor is called a *halt state*. A state s' is called a *successor* of s whenever there is a sequence of states starting with s and ending with s' in which each state is an immediate successor of the preceding.

Results of Computations and Safety

To characterize the effects of adding composite productions, it is necessary to have a means of describing the results of computations. Since a computation may not halt, one cannot identify results with halt states.

Given a state s, a *necessary permanent result* of s in a production system (PS) is a predicate r on states satisfying these conditions:

1. If s' is a halt state that is a successor of s in PS, then r is TRUE of s'.

2. There is a *limiting number* n such that if $s(1), \ldots, s(m)$ is any sequence of states with $s(1) = s$, and each $s(i + 1)$ is a successor of $s(i)$, and m is greater than n, then r is TRUE of $s(m)$.

Intuitively a necessary permanent result (abbreviated *npr*) is anything that is bound to become true of the state of the data base, and remain true, once s is reached.

The predicate r might be a test for a particular memory trace, for the absence of a particular structure, or for any other test on the data base. The particular sort of test that would be of interest in a given case would depend on the nature of the data base that the production system uses, and the nature of the computation being modeled.

The set of necessary permanent results of a state will be taken to define the outcome or outcomes of a computation that starts at that state. A transformation of a production system will be called *safe* if it preserves all the *npr*'s of states.

Sufficient Conditions for Safety Let PS be a production system, and let $T(PS)$ be a transformed version of it.

LEMMA 1 Preserving necessary permanent results:

Any *npr* of a state s in PS will be an *npr* of s in $T(PS)$:

1. If any halt state of $T(PS)$ is a halt state of PS.
2. If s' is a successor of s in $T(PS)$ (then it is a successor of s in PS).

Proof Let r be an *npr* of s in PS. If h is a halt state of s in $T(PS)$ that is a successor of s in $T(PS)$, then h must be a halt state of PS and must be a successor of s in PS. So r must be true of h.

Let n be the limiting number for r in PS, and let $s(1), \ldots, s(m)$ be a sequence of states with $s(1) = s$, each $s(i+1)$ a successor of $s(i)$ in $T(PS)$, and m greater than n. Each $s(i+1)$ must be a successor of $s(i)$ in PS, so r must be true of $s(m)$. So n is a suitable limiting number for r in $T(PS)$. □

These conditions for preservation of *npr*'s are *not* necessary. For example, it can happen that $T(PS)$ introduces new successors for s, but these are all transient, so that in the long run the successors of s settle down to be the same as those in PS. Nevertheless, the conditions are useful in sorting out conditions under which results are preserved by a transformation of a production system and when they may not be.

Composition of Productions

Let $p1$ and $p2$ be any two productions. A *composite* of $p1$ and $p2$ is any production p for which

p maps s to s' iff there exists a state s'' for which $p1$ maps s to s'' and $p2$ maps s'' to s'.

This definition is adapted from Vere (1977). As intuition would suggest, a composite production maps s to those states that could have been reached by applying $p1$ and then $p2$.

More than one p can satisfy this definition for a given $p1$ and $p2$, but the variation is trivial. As the following theorem shows, all the possible composites have the same condition, and the actions must agree on any state that satisfies the condition.

THEOREM Uniqueness of composition: Let $p1$ have condition $c1$ and action $f1$, and $p2$ have condition $c2$ and action $f2$. Let $p3$ be any composite of $p1$ and $p2$ with condition $c3$ and action $f3$. Then

1. $c3(s)$ is TRUE iff $c1(s)$ is TRUE, and there exists s' in $f1(s)$ such that $c2(s')$ is TRUE.
2. If $c3$ is TRUE for s, then s' is in $f3(s)$ iff there exists s'' in $f1(s)$ such that $c2(s'')$ is TRUE and s' is in $f2(s'')$.

Proof of Property 1 Suppose $c3$ is true of s but $c1(s)$ is FALSE. Then $p3$ maps s to some state or states (recall that the action of a production must produce a *nonempty* set of states for any state satisfying its condition). But $p1$ doesn't map s to anything, so $p3$ is not a composite of $p1$ and $p2$. Suppose $c3(s)$ is TRUE, but there is no s' in $f1(s)$ such that $c2(s')$ is TRUE. Let s^* be a state to which $p3$ maps s. Let s'' be any state for which $p1$ maps s to s''. Since s'' is in $f1(s)$, $c2(s'')$ is FALSE, and so $p2$ does not map s'' to s^*. So $p3$ is not a composite of $p1$ and $p2$.

Conversely, suppose there is an s for which $c1(s)$ is TRUE, and there is an s' in $f1(s)$ for which $c2(s')$ is TRUE, but $c3(s)$ is FALSE. There must be some state s^* to which $p2$ maps s', so $p1$ maps s to s' and $p2$ maps s' to s^*. But, since $c3(s)$ is FALSE, $p3$ fails to map s to s^*. □

Proof of Property 2 Let s be a state for which $c3$ is TRUE.

Suppose s' is in $f3(s)$ but there is no s'' in $f1(s)$ for which $c2(s'')$ is TRUE and s' is in $f2(s'')$. Then $p3$ maps s to s', but there is no s'' for which $p1$ maps s to s'' and $p2$ maps s'' to s'.

Conversely, suppose there are s'', s' for which $c2(s'')$ is TRUE, s'' is in $f1(s)$, and s' is in $f2(s'')$, but s' is not in $f3(s)$. Since s satisfies $c3$, $c1(s)$ is TRUE, and so $p1$ maps s to s''. Since $c2(s'')$ is TRUE, and s' is in $f2(s'')$, $p2$

maps s'' to s'. Then $p1$ maps s to s'', and $p2$ maps s'' to s', but $p3$ does not map s to s'. □

Special Case Suppose the action of $p1$ is a *function* so that it always produces just one new state when applied to a given state. This will be the case for most productions without variables in their actions. Then a composite of $p1$ and $p2$ can be expressed by

If $c1$ and $c2f1$, then $f2f1$

where juxtaposition indicates ordinary functional composition. Recall that $c2$ is a mapping from states to the values TRUE and FALSE, so it can be composed with $f1$, as can $f2$. Intuitively, the condition of the composite checks that $c1$ is true and that $c2$ would be true if $f1$ were applied. The action gives the effect of applying $f2$ after $f1$.

Because of the simplicity of this special case, all of the examples used for illustration in this chapter are chosen to come under it. All the actions used are simple functions of states. Note that although $f2f1$ and $c2f1$ are defined as compositions, there is no requirement that they actually be *computed* by applying $f1$ first and then $c2$ or $f2$. *Any* computation that gives the defined effect can be used. For example, if $f1$ added 2 to a counter and $f2$ subtracted 2, $f2f1$ is just the identity, and neither addition nor subtraction need actually be carried out. Similarly, if $f1$ is

give the fish to Lucy

and $c2$ is

Lucy has the fish

then $c2f1$ is just TRUE.

When Composition Is Safe

A few more notions must be defined in tackling this issue. A production p is *consistent* with a production system *PS* if s' is a successor of s in *PS* whenever p maps s to s'. That is, a consistent production, acting on its own, produces a successor that *PS* as a whole might produce. To illustrate this idea, consider these productions:

$p1$: *If* Lucy has the fish, *then* pass it to Ethel.

$p2$: *If* Ethel has the fish, *then* pass it to Fred.

The production

If Lucy has the fish, *then* pass it to Fred

is consistent with this system: if Lucy has the fish, this production gives it to Fred, which is where the system would put it. On the other hand, the production

If Lucy has the fish, *then* pass it to Ricky

is not consistent with the system. If Lucy has the fish, this production gives it to Ricky, which is not a state that can be reached by the system.

A production system is called *free* if all of its productions are consistent with it. That is, productions of a free production system considered independently do not produce any successors that they do not produce working together. For example, any production system in Anderson's ACT model is free because it can be applied if its condition is satisfied by a state. A system with parallel application discipline might not be free because any one production that is applicable to a state might carry out only part of the transformation of the state the whole set of applicable productions would impose. The partially transformed state created by the single production might not be a valid successor for the whole production system.

For example, suppose the following productions are used with a parallel production system:

$p1$: *If* Lucy has the fish, *then* pass it to Ethel.

$p2$: *If* Ricky has the duck, *then* pass it to Fred.

This system is not free, because $p1$ is not consistent with it. To see this, suppose that in the state s Lucy has the fish and Ricky the duck. Since the system has a parallel application discipline, both $p1$ and $p2$ are applied at once, and in the next state Ethel has the fish and Fred the duck. But if $p1$ alone had been applied to s, the resulting state would have seen Ethel with the fish and Ricky still holding the duck. This is not a possible successor for s in the production system.

LEMMA 2 Composition of consistent productions: If two productions are consistent with a production system *PS*, so is any composite of them.

Proof Let the productions be $p1$ and $p2$, and let $p3$ be a composite of them. Suppose $p3$ maps some state s to s'. There must be some state s'' such that $p1$ maps s to s'' and $p2$ maps s'' to s'. But since $p1$ and $p2$ are compatible with *PS*, s'' must be a successor of s, and s' a successor of s'' in *PS*. Since the successor relation is transitive, s' is a successor of s in *PS*. □

THEOREM Safety of adding consistent productions: Let *PS* be any free production system, and let *T*(*PS*) be a production system formed from it, satisfying the following conditions:

1. All productions in *T*(*PS*) are consistent with *PS*.
2. Any halt state of *T*(*PS*) is a halt state of *PS*.
3. *T*(*PS*) is serial.

Then any *npr* of a state s in *PS* is an *npr* of s in *T*(*PS*).

Remark Since composites of consistent productions are consistent, and *PS* is free, the theorem will apply when *T*(*PS*) is formed from *PS* by adding composites of its productions, as long as the condition of seriality is met.

Proof Given lemma 1, and hypothesis 2 of the theorem, it is only necessary to show that any successor of s in *T*(*PS*) must be a successor of s in *PS*. Let s' be a successor of s in *T*(*PS*). There must be a sequence of states $s(1), \ldots, s(m)$ with $s(1) = s$, $s(m) = s'$, and each $s(i+1)$ the immediate successor of $s(i)$ in *T*(*PS*). Since *T*(*PS*) is serial, each $s(i+1)$ must result from the application to $s(i)$ of the action of some *one* production whose condition is satisfied by s. But since every production of *T*(*PS*) is consistent with *PS*, $s(i+1)$ must be a successor of $s(i)$ in *PS*. □

Safety: Cases and Noncases

Here are situations where the safety theorem does and does not apply, so adding composite productions may or may not be safe.

Refractoriness Some application disciplines, such as in OPS2 (McDermott and Forgy 1978), have a rule that a production cannot apply if it has already applied once and the portion of the data base tested by its condition has not been altered. This is called the *refractoriness* principle of conflict resolution. Such an application discipline is not nonblocking; that is, the application discipline may produce no new state even though there is a production whose condition is satisfied. Production systems with this discipline can easily fail to be free, and composition will in general be unsafe.

For example, consider the productions:

$p1$: *If* Lucy has red hair, *then* give a fish to Ethel.

$p2$: *If* Ethel has a fish, *then* take the fish away, and give it to Fred.

Consider a starting state in which Lucy has red hair, and neither Ethel nor Fred has a fish. Production $p1$ will fire, giving Ethel a fish. Production $p2$ will then pass the fish from Ethel to Fred, and the system halts with Fred having a fish and Ethel not having one. Refractoriness prevents $p1$ from firing again because the original information about Lucy's hair has not been altered. Note that this means the system is not free: $p1$'s condition is satisfied, but its action would not produce a valid successor of this state if it were applied.

A composite of $p2$ and $p1$ is

$p21$: *If* Ethel has a fish *and* Lucy has red hair, *then* take the fish away from Ethel, give it to Fred, *and then* give a fish to Ethel.

From the same initial state, a system with $p21$ added can reach a state in which both Fred and Ethel have fish, which cannot happen with the original productions. What has happened is that the restriction imposed by refractoriness on $p1$ is not inherited by $p21$, and so $p1$'s action can get applied twice in the new system. So adding the composite is not safe.

Mutually Exclusive Conditions If the conditions of *PS* are mutually exclusive, it is easy to see that *PS* must be free, in any nonblocking application discipline. There is never any discrepancy between what individual productions do and what the system as a whole does, because only one production can be applied at a time, and any production whose condition is satisfied can be applied. For the same reason, such a *PS* is always serial.

Let

$p1$: *If* $c1$, *then* $f1$,

$p2$: *if* $c2$, *then* $f2$,

be two productions in *PS*. The condition of a composite $p3$ will be

$c1(s)$ *and* there exists s' in $f1(s)$ for which $c2(s')$ is TRUE.

Though the action of $p3$ is subject to trivial variation, in that there is more than one composite possible for $p1$ and $p2$ (the uniqueness theorem), assume that it is $f3$, given by

$f3(s)$ = all s' such that there exists s'' for which s'' is in $f1(s)$, $c2(s'')$ is TRUE, and s' is in $f2(s'')$.

Now the condition of $p3$ is not exclusive with $c1$, so if $p3$ is simply added to *PS*, the resulting system will not have mutually exclusive conditions. As discussed earlier, this problem can be avoided by replacing $p1$ by

If $c1(s)$ is TRUE *and* there is no s' in $f1(s)$ for which $c2(s')$ is TRUE, *then* $f1$.

If *T*(*PS*) is formed from *PS* by adding $p3$ and modifying $p1$ as shown, it is easy to check that all of the productions in *T*(*PS*) are consistent with *PS*, that *T*(*PS*) has no new halt states, and that *T*(*PS*) is serial, since it has mutually exclusive conditions. So *T*(*PS*) preserves the *npr*'s of *PS*, and adding composites in this way is therefore safe.

This application of the safety theorem is attractive because it is largely independent of the application discipline concerned and hence may be useful in a wide variety of production system schemes. Further it shows that any case in which adding composites is *not* safe must exploit nonexclusive conditions or blocking in the application discipline in some way, and hence hinges on logic that is implicitly embedded in the application discipline rather than being represented explicitly in the conditions of productions.

Priority schemes To illustrate this point, consider a production system in which an ordering is imposed on the productions and used in conflict resolution. The ordering could be based on specificity of conditions or any other consideration; suppose the three productions shown here are ordered so that a production earlier in the list will apply in preference to a later one:

$p1$: *If* A has the fish, *then* give it to B.

$p2$: *If* B has the fish *and* it is a herring, *then* give it to C.

$p3$: *If* B has the fish, *then* give it to D.

If a herring is started at A, these productions will pass it to C ($p2$ applies over $p3$) and halt.

The composite of $p1$ and $p3$ is

$p13$: *If* A has the fish, *then* give it to D.

Suppose *p*13 is formed and added to the original set of productions. If it is given a priority less than that of *p*1, it will never apply. But if it is given a priority greater than *p*1, the operation of the system is seriously disturbed. In particular, if a herring is started at A, it is passed to D by *p*13, not to C as in the original production system.

Why does this happen? Essentially, *p*3 has a hidden condition, implicit in the priority ordering: the fish must *not* be a herring. This implicit condition is lost when the composite production is formed, since the composition definition only takes into account the condition *explicitly given* for *p*3.

Refractoriness, Again As discussed earlier, use of refractoriness in conflict resolution can lead to blocking in the application discipline, which in turn can make a production system fail to be free, even if it has mutually exclusive conditions.

The effect of refractoriness can be approximated in a nonblocking application discipline if a *relative*, rather than absolute refractoriness penalty is imposed on a recently applied production, as Langley, Neches, Neves, and Anzai (1980) propose. In their scheme a less recently applied production will apply in favor of a more recent one, but a production can always be applied if it is the only one whose condition is satisfied.

In such a system, production systems with mutually exclusive conditions will be governed by the theorem, and composition will be safe. But if conditions are not mutually exclusive, problems can arise in this sort of system that are analogous to the priority problems just discussed.

Consider the two productions:

*p*1: *If* Lucy has the fish, *then* increment the fish counter.

*p*2: *If* Lucy has the fish, *then* take the fish away from Ethel.

Starting with the fish in Lucy's possession and the fish counter at zero, if even a relative refractoriness rule is in force, the counter cannot be incremented past one. This is because *p*1 can apply at most once before *p*2 applies, blocking *p*1. But the composition of *p*1 with itself is

If Lucy has the fish, *then* increment the fish counter by two.

If this production is added, the fish counter could reach two before *p*2 is applied, and possibly three if *p*1 is left in the system. The problem is that there are states satisfying the condition of *p*1 in which *p*1 will not be applied because of refractoriness, so the production system is not free.

Parallel Application In parallel application disciplines it can happen that the actions of several productions are all applied to give the next state. In some cases the total set of productions may be divided into classes, and a single production is chosen from each class to be applied to a given state.

Such parallel application can violate the condition of effective seriality of the theorem. Here is a production system that illustrates how this can make composition unsafe.

Let PS have three classes of two productions:

1. *Fish class.*

*pf*1: *If* A has the fish, *then* give it to B.

*pf*2: *If B* has the fish, *then* give it to C.

2. *Duck class.*

*pd*1: *If* A has the duck, *then* give it to B.

*pd*2: *If* B has the duck, *then* give it C.

3. *Control class.*

*pc*1: *If* C has the fish and duck, *then* eat the fish *and* announce "success!"

*pc*2: *If* C has the fish but no duck, *then* eat the fish *and* announce "fail!"

If a fish and duck are started at A, they will be passed simultaneously to C (*pf*1 and *pd*1 apply simultaneously, followed by *pf*2 and *pd*2), at which point the fish will be eaten, success will be announced, and the system halts.

The composite of *pf*1 and *pf*2 is

*pf*12: *If* A has the fish, *then* give it to C.

If this production is added to the fish class, and applied instead of *pf*1, the action is different. At the first application the fish goes to C, but the duck only reaches B. The control production *pc*2 now applies, and not *pc*1 as before, so the system halts after announcing "fail!"

The problem here is that even though composition acted only within the fish class of productions, which are independent of the duck class, the control productions can access aspects of the state modified by both classes. The control productions can thus check the synchronization of the fish and duck operations, which can be disrupted by composition within either class.

The ACT Model As a final example, consider Anderson's ACT model (Anderson 1976). It has a serial application discipline, since only one production is actually applied to a given state. Any production whose condition is satisfied by a given state *could* be applied (though the probability that a production is applied varies), so that any ACT production system is free. Consequently composition is always safe in ACT, provided only that when composites are added no original productions are removed or altered in such a way as to create new halt states.

Problems in Expressing Composites

As with any formal analysis, care is needed in applying these ideas to real production systems. Though it is usually easy in informal examples to form the composite of two productions, it is quite difficult to do so with formal accuracy in most production system languages. In fact it may be impossible to form a composite in some systems.

In ACT a condition can test for a network structure in which a node *A* is connected to a node *B* through some unspecified third node. In a simplified notation one might express this condition by *A*–?–*B*, where ? represents the unspecified node. An action may add a connection between *A* and another node, say *C*. In composing two productions, it may be necessary to compose this condition with this action: that is, to express the condition that *after* the link from *A* to *C* is placed, then *A* will be linked to *B* through an intermediate node. This will be true if *either A* is already linked to *B* through an intermediate *or C* is linked to *B*. Unfortunately there is no way to express this disjunction in the condition of a single ACT production.

Vere (1977) permits composites to be represented by *sets* of productions, since single productions in his scheme cannot express the logic required. Even then, he shows that special provision had to be made in the form of his productions to permit composites to be represented in the general case even by sets of productions.

Apart from restrictions on the logic that can be expressed in conditions or actions in a given scheme, there may be other problems in forming desired compositions. Suppose for example that one production has as its action, "assert goal is SUBTRACT," while another has as a condition "goal is MULTIPLY." Is the composition of this action with this condition FALSE? Only if just one assertion about "goal" can be present in the data base. Often the data base could hold two or more such assertions, and it is only an examination of the complete set of productions, together with the initial condition of the data base, that reveals that only one setting for goal will occur at a given time.

Consider the action "give Lucy the fish" and the condition "Lucy has the fish." Is their composition TRUE? Only if one can tell from whatever formalism is employed that giving Lucy the fish means that she has it. This sort of analysis is easy to do unconsciously in making composites informally; when one implements an algorithm that has to work mechanically, one may find lots of conditions being carried along that the mechanical procedure couldn't reduce to TRUE or FALSE.

Devising a representation for productions that allows compositions to be simply expressed, in the general case, and allows inferences of the kind just discussed to be made mechanically, is a challenge for production-system architects.

7.3 Beyond Safety: Problems in Controlling Risk

Proceduralization and the Elimination of Unneeded Tests

When a production system carries out a computation, each production that applies has in its condition one or more tests. In modeling the effects of practice, it is reasonable to look toward some reduction in the number of these tests as the computation is repeatedly carried out.

Typically some of the tests carried out during any computation are satisfied by virtue of actions carried out by earlier productions in the computation. These may be removed by composition. But what about the remaining tests, which access aspects of the data base not changed by earlier productions?

To return to an earlier example, the word-recognition productions in figure 7.1 test for the presence of links and markers in the stored lexicon. Though composition rearranges the order in which these tests are carried out, it does not eliminate them. Thus no matter how often ABA is recognized as a word, composition will never permit it to be recognized without actually checking its elements against the lexicon.

Neves and Anderson (1981; see also Anderson, Greeno, Kline, and Neves 1981) have proposed a mechanism called *proceduralization* that allows some such tests to be eliminated. Under their proposal the data base is segmented into permanent and temporary memory. When a condition is satisfied by a structure, a part of which is in permanent memory, a modified version of the condition is created with the test of permanent structure eliminated. At the same time any variables in the condition that were bound to elements in permanent memory are replaced by constants that refer directly to these elements. An example adapted from Neves and Anderson (1981) will make this process clearer.

The production considered in the example is part of a system that compares a probe letter against a fixed list of target letters. The target list, *A*, *Q*, *R*, *T*, is represented in permanent memory by structures which can be represented informally as

A is before *Q*,

Q is before *R*,

R is before *T*.

During processing there is in temporary memory the information

probe is *T*

and

considering *A*.

The latter structure is a marker that indicates which target is being examined at the moment. Actually only the marker "considering" is in temporary memory; the target A itself is in permanent memory.

The production to be analyzed is

If considering *x and* probe is *y and x is* different from *y and x* is before *z*, *then* considering *z*.

Here *x*, *y*, and *z* are all variables that can match letters. When the production applies to the present state of the data base, *x* will be bound to *A*, *y* to *T*, and *z* to *Q*.

Proceduralization generates the following new production:

If considering *A and* probe is *y and A* is different from *y*, *then* considering *Q*.

How this is done can be traced in two steps. First, the variables *x*, *y*, and *z* are considered. Since *x* and *z* were matched to elements in permanent memory, they are replaced by specific references to those elements. Since *y* matched an element in temporary memory, it is left alone. This gives the production

If considering *A and* probe is *y and A* is different from *y and A* is before *Q*, *then* considering *Q*.

Now, since the whole structure

A is before *Q*

is in permanent memory the test for it is dropped, leaving only those tests that refer to something in temporary memory. This gives the generated production.

This example shows that proceduralization can eliminate tests, like "*A* is before *Q*," that composition cannot. Plainly proceduralization is an unsafe operation, insofar as "permanent" information isn't truly permanent. As long as there is some way to modify the lexicon, productions generated by proceduralization may make incorrect judgements.

If unsafe operations are carried out, whether proceduralization, composition in an unsafe case, or any other, there must be some means of recovering if the transformation proves disruptive. One approach is to allow productions to have *strength*, with weak productions having a lower probability of application. When new productions are generated by a potentially unsafe operation they can be given low strength initially. Their strength can then be increased by some means only if they prove satisfactory (Anderson 1976; Anderson, Kline, and Beasley 1979). This gives a way of dealing with trouble in introducing new productions, but it doesn't handle problems that occur after the new productions are established.

If proceduralized productions are formed that judge *ABB* to be a nonword, what happens if it becomes a word? There will be difficulty in suppressing the nonword judgment. This might seem to be a psychologically plausible failing. If one is used to driving according to one set of traffic laws, one does not expect to adjust immediately when one is given a different set. The adjustment would be immediate if each driving procedure accessed a stored representation of the laws, but would be halting if some procedures had been developed from which tests of the laws had been eliminated.

Having recently changed from left-hand to right-hand drive, I can testify that the transition is not perfectly smooth. But it is clear that the massive interference that would be expected from productions that no longer test the rules doesn't show up. If productions specialized to driving unconditionally on one side of the road are built up, there is evidently a remarkably effective means for supplanting or overriding them when circumstances change.

The production-system architect is thus faced with conflicting challenges. On the one hand, the impact of incorrect new productions must be tempered, leading to the idea that new productions should have low strength. On the other hand, new information can suddenly change even established behaviors, leading to the idea that newly created productions should preempt older ones. This seems to be an open problem in production-system design.

Conversion of Multipass Algorithms to Single Pass

Consider two algorithms for setting a table. In the first, a *multipass* algorithm, the setter circles the table putting a napkin at each place, then goes around again putting a fork at each place, and so on until all required items are distributed. In the second algorithm, a *single-pass* version, the setter goes around the table just once, putting all the required items at each place before moving to the next. Clearly the *single-pass* method requires less running around and in that sense is more efficient.

The relationship between these two algorithms is quite a common one. For example, Lewis (1981) describes two algorithms used in solving equations in elementary algebra that are analogous to these.

Given a multipass algorithm, can the single-pass version evolve from it? In particular, can composition of productions convert multi- to single-pass algorithms as it can serial to parallel?

It is easy to adapt the analysis of composition to give at least a partial answer to the latter question and shed some light on the former. The crux of the matter is that although the single-pass algorithm may seem entirely identical in its effects to the multipass one, it is not, and the change from one algorithm to the other is not safe.

To see this, consider setting a table of infinite length. The multipass algorithm will *never* place any forks on such a table, since it will never finish laying out the napkins. But the single-pass algorithm puts out its first fork right after the first napkin. To put this more technically, under the multipass algorithm it is a necessary permanent result of starting with an infinite table that there are no forks on the table, but this result is not preserved under the single-pass one.

This difference between the two algorithms means that the single-pass algorithm cannot evolve from the multipass by any safe transformation. In

IF now placing napkins and there is no napkin here,
THEN place a napkin and move to the next place.

IF now placing napkins and there is a napkin here already,
THEN start placing forks.

IF now placing forks and there is no fork here,
THEN place a fork and move to the next place.

IF now placing forks and there is a fork here already,
THEN stop.

Figure 7.3
Production system for setting tables.

particular, it cannot evolve by composition of productions under any conditions in which this is safe, for example, when the productions have mutually exclusive conditions, or in an ACT-like system.

On further reflection, it is hard to see how any *local* analysis of the multipass algorithm could ever lead to a single-pass version, even if the safety of the transformation were ignored. Consider the production system in figure 7.3.

This system works for tables where the row of places is closed into a loop, like most actual tables. But this information is not stated anywhere in the algorithm, and no analysis of the algorithm itself can show that any forks will be placed at all! Forks won't be placed unless a napkin is reached while placing napkins, and this is not guaranteed by the productions. So one cannot suggest a multipass replacement of this algorithm without an analysis that has access to information outside the statement of the algorithm itself.

This is of course not a decisive argument. There may be some other production system in which the regime of control can be analyzed differently and from which the applicability of a single-pass replacement can be deduced. But one would then have to assume that in any case in which the transition to single-pass operation occurs, the original algorithm has this special kind of expression. It seems more plausible that this transformation, and perhaps others as well, arises from observation of the *operation* of a procedure, rather than on analysis of the procedure itself. It seems fairly easy to suggest a single-pass algorithm from an analysis of the *trace* of the multipass one. For further consideration of the role of traces, see Langley, Neches, Neves, and Anzai (1980), Neches (chapter 4), and Wallace, Klahr and Bluff (chapter 8).

Even if a trace is available there remain some subtleties. The trace of the multipass procedure of course has moves of the setter that are to be eliminated in conversion to single-pass operation. But then the analyzer has to *know* that these moves are inessential! If the whole operation were a dance, performed for visual effect, it would be silly to convert to single pass. Here again, it seems that information from outside has to be brought to bear, in this case not just from outside the statement of the algorithm but outside its trace as well.

One approach to this problem might be to distinguish essential from auxiliary actions in stating productions, if one wished to bring such questions within reach of the production system machinery itself. Alternatively, one could accept the need for some kind of control system that monitors and governs the action and creation of productions.

7.4 Discussion

Value of Formal Analysis

The chief aim of this analysis has been to outline what composition as a mechanism can and cannot do. It has been possible to do this is way that can be applied to some nontrivial problems, such as *Einstellung* and conversion of multipass algorithms, and that has some generality across particular production-system schemes.

This generality is important in view of the wide variety of different schemes in use in the field. It is hard to know what to make of analyses that rest on simulations carried out within some one particular scheme, since it is hard to assign credit for the demonstration among the productions used, the details of the application discipline, and perhaps other learning mechanisms that may be at work. In fact the formal analysis underscores the seriousness of this problem, since it compels consideration of the complexity of interaction between the logic stated explicitly in the conditions and actions of productions and the logic implicit in the application discipline.

It would be useful if this kind of analysis could be extended to proceduralization, generalization, discrimination, and other learning mechanisms that have been proposed. It would be useful as well if the analysis could treat the effects of such mechanisms when more than one is at work, as happens in most learning proposals. Such analysis would make it easier to sort out the contributions these mechanisms can make to a theory of learning and would develop a less theory-bound understanding of their action.

The point here is not that we need a theory of learning that is independent of assumptions about application discipline or data base, or whatever. As Richard Young argues (personal communication), these assumptions are really the core of what production systems are as psychological theories. Just because of that we have to understand what the assumptions do in a way that has some generality. Without such understanding we cannot effectively recombine the elements of the differing theories we now have into better new ones.

It is also possible, as Vere (1977) urges, that such analysis might shape the production-system formalism itself. Expression of composition pushes the syntax and permitted semantics of conditions and actions, and exposes to view limitations that may be desirable or not. Clean treatment of other learning mechanisms might have similar effect.

Productions: Answers and Questions

Returning to the observations about practice that opened this discussion, it has been possible to propose simple but definite models for many of them. Production-system formalism has provided a clean and explicit means of exposing the logic of these models and discovering some general properties of them. That is an endorsement for any theoretical framework.

The analyses suggest, however, that there are questions of control that need further thought. When is an unsafe transformation permissable? If an unsafe transformation is carried out, how can the resulting productions be suppressed when necessary? How is it determined which aspects of a computation are essential and which may be rearranged for efficiency? Can control be based on analysis of productions themselves, or must information about tasks and goals from outside the productions be brought to bear?

References

Anderson, J. R. 1976. *Language, Memory, and Thought*. Hillsdale, N.J.: Lawrence Erlbaum Associates.

Anderson, J. R., Kline, P. J., and Beasley, C. M. 1979. A general learning theory and its application to schema abstraction. In G. H. Bower (ed.), *The Psychology of Learning and Motivation*, Vol. 13. New York: Academic Press, pp. 277–318.

Cocke, J., and Schwartz, J. T. 1970. *Programming Languages and Their Compilers: Preliminary Notes*. New York: Courant Institute of Mathematical Sciences.

Lewis, C. 1978. *Production system models of practice effects*. Dissertation, University of Michigan.

Lewis, C. 1981. Skill in algebra. In J. R. Anderson (ed.), *Cognitive Skills and Their Acquisition*. Hillsdale, N.J.: Lawrence Erlbaum Associates.

Luchins, A. S. 1945. Mechanization in problem solving. *Psychological Monographs* 58, No. 270.

Langley, P., Neches, R., Neves, D. and Anzai, Y. 1980. A domain-independent framework for procedure learning. *International Journal of Policy Analysis and Information Systems* 4, 163–197.

McDermott, J., and Forgy, C. L. 1978. Production system conflict resolution strategies. In D. A. Waterman and F. Hayes-Roth (eds.), *Pattern-Directed Inference Systems*. New York: Academic Press, pp. 177–179.

Newell, A., and Rosenbloom, P. S. 1981. Mechanisms of skill acquisition and the law of practice. In J. R. Anderson (ed.), *Cognitive Skills and Their Acquisition*. Hillsdale, N.J.: Lawrence Erlbaum Associates, pp. 1–55.

Vere, S. A. 1977. Relational production systems. *Artificial Intelligence* 8, 47–68.

8 A Self-Modifying Production System Model of Cognitive Development

Iain Wallace, David Klahr, and Kevin Bluff

8.1 Goals and System Overview

Our overall goal is the construction of a theory of cognitive development in the form of a self-modifying information processing system. This chapter describes a system, called BAIRN (a Scottish word for "child"), that represents our current progress toward that goal. In formulating the theory, we have adopted *developmental tractability* as a fundamental constraint. This means that the features of the theory must be consistent not only with performance at each developmental level but also with prior developmental states. Originating with an innate kernal, these states emerge from their predecessors and give way to their successors during the course of environmental interaction.

As a result of this constraint, BAIRN departs radically from conventional production-system architectures. The depàrtures include, among other things, a complex node structure that represents information about previous interaction with other nodes, a limited amount of distributed parallel processing, and an explicit treatment of consciousness, motivation and emotion.

The BAIRN System

BAIRN is an integrated model of performance and learning. Performance is generated by a "world model" that represents BAIRN's knowledge, and learning derives from processes that monitor the interaction between the world model and BAIRN's performance in the current environment. Development starts when the initial "kernal" world model begins to interact with the environment, and the learning processes monitor and react to the symbolic products of that interaction, producing a revised world model. This integrated cycle of performance and learning continues indefinitely.

BAIRN's Representation of Knowledge BAIRN's world model takes the form of a network of interconnected nodes in long-term memory (LTM). A node represents a basic unit of knowledge about a feature of the world. Each knowledge unit is defined in the form of several productions as well as information about the node's connectivity within the network. This permits it to spread activation in LTM at the conclusion of its own activity. A limited number of nodes can be active simultaneously.

BAIRN departs from conventional production system architectures in its use of nodes, rather than individual productions, as the basic elements for knowledge representation. The core constituent of each node is a production system, and the nodes resemble productions in possessing activation conditions and in changing knowledge states. But in addition each node possesses information regarding its functional relationships with other nodes. In contrast, in a classic production system, individual productions are entirely ignorant of one another's existence and only interact via a shared working memory. In BAIRN, nodes use their relational knowledge in passing information directly to other nodes. However, the conventional feature of a shared working memory is retained in BAIRN. It is used both as a means of limiting the amount of processing proceeding at any point in time and of enabling nodes to interact in the absence of direct connections between them.

BAIRN does not represent declarative and procedural knowledge in a separate propositional network and production repertoire (see Anderson 1983). There is a single network of nodes, each of which contains representations of procedural knowledge and related declarative knowledge. When spreading activation occurs, *information*, rather than activation potential, is passed between nodes. Subsequent activation of nodes is determined by their relative potency in the context of the specific information available to each of them as they compete for a limited number of parallel processing channels.

How Does BAIRN Learn? A detailed account of BAIRN's learning mechanisms is presented in sections 8.8 through 8.11. Here we present an overview. When a node is activated, details about the information that triggered its activation and about the end state produced by its operation are placed in LTM. This information becomes part of an episodic memory—or "time line"—that provides a sequential record of processing activity. (See section 8.1). Additions and modifications to the network are made by learning processes capable of detecting significant and/or consistently recurring segments of the time-line record.

BAIRN learns about the world by processing the information in the time line. That is, it learns about the world by analyzing the regularities produced by the interactions between its current knowledge and the environment. At first, this information is very primitive, being based only the results of BAIRN's innate endowment of primitive perceptual and motor nodes. As the world model gets more elaborated, so does the information available for processing in the time line as richer and more powerful nodes are added to LTM.

Four fundamental learning processes are employed by BAIRN:

1. *Node creation* involves the addition of new nodes to LTM. This happens when the time-line processes detect similar patterns of information in close temporal contiguity. The new node is constructed to capture the essential features of the nodes that gave rise to the detected patterns.

2. *Node combination* occurs when the system discovers two or more nodes that co-occur and that appear to be functionally equivalent. A new, superordinate node is produced which may vary from a totally conjunctive to a totally disjunctive combination of its precursors. The type of combination depends on their degree of similarity.

3. *Redundancy elimination* produces more efficient processing at a node by modifying the productions that define that node so as to avoid the unnecessary activation of some productions.

4. *Node modification* involves the detection of a regularity immediately preceding or following the activation of a node and the subsequent addition to that node of productions reflecting the regularity. It may also reflect the results of node combination. A token for a new superordinate node is substituted at other nodes for tokens representing its precursors or subordinates.

What Does BAIRN Learn? BAIRN is proposed as a general model of cognitive development, and we have designed it with the goal of accounting for a very broad range of acquisitions. In this chapter, although we allude to several different domains, we present a detailed example of only one important domain: the acquisition of quantitative concepts and their related operators. The account starts with rudimentary perceptual encodings of discontinuous quantity and goes through the acquisition of quantity conservation rules.

Chapter Organization

Having provided the broadest of broad brush pictures of the system as a whole we will now undertake a more detailed consideration of BAIRN's structure. We first provide an account of the already developed, or "adult" system, and then focus on the general learning processes involved in its self-modification capability. In describing BAIRN, we face the problem of selecting a starting point for an account of a complex system traversing a dynamic, continuous sequence of interdependent phases. Any solution to such a narrative problem must be a compromise and produces its share of awkwardness.

We begin by considering the structure of nodes (section 8.2). In subsequent sections we deal with the within-node processing involved when an individual node is operating (section 8.3), with the spread of activation between nodes that occurs when a node completes its operation (section 8.4), with the control mechanisms governing parallel processing and channel allocation (section 8.5). Then we turn to the self-modification process. The specific context for learning represents an important developmental milestone: the aquisition of knowledge about quantity conservation. Sections 8.6 and 8.7 give the relevant background, and sections 8.8 to 8.12 describe the learning processes in detail.

8.2 Node Structure

Each node represents a knowledge unit comprised to associations that help the system achieve its objectives. In this section we describe how that knowledge is represented in individual nodes. The source of this knowledge, and its subsequent utilization, will be considered in later sections.

Association via Temporal Contiguity

The structure of a node incorporates representations of two broad types of association: one based on temporal contiguity and the other based on functional equivalence. *Contiguity-based functional relatedness* represents relationships in which the functioning of processes in close temporal contiguity has produced successful outcomes. Every production in the node structure exemplifies this type of association. The direct linkage between a state and a sequence of actions—as represented in the condition and action of a production—is the closest form of functional relationship in LTM.

Although productions in BAIRN resemble those employed in classic production systems, they differ significantly in their structure and mode of operation. In a classic system conditions are compared with the current contents of a shared working memory. This test proceeds on a straight match or mismatch basis, and productions have no knowledge of the sources of the information relevant to the satisfaction of their conditions.

BAIRN productions, in contrast, do contain knowledge about sources of information required to satisfy conditions, and are capable of initiating processing aimed at acquiring such information. The basis of this capability will be clarified by a description of the general structure of a BAIRN production.

An element in the condition side of a BAIRN production may be either a token for another node or a representation of a specific result of node activation, such as a relational expression. Actions either insert elements into working memory by simple assertion or else they activate processes that will result in the construction and insertion of elements. As a consequence *each element in the condition and action of a production is semantically defined at a node elsewhere in the network*. Exceptions to this principle are elements asserted by productions that represent their own semantic contribution. All other elements have the location of their semantic definitions included in their representations. The resulting general form of productions is as follows (the italicized phrases represent variables):

IF the token for *node 1* is present
and *relational outcome x* produced by *node 2* is present,

THEN assert *element 1*
and call *node 3* to operate on *element 2*.

All variables in productions represent class variables, and the classes or concepts are defined at other nodes or at the node under consideration. Consequently BAIRN productions do not use free variables that can match and bind to any working memory element. The nature and extent of the classes reflect the developmental state of the system. Two general developmental sequences can be distinguished. In one, classes are initially very broad and globally defined. Subsequent experience results in the derivation and representation of more specifically defined subordinates. The class of environmental features distinguished as figures against ground provides an example of an initial, global concept.

An alternative development sequence commences with narrow classes defined by specific primary processes such as sensorimotor responses. These enable the detection of classes or environmental features defined in terms of combinations of primary process classes. Subsequently classes of environmental features become subordinates of new superordinate classes derived by abstraction.

So far our discussion has emphasized individual productions. The *group* of productions forming the basis of the definition of a unit of knowledge at a node also exemplifies association via temporal contiguity. As in the case of the constituents of individual productions, the members of the group become associated as a result of successful operation in close temporal proximity. Their functional relationship is less close since, unlike the constituents of productions, they are not directly linked but interact via a shared work space.

In BAIRN each node is provided with its own unconstrained local work space. Our system-building strategy has been to impose space constraints on the working memories employed in between-node, rather than within-node, processing. We restrict the amount of parallel processing to a level consistent with the capacity of sensorimotor channels and the requirements for learning by limiting the number of processing channels and the number of nodes simultaneously vying for them. With these objectives achieved, and given the operationally infinite capacity of LTM, there appears to be no reason why the benefits of unrestricted work space should not be conferred on within-node processing.

Within-Node Processing The productions stored at a node make up its **definition list**. As figure 8.1 indicates, the **definition list**(1) is one of three main constituents of node structure.[1] The *activation conditions*(2) represent conjunctions of the conditions of those individual productions which, in the past, have served as alternative beginnings of successful operation by the **definition list** productions. Satisfaction of at least one set of activation conditions is necessary before a node can participate in the limited amount of parallel activity allowed in the network. Further details about how the activation conditions operate will be provided in section 8.3.

There are two categories of productions on the **definition list**. The first, and developmentally prior, category includes productions representing *procedural knowledge*(3) or "knowing how." Since the final sections of this chapter are devoted to an account of the learning of quantification processes, we will set the scene by stating examples in quantitative terms:

IF the objective is to produce a *quantitative symbol* for a *collect*,
THEN select an appropriate *quantifier*
and apply it to the *collection*.

The second category includes productions representing declarative knowledge or "knowing that." The associations that they represent derive

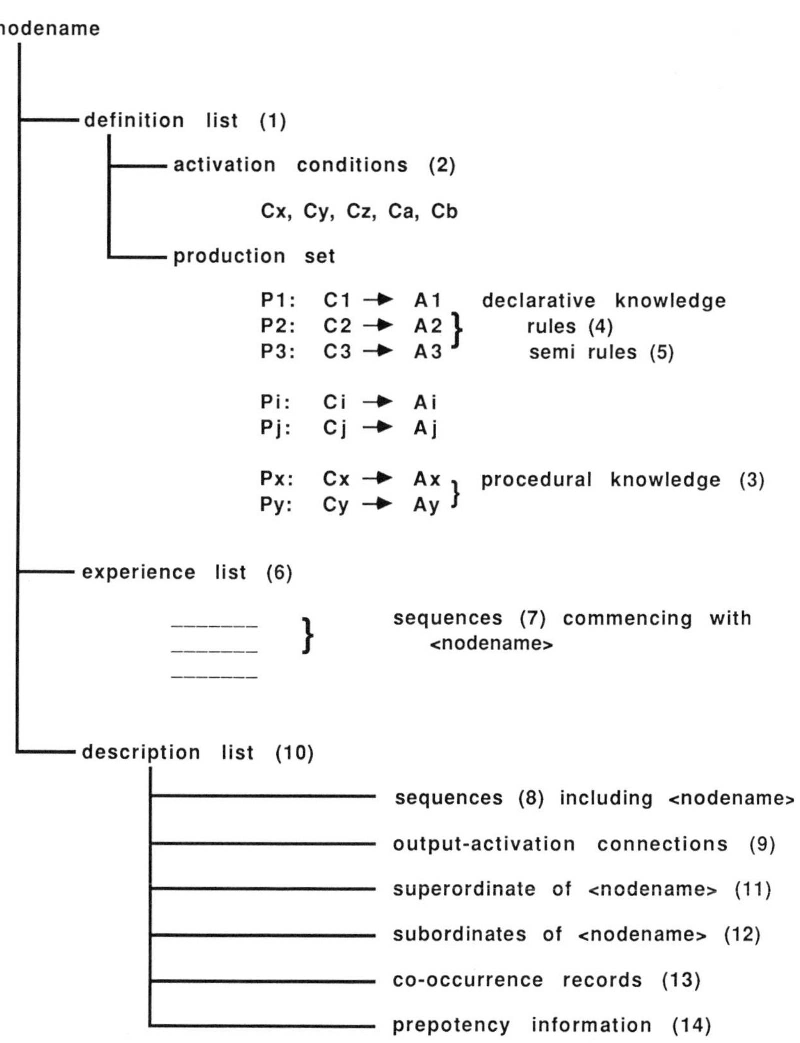

Figure 8.1
Schematic of information contained in node structure

from two sources. The first source comes from the results of processing by procedural productions. Learning from such results produces declarative knowledge in the form of situation-linked propositions expressed as productions. These productions provide results from node activation with little or no involvement of procedural productions. In some cases they directly link state descriptions to node results:

IF the value of *object 1* is Fred
and the value of *object 2* is Joe
and the objective is quantitative comparison,
THEN Fred is bigger than Joe.

IF *collection 1* has more than *collection 2*
and a *quantity* is added to *collection 1*
and the objective is quantitative comparison,
THEN *collection 1* is more than *collection 2*.

Declarative productions on the **definition list** of a quantitative comparison node "short circuit" the procedural productions entirely. Productions directly generating node output without procedural processing are referred to as *rules*(4). In other cases involvement of procedural knowledge is reduced, but not entirely avoided, by productions that provide as declarative knowledge intermediate, rather than final, processing results:

IF the objective is length estimation of *object 1*
and an *estimation standard* is required for quantitative comparison,
THEN the *length* of my car is 4 meters.

Productions facilitating processing by generating intermediate results are termed *semirules*(5).

The second source of declarative knowledge is linguistic input. Results that would be obtained by applying procedural productions to specific input can be communicated to the system in linguistic form without the necessity of direct derivation. When applied to records of decoded linguistic input, learning processes add declarative productions to **definition lists**. The new productions represent situation-linked propositions and reduce the need to call on procedural knowledge.

Between-Node Processing Two other features of node structure provide representations of contiguity-based functional relatedness. Unlike the information stored on the **definition list**, these features are entirely concerned with between-node rather than within-node associations:

1. Each node possesses an **experience list**. Each entry on the **experience list** (6) describes a sequence of node activations commencing with an activation of the node under consideration. These sequences (7) are derived from BAIRN's previous experience. They represent a degree of association that justifies sequential connections between nodes but is not yet sufficient to warrant construction of a new node incorporating these associations in its **definition list**. The connection between a pair of nodes in a sequence may be of a direct form in which the second node receives the output from the first node and operates on it. Alternatively, it may involve contiguous activation with the first node prompting the second to operate but not providing it with direct input (see section 8.4).

   The complete specification of sequences appears only on the **experience list** of the initial node. Subsequent nodes have increasingly truncated representations containing information on the immediately preceding node and the remainder of the sequence after their own operation. This information (8) is stored in each node's **description list**.

2. The second form of association between nodes is confined to pairs of nodes rather than sequences. It relates to cases in which the output of a node appears as an element in the activation conditions of another node (9). This output may take the form of the name token of the first node, or it may represent a more elaborate result of its processing, such as a relation. A complete record of such connections between output and activation conditions is maintained on the **description list** (10) of the first node.

Association via Functional Equivalence

As indicated earlier, node structure incorporates representations of two types of association. So far, we have confined our attention to the first: contiguity-based functional relatedness. The second type of association arises from *co-occurrence due to functional equivalence*. Nodes are regarded as co-occurring when experience indicates that they occupy the same locations and perform the same functions in sequences of processing. These co-occurrences enable the mapping of category, class, or concept relationships between nodes. In some cases two or more co-occurring nodes indicate the need for a new node representing a superordinate class of which they are subordinates. In others co-occurrence of two nodes indicates that one should be added to the list of subordinates of the other. Information covering the superordinate (11) and subordinate (12) class relationships of each node is stored on its **description list**. The representation of each relationship includes information about the contexts in which that relationship has applied. Contextual descriptions comprise the node input and output and sequence and states associated with functional equivalence. In addition to information on superordinate and subordinate relationships, the **description list** also contains records of co-occurrences (13) of the node with others. These records may give rise to new relationships as further experience is obtained.

8.3 Node Operation

Our account begins with the node inactive. Node activation is determined, in part, by the node's activation conditions. The minimum requirement for satisfying these conditions is, first, availability of information that satisfies the conditions of one of the "alternative beginning" productions and, second, availability of all information required during operation of the node that is neither created by production actions nor acquired via calls to sensoriperceptual nodes incorporated in the conditions of productions.

The processes by which information is inserted in a node's work space will be covered in section 8.5. Even if these processes do satisfy the node's activation conditions, it is not immediately activated. Rather, it enters the phase prior to operation and bids for one of a limited number of processing channels. The result of this bid depends on a comparison of the node's potency with that of other nodes seeking to act at the same time. The nature and source of potency will also be considered in section 8.5. For our present purpose it is sufficient to indicate that it is determined by matching the current activation information with records of specific sets of activation information linked to end states and potency. These co-occurrence records (13) are derived from previous experience and are stored on the **description list**.

When information in the work space is insufficient to satisfy the activation conditions, the node does not cease its attempt to operate. The alternative beginning production closest to having its conditions satisfied is identified, and an attempt is made to acquire the additional input required a complete its satisfaction. This process utilizes knowledge, included in the conditions of BAIRN productions, about sources of information that can satisfy them. The node linked as a source to the first unsatisfied condition is prompted to attempt to act.

The result of the prompt depends on both the availability of information relevant to its activation conditions and the basic level of potency of the original prompting node, since the "slave" node is assigned this potency during its attempt to acquire a processing channel. If the prompt successfully procures the missing information, the procedure is repeated with the next unsatisfied condition. To maintain the current contextual relevance of the activation information available to nodes, a check is conducted on each occasion that new information is received by insertion or as a result of prompting. All of the activation information is compared with the current contents of the appropriate working memories employed in between-node processing. These short-term memory (STM) stores have been referred to earlier, and at this point we give a brief indication of their place in BAIRN.

STM Stores

In the current version of BAIRN primary emphasis is placed on between-node processing conducted via a semantic short-term memory (SSTM). This is assumed to be a store for information which has been preprocessed to a point where it is represented in the same general semantic form regardless of the sensoriperceptual modality by which it entered the system. The function of SSTM in limiting the amount of parallel processing has already been touched on and will be considered further in section 8.4. For the moment it will suffice to indicate that in exploration of BAIRN's performance to date, it has not proved necessary to assign SSTM a capacity greater than ten chunks of information.

In addition to SSTM it is assumed that buffers are available to the sensoriperceptual nodes responsible for the preprocessing. These nodes have the same structure as those interacting via SSTM. Although the sensoriperceptual buffers have decay characteristics that constrain the availability of information for processing, the sensoriperceptual nodes are considered to operate in a highly parallel fashion employing many more channels than are available to the nodes in the orbit of SSTM.

Activation sequence

We return to the sequence of events that ensues when a node's activation conditions have been satisfied and its potency is sufficiently high to secure an operating channel:

EVENT 1 A record is opened in the time line and the name of the node and a representation of the input responsible for its activation are inserted in it.

EVENT 2 The initial information in the node's work space is reviewed by any rules on the **definition list**. If a rule's conditions are satisfied, the operation of the node can be short-circuited and an end state generated immediately.

EVENT 3 If no rule is applicable, the necessary variable bindings are established using the specific values of the class variables derived from the information satisfying the activation conditions.

EVENT 4 The rest of the productions on the **definition list** commence processing the information in the work space. A number of features of their operation merit comment:

1. The recognition phase of the recognition-act cycle involves a parallel review of the contents of the work space by the conditions of all of the productions.

2. Sensoriperceptual conditions not satisfied by information obtained via the activation conditions are permitted to check the appropriate buffer and, if necessary, prompt their source node. Under these circumstances a source node may operate in the channel already secured. There are two qualifications on the exercise of these privileges by sensoriperceptual conditions: all of the conditions in the production must be sensoriperceptual, or any conditions that are not sensoriperceptual must be already satisfied.

3. If the conditions of one or more semirules are satisfied, they operate and no other productions are permitted to act in that cycle.

4. If no semirules can operate, all satisfied productions are applied.

5. Information in the work space is available for use by any of the productions during a cycle. At the end of a cycle all information employed by one or more productions is deleted from the work space.

6. The near absence of conflict resolution principles in the within-node processing is attributable to three features, two of which have been previously mentioned: the architecture of the network, which resolves conflict sets at the between-node level and distributes processing among a large number of relatively small production systems derived from consistencies

detected in BAIRN's experience; the avoidance of the use of free variables in the conditions of productions, which results in a reduction in the number of instantiations; and the prevention of immediate repetition of the activation of productions by deletion from the work space of expressions involved in successful matches at the conclusion of each cycle.

EVENT 5 When a series of recognition-act cycles has brought processing by the productions to a conclusion, the information remaining in the work space is reviewed to assess whether the end state is consistent with expectations. This is achieved by comparing it with information on the **description list** on the end states previously produced by the type of input that initiated the current activation. If the end state is unexpected, the time-line entry is marked for later consideration by the learning processes.

EVENT 6 The time-line entry is completed by inserting a representation of the end state produced by the node's operation.

EVENT 7 A representation of the node's output is placed in the appropriate buffer. In the case of SSTM this record is not simply accompanied by the node's name. Each constituent of the output is accompanied by the name of the node defining the process that produced it. These names are derived from the actions of individual productions. The reason for the inclusion of this information will become clear as we move to consider the next phase of the node's operation. Having successfully completed its processing, the node proceeds to spread activation to other nodes. Since this is a complex and fundamental procedure, it will be given an extended treatment in the next section.

8.4 Activation Spread

The approach to activation spread adopted in BAIRN is consistent with the integration of procedural and declarative knowledge in node structure and the emphasis on context-based determinants of node connectivity. Variations in activation spread are represented not by passing varying amounts of strength from node to node but by variations in the nature of information and the methods by which it is passed between nodes. There are three modes of activation spread. The standard mode operates during "normal" arousal level, and relatively high or low arousal levels result in one or the other of two alternate modes.

Spread during "Normal" Arousal

In the standard mode a node uses three methods of passing information to other nodes. All three methods operate in parallel:

1. Using the entries on the **experience list**, a copy of the node's end state is placed in the work space of each node occupying the second position in an activation sequence. This action represents an activation prompt. In some cases the information received will become direct input to the second node if it makes a successful bid to act. In others the information is not required as direct input since the association is one of contiguous activation rather than an output-input link. In such cases information passed functions purely as an activation prompt and the result of the attempt to act depends on the availability of appropriate input from other sources. Information passed as a prompt is retained and becomes part of the output package to be passed to the next node in the sequence, if the bid to act and subsequent activation are successful.

2. The second method employs the record on the **description list** of the connections between the node's output and the activation conditions of other nodes. When a node's end state contains elements that appear in other nodes' activation conditions, representations of those elements are placed in the work spaces of the relevant nodes. As indicated earlier, the elements may simply be the name or token of the node spreading activation or more complex forms of output such as relations.

3. The **description list** also supplies the connectivity information used in the third method of spreading activation. The list is searched to discover if the node has a subordinate-superordinate relationship with another node in the context represented by the current output. If such a relationship is discovered the process is repeated using the **description list** of the superordinate node to determine if it in turn functions as a subordinate in a relationship concerned with the current context. The search for relevant superordinates is restricted to two levels to constrain the amount of computation. The highest superordinate node discovered is used as a basis for spreading activation in the way described as the second method. The elements placed in node work spaces reflect the output of the original, subordinate node.

The three methods making up the standard mode of spreading activation endow it with a "middle of the road" or compromise flavor. Methods one and two emphasize depth or continuity of the current line of processing, and the third method provides for breadth and switching of processing direction. They also provide for both functional relatedness and functional equivalence to play a part. The first two methods and the final step in the third method rely on connections representing functional relatedness. The core of the third method employs between-node connections established as a result of experience of functional equivalence.

Spread during High or Low Arousal

In contrast to the standard mode the two alternative modes of spreading activation emphasize, respectively, depth and breadth. The first alternative replaces the standard mode when operation of a node is associated with a high level of arousal. High arousal is caused by the presence on the **definition list** of productions that provide direct access to primary emotion generators (see section 8.5). These generators link sensoriperceptual conditions with physiological actions defining primary emotions such as pleasure, fear, anger, and so on. The general function performed by primary emotion generators will be considered in section 8.5. For the present purpose, it is sufficient to indicate that nodes with such productions on their **definition lists** are designated as high arousal nodes and adopt a characteristic mode of spreading activation. The mode permits the node to use only the first two methods included in the standard mode. The effect of this restriction is to limit spread to connections emphasizing continuity of the current line of processing and functional relatedness between nodes. Such limitation is appropriate when high arousal nodes representing, for example, "fight or flight" behavior are in operation, since the general effect is to dampen diversive, cognitive activity in favor of nodes providing more direct, sensorimotor reactions. The mode is less adaptive if primary emotion generators appear on the **definition lists** of nodes associated with contexts requiring flexibility and sustained cognitive processing for solution.

The standard mode gives way to the second alternative when operation of a node is associated with low arousal. Low arousal, unlike high arousal, is not considered to be a continuing feature of the operation of specific nodes. It is a feature of the system's treatment of two types of novelty. The first is represented by new nodes added to the network as a result of experience. In the interests of facilitating construction of connections between them and other nodes, a modified mode of spreading activation is adopted. The duration of the use of the modified mode is linked to the value of a parameter that determines the potency of a node's bid to act when its activation conditions are satisfied. Further details of this process will be provided in section 8.5. In the case of each new node the parameter is assigned a value reflecting the nature of the experience resulting in its construction. This value is then temporarily raised to increase the initial likelihood of the node's activation. Repeated activation results in decrements of the value until it reaches the level originally assigned. At this point the node reverts from the modified to the standard mode of spreading activation.

The second type of novelty associated with low arousal is not confined to nodes newly added to the network. It applies to any node that is activated after a minimum period of inactivity (defined by the value of a parameter). In order to attend selectively to novel features of the current situation, such nodes produce a state of low arousal and spread activation by the modified mode. This maximizes their influence in determining the range of possible events following their successful operation. As in the case of new nodes the value of their potency parameter is raised and subsequently diminished on a decrement with activation basis. Since the rate of decrement employed is greater than in the case of newly constructed nodes, fewer repetitions are required to produce a return to the original value assigned and reversion to the standard mode.

The low arousal mode enables BAIRN to cope with the two types of novelty by adding a method of spreading activation to the three included in the standard mode. Like all other nodes low arousal nodes, at the conclusion of their operation, place a copy of their output in SSTM (or a sensory buffer, if appropriate). We have already described the function of this information: it facilitates the checking of the recency of information available to nodes considering a bid to act. In the standard mode this is the only contribution made by the information to determining the results of activation spread. In the modified mode the breadth of the effects of a node's output on subsequent events is maximized by spreading activation from the current contents of SSTM. This adds to the effects of spreading activation on the basis of **description list** connections between the node's output and the activation conditions of other nodes in two ways. The **description list** connections are defined entirely in terms of links to the node producing the output. Figure 8.2 illustrates how SSTM utilizes the connections between nodes responsible for producing *constituents* of the output and the activation conditions of other nodes. The nodes in question feature on the

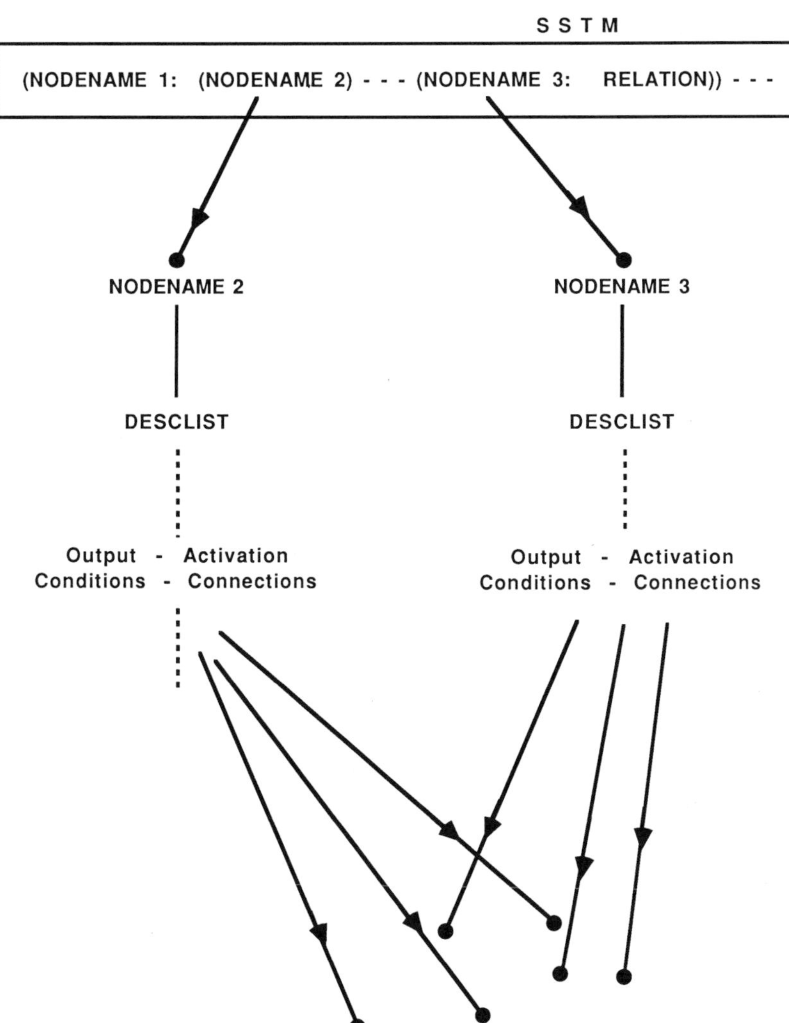

Figure 8.2
Activation spread from elements in SSTM

definition list of the node that produced the output. Further breadth is obtained by permitting spread of activation on the same basis from the outputs of any other nodes which are currently present in SSTM. By spreading activation from SSTM in these two ways, BAIRN uses both output-input and contiguous relationships between nodes in obtaining the desired increase in the breadth of the effects of a node's output.

We have now considered the structure of individual nodes (section 8.2), their method of internal operation (section 8.3), and the modes by which they spread activation to other nodes (section 8.4). Throughout these discussions we have referred to processes that determine the results of bids to act made by nodes whose activation conditions are satisfied. We conclude this review of BAIRN's structure by considering these processes as part of the general mode of operation that ensures that only a limited number of nodes are simultaneously active.

8.5 Parallel Processing and Channel Allocation

BAIRN's design represents a compromise between two conflicting requirements. On the one hand, the complex communication among nodes requires a certain amount of parallel processing. On the other hand, we do not want to raise the complexity of the trace data in the time line to a level which inhibits effective operation of the self-modification processes. The optimal amount of parallelism is yet to be determined. At present it is set at three channels of parallel processing.

Focal Consciousness

Simultaneously active nodes operate in either of two different processing modes, corresponding to different levels of consciousness. At any point in time, only one of the active nodes operates in a *focally conscious* mode. This status enhances the node's influence on subsequent processing. Output from a focally conscious node has priority in relation to the limited capacity of SSTM. Output from nonfocally conscious nodes can only be inserted into SSTM if unoccupied space remains after the insertion of focally conscious output.

Priority use of SSTM increases the influence of focally conscious output in two ways. Nodes considering activation on the basis of information received via focally conscious processing are more likely to succeed when they check the contextual recency of information by comparing it with the current contents of SSTM. In addition, when activation spreads from a node in low-arousal mode, the dominance of focally conscious output is directly reflected in spreading activation from the current contents of SSTM.

Focal consciousness is also distinguished by the ability to "attend" to processing one level below the level of aggregation represented by the focally conscious node. The nature of this feature is most clearly indicated in relation to the time-line record. In the general mode of node operation, a single episodic record is inserted in the time line. The record contains the information that satisfied the activation conditions of the node and tokens representing the contents of its work space at the conclusion of its activation. In the case of a node in focal consciousness, an expanded episodic record is produced that provides an account of the processing sequence determined by the node's **definition list**. This is precisely the type of comprehensive trace information required when the system experiences operational difficulties. Absence of such information, in the case of nodes lying without focal consciousness, impedes on-line tackling of difficulties and may lead to the deferral of effective intervention until the necessary information can be obtained by reactivating a problem node off-line as part of a subsequent time-line review process (see section 8.8).

There is a second advantage of the more detailed time-line records of nodes lying within the focally conscious stream of processing: they facilitate the system's attempts to generalize by combining two existing nodes to produce a third at a higher level of aggregation, and to achieve economies by detecting and eliminating redundant processing. These processes will be considered in an account of the system's self-modification capability in section 8.8.

The ability to attend to processing one level below the level of aggregation represented by the node can be viewed as the operational basis of the experience of subjective awareness. The core content of consciousness is the processing occurring in the work space of the focally conscious node.

Unconscious Processing

Two other nodes are permitted to operate in parallel with the node occupying focal consciousness. They are considered to be engaging in unconscious processing. As already indicated, their influence on subsequent node activation is restricted by the precedence accorded to focally conscious output in SSTM. Output from unconscious nodes can only be inserted in SSTM if unoccupied space exists after the needs of current focally conscious output have been met. Provided this constraint is observed, new unconscious output is permitted to force the results of previous focally conscious and unconscious processing out of SSTM. As a second operational distinction from focal consciousness, nodes engaging in unconscious processing do not attend to processing one level below the level of aggregation that they represent, and their time-line entry is limited to an unexpanded episodic record.

Although the processing activity of unconscious nodes lies outside of the bounds of consciousness, it may contribute to psychological experience through its output. The core of subjective awareness is ongoing focally conscious processing. But BAIRN also possesses a general awareness of the current context, as defined by the contents of SSTM. Output from unconscious processing that is inserted in SSTM thus forms part of the content of subjective awareness.

Having reviewed the number and mode of operation of the channels available for parallel processing, we turn now to the processes responsible for allocating nodes to channels. First, we describe the method of assigning relative potency or *prepotency* to nodes. Then, we consider the timing and interactive relationships of channel allocation, node operation and activation spread.

Node Potency: Motives and Emotions

Assignment of prepotency values to nodes is a fundamental feature of BAIRN, since it is the interaction of nodal prepotencies and the transfer of information by activation spread that determines the "purposes" or goal directedness of the system. In production system terms the results of the interaction represent the resolution of the between-node conflict set. In specifying the assignment process, our starting point is an appraisal of the functions performed by motives and emotions in an information processing system.[2]

The existence of motives is a consequence of the need for directionality in adaptive, flexible, intelligent systems. Constraints on possible courses of action are essential for the establishment and maintenance of successful environmental interaction. In BAIRN the first step toward fulfilling this function is the inclusion of *motive generators* in the innate kernal. Motive generators bias the construction of the system's representation of its world in particular directions and as a result constrain and direct its behavior.

They operate by scanning the time-line trace for sequences representing experience falling within the area of their motives and initiating appropriate additions or modifications to LTM. This process is conducted both on-line and off-line.

Emotions can be regarded as "hard-wired" sources of information that assist in a continuing process of discrimination that is crucial in canalizing the behavior of the system in appropriate directions. Episodic records of physiological activity associated with emotions assist motive generators in performing their function by facilitating rapid direction and discrimination of time-line segments both on-line and off-line. These records initially reflect the operation of *primary emotion generators* included in the system's "innate" repertoire. These are productions linking sensoriperceptual conditions with physiological actions defining primary emotions such as pleasure, fear, and anger. The physiological trace data is detected and reacted to by the innate motive generators. Their conditions include patterns of physiological activity defining primary emotions, indications of the level of emotional intensity derived from the intensity of sensory stimulation, and other situational features defining the area of the motive. In innate motive generators these situational features are of a relatively global nature, such as the perception of human contact or movement in the environment and the occurrence of problems in the system's operation.

Interaction between the initial repertoires of generators for emotions and motives produces the episodic records that are selected as starting points for processing of the time line in a search for consistent sequences.[3] In some cases motive generators representing highly significant motives directly determine that a new node will be added to LTM on the basis of a single occurrence of a sequence. In other cases the decision depends on the result of time-line processing by consistency detection processes carried out after a motive generator has indicated the starting point for analysis. When an addition to LTM occurs, an initial prepotency value is assigned to the new node by the motive generator(s) involved in its creation. The prepotency reflects the status of the motive generator(s) in a hierarchy of primary motives and specific values of the emotional intensity and situational feature variables included in the sequence. As figure 8.1 indicates, this initial prepotency (14) is stored on the **description list** of the new node.

Prepotency assignment is not confined to newly created nodes. Individual nodes compare the results of their activations with expectations based on previous input/output conjunctions stored on their description lists.

Unexpected or novel outcomes are flagged in the time-line record to enable processing by motive generators and assignment of a prepotency value. During the course of interaction with the environment, this procedure provides each node with a range of context-linked prepotencies. The process differentiates the initial global prepotency and reflects variations in the node's significance in different contexts. In addition, as indicated earlier, prepotency levels can be temporarily increased during the mode of spreading activation used when nodes operate with low arousal due to novelty.

Interaction of the innate repertoires of emotion and motive generators not only contributes to construction of the system's LTM world model but also results in the learning of further emotions and motives. Representations of higher-level or compound emotions are derived from the time-line sequences revealing the functional relatedness of two or more primary emotion generators. Higher-level motive generators capable of processing the more complex physiological trace data produced by the compound emotion generators are derived from time-line sequences, including associated activations of the initial motive generators which process primary emotions. These compound motive generators provide a capability to assign initial prepotency values to new nodes derived from sequences featuring compound emotions.

Our approach clearly owes a heavy theoretical debt to Allport's (1955) views on the functional autonomy of experientially derived motives and to the work of Cattell (1950). It places great explanatory weight on the learning processes responsible for the construction of experience-based motive generators and the assignment to them of a prepotency-granting capability consistent with the hierarchical positions of the primary motives involved in their creation. The nature of the repertoire of primary motives selected and the hierarchy determining their relative status are also critical.

Some Simplifying Assumptions

Our investigation of the practical feasibility of learning motives and of the relative merits of alternative motivational repertoires and structures is at an early stage. In implementing network segments, we use parameter settings to establish prepotencies on the **description lists** of individual nodes, and operator calls to provide additional prepotencies when unexpected outcomes occur. The operational function of emotion is simulated by including, where necessary, emotion generator productions in the **definition lists** of individual nodes.

Implementation of the timing and interactive relationships of channel allocation, node operation and activation spread poses the intractable problems of simulating parallelism on a sequential processor. In the current version of BAIRN we make several simplifying assumptions. We assume that the "normal" situation is one in which each node occupying a channel continues its processing to completion without interruption, engages in activation spread and is succeeded in the channel by the node with the highest prepotency of those activated by the spread. The ability to interrupt within-node processing and take over a channel before completion by the current node is confined to nodes representing sensoriperceptual processes that register environmental emergencies.

Due to variations in within-node processing time and in the duration of the activation spread initiated by each node, it is highly unlikely that more than one node will complete its processing at any instant. In the rare event of a double or triple tie we permit the nodes to insert output in SSTM in an order of precedence based on their relative prepotency. A combined spread of activation is then carried out and the available channels are occupied by the two or three nodes with the highest prepotency.

Combined activation spread might enable the results of processing in a single channel to determine the next phase of processing in two or all three channels. We are currently reviewing the merits and demerits of permitting cross-channel influence. The specific approach being considered would involve identifying three nodes with the highest prepotencies in each activation spread. The node with the highest prepotency would commence processing in the channel vacated by the node responsible for the spread of activation. The remaining two nodes would be retained until occurrence of the next spread of activation initiated from another channel and would be permitted to compete for the vacancy with the nodes involved. This would create the possibility of more channels—and processing power—being devoted to aspects of the network with relatively high prepotency.

The obvious advantages of this situation must, however, be weighed against the possible degradation of the system's effectiveness. Overdominance of a single stream of processing might produce an undue narrowing or tunneling effect on the range of activity. One way to minimize the risk would be to increase the number of processing channels beyond three. Determination of the feasibility of this approach must await the outcome of investigation of the maximum degree of parallel processing which is possible before the complexity level of the trace data recorded in the time-

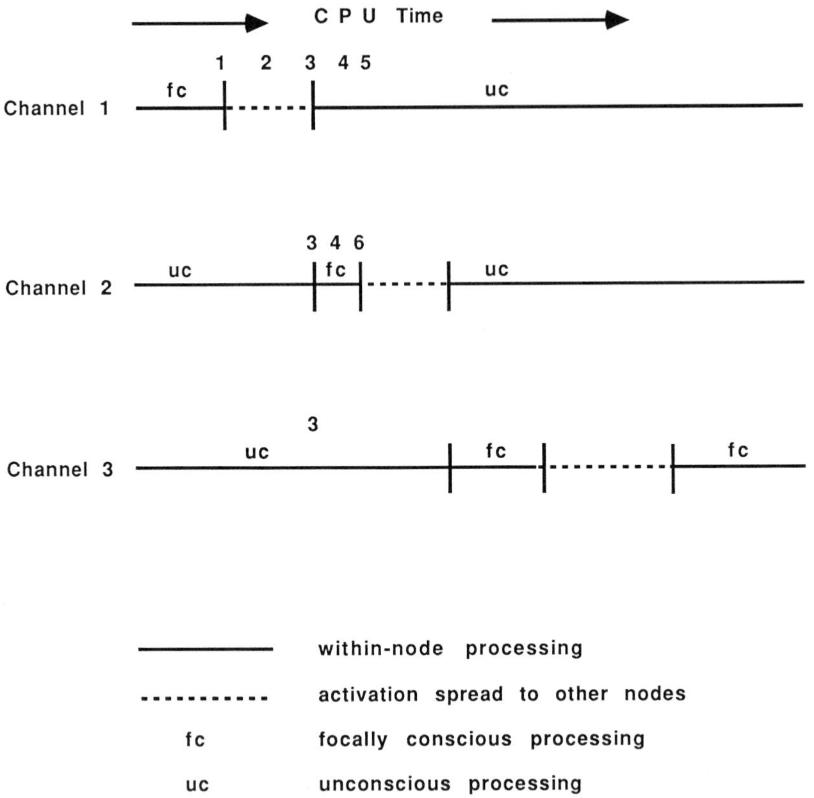

Figure 8.3
Temporal sequence of channel allocation: consciousness levels in parallel processing

line begins to affect adversely the functioning of the system's general learning processes.

Temporal Sequence of Channel Allocation

Having considered the nature of the simplifying assumptions and some of their implications, we will now turn to a description of the interactive relationship among channel allocation, node operation, and activation spread as it proceeds from moment to moment. The events detailed cover the first of three sequential occurrences of activation spread shown in figure 8.3. The timing relationship between the processing proceeding in the three channels is defined in terms of the time required for each spread of activation and the duration of the processing carried out by each node occupying a channel. In each case CPU time is used as an estimate of real time.

EVENT 1 The node occupying channel 1 and operating in focal consciousness completes its processing and therefore requires no further time for the production of output. This is indicated by the switch from within-node processing to activation spread.

EVENT 2 Activation is spread from the node on the basis of its current output and in the mode consistent with its arousal status. The next node to occupy the channel is identified as a result of the interaction between prepotency values and the information contained in the output.

EVENT 3 A review is conducted of the levels of consciousness assigned to the nodes occupying the three channels. If the prepotency of the new node exceeds the prepotencies of the two nodes operating in the other channels, it will achieve focally conscious status like its predecessor. If it does not, the node with the highest prepotency changes status from unconscious to focally conscious processing. This elevation does not disrupt the node's processing since its effects are confined to time-line entries and the insertion of output in SSTM. In the example, the node occupying channel 2 achieves focally conscious status.

EVENT 4 The time required to carry out the spread of activation is computed and added to the operating time of the last node to complete processing. The sum obtained is then subtracted from the processing time required for the nodes operating in the other channels to produce their output. The result of this calculation indicates that the node in channel 2 will be the next to complete processing.

EVENT 5 Within-node processing defined by the new node occupying channel 1 is carried out to completion and the time required is recorded. If necessary, records of the relative completion times of concurrently active nodes are used to determine whether information not provided via the activation conditions and required by sensoriperceptual conditions can be assumed to be already available without additional processing.

EVENT 6 The node in channel 2 is considered to have completed its processing and it becomes the starting point of activation spread.

The remaining events depicted in figure 8.3 will not be described step by step. They represent two further cycles through the sequence of activation spread, node identification, consciousness review, time computation to determine the next node to complete processing, running of the new node and recording of the time necessary for its operation.

This description of the interactions among channel allocation, node operation, and activation spread concludes our consideration of BAIRN's general architecture and control structure. With this account of the already developed—or "adult"—system as background, we will focus on the general learning processes that provide BAIRN with its self-modification capability. We will describe these processes in the context of a specific series of learning events, each contributing to revision of the system's world model and modification of its performance. The example is concerned with the acquisition of quantification processes and, in particular, the sequence of learning events culminating with the ability to conserve discontinuous quantity.

8.6 BAIRN and Conservation of Discontinuous Quantity

BAIRN characterizes the attainment of conservation of discontinuous quantity as the result of adding rules to a node's **definition list**. Recall that rules represent declarative knowledge and that they take the form of situation-linked propositions expressed as productions. In the case of conservation of discontinuous quantity the rules directly link state descriptions to node results and avoid the need for activation of the procedural productions on the **definition list**. The node involved represents the knowledge underlying the ability to make quantitative comparisons. The rules have the general form

IF two *collections* have a specific *quantitative relationship*
and one of the *collections* undergoes a *perceptual transformation*,

THEN the *transformed collection* and *untransformed collection*
have the same *quantitative relationship*.

This general form does not cover all of the cases where discovery of the conservation principle leads to processing economy. It excludes sequences of events involving quantity-changing transformations and a single rather than two collections. Ten rules are required to cover the range of variations in number of collections, initial quantitative relationships, and transformations. A comprehensive account of the full definition in processing terms of attainment of conservation of discontinuous quantity is presented in

Klahr and Wallace (1976) and a summary can be found in Klahr (1984). Because our goal here is to illustrate BAIRN's learning processes, we will restrict our example to situations involving two collections and selected quantitative relationships and transformations.

Quantification Processes in Adults and Children

The process culminating in the appearance of conservation of discontinuous quantity begins with the quantification processes that generate symbols representing quantitative properties of perceived collections. Comparison of such internal symbols establishes the quantitative relationship between their external referents. Construction of a node representing the process of quantitative comparison sets the scene for the achievement of greater economy in functioning by the discovery of conservation.

The nature and development of quantification processes are currently popular and controversial research topics. Klahr and Wallace (1976) present an empirical and theoretical case for the existence of three quantification operators: subitizing (Q_s), counting (Q_c), and estimation (Q_e). When asked to quantify collections of fewer than four objects, adults employ Q_s and respond rapidly and accurately with no conscious awareness of intermediate processing. This experience is completely different from quantification based on Q_c, which requires conscious management of attention for effective application of the technology of counting by ones. Quantitative symbols can be produced in situations involving great numbers, limited exposure duration, or continuous quantity, where neither Q_s nor Q_c can function. This is the province of Q_e, the estimation quantifier.

In adults, Q_s, Q_c, and Q_e are fully developed. For very small n, Q_s is used; for very large n, or for continuous quantity, Q_e is used; for intermediate situations, Q_c is used. Klahr and Wallace (1976) argue that development of the three quantifiers proceeds concurrently but that Q_s is the first to attain the status of a reliable indicator of quantity. Q_s is constructed by the child as a result of experience with small collections of objects. In contrast, Q_c is acquired as a socially transmitted technology and remains essentially a ritual without semantic basis until realization that it performs the same function as Q_s confers the status of an indicator of quantity. This event must be preceded by reliable performance of the complex counting technology. Q_e achieves the status of a reliable indicator of continuous quantity independently of Q_s and Q_c. Its function in estimation of the relative quantity of large or briefly viewed discontinuous collections does not appear until relatively late in development and as a result of the interaction between Q_c and Q_e.

The primacy of Q_s is rejected by Gelman and Gallistel (1978) who present a case for the prior development of Q_c and the subsequent appearance of Q_s as a shortcut method of rapidly quantifying small collections. The empirical and theoretical arguments for and against this position cannot be reviewed here, but a few salient features will be mentioned. There can be no doubt about the qualitative distinctiveness of the quantification process in the Q_s and Q_c domains. When kindergarten children quantify random dot patterns, their reaction times and error rates reveal a clear discontinuity at $n = 3$ or 4 (Chi and Klahr 1975). It is clear that they possess both Q_s and Q_c, although both are substantially slower than the adult versions. The increase in reaction time with n suggests that Q_s resembles Q_c in drawing on sequential processes concerned with attention management and symbol generation. The increase in the reaction time slope from 200 msec to 1000 msec, with the move from the Q_s to Q_c numerical range, however, appears to rule out rapid subvocal counting by ones as an explanation of Q_s. In addition the view that Q_s is based on pattern recognition, with, for example, collections of three being processed as a triangular gestalt, is not supported by empirical findings. Chase (1978) obtained the typical discontinuity in reaction time at $n = 3$ or 4 when subjects had to quantify complex block configurations, which clearly did not conform to "good" quantification patterns. More recently van Oeffelen and Vos (1982) found that people can subitize groups of dots as well as individual dots. They used displays of from 13 to 23 dots that could be grouped into from one to 8 clusters. The clusters were displayed for brief durations, and the subjects had to report how many clusters of dots they saw. When the number of clusters was within the subitizing range, subjects were very accurate, but their performance deteriorated sharply when there were more than 4 clusters.

Thus Q_s appears to be partially controlled by high-order cognitive processes that determine the target of the quantification effort (e.g., dots, cubes, dot clusters), and some inherent limitation on rapid segmentation of the visual field into three or four perceptual chunks. It is likely to be a side effect of a more general hierarchically organized perceptual process (see Palmer 1977).

Quantification Processes in Infants

Reliable data on quantification ability in infants is necessary if the vexed question of the developmental relationship of Q_s and Q_c is to be resolved.

Such data have only begun to become available in the last two years with a sequence of studies of infants' ability to discriminate small numerosities. The results indicate that infants possess such ability and that the discrimination is based on number *per se* rather than other properties such as brightness, total contour, extent, density or surface area (Cooper 1984; Starkey and Cooper 1980; Starkey, Spelke, and Gelman 1980; Strauss and Curtis 1981, 1984). The procedure adopted involves initially habituating infants to a particular numerosity (e.g., $n = 2$) and then presenting them with posthabituation arrays of the same numerosity or one very close to it (e.g., $n = 2$ or 3). The results are interpreted on the basis that, if subjects dishabituate to the novel numerosity but not the familiar one, they have demonstrated the ability to discriminate between the two quantities. On this criterion the studies demonstrate that infants as young as four months are able to discriminate 2–3, 3–4, but not 4–5.

What is the nature of the process underlying these data? Strauss and Curtis (1981) point out that, although their "results demonstrate that some numerosities can be discriminated by infants even though they possess no knowledge of counting," they "do not necessarily imply that the infant has a cognitive awareness of number and can 'represent' numerosity" (p. 1151). Despite this commendable caution, it appears to be necessary to attribute habituation to a particular numerosity, when many other perceptual dimensions are being varied, to some form of repeated encoding of the cardinality of the set size.

Starkey et al. (1980) on the basis of their infant studies, conclude that "infants possess a primitive form of nonverbal counting" that "may underlie (some) subitizing phenomena" and that might "share some component processes with verbal counting." Whether "nonverbal counting" is an appropriate label for the processes responsible for a primitive form of cardinal quantification is a moot point. Clearly the processes must include attention management and symbol generation, but these are common to both counting and subitizing. Similarity to the processes underlying subitizing is suggested by the finding that infants can discriminate 3–4 but not 4–5. This ceiling on their performance coincides with the discontinuity in the child and adult reaction time data that defines the upper bound of the subitizing range.

Any attempt to characterize this initial form of quantification must take account of preliminary results reported by Starkey, Spelke, and Gelman (1983). Their data suggest that for $n = 2$ or 3, infants can do cross-model matching between simultaneous visual and sequential auditory patterns. The range (2–3) and the rate of presentation of the auditory patterns are consistent with the characteristics of the slower, child version of Q_s (Chi and Klahr 1975).

The data provided by the infant studies to date are highly intriguing, but far from providing a clear prescription for the process definition of an initial quantifier. They suggest, however, that it may reasonably be viewed as a direct precursor of Q_s, sharing many of its processing features. These would include the attention management and symbol generation processes which Q_s shares with Q_c. If the implications of the cross-model data are to be accommodated, the quantitative symbols produced by an initial mode of quantification must exhibit a high degree of abstractness and generality.

8.7 Development of the Quantifiers: A Preliminary Overview

Innate Processes

As already indicated, the task of defining innate quantification processes is far from straightforward. We take as our starting point two inferences derived from the empirical studies. The first is the existence of innate processes that can segment the perceptual field into chunks. The perceptual field may be visual or auditory and the size of segment composing each chunk may vary with the current objectives of environmental interaction. For example, a visual chunk may, at different times, contain a dot, a cube, or a cluster of dots.

The concept of a chunk of variable size as a basis for segmentation can be formally described in terms of the topological concept of a *tolerance space* (Zeeman and Buneman 1968). If two objects *a* and *b* are not distinguished, then they are considered to be *within tolerance* ($a \sim b$). Identification of a chunk with a tolerance space produces the required characteristics. If each tolerance space comprises a single dot or cube all pairs of dots or cubes in a display or collection are outside tolerance. Chunking of a cluster of dots or group of cubes is represented by a change which brings number of pairs of dots or cubes within tolerance and renders them occupants of a single tolerance space. Our account of the initial quantification processes will be based on the co-occurrence of a number of tolerance spaces in the visual or auditory field.

The second inference from the empirical studies is the existence of a limit on the number of tolerance spaces which can be registered simultaneously. Tolerance spaces are regarded as the results of processing of the contents of visual and auditory STM stores. Capacity and decay characteristics of these buffers restrict the number of tolerance spaces in the visual or auditory field that can be registered as co-occuring. As we have seen, a considerable weight of evidence suggests that the visual perceptual limit is three tolerance spaces. There is a tenuous basis for the conclusion that a similar constraint operates in auditory perception.

Innate Quantifier Nodes In BAIRN the initial quantifier is represented by three nodes that provide an ability to produce representations of small, cardinal quantities. Consistent with the hypothesis that they are developmental precursors of Q_s, the nodes will be referred to as SUBIT-ONE, SUBIT-TWO, and SUBIT-THREE. The core of the **definition list** of each node is a single production that registers the occurrence or co-occurrence of tolerance spaces in the visual or auditory STM stores and generates a representation of cardinal quantity. This takes the same form regardless of which modality has registered the tolerance spaces. In the case of SUBIT-TWO the core production takes the form

((TOLERANCE-SPACE-DETECTOR TS1)(TOLERANCE-SPACE-DETECTOR TS2) → (TSA TSA))

The TOLERANCE-SPACE-DETECTOR provides an example of a node representing a very broad and globally defined class or concept. It defines the class of environmental features that can be distinguished as figures against ground in either a visual or auditory context. The processes that make up its **definition list** monitor the contents of VSTM and ASTM for the presence of discriminable figures. In the initial stages of development, perception of these global figures provides the only examples of tolerance spaces. As already indicated, we assume that the monitoring processes are unable to register more than three tolerance spaces in the contents of VSTM arising from a single visual fixation or in a segment of auditory input sufficient to fill ASTM. They are, however, able to preserve the identity of single figures and the resulting tolerance spaces and to avoid double processing of the same VSTM or ASTM content. Detection of each tolerance space results in a representation, in the general form TS*n*, being placed in the work spaces of the SUBIT nodes since they appear on the **description list** record of the connections between the output of the

TOLERANCE-SPACE-DETECTOR and the activation conditions of other nodes. The presence of two tolerance space representations (TS1 and TS2) satisfies the conditions for the successful operation of SUBIT-TWO and results in the generation of a *tolerance space atom* (TSA) for each tolerance space detected. Expressions containing combinations of TSAs are the initial representations of cardinal quantity.

Elaboration of Quantifiers

As development proceeds, nodes such as the TOLERANCE-SPACE-DETECTOR become linked in a superordinate-subordinate relationship to new nodes added to LTM. The learning processes involved will be illustrated shortly. The new nodes represent specific classes of objects that have been consistently detected in the environment on the basis of a range of features in addition to those that define global figures against a background.

As the range of subordinates increases, the output from the TOLERANCE-SPACE-DETECTOR reflects the ability to register tolerance spaces in a more discriminated and specific form. This arises from one of the methods of spreading activation included in the standard mode. Recall that the **description list** of a node that has operated successfully is searched (search is currently limited to just two levels) to discover if it has a subordinate-superordinate relationship with another node in the context represented by the current output (see section 8.4). The highest superordinate node discovered spreads activation on the basis of its connections with the activation conditions of other nodes. The information placed in their work spaces is the output of the subordinate node that initiated the process.

These developments directly affect the relationship between the TOLERANCE-SPACE-DETECTOR and the SUBIT nodes. For example, books, paragraphs, words, and letters are all initially registered as examples of global figures against a background and result in TS*n* tolerance space representations being placed in the work spaces of the SUBIT nodes. With experience these classes of objects are discriminated and new nodes representing them are added to LTM in a subordinate relationship to the TOLERANCE-SPACE-DETECTOR. When activation spreads from one of the new nodes, the input received by the SUBIT nodes via the TOLERANCE-SPACE-DETECTOR reflects the level of tolerance represented in the node. If the BOOK node is activated, then the expression

(TOLERANCE-SPACE-DETECTOR BOOK)

will be placed in the work space of the SUBIT nodes. For the moment the paragraphs, words, and letters in the book are within tolerance and subsumed in a single tolerance space. If attention is directed to the words on a page, the tolerance level alters. Spread of activation from the WORD node results in each word being registered as a tolerance space. In this case, the input passed to the SUBIT nodes by the TOLERANCE-SPACE-DETECTOR takes the general form

(TOLERANCE-SPACE-DETECTOR WORD).

We will now summarize and complete our account of the innate quantification processes. The initial ability to quantify discontinuous collections of elements is entirely attributable to the three SUBIT nodes. The development of Q_c, which is dependent on social transmission, has not yet started. Quantification is restricted to the generation of representations of cardinal quantity, since Q_c is absent, and the three SUBIT nodes are initially unconnected except for their mutual dependence on the operation of the TOLERANCE-SPACE-DETECTOR.

We also assume an innate ability to represent continuous quantity. The initial version of Q_e consists of processes capable of generating an internal symbol representing the relative extent of the space continuously occupied by an element in the environment. The symbols can be conceptualized as TSA-like discrete element indicators linked to some form of analog representation of continuous quantity. Processing by Q_e of the information arising from perception of a plate and a table top would, for example, result in generation of two TSAs representing their discrete nature as environmental features. The disparity in the continuous space which they occupy would be reflected in the nature of an analog representation constructed and linked to each TSA.

From Innate Quantifiers to Quantity Conservation: BAIRN's Basic Processes

These assumptions provide the starting point for the description of the development of conservation of discontinuous quantity. Our prime objective is to demonstrate BAIRN in operation; therefore, in the interests of necessary abbreviation, we will not give an extended account of every developmental step. The major omissions are accounts of the acquisition of

Q_c and of the final stages of generalization of conservation to Q_e. In the case of other omissions we will refer to earlier examples of similar developmental events.

BAIRN's developmental path to acquisition of discontinuous quantity conservation is indicated in figure 8.4. Parallel strands are considered to be developmentally concurrent, and developmental sequence is represented by relative position from left to right. We will provide a brief overview of the complete sequence of events before offering a more detailed account of the processes contributing to each step.

Recall that BAIRN's node structure (section 8.2), incorporates two broad types of association. Contiguity-based functional relatedness represents relationships in which the functioning of processes in close contiguity or proximity in time has produced successful experience. The second type of association, co-occurrence due to functional equivalence, arises when BAIRN notices that nodes occupy the same locations and perform the same functions in sequences of processing. Each type of association gives rise to a general learning process employed by BAIRN, and the conservation context provides excellent examples of both learning processes in operation:

1. *Node creation* involves the detection of continguity-based functional relatedness and the addition to LTM of new nodes representing the relationships.
2. *Node combination* arises from the discovery that nodes co-occur and appear to be functionally equivalent. In some cases, co-occurrence results in the establishment of a new superordinate-subordinate relationship between already existing nodes. This is the process by which the TOLERANCE-SPACE-DETECTOR node acquires its subordinates. In other cases two or more co-occurring nodes indicate that a new node should be constructed representing a superordinate class of which they are subordinates.

As figure 8.4 indicates, two of the steps in the acquisition of conservation of discontinuous quantity result from node creation, and three are the result of node combination.

Two of the developmental steps are not accounted for by either node creation or combination. They are attributed to *redundancy elimination* and *node modification*. Redundancy elimination is a learning process resulting

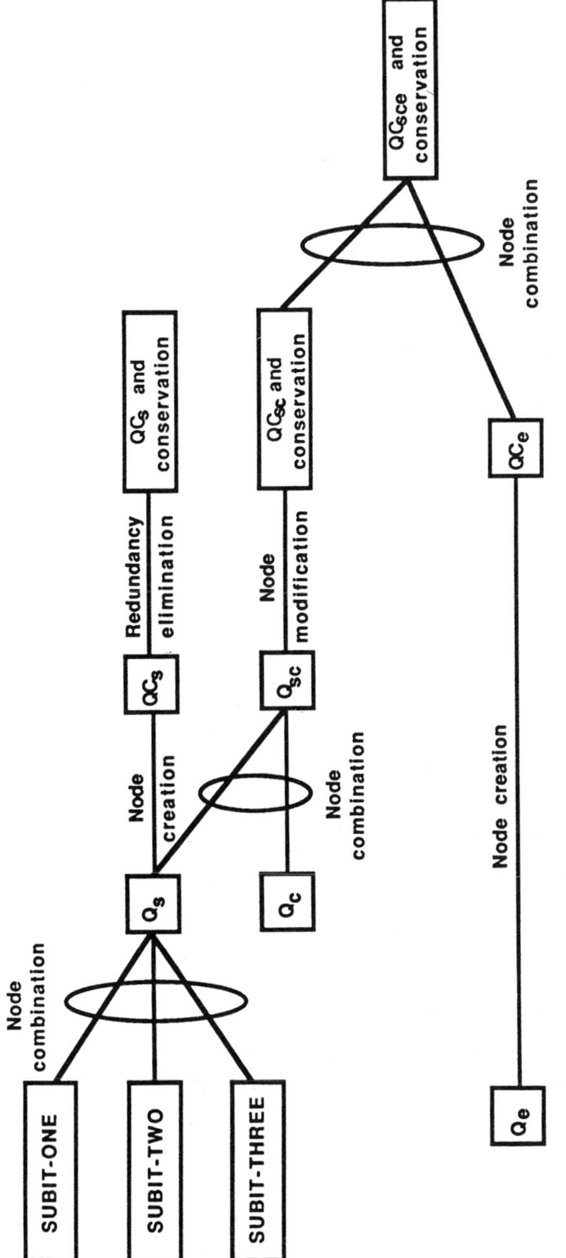

Figure 8.4
Developmental path to conservation of discontinuous quantity. Closed figures show node names; connecting lines show learning processes.

in LTM additions and modifications that produce more efficient processing. In the attainment of conservation of discontinuous quantity, redundant processing is eliminated by the addition of rules to the **definition list** of the quantitative comparison node. As already indicated in section 8.2, these rules eliminate the need for activation of the procedural productions on the **definition list**.

Node combination may result in the operation of *node modification*. When a new superordinate-subordinate relationship is being established, BAIRN reviews the range of contexts included in the records of co-occurrence giving rise to the new superordinate node. If the contexts span the complete applicability range of the subordinate nodes, and the form of node combination complies with criteria that will be outlined later, then node modification takes place. This entails substitution of the token or name of the new superordinate node for those of the subordinate nodes wherever they appear in the **definition lists** of nodes in LTM. Node modification is responsible for the extension of the scope of the conservation rules from quantitative comparisons involving quantitative symbols produced by Q_s to those involving symbols generated by Q_c.

Emergence of the Quantifiers

Having introduced BAIRN's general learning processes in the context of conservation acquisition, we will complete our overview by considering the sequence of events presented in figure 8.4 from a developmental perspective. The developmental sequence is determined by the interaction among Q_s, Q_c, and Q_e, with Q_s playing the primary role. The first step in the developmental sequence is the combination of the three nodes representing the innate quantifiers, SUBIT-ONE, SUBIT-TWO and SUBIT-THREE into a new superordinate node: the subitizing quantifier, Q_s. It provides the first integrated representation of a reliable indicator of cardinal quantity. With Q_s in place, the construction of an initial process for comparison of discontinuous quantity is possible. When applied to records involving Q_s, the node creation processes detect continguity relationships, and represent them in the form of a new node, QC_s (an abbreviation for *Q*uantitative *C*omparison based on *S*ubitizing). QC_s can reliably compare the quantity of discontinuous collections that lie within the range of Q_s. The availability of a quantitative comparison process paves the way for the construction of the first conservation rules as a result of the application of the redundancy elimination process to records of the operation of QC_s. The rules added to the **definition list** of QC_s establish conservation, but it is confined to discontinuous collections in the Q_s range.

The development of Q_c and Q_e proceeds in parallel with these events. The acquisition of the constituent skills of counting, Q_c, is a relatively protracted process due to their complexity and the difficulty of achieving the appropriate interrelationships. The node, Q_c, representing the first counting quantifier, is normally constructed between two and three years. Its reliability is initially confined to small collections. Applications of Q_s and Q_c to small collections produce experience records that enable discovery of their functional equivalence by the node combination process. The result is the addition to LTM of a new superordinate node, Q_{sc}, with Q_s and Q_c as subordinates.

The combination of Q_s and Q_c marks a fundamental advance in the development of quantification. The new node created, Q_{sc}, is a reliable indicator of both cardinal and ordinal discontinuous quantity, has a potentially unconstrained numerical range, and enjoys relatively high prepotency. Only one of these attributes, but the most critical of all, is supplied by Q_s. This is the status of an indicator of cardinal quantity. Despite its relatively protracted development and the complexity of the skills involved, Q_c is a socially transmitted technology without a semantic basis in environmental validity until establishment of its functional equivalence with Q_s.

Recall that when node combination takes place, a review of the contextual range of the co-occurrence records and the form of the combination is carried out to determine if node modification is appropriate. In the case of Q_{sc}, the review returns a positive verdict, because the contexts appear to span the range of applicability of Q_s and Q_c and the form of combination complies with the criteria. Node modification results in the substitution of Q_{sc} for Q_s in the **definition list** of QC_s. This has the effect of broadening the applicability of the node in general and of the conservation rules in particular to include quantitative comparisons involving Q_c. We mark the increased range of the node by changing its name from QC_s to QC_{sc}.

Development of the estimation quantifier, Q_e, proceeds on the basis of the innate ability to generate internal symbols representing the relative extent of the space continuously occupied by environmental elements. As indicated earlier, its initial relevance is to recording the characteristics of single objects in the environment. Quantitative comparison involving Q_e emerges as a means of determining the relative amounts of continuous space occupied by single objects. Development of a Q_e comparison process concerned with discontinuous collections proceeds independently and relatively slowly because the method of generating and comparing single analog symbols adopted with objects is less suited to comparisons of discontinuous collections. It is assumed that despite its deficiencies, application of the single analog method eventually produces experience records that enable the node creation process to construct a new node, QC_e. As in the case of Q_s and Q_c, records of the co-occurrence of QC_{sc} and QC_e result in node combination and the construction of a new node, QC_{sce}, which integrates quantitative comparison of discontinuous collections involving Q_s, Q_c, and Q_e. A particular feature of the **definition list** of QC_{sce} is the construction of rules that extend the range of conservation of discontinuous quantity to operations involving quantitative symbols generated by Q_e.

Introduction of the new rules is much less straightforward than in the case of the extension of conservation to the operation of Q_c. The relative unsuitability of the single analog method for application to discontinuous collections ensures that the rules operate far from smoothly on symbols produced by Q_e. It is argued elsewhere (Klahr and Wallace 1976) that these difficulties and the resulting error feedback produce a modification that permits the generation and comparison of more than a single analog symbol for each collection. These developments, however, lie beyond the scope of the present example.

We have now completed our introduction of the general learning processes employed by BAIRN in deriving conservation of discontinuous quantity and our account of the cognitive developmental background to the sequence of events. In the remaining sections we will provide a more detailed description of each developmental step shown in figure 8.4.

8.8 Node Combination

As already indicated, Q_s is added to the LTM network as a superordinate node created by the combination of SUBIT-ONE, SUBIT-TWO, and SUBIT-THREE. Like the other general learning processes, node combination depends on the results of processing the time-line records of node activity. Figure 8.5 illustrates the type of time-line content that would eventually lead to the construction of Q_s. This simplified example does not contain a trace of the processing in all three parallel channels. The sequence represents a record of environmental interaction in which a limited reper-

```
(BLOCK    VIS - STIM \ BLOCK)

(SUBIT - THREE(TOLERANCE-SPACE-DETECTOR(BLOCK)\(TSA TSA TSA))

(PICKUP (OBJECT(BLOCK))\ (OBJECT PICKED-UP))
(PUTDOWN(OBJECT(BLOCK))\ (OBJECT PUT-DOWN))
(BLOCK    VIS-STIM\BLOCK)
(SUBIT-ONE(TOLERANCE-SPACE-DETECTOR(BLOCK))\ (TSA)

(SUBIT-TWO(TOLERANCE-SPACE-DETECTOR(BLOCK))\ (TSA TSA))

(PICKUP(OBJECT(BLOCK))\ (OBJECT PICKED-UP))

(PUTDOWN(OBJECT(BLOCK))\ (BLOCK PUT-DOWN))
```

Figure 8.5
Example of time-line content resulting in construction of Q_s

toire of actions is applied to a collection of four blocks. The spatial layout of the blocks comprises a group of three and a single block. This provides the context for intermittent activation of one or another of the SUBIT nodes.

The record of activation of each node is termed an *episode* and has the general form

(NODENAME INPUT \ OUTPUT)

The first episode in the sequence, for example, records an activation of BLOCK, a node providing a crude representation of the perception of a block. The activation conditions were satisfied by registration of visual features, and the output at the termination of processing was a name token indicating detection of a block.

The connections in the LTM network that determine the processing following successful activation of BLOCK are indicated in figure 8.6. Because experience has resulted in BLOCK becoming one of the subordinates of the TOLERANCE-SPACE-DETECTOR, its output is passed to all three SUBIT nodes. BLOCK has also acquired the status of a subordinate of OBJECT, a node representing a global definition of graspable objects. As a consequence the output of BLOCK reaches PICKUP via an activation condition connection with OBJECT. Operation of PICKUP produces the motor movement necessary to select, grasp, and raise one of the blocks in the group of three.

Continuing the example shown in figure 8.5, SUBIT-THREE obtains one of the channels available for parallel processing and generates a quantitative symbol representing the group of three objects. SUBIT-ONE

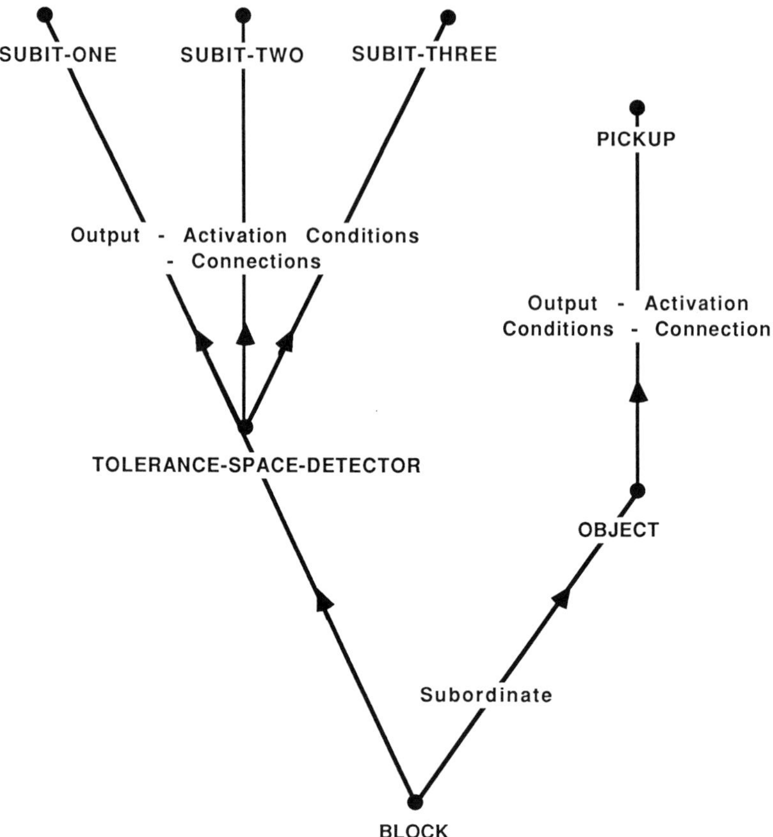

Figure 8.6
Activation spread following operation of BLOCK node

and SUBIT-TWO do not operate despite their activation conditions being satisfied. In the early stages of development the frequency of activation of the SUBIT nodes is relatively low. This is due to their relatively low prepotency until experience results in the appearance of specific subordinates of the TOLERANCE-SPACE-DETECTOR that provide a range of differentiated objects for association with agreeable end states. Nodes concerned with perception (BLOCK) and execution of movement (PICKUP) and functional relationships in the environment enjoy higher initial prepotency and compete successfully with the SUBIT nodes for the processing channels. The SUBIT nodes themselves are initially ranked in prepotency on the basis of the number of connections to other nodes included in their **definition lists**. This produces the order SUBIT-THREE, SUBIT-TWO, SUBIT-ONE. **Definition list** connectivity determines prepotency wherever values based on the processing of end states by motive generators are unavailable.

The sequence continues with the activation of PUTDOWN which returns the block to the spatial layout but places it alongside the single block. This is followed by episodes representing a further activation of BLOCK and the operation of SUBIT-ONE and SUBIT-TWO in response to the group of two blocks. The time-line segment ends with the activation of PICKUP and PUTDOWN prompted, as before, by output from BLOCK reaching PICKUP via its activation condition connection with OBJECT.

Some General Comments on the Time Line

Figure 8.5 illustrates the type of sequential record of parallel processing that provides input to BAIRN's learning processes. The decision to represent the complete sequential record of BAIRN's processing as a distinct segment of LTM was one of our most significant architectural decisions, because an effective method of processing trace data is crucial to the viability of a learning system. The decision reflects the influence of psychological research (Tulving 1972) but was made principally on operational grounds. The major alternative is the incorporation of trace data with other information in a consolidated LTM structure. Neches (1981) has explored this approach in an ACT-like system by inserting trace data in the declarative/propositional network that is the basis for the operation of the production repertoire. His experience indicates that as the amount of trace data in the network increases, the general effectiveness of the system decreases. The fall-off in performance is due to the diffuse spread of activation resulting from the presence of the trace data. Neches' resolution of this problem was to use a goal-driven scheme for dealing with traces.

In its present form BAIRN has a single time line that receives episodic records of the functioning of all of the parallel streams of processing. We considered an approach involving separate time lines for each stream or channel but rejected it on the grounds that detection of the interaction between streams of processing is critical for the learning of fundamental forms of human performance. The syntactic-semantic mapping essential to the acquisition of oral language, reading and writing, for example, requires the detection of functional relatedness of processes that initially occur in close contiguity in time but in separate processing streams.

We are currently investigating the consequences of recording trace data from parallel processing in a single, sequential record. The interweaving of sequences of episodes derived from separate channels facilitates the discovery of interaction, but it complicates the detection of significant sequences in a single channel. When monitoring of records from a single channel is the objective, episodes derived from other channels become "noise." Learning processes must be designed to retain the capability of detecting interaction while exhibiting resilience in the discovery of sequences against noisy backgrounds.

The methods adopted in BAIRN in pursuit of these ideal operating characteristics will become evident as we proceed with our description of the general learning processes. Our concern in this section is primarily with node combination, but the first steps in processing the contents of the time line are common to node combination, node creation, and redundancy elimination. It is assumed that time-line processing requires a channel and that it has a low prepotency. As a consequence it typically occurs during periods of rest or sleep or when processes with a high degree of automaticity are sufficient to cope with the current demands of the environment. The extent to which stretches of the time line undergo a complete review is dependent on the duration of retention of a channel by the learning processes. The maximum scope of a review is bounded by the point in the time line at which the previous review terminated and the location of the first episode recording the conducting of the current review.

Identifying Novel Experience Recall that the **experience list** of each node contains details of node activation sequences beginning with its own activation (section 8.2). They are derived from the system's previous experience and represent association between nodes viewed as justifying sequential connections but not their incorporation in a new node. As already indicated, these **experience list** sequences provide the basis for one of the three methods used in the standard mode of spreading activation. Where successive node activations occur as a result of their inclusion in an **experience list** sequence, this is indicated in their time-line records. This facilitates the first phase of the time-line review, which is devoted to identifying stretches representing novel experience. The process of novelty detection begins with the first episode marked as initiating an **experience list** sequence. The representation of the appropriate sequence is obtained from the **experience list** and compared with the contents of the time line. The matching process used is a generally applicable one. A successful match indicates that the time-line stretch does not represent novel experience. Non-novel stretches of the time line are identified as a residual of repeating this procedure for each episode marked as commencing an **experience list** sequence.

Motivational Analysis The remaining stretches, identified as representing novel experience, become the input for the second phase of the time-line review. This involves a qualitative scan of the episodes by the motive generators. As indicated earlier, they operate by scanning the time-line trace for sequences falling within the area of their motives and subsequently, initiating appropriate additions or modifications to the work. They are assisted in this process by episodic records of the operation of emotion generators that provide markers guiding them to relevant sequences. The qualitative scan may result in an immediate decision to submit a sequence to the procedure for node creation. This occurs when an episode is discovered that represents an end state falling within the area of a motive generator designated as being of the highest importance to the system. The number of motive generators accorded this status is a system design decision of considerable importance.

A second result of the qualitative scan is the identification of episodes that indicate that the time-line stretches in their vicinity should be submitted to a quantitative scan aimed at the detection of consistency. The motive generators involved in the discovery of these episodes, though not falling in the category of highest importance, occupy positions in the hierarchy of motives that endow them with high significance, or salience. Once again, determining the cutoff level in the motivational hierarchy for the conferring of high significance is an important decision in designing the system.

The next step involves searching the time-line segment under review for episodes matching those identified as starting points by high-significance motive generators. The episodes are processed in descending order of the significance of the motive generators that identified them. The matching process employed is the generally applicable one mentioned earlier. Two episodes are declared a match only after the comparison processes determine that their outputs match exactly when class variable tokens included in the conditions of the **definition list**'s productions have been substituted for their specific value bindings. The effect of this substitution is illustrated in the time-line segment presented in figure 8.5. For example, the input recorded in the episode

(PICKUP (OBJECT(BLOCK)) \ (OBJECT PICKED-UP))

indicates that the specific value of the class variable OBJECT during this activation was BLOCK. However, the class variable token OBJECT rather than the specific value BLOCK appears in the output record and participates in episodic comparisons. This substitution ensures that matching occurs at the highest level of generalization justified by the **definition list** contents of the nodes responsible for the comparison.

Comparison of Episodic Sequences When individual episodes that match one of the initial episodes are discovered, then the consistency detection process compares the time-line segment adjacent to the initial episode with the region incorporating the first matching episode. If this match succeeds, then the resulting sequence is compared with the region around the second matching episode.

The decision about whether two episodic sequences are regarded as matching depends on a parameter called the matching index criterion (MIC). The MIC varies between 0 and 1 and is considered to have a constant, "innate" value for each individual. It specifies the proportion of individual episodes in two sequences that must match before the sequences are regarded as matching. That is, the MIC permits *partial matching* of sequences. If the proportion of matching episodes in two sequences exceeds the prevailing MIC value, information on the co-occurrence of mismatching episodes is included in the sequence representing the result of the successful match. As we shall see, the ability to acquire such co-occurrence data embedded in consistent contexts is the basis for the process of node combination. In addition to the MIC, several parameters are used by BAIRN's learning processes. They will be described in detail in the next several sections, and they are listed, in summary form in table 8.1.

Table 8.1
Parameters used by BAIRN's learning processes

Name	Function	Source
MIC (matching index criterion)	Specifies the proportion of individual episodes that must match for two sequences to be considered as matching.	Innate, constant in each individual version of the system.
CCL (critical consistency level)	Criterion for deciding whether or not the sequences being compared are sufficiently novel to trigger learning processes.	Limits set innately, in each individual version of the system. Current value based on recent experience. (Similar to changing aspiration levels.)
ccl (current consistency level)	Index for the degree of match for current sequences.	Product of number of sequences being compared and number of matching episodes.
LTM addition factor	Proportion of CCL necessary for new sequence to be added to **experience list** of initial node.	Innate, constant proportion of CCL.
Sequence frequency	Total number of individual sequences subsumed by a consistent sequence. Used in cleaning up consistent sequences.	Determined by system's experience.
Highest COG member frequency	Highest frequency of occurrence of any individual episodic record included in a COG. Used in cleaning up consistent sequences.	Determined by system's experience.
Generality criterion	Employed in determining range of applicability of new nodes	Innate, constant in each individual version of the system.

The results of each successful match are reviewed to determine if a sequence representing a significant level of consistency has been constructed. The outcome depends on the second parameter in the consistency detection process: the critical consistency level (CCL). We assume that at any point in time, the CCL of an individual's learning processes lies within a range that is part of the individual's innate endowment. The current CCL value reflects the results of a process of adaptation to immediately previous experience. A time-line review resulting in successful consistency detection leads to an upward revision of the CCL value, whereas failure produces a CCL reduction. Thus the definition of what constitutes a significant level of consistency is a continuous function of the outcome of the time-line processes.

A current consistency level (ccl) is computed at the conclusion of matching each pair of episodic sequences. Its value reflects both the number of sequences compared and the number of matching episodes. A high ccl can be produced by relatively few sequences with a large number of matching episodes or a larger number of sequences with relatively fewer matching episodes. If the value of the ccl continues to rise after each matching of a pair of sequences, a further comparison is carried out of the sequences resulting from the previous matches and the time-line stretch containing the next target episode. When the value of the ccl ceases to rise, attempts to subsume additional time-line stretches within the current sequence are discontinued, and the ccl is compared with the CCL. If ccl > CCL, significantly consistent experience has been detected and the sequence becomes an input to the processes of node combination, node creation and redundancy elimination.

If ccl exceeds a proportion of CCL determined by the current value of a third parameter, the *LTM addition factor*, the sequence is added to the **experience list** of the node responsible for the first episode in the sequence. In order to enable the new sequence to influence the spreading of activation the **description lists** of the nodes responsible for subsequent episodes in the sequence are then modified. The information they receive consists of increasingly truncated representations comprising information on the identity of the immediately preceding node and the remainder of the sequence after their own operation.

As indicated earlier, sequences placed on **experience lists** are employed in processing the time line to eliminate non-novel experience. The matching process is identical to that used when two novel stretches of the time line are compared in the search for consistency. A ccl stored with each **experience list** sequence is revised whenever it figures in a successful comparison. When, as a result of a series of comparisons, a sequence reaches a point at which ccl exceeds the current value of CCL, it becomes the basis of modification of LTM. During the comparisons additions to the sequence may occur by interpolation or extrapolation of additional episodes.

The Construction of Q_s

Having concluded our description of the initial phases of time-line analysis common to all of the learning processes, we will return to the specific example of the construction of Q_s via node combination. A simplified example of time-line content resulting in the appearance of Q_s was shown in figure 8.5. Continued environmental interaction involving further processing of block collections by a range of perceptual, motor and quantification nodes leads to the insertion in the time line of episodic records likely to produce positive results when reviewed by the consistency detection processes. Although, as already indicated, the three SUBIT nodes are considered to possess relatively low prepotency, it is a reasonable assumption that a perceptual node, like BLOCK, and motor movement nodes, such as PICKUP and PUTDOWN, have sufficiently high prepotency levels early in cognitive development for one or more of their episodic records to be identified as a starting point for the process of consistency detection. The result obtained is illustrated in figure 8.7.

Formation of the Co-Occurrence Group (COG) The sequence in figure 8.7 was constructed by the successive paired matching of 12 time-line stretches in which the sequence derived from matching the first two stretches was compared with the third stretch and the resulting sequence was matched with the fourth stretch, and so on. The process was continued until ccl ceased to rise and the subsequent comparison indicated that ccl > CCL. As a consequence the sequence is submitted to the general learning processes. In this example CCL = 40 and MIC = 0.5 were selected as the parameter values for the review process.

Detailed examination of the final sequence reveals that episodic records for BLOCK, MOVE, PICKUP, HAND-MOVE, and PUTDOWN appeared in the same relative positions in all 12 contributing sequences. This consistency accounts for the final sequence satisfying the significance criteria. Recall that information on the co-occurrence of mismatching

```
(BLOCK VIS-ST!M\BLOCKS)
(COG (*INT. 7) ((SEM-NODE-S15 SEM-NODE-S15 -INPUT\SEM-NODE-S15) 2)
               ((AUD-NODE-A13 AUD-NODE-A13 -INPUT\AUD-NODE-A13) 1)
               ((SEM-NODE-S29 SEM-NODE-S29 -INPUT\SEM-NODE-S29) 1)
               ((SEM-NODE-S21 SEM-NODE-S21 -INPUT\SEM-NODE-S21) 1)
               ((VIS-NODE-V1 VIS-NODE-V1 -INPUT\VIS-NODE-V1) 1))

(COG (*INT. 2) ((SUBIT-TWO(TOLERANCE-SPACE-DETECTOR(BLOCK))\(TSA TSA)) 4)
               ((SUBIT-ONE(TOLERANCE-SPACE-DETECTOR(BLOCK))\(TSA)) 3)
               ((SUBIT-THREE(TOLEANCE-SPACE-DETECTOR(BLOCK))\
                                                  (TSA TSA TSA)) 3))

((MOVE INIT-LOC\(AT TARGET-LOC))

(COG (*INT. 8) ((SEM-NODE S16 SEM-NODE-S16 -INPUT\SEM-NODE-S16) 2)
               ((VIS-NODE-V16 VIS-NODE-V16 -INPUT\VIS-NODE-V16) 1)
               ((VIS-NODE-V17 VIS-NODE-V17 -INPUT\VIS-NODE-V17) 1)

((PICK UP (OBJECT (BLOCK))\(OBJECT PICKED UP))

(COG (*INT. 7) ((AUD-NODE-A13 AUD-NODE-A13 -INPUT\AUD-NODE-A13) 1)
               ((AUD-NODE-A35 AUD-NODE-A35 -INPUT\AUD-NODE-A35) 1)
               ((VIS-NODE-V9  VIS-NODE-V9  -INPUT\VIS-NODE-V9-) 1)
               ((VIS-NODE-V10 VIS-NODE-V10 -INPUT\VIS-NODE-V10) 1)
               ((VIS-NODE-V36 VIS-NODE-V36 -INPUT\VIS-NODE-V36) 1)

(HAND-MOVE INIT-LOC TARGET-LOC\(HAND MOVED))

(COG (*INT. 8) ((SEM-NODE-S3  SEM-NODE-S3  -INPUT\SEM-NODE-S3 ) 1)
               ((SEM-NODE-S26 SEM-NODE-S26 -INPUT\SEM-NODE-S26) 1)
               ((AUD-NODE-A2  AUD-NODE-A2  -INPUT\AUD-NODE-A2 ) 1)
               ((VIS-NODE-V23 VIS-NODE-V23 -INPUT\VIS-NODE-V23) 1)

(PUT-DOWN (OBJECT (BLOCKS))\(OBJECT PUT-DOWN))
```

Figure 8.7
Consistent sequence leading to construction of Q_s by node combination

episodes is incorporated in sequences if there are sufficient matching episodes in the vicinity to provide a consistent context. Information on mismatches takes the form of a list, termed a *co-occurrence group (COG)*. Each COG in a final sequence includes all of the episodes which have participated in a mismatch at a specific point in the sequence during any of the matches. The most important COG in our example is the second one in the sequence, since it records the co-occurrence of activations of each of the three SUBIT nodes. The other COGs comprise information intended to demonstrate the effect of interweaving in the time line of sequences of episodes derived from separate processing channels. These episodes, unlike the records for BLOCK, MOVE, and the other nodes, do not contain reference to recognizable, real world features. They are intended to represent a range of unspecified auditory (AUD-NODE) and visual (VIS-NODE) perceptual events leading to activation of nodes (SEM-NODE) which process information represented in the general semantic form required for storage in the semantic short term memory (SSTM). The content of their records conforms with the general structure of an episode:

(NODENAME	INPUT	\	OUTPUT)
(AUD-NODE-An	AUD-NODE-An-INPUT	\	AUD-NODE-An)
(VIS-NODE-Vn	VIS-NODE-Vn-INPUT	\	VIS-NODE-Vn)
(SEM-NODE-Sn	SEM-NODE-Sn-INPUT	\	SEM-NODE-Sn)

Each item in a COG is tagged with an indication of its frequency of occurrence. For example, the list recording co-occurrence of the SUBIT nodes shows relative frequencies for SUBIT-TWO, SUBIT-ONE, and SUBIT-THREE of 4, 3, and 3, respectively. This establishes that activation of a SUBIT node in that location has been a feature of as many as 10 of the 12 time-line stretches. In contrast, the sum of the individual frequencies of individual entries in the COGs containing AUD-NODE, VIS-NODE, and SEM-NODE entries falls far short of 12. This reflects the intermittent and varied nature of the episodic records interwoven with the block-handling sequence as a result of concurrent activity in other processing channels. The entry (*INT. *n*) at the start of these COGs indicates the number of occasions on which time-line stretches did not have an episodic record in this location.

Cleaning Up the Consistent Sequence As indicated earlier, restricting trace data to a single time-line record requires that learning processes display resilience in disentangling sequences from noisy backgrounds. In the current example, resilience is assessed by the extent to which the BLOCK, SUBIT, MOVE sequence can be separated from the interwoven AUD-NODE, VIS-NODE, SEM-NODE episodes. The processes that undertake this task operate before node combination, node creation or redundancy elimination are attempted. They begin by accessing appropriate **description lists** to determine whether any of the nodes responsible for entries on individual COGs are known to be subordinates of a common superordinate in the specific context of the final sequence. If subordinate-superordinate relationships are found, the superordinate is substituted in the episodic records. This has two desirable results. Unnecessary attempts at node combination are avoided. It also prevents inappropriate deletions of COGs from the sequence during the purging process which follows. In our example no change is made to the final sequence since the SUBIT nodes are not linked to a common superordinate, and it is assumed that the situation is the same for the nodes responsible for the AUD-NODE, VIS-NODE, and SEM-NODE entries on COGs.

The final sequence is now submitted to a purging process that carries the major responsibility for removing any remaining background noise that might impede operation of the general learning processes. The first phase of the purge is aimed at the detection and removal of complete COGs. The frequencies attached to individual entries on each COG are summed and compared with a criterion value. If a frequency total falls below the criterion level, the corresponding COG is deleted from the sequence. The criterion value used in reviewing each sequence is derived from the following formula:

$(1 - \text{MIC}) \times$ Sequence frequency.

The sequence frequency is the total number of sequences involved in the matching comparisons from which the final sequence was obtained; in our example it has a value of 12. This establishes the maximum frequency of occurrence of an individual episode in the sequence. The extent to which the criterion value falls below the maximum is determined by a weighting factor. Weighting the sequence frequency by (1 − MIC) reflects the view that employment of a relatively high MIC value in the comparisons involved in deriving a sequence enables a corresponding relaxation in the consistency level demanded during the purging process. Application of the formula to our example yields a criterion value of 6 (0.5×12). This results in the deletion from the sequence of all of the COGs except the list recording the co-occurrence of the SUBIT nodes.

The aim of the second phase of the purge is the removal of individual episodic records from the COGs that have survived the first review. The frequencies attached to each record are compared with a criterion value, and records with frequencies below the value are deleted from the list. The criterion value for each COG is produced by the formula:

$(1 - \text{MIC}) \times$ Highest list entry frequency.

The highest list entry frequency is the highest frequency of occurrence attached to an individual episodic record on the COG under review. The rationale for employment of (1 − MIC) as a weighting factor is the same as

```
(BLOCK VIS-STIM\BLOCKS)

(COG (*INT. 2) ((SUBIT-TWO(TOLERANCE-SPACE-DETECTOR(BLOCK))\
                                                  (TSA TSA))4)

               ((SUBIT-ONE(TOLERANCE-SPACE-DETECTOR(BLOCK))\
                                                      (TSA))3)

               ((SUBIT-THREE(TOLERANCE-SPACE-DETECTOR(BLOCK))\
                                              (TSA TSA TSA))3))

(MOVE INIT-LOC TARGET-LOC \ (AT TARGET-LOC))

(PICK UP (OBJECT (BLOCK ))) \ (OBJECT PICKED-UP))

(HAND-MOVE INIT-LOC TARGET-LOC \ (HAND MOVED))

(PUT-DOWN (OBJECT (BLOCK)) \ (OBJECT PUT-DOWN))
```

Figure 8.8
Consistent sequence after elimination of elements below criterion

in the first phase of the purge. The solitary remaining COG in our example is unaffected by this review process since all of the records have a frequency in excess of the criterion value of 2 (0.5×4) derived from the formula.

The purged version of our sequence is presented in figure 8.8. Survival of one or more COGs in the final sequence after the purge is the cue for activation of the node combination process. The objective is to determine whether the degree of functional equivalence of the nodes underlying the entries on each COG is sufficient to warrant addition of a new node to the LTM network. This is the point at which the reason for maintaining records of co-occurrence on the **description list** of each node becomes clear. These records provide a history of the functional equivalence of nodes as revealed in their previous membership of COGs. This information is combined with the contents of the current COG in reaching a decision.

Frequency of co-occurrence is the criterion adopted in assessing degrees of functional equivalence. A co-occurrence frequency is calculated for all possible pairings of the nodes responsible for entries on the current COG. The number of co-occurrences recorded in the COG is combined with the number stored in the **description list** records to yield a total frequency. If only two nodes are under review and the total frequency of co-occurrence > CCL, the decision to combine them is taken. When three or more nodes are involved, the pair with the highest total frequency are considered first. If the frequency > CCL, the combination decision is taken, and the total frequency of co-occurrence of each of the remaining nodes with both members of the initial pair is calculated. The highest total frequency is compared with the CCL, and, if it is greater, the corresponding node will be combined with the initial pair. The process of calculating total frequencies of co-occurrence with all of the members of the current group of nodes to be combined and comparing the highest total with the CCL continues to produce additions to the node combination group until a highest total < CCL is obtained or no further nodes remain for consideration. In the case of the three nodes in our example, the co-occurrence frequencies recorded in the current COG are insufficient to satisfy the > CCL criterion. Node combination is therefore dependent on the frequency information stored in the **description list** records. If we assume that previous COGs have produced the following co-occurrence frequencies

SUBIT-ONE/SUBIT-TWO	39
SUBIT-ONE/SUBIT-THREE	38
SUBIT-TWO/SUBIT-THREE	38

then combination with the current COG frequencies produces a situation in which node combination will proceed.

SUBIT-ONE/SUBIT-TWO	(3 + 39)	42 > CCL (40)
SUBIT-ONE/SUBIT-THREE	(3 + 38)	41 > CCL (40)
SUBIT-TWO/SUBIT-THREE	(3 + 38)	41 > CCL (40)

The decision to combine SUBIT-ONE and SUBIT-TWO is made first since they are the pair with the highest total frequency. There follows consideration of the total frequency of co-occurrence of the remaining node, SUBIT-THREE, with both members of the initial pair. This exceeds the criterion level by a wide margin since the frequencies individually are > CCL.

Constructing the Definition List The process of constructing a new node involves two phases. Each poses problems which arise from fundamental issues in the operation of self-modifying systems. The first phase involves determining how to form the **definition list** for the new node from the **definition lists** of the nodes to be combined. The range of possibilities will be discussed in terms of the combination of two **definition lists**, but is equally applicable to any number. At one extreme is total conjunction. This requires complete functional equivalence between the nodes at the level of individual productions. Each production has a matching production on the other **definition list**. The process by which such a match is determined poses considerable difficulties, but we will postpone consideration of them for the moment.

At the other extreme is total disjunction. Functional equivalence is entirely confined to the node level, and no matches are obtained between individual productions on the **definition lists**. Between the extremes lies the range of situations in which some pairs of productions match and others do not and a partially conjunctive and partially disjunctive structure is appropriate for the **definition list** of the new node.

An exhaustive approach to identifying the optimal mode of combination entails systematic comparison of all possible pairs of productions on the **definition lists**. The computational cost of this procedure must be weighed against any disadvantages imposed on the system by creation of a new node with a structure that is suboptimal on the conjunctive-disjunctive dimension. In BAIRN the exhaustive approach has been rejected in favor of a fallible, but more efficient, procedure. We assume that any suboptimality in node structure is unlikely to affect seriously the performance of the system and is likely to be corrected by subsequent node creation and modification.

The procedure involves the use of two heuristics. The first heuristic is employed when the co-occurrence information in the current COG or in the **description list** records provides one or more pairs of episodes in which both nodes operated in the focally conscious channel. Recall that the time-line entry for a focally conscious node provides a trace of the within-node processing in addition to the information that satisfied the activation conditions and the final contents of the scratch pad working space. Each pair of episodic records is submitted to the standard matching process employed in the time-line review. If they match on the > MIC criterion, an attempt is made to conjunctively combine the nodes; if not, a new node with a disjunctive structure is constructed.

As there is a high probability that at least one pair of focally conscious records will be available when node combination is undertaken, the first heuristic can be regarded as the dominant method. In the absence of even a single pair of focally conscious records, an alternative heuristic is used. It involves paired comparisons of the input and output information contained in the abbreviated time-line records of unconscious processing on the current COG or the **description lists**. A group of eight productions links specific profiles of matches and mismatches obtained from these comparisons with a conjunctive or disjunctive approach to node combination. Since details of the second heuristic are not required for our example, in the interests of brevity, we will not consider it any further.

Deciding on the mode of combination to be adopted in relation to SUBIT-ONE, SUBIT-TWO, and SUBIT-THREE is relatively straightforward. Since their **definition lists** comprise only a single production, detailed time-line records arising from focally conscious processing are identical to the node input-output records produced by processing taking place outside of focal consciousness. Application of either heuristic indicates the appropriateness of a disjunctive combination of the three nodes since the standard matching process yields a > MIC result in all cases and the second heuristic recommends disjunction when applied to a matching profile entirely composed of results in the form

(INPUT1 is not equal to INPUT2) AND (OUTPUT1 is not equal to OUTPUT2).

Disjunctive combination of the three nodes results in the addition to the LTM network of the new superordinate node, Q_s, with a **definition list** featuring the three core productions derived from its subordinates. SUBIT-ONE, SUBIT-TWO, and SUBIT-THREE as procedural knowledge:[4]

((TOLERANCE-SPACE-DETECTOR TS) → (TSA))
((TOLERANCE-SPACE-DETECTOR TS1) (TOLERANCE-SPACE-DETECTOR TS2 → (TSA TSA))
((TOLERANCE-SPACE-DETECTOR TS1) (TOLERANCE-SPACE-DETECTOR TS2) (TOLERANCE-SPACE-DETECTOR TS3) → (TSA TSA TSA))

Consistent with the disjunctive structure, all three productions are considered to represent alternative beginnings to processing by Q_s. As a consequence the conditions of all three productions are treated as activation conditions for the node. Nodes produced by disjunctive combination are assigned initial prepotencies derived by summing the initial prepotency values of the subordinate nodes. Specific values linked to specific inputs during previous operations of the subordinates are retained and used by the superordinate node.

Although our account of the development of conservation of discontinuous quantity will not provide examples of conjunctive node combination, a brief description of the procedure adopted will be included since it provides an indication of the strategy being employed in tackling some of the more intractable problems in system construction. If the results obtained with either heuristic are consistent with conjunctive combination, an attempt is made to produce a single **definition list** for the new node by detecting and combining corresponding productions on the **definition lists** of the nodes being combined.

Identifying pairs of productions for combination in a large repertoire without incurring unacceptable computational costs and producing many spurious generalizations is a difficult task (Anderson, Kline and Beasley, 1980). BAIRN relies on the context-based consistency-detection procedures to limit the search to **definition lists** which can be considered highly promising areas. Within **definition lists**, the detection process is facilitated if the first heuristic is used in deciding the mode of node combination, since pairs of productions underlying matching episodic records can be regarded as prime candidates for combination.

Combining pairs of productions is also fraught with difficulty. It is necessary to establish appropriate correspondence between the elements composing the two productions and to decide whether elements without a corresponding member can be omitted from a new, more general production without adverse results on performance. These steps are facilitated in BAIRN by the avoidance of the use of free variables in **definition lists**. Recall that all variables in productions represent class variables defined at nodes. The node modification process ensures that the class variables included in **definition lists** represent the highest level of generality supported by the experience of the system to date. This diminishes the likelihood of the matching process yielding inappropriate correspondence results.

The general strategy adopted in comparing productions is consistent with currently accepted practice (Langley et al. 1981) in requiring an exact correspondence between the actions of the two productions. If a mismatch results, the productions are inserted in the combined **definition list** as disjunctive items without a comparison of their conditions. If the actions match, the conditions are compared. Results are determined by the following four productions:

PD1
IF all *PDx conditions* match *PDy conditions*
and no *PDx conditions* or *PDy conditions* remain unmatched,
THEN insert the PDx/PDy common form production in the combined definition list.

PD2
IF all *PDx conditions* match *PDy conditions*
and some *PDy conditions* remain unmatched,
THEN add a new production containing only the matching conditions to the combined definition list.

PD3
IF some *PDx conditions* match some *PDy conditions*
and some *PDx conditions* remain unmatched
and some *PDy conditions* remain unmatched,
THEN insert *PDx* and *PDy* in the combined definition list as disjunctive items.

PD4
IF no *PDx conditions* match *PDy conditions*,
THEN insert *PDx* and *PDy* in the combined definition list as disjunctive items.

At the conclusion of the comparison process each of the categories of productions on the two **definition lists**—rules, semirules, and procedural knowledge—may have resulted in the construction of new, combined productions and/or the identification of productions that are to continue as disjunctive items.

The **definition list** established for the new superordinate node is composed of the rules, semirules, and procedural knowledge produced by successful combination of productions. None of the disjunctive productions are included. They continue to feature on the **definition lists** of the nodes being combined and are linked to the superordinate node via the record of subordinate-superordinate relationships maintained on their **description lists**. Our rationale is that the **definition list** of the superordinate node enables recognition of new subordinates as environmental interaction proceeds. Meanwhile the subordinate-superordinate links maintain access to subordinate nodes whose **definition lists** may exhibit "the complex, overlapping and only partially specified feature structures of natural categories" (Anderson, Kline, and Beasley 1980).

A decision on the activation conditions to be assigned to the superordinate node is reached by a procedure similar to that adopted in relation to the productions. The activation conditions of the nodes being combined are compared, and those that match become activation conditions of the new node.

Consistent with the rationale, a new superordinate node resulting from a partial conjunctive combination is assigned an initial prepotency level lower than the prepotencies of its subordinates. This ensures that the more specific subordinates continue to be activated in the environmental situations to which they are relevant while the superordinate with its more generalized activation conditions takes precedence in novel situations. On the rare occasions, when a completely successful matching of productions and activation conditions permits a totally conjunctive combination, the new node is treated in the same fashion as in disjunctive combination and assigned an initial prepotency derived by summing the initial prepotencies of the subordinate nodes.

Determining the Scope of the New Node We have reviewed the process for deciding on the appropriate mode of combination to be adopted in deriving the **definition list** of a new node from the **definition lists** of the nodes to be combined, and we have considered its implementation. Now we turn to the second significant phase in the construction of a node by combination—determining the range of applicability of the new node. In the BAIRN system this involves decisions about the scope defined by the activation conditions of the new node once a disjunctive, partial, or total conjunctive combination has occurred: Is its area of potential application to be restricted to the range of specific inputs that satisfied the activation conditions leading to the combination? Or, is the new superordinate node to apply across the entire area defined by the class variables included in the activation conditions?

The most convincing current approach to this problem is found in the machine-learning literature in the candidate elimination method of Mitchell (1983) and the closely related focusing algorithm of Young et al. (1977); more fully described by Bundy and Silver (1982). It involves zeroing in on the appropriate point on the specificity-generality continuum for application of a new rule by successive adjustments of separate specificity and generality indicators. At the outset the specificity indicator is placed at a point defined by the specific input to, or area covered by, the initial example submitted to the learning process. In contrast, the setting of the generality indicator includes the entire area of possible generalization defined by the tree of subordinate-superordinate conceptual relationships subtended by the specific values of the class variables incorporated in the initial example. As each successive example is received, the location of the indicators is reviewed. If a positive example confirms the appropriateness of application of a rule in a specific context, the specificity indicator is moved to include the new situation and increase the generality of application of the rule. When a negative example indicates that the rule is inappropriate in a context, the generality indicator is adjusted to exclude the unsuccessful situation and diminish the future area of application. If a sufficiently varied and extended sequence of examples is provided, the two indicators ultimately coincide and the applicability of the rule is exactly determined.

The method of determining the appropriate range of applicability of a new node currently adopted in BAIRN is operationally equivalent to the rule-learning approach. The range of specific inputs that satisfied the activation conditions during the experience leading to combination defines the current position of the specificity indicator. The location of the generality indicator is defined by the complete range of values of the class variables in the activation conditions.

In our example the range of specific inputs to the SUBIT nodes comprises BLOCKS, which are featured in the current COG and in the other environmental features involved in the earlier COGs that have contributed to the **description list** records. Since the activation conditions of all three SUBIT nodes are defined in terms of the TOLERANCE-SPACE-DETECTOR, the complete range of this class variable determines the location of the generality indicator.

In the present version of BAIRN the method of determining the range of the activation conditions of the new node places greater emphasis on generality than specificity. This is considered to be justified by the two stages of consistency monitoring, sequence derivation and list purging, which co-occurrence information must survive to reach this point. Activation conditions are stated in terms of the entire area of possible generalization if two conditions are satisfied. The first is the absence from the current COG and the relevant **description lists** of records of node failure involving specific values of the class variables in the activation conditions. The second is satisfaction of a quantitative *generality criterion.*

Two versions of the generality criterion are currently being explored. Satisfaction of the first requires that

Number of different specific inputs $> p \times$ Number of values of class variable.

This criterion is applied to each class variable in each of the activation conditions. The current number of values of a class variable is indicated by the number of subordinates recorded on the **description list** of the node representing the class variable. The number of different specific inputs is the number of distinct values of a class variable that contributed to satisfying the activation conditions during the experience leading to combination. The stringency of the criterion is dependent on the value of the parameter, p. Consistent with the decision to emphasize generality, the effectiveness of values in the 0.3 to 0.5 range is currently being investigated.

The alternative generality criterion is based on the degree of variety or variability of the values of a class variable exhibited in the records of the experience that produced combination. No reference is made to the current number of values of the class variable as indicated in its superordinate-subordinate connections. Variability is assessed by movement in the value of

$$\frac{\text{Average frequency of occurrence of class members}}{\text{Total frequency of occurrence of class members}}.$$

An increase in the value is associated with a decrease in the variety of the class members involved in node combination. The level currently adopted as a cutoff is 0.2. If a class variable yields a value < 0.2, the generality criterion is considered to have been satisfied.

As indicated earlier, if a class variable satisfies both the absence of failure and generality conditions, it is included in the activation conditions of the new node without restriction on its range of acceptable values. If all of the class variables satisfy both conditions, the range of potential applicability of the new node will span the entire area defined by the conjunctions of class variables in its activation conditions. The strategy adopted in cutting back the range of applicability if either or both conditions are not satisfied is indicated in the following productions:

IF there is one or more *failures*
and *generality* satisfies *criterion*,
THEN set *applicability range* of *class variable*
= complete range − *failing values*.

IF there are no *failures*
and *generality* does not satisfy *criterion*,
THEN set *applicability range* of *class variable*
= *values* occurring in experience leading to combination.

IF there are *failures*
and *generality* does not satisfy *criterion*,
THEN set *applicability range* of *class variable*
= values occurring in experience leading to combination.

It is reasonable to assume that in our example both the failure and generality conditions will be satisfied. Since the activation conditions of all three SUBIT nodes are defined in terms of the TOLERANCE-SPACE-DETECTOR and Q_s consists of a disjunctive combination of them, the only class variable that must be submitted to the applicability review is the TOLERANCE-SPACE-DETECTOR. In view of its status as an innate, globally defined class, it is highly improbable that the experiential record will contain any specific values that have caused the failure of a SUBIT node. In infancy and early childhood the experience resulting in construction of Q_s probably reflects in frequent encounters with a wide variety of objects rather than frequent interaction with a single environmental feature. This is precisely the type of experience that results in satisfaction of either version of the generality criterion. Satisfaction of the failure and generality conditions avoids the need to restrict the range of values of the TOLERANCE-SPACE-DETECTOR that will be accepted as satisfying the activation conditions of the new node, Q_s. It thus retains the very broad range of potential applicability defined by this global class.

In concluding our account of the process of node creation by node combination, it should be emphasized that it is a recurring procedure that makes a continuing contribution to increasing the effectiveness of the LTM network as a basis for environmental interaction. For example, if the system's experience underlying a particular node combination is unrepresentative and does not appropriately reflect the nature of the environment, the new node may combine fewer nodes than it ought to or be assigned limited applicability when generalization across the entire area of concern should have occurred. Such deficiencies are subsequently remedied as a result of additional experience leading to further node combination.

The effectiveness of the system may also suffer as a result of overgeneralization in constructing new nodes by combination. This takes the form of including areas in the range of applicability that should have been excluded. Once again, such errors are pinpointed by inappropriate application of nodes as experience proceeds and remedied by creation of or addition to lists of failing values employed in the processing of activation conditions.

Our lengthy description of node combination has included an account of procedures for reviewing time-line content that are also prerequisites for the operation of node creation and redundancy elimination. Therefore descriptions of these general learning processes which follow can be confined to more reasonable limits.

8.9 Node Creation: QC_s

The addition of Q_s to the LTM network paves the way for the construction of the first reliable process for comparing the quantity of discontinuous collections lying within the subitizing range, the operational zone of Q_s. The node representing this process, QC_s, is the result of node creation rather than node combination. As already indicated, node creation involves the detection of contiguity-based functional relatedness and the addition to LTM of a new node representing the relationships. This is accomplished by deriving a significantly consistent sequence via the time-line review process and defining the **definition list** of a new node in terms of the nodes responsible for the appearance of the consistent sequence in the time line.

The key feature in producing the time-line entries underlying detection of the consistent sequence is operation of the COMPARATOR, an important node in the LTM network that we have not previously encountered. The COMPARATOR plays an essential part in the learning processes that enables the system to increase the effectiveness of its environmental interaction. Its function is to determine whether segments of information derived from the system's interactive experience are the "same" or "different." Since this decision is the basis of the essential abilities of classification and discrimination, the COMPARATOR is considered to be innate.

In processing terms the COMPARATOR is a symbol comparing procedure that takes its input from the time line rather than an STM store. It acquires input by monitoring the time line while normal LTM network activity is proceeding and new episodic records are being added. The required input comprises two episodic records that must be selected from the ten most recent entries. This restriction of the access of the COMPARATOR to the time line to a comparatively narrow window has two objectives. It increases the likelihood that the episodes being compared are relevant to the same contexts. Second, since the COMPARATOR makes a time-line record of its own processing in the normal way, the restriction raises the possibility that a consistent relationship will be discovered between the previous activation of nodes and the production of particular outcomes by the COMPARATOR.

The creation of QC_s is the result of the COMPARATOR encountering episodic records arising from repeated activation of Q_s. This activation is produced by contact with a wide range of objects in environmental interaction. Operation of the COMPARATOR on the Q_s records results in consistency which is detected by the time-line review process. The type of sequence that emerges after the purge and becomes the input for node creation is illustrated in figure 8.9.

The specific events underlying the sequence are seven distinct occasions on which Q_s is applied to an environmental object, the object is moved, and Q_s is applied to it again. On each occasion the episodic records of the two activations of Q_s are processed by the COMPARATOR and the results inserted in the time-line record of its operation. The input to the COMPARATOR consists of two time-line entries such as

(TL-ENTRY(Q_s(TOLERANCE-SPACE-DETECTOR(KNIFE))
\TSA))
(TL-ENTRY(Q_s(TOLERANCE-SPACE-DETECTOR(KNIFE))
\TSA))

and the output comprises any elements in the episodic records that do not match. In our example there is a perfect match and a NIL return is reported for the input and output aspects of both records:

(* NIL\ * NIL)(* NIL\ * NIL).

This result represents the first appearance of an internal representation of quantitative equality. It seems probable that a representation for equality is derived before inequality since all comparisons of Q_s records for equal quantities produce the same result. In contrast, inequality can be represented in several different ways. The variants correspond to the size of the difference, one or two TSA symbols, and which of the episodes has the unmatched element or elements. The sequence of development is ultimately dependent on the nature of environmental experience. It is not critical for the construction of QC_s because it receives the same **definition list** as a consequence of the processing of consistent sequences incorporating equal or unequal quantitative relationships.

The presence of the episodic record for RESULTREVIEW in the se-

```
(Q-S (TOLERANCE-SPACE-DETECTOR (KNIFE SPOON TOY PLATE SAUCER TRAIN
                                                        BALL))\(TSA)))

(MOVE (MOVEABLE-OBJECT (KNIFE SPOON TOY PLATE SAUCER TRAIN BALL))\
                                              (MOVEABLE-OBJECT MOVED))

(RESULTREVIEW (NEW-SITUATION ((KNIFE MOVED) (SPOON MOVED) (TOY MOVED)
        (PLATE MOVED) (SAUCER MOVED) (TRAIN MOVED) (BALL MOVED)))\
                                   ((MOVEABLE-OBJECT MOVED) PLEASING)))

(Q-S (TOLERANCE-SPACE-DETECTOR (KNIFE SPOON TOY PLATE SAUCER TRAIN
                                                        BALL))\(TSA))

(COMPARATOR (TL-ENTRY (Q-S(TOLERANCE-SPACE-DETECTOR(KNIFE))\ (TSA))

                      (Q-S(TOLERANCE-SPACE-DETECTOR(SPOON))\ (TSA))

                      (Q-S(TOLERANCE-SPACE-DETECTOR(TOY))\ (TSA))

                      (Q-S(TOLERANCE-SPACE-DETECTOR(PLATE))\ (TSA))

                      (Q-S(TOLERANCE-SPACE-DETECTOR(SAUCER))\ (TSA))

                      (Q-S(TOLERANCE-SPACE-DETECTOR(TRAIN))\ (TSA))

                      (Q-S(TOLERANCE-SPACE-DETECTOR(BALL))\ (TSA))

           (TL-ENTRY (Q-S(TOLERANCE-SPACE-DETECTOR(KNIFE))\ (TSA))

                      (Q-S(TOLERANCE-SPACE-DETECTOR(SPOON))\ (TSA))

                      (Q-S(TOLERANCE-SPACE-DETECTOR(TOY))\ (TSA))

                      (Q-S(TOLERANCE-SPACE-DETECTOR(PLATE))\ (TSA))

                      (Q-S(TOLERANCE-SPACE-DETECTOR(SAUCER))\ (TSA))

                      (Q-S(TOLERANCE-SPACE-DETECTOR(TRAIN))\ (TSA))

                      (Q-S(TOLERANCE-SPACE-DETECTOR(BALL))\ (TSA))

           \(*NIL\*NIL)  (*NIL\*NIL))
```

Figure 8.9
Consistent sequence leading to construction of QC_s

quence reflects the reason that the time-line segments involving manipulation of objects attracted the attention of the consistency detection processes. It is an example of the physiological trace data inserted in the time line by primary emotion generators. RESULTREVIEW is a primary emotion generator that links the physiological action of pleasure to sensori-perceptual conditions satisfied by creation of a new, spatial relationship between environmental features. The occurrence of pleasure in one of the time-line records is detected by a PLEASURE motive generator that initiates the search for consistency culminating in the purged sequence presented in figure 8.8.

The purged sequence leads to the creation of a new node, QC_s. The core production on its **definition list** represents the relationship between activation of Q_s and the functioning of COMPARATOR:

$((Q_s(Q_s\text{-OUTPUT-CLASS}))(Q_s(Q_s\text{-OUTPUT-CLASS}))$
$\rightarrow$ COMPARATOR).

QC_s is, in effect, a specialized version of the comparison process added to the LTM network to deal with a context characterized by consistent comparison outcomes. Unlike the innate COMPARATOR with its source of input restricted to the time-line window, COMPARATOR in the service of QC_s receives input from the external environment via the activation of Q_s and processes it in the work space of QC_s.

The activation conditions for QC_s are identical with the conditions in the core production. The range of applicability is set at the full extent of the class of outputs produced by Q_s. This decision is taken on the same grounds as in node combination. There is no record of failure in the sequence and the range of specific inputs to Q_s is considered to be sufficiently broad and varied to satisfy either of the generality criteria.

8.10 Redundancy Elimination: QC_s

With the addition of QC_s to the LTM network, Q_s, as a reliable indicator of small quantities, has become linked to a comparison process capable of generating distinctive representations of quantitative relationships. The process of discriminating the full range of "equal," "more," and "less" relations arising from environmental interaction, and subsequently mapping language onto them, continues for a considerable period after creation of QC_s. Nevertheless, from is inception the new node opens the way to the identification and elimination of redundant processing by adding rules to the **definition list** of QC_s that circumvent the activation of the procedural productions.

As indicated earlier, ten rules must be derived to cover the range of variations in number of collections—initial quantitative relationships and transformations that collectively constitute a fully developed version of conservation of discontinuous quantity. Description of the construction of a single rule will be sufficient to illustrate how the general learning process incorporated in BAIRN account for the development of all ten. The example selected is the following rule:

IF two *collections* are equal in *quantity*
and one of the *collections* undergoes an *addition transformation*,
THEN the transformed *collection* is greater in *quantity* than
the untransformed *collection*.

The inclusion of two collections makes for a richer illustration, although it may not be consistent with the sequence of development. Cowan (1979), for example, found that the rules for identity conservation (one collection) are acquired prior to those for equivalence conservation (two collections).

Selection of an addition rather than a perceptual transformation is consistent with Siegler's (1981) findings on their developmental order with small collections. As Klahr (1984) points out, appreciation of the effects of addition, subtraction, and specific perceptual transformations may be preceded by a primitive, possibly innate, expectation that in the absence of a transformation the quantity of a small collection remains unchanged, whereas if a transformation has been observed, no such expectation exists.

Figure 8.10 illustrates the type of consistent sequence, after the purge, that gives rise to our rule. It arises from time-line records of repeated activations of QC_s interspersed with addition transformations. We will consider the sequence event by event:

EVENT 1 A successful activation of Q_s occurs with a single object in the environment as input. The nature of the object varies widely across the individual event which give rise to the sequence. Since (Q_s-OUTPUT-CLASS) appears in the activation conditions of QC_s the output, (TSA), is placed in the work space of QC_s.

EVENT 2 The first activation condition of QC_s is satisfied. To satisfy the second activation condition, another independent and successful operation

```
(Q-S(TOLERANCE-SPACE-DETECTOR(SAUCER KNIFE SPOON TOY GLASS BEAR
    FORK BLOCK TRAIN CUP))\(TSA))

(QC-S(TSA))(Q-S(TSA)) \ (*NIL)(*NIL))

(ADD (OBJECT(SAUCER FORK SPOON BLOCK GLASS DOLL FORK BLOCK COACH
CUP))\(OBJECT ADDED))

(Q-S(TOLERANCE-SPACE-DETECTOR((SAUCER SAUCER)(KNIFE FORK FORK)(SPOON
SPOON)(TOY BLOCK BLOCK)(GLASS GLASS)(BEAR DOLL DOLL)(FORK FORK FORK)
   (BLOCK BLOCK)(TRAIN COACH)(CUP CUP CUP)))\Q-S-OUTPUT-CLASS))

(QC-S ((Q-S(TSA TSA)) (Q-S (TSA)))
       ((Q-S(TSA TSA TSA)) (Q-S (TSA)))
       ((Q-S(TSA TSA)) (Q-S (TSA)))
       ((Q-S(TSA TSA TSA)) (Q-S (TSA)))
       ((Q-S TSA TSA)) (Q-S TSA)))          \ (Q-S-OUTPUT-CLASS) (*NIL))
       ((Q-S(TSA TSA TSA)) (Q-S (TSA)))
       ((Q-S(TSA TSA TSA)) (Q-S (TSA)))
       ((Q-S(TSA TSA)) (Q-S (TSA)))
       ((Q-S(TSA TSA)) (Q-S (TSA)))
       ((Q-S(TSA TSA TSA)) (Q-S (TSA)))
```

Figure 8.10
Consistent sequence leading to redundancy elimination

of Q_s is required. The relative prepotency of QC_s is sufficiently high to procure a processing channel, and Q_s operates in it as a slave node. Q_s operates successfully on another single object in the environment and passes the resulting (TSA) to QC_s. Since Q_s operated as a slave node to QC_s, no separate record of its activation is placed in the time line. QC_s can now operate, carries out the comparison via the COMPARATOR and returns an internal representation of quantitative equality, (* NIL) (* NIL).

EVENT 3 The environmental situation results in operation of the ADD node. This represents a qualitative rather than a quantitative form of addition in which an unspecified "amount" of objects are moved into the original area of focal attention and placed near one of the single objects already quantified. In the example the amount involved is either one or two objects, and, as before, their nature varies across the individual events.

EVENT 4 The altered situation results in another successful activation of Q_s with the objects moved into the area as input. As before, the output is passed to the QC_s work space. The record of this event in the consistent sequence has (QS-OUTPUT-CLASS) as its output. This illustrates another aspect of COG processing. In the unpurged sequence this episode is a COG list since it represents firings of Q_s, sometimes yielding (TSA TSA) and on other occasions (TSA TSA TSA). The purge process removes this type of COG by substituting a representation of the general class of results produced by the node, (*QS*-OUTPUT-CLASS), for the specific outputs that were responsible for the mismatches leading to the COG.

EVENT 5 The next step is a repetition of the processing described in EVENT 2. On this occasion the second activation condition of QC_s is satisfied as a result of application of Q_s to the single object located close to the objects moved into the area. Operation of the COMPARATOR returns an internal representation of quantitative inequality. In the individual sequences this would take the form (* NIL) (TSA) or (* NIL) (TSA TSA). It will be recalled that before the comparison of episodes in the search for consistent sequences, class variable tokens included in the conditions of productions on the **definition list** of the node responsible for the episode are substituted for any of their specific value bindings that appear in the episode output. In our example this results in the substitution of (Q_s-OUTPUT-CLASS) for the specific values (TSA) and (TSA TSA).

At the conclusion of the purge, the consistent sequence is submitted to a procedure for detecting redundant processing in addition to being reviewed for node combination and node creation. At present BAIRN's approach to discovering redundancy is severely limited. A search is carried out for repeated activations of the same node. This scan takes account of activation recorded in extended records of focally conscious processing. If there is a consistent relationship between the outputs produced on two occasions, a rule is generated on the assumption that under the circumstances represented in the sequence, the second output can in the future be produced by the node directly without engaging in its normal processing. A new rule is constructed by applying this procedure to the sequence in figure 8.10. It takes the following form:

((QC_s(* NIL) (* NIL)) (ADD(OBJECT ADDED))
(Q_s(Q_s-OUTPUT-CLASS)) → (QC_s(Q_s-OUTPUT-CLASS) (* NIL)).

Addition of this rule to the **definition list** of QC_s ensures that it will be scanned at the outset of the node's processing and that when its conditions are satisfied, the inequality result will be generated without involvement of the quantitative comparison procedure.

8.11 The Construction of Q_{sc}

The establishment of QC_s and the creation of redundancy elimination rules proceed as a consequence of the activation of Q_s. As indicated earlier, it is assumed that in the early stages of development, the frequency of activation of Q_s is likely to be relatively low. This is due to the dependence of its activation conditions on the TOLERANCE-SPACE-DETECTOR that generates undifferentiated representation of tolerance spaces that are unlikely to become associated with agreeable end states rating a high prepotency. The conditions for the activation rate of Q_s to increase are established as experience results in the appearance of specific subordinates of the TOLERANCE-SPACE-DETECTOR that provide a range of differentiated objects for association with agreeable end states. This also paves the way for social interaction to increase the prepotencies linked with certain inputs and end states. Adults, for example, may provide young children with the number names for small collections when they believe that environmental objects forming such collections are the current focus of the children's attention. As a result it is plausible that the prepotencies associated with the subitizing of groups of two or three identical objects will be raised since an adult is more likely to consider quantification appropriate when confronted with a homogeneous collection than with a range of heterogeneous, individual objects.

Although rising, the prepotency and thus frequency of activation of Q_s will not rival that of the developing counting quantifier, Q_c. Since the constituent skills of Q_c are acquired as a result of social interaction with adults and older children, they possess high prepotency. As a consequence, and in contrast to Q_s, they are readily applied to environmental collections regardless of their heterogeneity or homogeneity. Q_s does not share this prominence until node combination results in its integration with Q_c.

The Q_s and Q_c nodes are combined as a result of children employing sometimes one and sometimes the other in relation to environmental collections falling within the numerical range of Q_s. It is feasible that application in the same type of situations will produce a sufficient number of co-occurrences of the two nodes in consistent sequences to result in their combination. The process is greatly facilitated, however, if it is assumed that language labels have been mapped onto the outputs of Q_s before these co-occurrences.

Node Modification

Consideration of the process that enables BAIRN to map language labels onto node outputs provides us with an opportunity to introduce an additional feature of node creation and to begin our description of node modification.

In the construction of QC_s we have reviewed an example in which an entire consistent sequence resulted in creation of a new node. The general learning processes in BAIRN also make provision for basing the decision to create a new node on segments or subsequences of significant consistent sequences obtained by time-line processing. The method of identifying subsequences involves reviewing the STM buffers from which nodes may derive input. If a subsequence of nodes sharing the same STM buffer is discovered, then the subsequence is submitted to the node creation procedure. This is an important additional source of new nodes representing the auditory or visual perception of words. Such nodes can of course be constructed as a result of processing complete consistent sequences.

Node modification frequently plays a complementary role to this type of node creation. If a significant sequence reveals a consistent relationship between a subsequence and the output of a node occurring prior to the subsequence or the activation of a node following it, a production reflecting this relationship is added to the **definition list** of the node concerned. This procedure provides a means of mapping language onto the knowledge or semantic base represented in nodes already featuring in the LTM network. The mapping may link linguistic input to node activation or provide a linguistic means of communicating the results of a node's operation. The same consistent sequences through their subsequences may contribute to the creation of new nodes and to the modification of existing nodes by the addition of new productions.

We now return to our account of the part played by language in facilitating the combination of Q_s and Q_c. In addition to the existence of Q_s, we assume as a baseline that the child possesses auditory perceptual nodes capable of registering the phones composing the first three number labels and in addition that a mapping has already been learned between the representations of a range of objects in the environment and auditory versions of their linguistic labels.

The purged consistent sequence presented in figure 8.11 is the result of a number of occasions on which inspecting, manipulating, and subitizing

```
(AUD-T   AUD-T \ T)

(AUD-DO   AUD-DO \ DO)

(COG   (PLATE AUD-PLATE \ PLATE)
       (KNIFE AUD-KNIFE \ KNIFE))

(AUD-S   AUD-S \ S)

(LOOK-AT (OBJECT (KNIFE PLATE)) \ (OBJECT LOOK-AT-ED))

(COG (PICK-UP (OBJECT (SPOON SAUCER)) \ (OBJECT PICK-UP-ED))

     (TOUCH (OBJECT (CUP TOY KNIFE SOCK TRAIN)) \ (OBJECT TOUCH-ED))

(Q-S (TOLERANCE-SPACE-DETECTOR (KNIFE PLATE)) \ (TSA TSA)))

(VIS-NODE-A17    VIS-NODE-A17 - INPUT \ VIS-NODE-A17)

(Q-S (TOLERANCE-SPACE-DETECTOR (PLATE CUP TOY KNIFE SAUCER SPOON
                                 SOCK TRAIN)) \ (TSA TSA))
```

Figure 8.11
Purged consistent sequence leading to node modification

collections of two objects has been associated with a verbal commentary on the situations by an adult or older child. The purged version of the sequence provides the basis for modification of the LTM network. An auditory perceptual subsequence composed of the first four episodes is detected and found to have a consistent relationship with the output of Q_s, (TSA TSA). This results in a linguistic-semantic mapping which is achieved by adding a new production to the **definition list** of Q_s:

(TWO)(AUD-TS)(S) → (TSA-TSA).

This is equivalent to

IF the *word* 'two' has been heard
and the *word* for a tolerance space has been heard
and the *phone* 's' has been heard,
THEN generate the output of SUBIT-TWO.

In this fashion the appropriate verbal labels are linked with the three outputs of Q_s. This enables exploration by the child of the vocal output that must be produced to satisfy the auditory activation conditions of these new productions. Success is achieved when vocalization has been followed by auditory activation sufficiently frequently to produce a consistent sequence

```
(COG  Q-C (TOLERANCE-SPACE-DETECTOR (BLOCK BOOK FORK SHOE TOY
      Q-S                                   SPOON SAUCER))

                                   \(VOC TWO)(VOC TS)(VOC S))

(TWO (AUD-TWO) \ TWO)

(COG (TOY (AUD-TOY \ TOY)
     (SPOON (AUD-SPOON) \ SPOON))

(S (AUD-S) \ S)
```

Figure 8.12
Consistent sequence leading to construction of Q_{sc}

that results in the addition of further productions to the definition list of Q_s. These productions provide the ability to verbalize the results of subitizing. In the case of SUBIT-TWO, for example, the objective is achieved by

(TSA TSA → (VOC-TWO)(VOC-TS)(VOC-S)),

IF the output of SUBIT-TWO has been generated
THEN vocalize the *word* 'two,'
and vocalize the *word* for the *tolerance space*
and vocalize the *phone* 's,'

Addition of productions providing verbalization of results endows a node with a powerful check on the accuracy of communication of its outcomes. The check takes the form of deferring deactivation of the node until the vocalization has resulted in satisfaction of the conditions of the corresponding auditory perceptual production on its **definition list**. This linguistic feedback registers in the time line as word and single phone episodes in addition to satisfying the requirements of the communication check. This provides a powerful learning device as it facilitates detection of correspondence between nodes that have been derived separately but share the same linguistic mappings. The combination of Q_s and Q_c is facilitated in precisely this manner.

The type of purged consistent sequence arising from the occurrence of linguistic feedback in conjunction with the application of Q_s and Q_c to environmental collections within the subitizing range is illustrated in figure 8.12. The decision to combine the nodes arises from the co-occurrence recorded in the COG.

Since we will not offer a detailed account of Q_c, no illustration will be provided of the complete **definition list** of the new node, Q_{sc}. Its general structure is similar to that of Q_s, as they are both the result of disjunctive node combination. We assume that the range of contexts included in the co-occurrence records giving rise to the combination is sufficiently broad of endow Q_{sc} with the combined range of applicability of Q_s and Q_c. As a result it possesses the full range of applicability of the TOLERANCE-SPACE-DETECTOR.

8.12 Generalization of Conservation of Discontinuous Quantity

The addition of Q_{sc} to the LTM network is a prerequisite for a major advance in the development of conservation of discontinuous quantity. This is the result of interaction between node combination and node modification. Recall that the process of node combination (section 8.8) involves procedures for determining which type of combination is appropriate and how broad the range of applicability of the new node should be. The results of these procedures are employed in deciding whether a token for the new superordinate node should be substituted for those of its subordinates wherever they occur in the **definition lists** of other nodes in the LTM network. In the current version of BAIRN this general substitution is carried out if a disjunctive or totally conjunctive combination has taken place and the applicability review has indicated that the activation conditions of the new node should be stated in terms of the entire area of possible generalization.

In the case of Q_{sc} these conditions are satisfied, and a token for Q_{sc} is substituted wherever Q_s and Q_c appear on other **definition lists**. Accordingly Q_sC is substituted for Q_s on the definition list of QC_s. The modified node will be called QC_{sc}. This substitution results in modification of the conservation rules. The nature of the modification is indicated in the revised version of the rule covering the effect of an addition transformation on a situation with two collections equal in quantity:

((QC_{sc}(* NIL)(* NIL)) (ADD(OBJECT ADDED))
(Q_sC(Q_{sc}-OUTPUT-CLASS))) → (QC_{sc}(Q_{sc}-OUTPUT-CLASS)(* NIL)).

The processing underlying functioning of the conservation rules now involves application of the COMPARATOR in comparing pairs of episode records produced by Q_c as well as Q_s. This proceeds smoothly as soon as the specific Q_c comparison outcomes that fit in each of the slots in the rules are identified. This is easily accomplished during the first applications of the rules to specific pairs of Q_c records.

Explaining the appearance of conservation rules in the functioning of Q_c by node combination and subsequent generalization gives rise to a testable hypothesis. We predict that rules dealing with addition, subtraction, and perceptual transformations will become operative in children's counting performance at roughly the same point in development. Any asynchronous relationships will be short term, varying between individuals and attributable to differences in the order in which the appropriate Q_c comparison outcomes are identified and slotted into the rules. This hypothesis contrasts with the developmental primacy of addition/subtraction rules over perceptual transformation rules in dealing with collections within the subitizing range. Siegler's (1981) results include data supporting simultaneous appearance of all three rules in children's performance with larger collections falling within the range of Q_c and beyond the range of Q_s.

Consideration of a second major step in generalization of conservation of discontinuous quantity concludes our developmental account. As indicated earlier, the first node of quantitative comparison involving the estimation quantifier, Q_e, emerges as a means of determining the relative amounts of continuous space occupied by single objects. Development of a Q_e comparison process concerned with discontinuous collections proceeds independently and relatively slowly as the method of generating and comparing single analog symbols adopted with objects is less suited to comparisons of discontinuous collections. It is assumed that despite its deficiencies, application of the single analog method eventually leads to sufficient time-line consistency for the creation of a new node, QC_e, linking Q_e with the COMPARATOR in a quantitative comparison process geared to handling discontinuous collections.

The sequence of linguistic mapping, followed by the detection of node equivalence via sequences incorporating linguistic feedback, has already been described in relation to the combination of Q_s and Q_c to form Q_{sc}. This sequence of events cannot be applied to produce a further combination of Q_{sc} and Q_e, since the language mapped onto the analog results produced by Q_e does not overlap with the linguistic correlates of Q_s and Q_c. It does, however, provide a sufficient method of combining QC_{sc} and QC_e. The first step is the identification of consistent sequences, which result in the addition to LTM of new nodes representing auditory definitions of words such as "equal" and "more" as chains of phones and also the addition to QC_{sc} of productions representing an appropriate mapping of this linguistic input onto outcomes derived via both Q_s and Q_c. As in the previous example this is followed by vocal exploration, the eventual creation of nodes defining the process of vocalizing the words and the addition to QC_{sc} of productions providing the ability to verbalize its results. When, later in development, QC_e has the same words mapped onto its outcomes and auditory and vocal productions added to its **definition list**, the scene is set for node combination.

As in the case of Q_s and Q_c, it is assumed that QC_{sc} and QC_e are applied to the same environmental collections and facilitate consistency detection by generating vocal feedback. Node combination results in a disjunctive **definition list** being produced for the new node, QC_{sce}. The most important result of combination for the present purpose is the modification of the conservation rules in QC_{sc} to take account of the greater breadth of applicability of QC_{sce}. Since the combination is disjunctive, this entails constructing isomorphic rules for consideration when the activation conditions of QC_e lead to activation of QC_{sce}. In the case of the now familiar example, the new production would be as follows:

((QC_e(* NIL)(* NIL))(ADD(OBJECT ADDED))
(Q_e(Q_e-OUTPUT-CLASS))) → (QC_e(Q_e-OUTPUT-CLASS)(* NIL)).

Introduction of the new rules is much less straightforward than in the case of the extension of conservation to the operation of Q_c. The relative unsuitability of the single analog method for application to discontinuous collections ensures that the rules operate far from smoothly on symbols produced by Q_e. We have argued elsewhere (Klahr and Wallace 1976) that these difficulties and the resulting error feedback produce a modification that permits the generation and comparison of more than a single analog symbol for each collection. The significance of this modification extends beyond QC_{sce} because it paves the way for the extension of the addition, subtraction, and perceptual transformation rules from discontinuous quantity to continuous quantity. Given the developmental delay, it appears probable that complete conservation of continuous quantity emerges as a result of the construction of one or more additional quantitative comparison nodes based on the employment of Q_e, but defined in terms of the widely disparate environmental situations involved in the range of solid and liquid continuous quantity. This line of argument is supported by the clear distinction reported by Siegler (1981) between children's performance on discontinuous quantity conservation tasks on the one hand and conservation of liquid and solid quantity on the other.

8.13 Conclusion

The bulk is this chapter has been devoted to a demonstration of the sufficiency of BAIRN's learning processes to account for the development of conservation of discontinuous quantity. Since much of the emphasis has been placed on the constraints that the learning processes impose on the possible relationships between developmental states, it seems appropriate to end with a comment on variability and flexibility. Although the emerging picture of cognitive development exhibits numerous relations between states that appear to be general and stable, the overriding impression left by empirical studies is of widespread diversity in individual developmental paths. The memory architecture, control structure, and, above all, learning processes incorporated in BAIRN combine to form a system with a high degree of potential variations. BAIRN is sensitive to variations in environmental experience, and also through adjustment of the parameters it is able to reflect individual differences in innate endowment. This flexibility enhances the possibility that BAIRN may make some small contribution in the developmental area toward meeting the general need in cognitive psychology for "a language, a repertoire of concepts that is sufficiently rich to enable the formulation of interesting and testable propositions in a wide variety of areas, all of which spring from the same underlying cognitive view, and which are therefore mutually informative" (Claxton 1978, p. 513).

Notes

1. The bracketed numbers in the text and in the figure correspond to the order in which features will be discussed.

2. Although this approach has the advantage of grounding the process in fundamental theory, it increases the complexity of its implementation. We believe that the strategic advantages will outweigh the practical difficulties in the medium to long term. The approach differs widely from that adopted in ACT. In ACT all productions are assigned the same value of a strength parameter when first created. When it applies successfully or receives negative feedback, the initial strength of a production is increased by a standard amount or decreased by a standard factor. In contrast, new nodes in BAIRN are assigned widely differing initial prepotency levels on the basis of their relationship to achievement of the system's 'purposes'

or goals. As environmental interaction proceeds, novel outcomes produced by nodes are evaluated and each node is provided with a range of specific context-linked prepotencies.

3. As we will see in section 8.8, the detection of such sequences plays an important part in the learning process.

4. An example of the method of coping with rules in disjunctive combination will be provided in section 8.12.

References

Allport, G. W. 1955. *Becoming: Basic Considerations for a Psychology of Personality*. New Haven: Yale University Press.

Anderson, J. R. 1983. *The Architecture of Cognition*. Cambridge, Mass.: Harvard University Press.

Anderson, J. R., and Kline, P. J. 1979. A learning system and its psychological implications. *Proceedings of the Sixth International Joint Conference on Artificial Intelligence*, Tokyo.

Anderson, J. R., Kline, P. J., and Beasley, C. M., Jr., 1978. *A general learning theory and its application to schema abstraction*. (Technical Report No. 78-2). Department of Psychology, Carnegie-Mellon University.

Bundy, A., and Silver, B. 1982. A critical survey of rule learning programs. *Proceedings of the European Conference on Artificial Intelligence*.

Cattell, R. B. 1950. *Personality: A Systematic, Theoretical, and Factual Study*. New York: McGraw-Hill.

Chase, W. G. 1978. Elementary information processes. In W. K. Estes (ed.), *Handbook of Learning and Cognitive Processes*, Vol. 5. Hillsdale, N.J.: Lawrence Erlbaum Associates.

Chi, M. T. H., and Klahr, D. 1975. Span and rate of apprehension in children and adults. *Journal of Experimental Child Psychology*, 19, 434–439.

Claxton, G. 1978. Special review feature: memory research. *British Journal of Psychology*, 69, 513–520.

Cooper, R. 1984. Number development: Extensions from intuitive concepts. In C. Sophian (ed.), *Origins of Cognitive Skills*. Hillsdale, N.J.: Lawrence Erlbaum Associates.

Cowan, R. 1979. A reappraisal of the relation between performances of quantitative identity and quantitative equivalence conservation tasks. *Journal of Experimental Child Psychology*, 28, 68–80.

Gelman, R., and Gallistel, C. R. 1978. *The Child's Understanding of Number*. Cambridge, Mass.: Harvard University Press.

Klahr, D. 1984. Transition processes in quantitative development. In R. Sternberg (ed.), *Mechanisms of Cognitive Development*. San Fransisco: Freeman.

Klahr, D., and Wallace, J. G. 1976. *Cognitive Development: An Information Processing View*. Hillsdale, N.J.: Lawrence Erlbaum Associates.

Langley, P., Neches, R., Neves, D. M., and Anzai, Y. 1981. A domain-independent framework for procedure learning. *Policy Analysis and Information Systems* 4(2), 163–197.

Mitchell, T. 1983. Learning and problem solving. *Proceedings of the Eighth International Joint Conference on Artificial Intelligence*.

Neches, R. 1985. Models of heuristic procedure modification. Dissertation. Department of Psychology, Carnegie-Mellon University.

Palmer, S. 1977. Hierarchical structure in perceptual representation. *Cognitive Psychology* 9, 441–474.

Siegler, R. S. 1981. Developmental sequences within and between concepts. *Monographs of the Society for Research in Child Development* 46(2), Serial Number 189.

Starkey, P., and Cooper, R. G., Jr. 1980. Numerosity perception in human infants. *Science* 210, 1033.

Starkey, P., Spelke, E., and Gelman, R. 1980. *Number competence in infants: Sensitivity to numeric invariance and numeric change*. Paper presented at the International Conference on Infant Studies, New Haven, Conn.

Starkey, P., Spelke, E., and Gelman, R. 1983. Detection of intermodal numerical correspondences by human infants. *Science* 222, 179–181.

Strauss, M. S., and Curtis, L. E. 1981. Infant perception of numerosity. *Child Development* 52, 1146–1152.

Strauss, M. S., and Curtis, L. E. 1984. Development of numerical concepts in infancy. In C. Sophian (ed.), *The Origins of Cognitive Skills*. Hillsdale, N.J.: Lawrence Erlbaum Associates.

Tulving, E. 1972. Episodic and semantic memory. In E. Tulving and W. Donaldson (eds.), *Organization of Memory*. New York: Academic Press.

Van Oeffelen, M. P., and Vos, P. G. 1982. Configuration effects on the enumeration of dots: Counting by groups. *Memory and Cognition* 10, 396–404.

Young, R. M., Plotkin, G. D., and Linz, R. F. 1977. Analysis of an extended concept-learning task. *Proceedings of the Fifth International Joint Conference on Artificial Intelligence*.

Zeeman, E. C., and Buneman, O. P. 1968. Tolerance spaces and the brain. In C. H. Waddington (ed.), *Towards a Theoretical Biology*. Chicago: Aldine.

9 Production Systems, Learning, and Tutoring

John Anderson

The preceding chapters document the role of production systems in modeling human cognition and learning. If such systems, are in fact, good models, they could form the bases for pedagogical applications. This chapter focuses on the role of production-system models in the design of a certain type of computer-based tutor. We have developed two instances of this type of tutor—one to tutor introductory LISP programming (Reiser, Anderson, and Farrell 1985) and one to tutor doing proofs in geometry (Anderson, Boyle, and Yost 1985). There is evidence that these tutors are effective relative to standard classroom instruction. However, the purpose of this research effort is as much to test the psychological reality of production-system architectures as it is to yield practical application. The specific architecture being tested is that of the ACT* production system (Anderson 1983), although many of the issues are not specific to that system.

A basic premise is that in order to be effective, the tutor needs to have a cognitive process model of the student. Instruction can only be truly principled if the tutor has (1) an accurate interpretation of the current cognitive state of the student, (2) a precise definition of the desired cognitive state of the student, and (3) a learning thory that describes how experience changes the cognitive state of the student. Then both the actual student and an ideal student should be cast as production systems—one capable of simulating the current behavior of the student, and the other capable of simulating the desired state. These are called the current and ideal student models, respectively. A learning theory should be one concerned with changes in the production set.

9.1 Production Systems

The Model-Tracing Methodology

Model tracing is an instructional paradigm whose basic feature is that it tries to simulate dynamically a student's problem-solving and use that simulation to interpret the student's behavior. The simulations take the form of production systems. The model of the student is a nondeterministic production system, in which any one of a number of productions can fire at each point. Our objective is to try to find the one allowable sequence of productions that will uniquely reproduce the surface behavior of the student. This sequence of productions becomes our interpretation of that student. Instruction focuses on the points where the sequence deviates from the prescriptions of the ideal model.

This enterprise is predicated on the assumption that we can correctly model the student at two levels. First, and transparently, we have to be able to model the input-output behavior of the student. Second, and not so transparently, the productions we use must correspond to the steps in which the student actually solves the problem. This second requirement is necessary because part of our instructional strategy is to interrupt the student after a production step and engage in instruction on the previous activity. This only makes sense if we have caught the student between steps of problem solution and the previous step corresponds to what our theory claim. Thus, tutoring forces us to address seriously the grain size with which we model a student in a production system.

Ideally, we would like to have a situation in which we could monitor this student after each production firing. By hypothesis, each production firing produces a change in working memory, and we potentially could monitor for that change. There are two major advantages to monitoring a problem solution production by production. First, this minimizes the ambiguity in interpreting the student in terms of the nondeterministic model. (If we only sample the student's performance every n firings, and the average non-determinism per firing is m, we have to use the students response to select from among m^n interpretations.) Second, as we will see, our learning theory places a premium on immediacy of feedback. Therefore, it is important to be able to respond to an error as soon as it occurs.

Success at monitoring student performance depends on our defining a suitable interface. We would like to design an interface where a subject can easily deposit a record of every step of a problem's solution. For instance, in tutoring addition, it is easy to get a written record of the final answer in digits but not of the process of the calculation, of running totals and carrying. In a non-computer-based system we might encourage the student to verbalize out loud the running total and put marks on the paper to indicate carrying. In a computer tutor, natural language cannot be understood, and the student cannot really write as he calculates. Yet we want to fashion an interface where activities giving the intermediate information will be at least as easy and natural as verbalization. It is not always the case that the computer is at a disadvantage to standard methodology. For instance, standard methodology has no means for a student to plan the proof for a geometry problem, but we have created a graphical formation for this purpose in our geometry tutor (Anderson, Boyle, and Yost 1985).

One of the realities of tutoring is that the student can generate behavior that cannot be interpreted in terms of our student model. As simple examples of this, the student's hands may wander off base on the keyboard and enter a sequence of garbage, or he might enter a term from another programming language or a term that makes no sense such as referring to "adjacent supplementary segments" when doing a geometry proof. In principle, such perturbations could be modeled, but in practice they cannot. In our experience, about 20 percent of all errors fall in this category. Once a student has made such an error, our ability to interpret his future problem solving can be severely limited. This is because if one cannot find a production to simulate that behavior, one cannot define the next state in the simulation. Therefore, in order to continue the model tracing, we are forced to stop the student when we detect such an error and ask him to reconsider it. Frequently, such errors are slips, and students will spontaneously correct themselves. However, if they do not, we force them to take a step which is along a correct solution path.

If one believed that such correction was harmful to the learning, one would be in a situation where the learning theory and methodology were in opposition. However, fortunately our learning theory implies that immediate feedback is important. Even in the 80 percent of the cases where we can interpret the error in the model, we point the error out to the student and encourage the student to return to a correct path.

An Example of Tutorial Interaction

We can use the model-tracing methodology I have outlined to interpret the student's learning behavior. We now provide an example of our model-tracing methodology in action from the LISP tutor and then discuss some of its important features.

Our LISP tutor is based on our earlier efforts to model learning to program in LISP (Anderson, Farrell, and Sauers 1984). Figure 9. 1 presents a dialogue we between computer tutor and a student coding recursive functions to calculate factorial. This does not present the tutor as it actually appears. Instead, it shows a "teletype" version of the tutor in which the interaction is linearized. In the actual tutor, the interaction involves updates to various windows. In the teletype version shown in the figure the tutor's

Define the function fact. It takes a number argument, n, and computes the factorial of n, which is the result of multiplying n × n − 1 × n − 2... × 1. For instance, (fact 3) = 3 × 2 × 1 = 6. by definition, the factorial of 0 is 1.

1. **(defun fact (n)**
(cond ((equal) *⟨ACTION⟩)*
⟨RECURSIVECASE⟩))

I assume that you are trying to test if the number argument is equal to the number zero. There is a special function for testing equivalence to zero. Try to use that function instead of EQUAL.

What code can you write to test if the condition for terminating case is true? Try writing a predicate.

2. (defun fact (n)
*(cond ((***zero** *⟨ACTION⟩)*
⟨RECURSIVECASE⟩))

Did you mean zerop (y or n)? **y**

3. (defun fact (n)
*(cond ((***zerop n) 1)**
⟨RECURSIVECASE⟩))

Is the value of fact in the recursive cases calculated by:

PRESS:	IF YOU WANT TO:
1	Calling fact recursively with n.
2	Multiplying n by fact of n minus 1.
3	Getting 1 2 . . . n and then multiplying the results.
4	have the tutor choose

Menu choice: **3**

That is a reasonable way to think of doing factorials but it is not a plan for a recursive function. Since you seem to be having trouble with the recursive cases, let us work through some examples and figure out the conditions and actions for each of these cases.

The recursive relationship is the relationship between fact called with n and fact called with

PRESS	IF YOU WANT TO
1	n minus 1
2	n equal to 0
3	n plus 1
4	have the tutor choose

Menu choice: **1**

We will consider some concrete examples. We will characterize the recursive relationship between fact called with 1 and fact called with 0

What is the value of (fact 1)?
Answer: **1**

What is the value of (fact 0)?
Answer: **1**

EXAMPLES

	fact (n)	fact (n − 1)
A.	(fact 1) = 1	(fact 0) = 1

Figure 9.1

We will consider some more concrete examples. We will characterize the recursive relationship between fact called with 3 and fact called with 2

What is the value of (fact 3)?

Answer: **6**

What is the value of (fact 2)?

Answer: **2**

EXAMPLES

	fact (n)	fact (n − 1)
A.	(fact 1) = 1	(fact 0) = 1
B.	(fact 3) = 6	(fact 2) = 2

Since there is only one recursive case characterized by the examples you have just worked out the condition in this case can be just coded as T. We will just focus on characterizing the action in this case.

In examples A and B what do you have to do to get the result of fact called with n?

PRESS:	IF YOU WANT TO:
1	Multiply n by one less than n.
2	Multiply n by fact of one less than n.
3	Add n to the result of fact called with one less than n
4	have the tutor choose

Menu choice: **2**

We have now worked through a series of examples that illustrate the recursive relation. We will now return to the goal of trying to produce LISP code that specifies the recursive relation.

4. *(defun fact (n)*
   (cond ((zerop n) 1)
   (t (fact)))

   You will have to use fact at some point but right now you want to multiply.

5. *(defun fact (n)*
   (code ((zerop n) 1)
   (t **(times** *⟨NUM⟩ ⟨NUM2⟩)))))*

What do you want to do first?

PRESS:	IF YOU WANT TO:
1	Write code to get the number argument
2	Write code to get the recursive part

Menu choice: **1**

6. *(defun fact (n)*
   (cond ((zerop n) 1)
   (t (times **n (fact n))** *)))*

   You cannot just code n at this point. What you want to do is subtract one from n.

7. *defun fact (n)*
   (cond ((zerop n) 1)
   (t (times n (fact **(difference)** *))))*

   Difference would work in this case but it is more appropriate to use the function SUB1 when you are subtracting 1 from a number.

Figure 9.1 continued

8. *(defun fact (n)*
(cond ((zerop n) 1)
(t (times n (fact **(sub1 n))***))))*
... YOU ARE DONE. TYPE NEXT TO GO ON AFTER ...
... TESTING THE FUNCTIONS YOU HAVE DEFINED ...
THE LISP WINDOW

= > **(trace fact)**
(fact)
= > **(fact 3)**
1 ⟨Enter⟩ fact (3)
2 ⟨Enter⟩ fact (2)
3 ⟨Enter⟩ fact (1)
4 ⟨Enter⟩ fact (0)
4 ⟨EXIT⟩ fact 1
3)EXIT⟩ fact 1
2 ⟨EXIT⟩ fact 2
1 ⟨EXIT⟩ fact 6
6

Figure 9.1 continued

output is given in normal type while the student's input is shown in bold characters. These listings present "snapshots" of the interaction; each time the student produces a response, we have listed his input along with the tutor's response (numbered for convenience). The total code as it appears on the screen is shown, although the student has added only what is different from the previous code (in boldface type). For instance, in line 2 he has added "**zero**" as an extension of "*(defun fact (n)* (*cond*(."

In the first line, when the subject typed "(*defun*," the template

(defun ⟨name⟩ ⟨parameters⟩ ⟨body⟩)

appeared. The terms in ⟨—⟩ angle brackets denote pieces of code he will apply. The subject then filled in the ⟨name⟩ slot and the ⟨parameters⟩ slot and had started to fill in the ⟨body⟩ slot. Note that, at all points, parentheses are balanced and syntax is checked.

Although the student has some difficulty with the syntax of the conditional tests in lines 1 and 2, he basically codes the terminating case for the factorial function correctly. We find that students usually have little difficulty with terminating cases, but great difficulty with recursive cases. The dialogue after line 3 illustrates how the tutor guides the student through a design of the recursive function. Basically, it leads the student to construct a couple of examples of the relationship between fact (n) and fact (n − 1),

```
In examples A and B what do you have to do to get the result
of fact called with n?
PRESS:              IF YOU WANT TO:
1.      Multiply n by one less than n.
2.      Multiply n by fact of one less than n.
3.      Add n to the result of fact called with one less than n.
4.      Have the tutor choose.
Menu Choice: 2
                        CODE FOR fact
(defun fact (n)
    (cond ((zerop n) 1)
          <RECURSIVE-CASE>))

                        EXAMPLES
      fact (n)        fact (n-1)
A.  (fact 1) = 1    (fact 0) = 1
B.  (fact 3) = 6    (fact 2) = 2
```

Figure 9.2
The screen configuration before line 4 in figure 9.1

and then gets the student to identify the general relationship. Figure 9.2 shows the screen image at a critical point in the design of this function.

The dialogue after this point shows two errors students often make in defining recursive functions. The first, in line 4, is to call the function directly without combining the recursive call with other elements. The second, in line 6, is to call the function recursively with the same argument rather than a simpler one.

When the student finishes coding the function, he goes to the LISP window and experiments. He is required to trace the function, and the recursive calls embed and then unravel. Figure 9.3 gives the screen image at this point, with the code appearing on top and the trace below it.

Features of the Model-Training Methodology

This example illustrates a number of features of our tutoring methodology.

1. The tutor constantly monitors the student's problem solving and provides direction whenever the student wanders off path.

```
--- YOU ARE DONE.  TYPE NEXT TO GO ON AFTER ---
--- TESTING THE FUNCTIONS YOU HAVE DEFINED  ---

(defun fact (n)
    (cond ((zerop n) 1)
          (t (times n (fact (sub1 n))))))

                    THE LISP WINDOW

= > (trace fact)
(fact)

= > (fact 3)
1 <Enter> fact (3)
|2 <Enter> fact (2)
| 3 <Enter> fact (1)
| |4 <Enter> fact (0)
| |4 <EXIT>  fact  1
| 3 <EXIT>  fact  1
|2 <EXIT>  fact  2
1 <EXIT>  fact  6
6
```

Figure 9.3
The screen configuration at the end of the dialogue in figure 9.1

2. The tutor tries to provide help with both the overt parts of the problem solution and the planning. However, to address the planning, a mechanism had to be introduced in the interface (in this case menus) to allow the student to communicate the steps of planning.

3. The interface tries to eliminate aspects like syntax checking, which are irrelevant to the problem-solving skill being tutored.

4. The interface is highly reactive in that it does make some response to every symbol the student enters.

The Mechanics of Model Tracing

Sitting within this computer tutor is a production system consisting of hundreds of ideal and buggy rules. In this section, we present examples of a production rule that codes APPEND and two bugs. Associated with bug is an example of the feedback we would present to the student should the student display that bug:

Production Rule in Ideal Model:

IF the goal is to combine *LIST1* and *LIST2* into a single list,
THEN use the function APPEND and set subgoals to code *LIST1* and *LIST2*.

Related Bugs:

IF the goal is to combine *LIST1* and *LIST2* into a single list,
THEN use the function LIST and set subgoals to code *LIST1* and *LIST2*.

You should combine the first list and the second list, but LIST is not the right function. If you LIST together (a b c) and (x y z), for example, you will get ((a b c) (x y z)) instead of (a b c x y z). LIST just wraps parens around its arguments.

IF the goal is to combine *LIST1* and *LIST2* into a single list and *LIST1* = *LIST2*,
THEN use the function TIMES and set subgoals to code *LIST1* and the number 2.

You want to put together two copies of the same list, but you can't make two copies of a list by using the function TIMES. TIMES only works on numbers. You should use a function that combines two lists together.

The tutor determines which rule fired in the student's head by seeing which rule action matches the behavior of the student. Attached to the rules are templates for dialogues such as the two we have given here.

Altogether we have over 1,000 productions (correct and buggy) to model student performance in our lessons, which cover all the basic syntax of LISP, design of iteration and recursive function, use of data structures, and means-ends planning of code. The majority of these productions are like the APPEND production above, in that they are directly connected to the generation of code. Another example of such a production is

IF the goal is to test if *arg1* is zero
THEN use the LISP function ZEROP, and set a subgoal to code *arg1*.

Because they are connected to the generation of code. It is very easy to monitor for their execution. However, many productions are concerned with planning such as that involved in the design of a recursive call. Normally, students are very quiet at such times. We were faced with the task of finding some way of getting students to express their planning processes. The example illustrates the solution that we adopted in the LISP tutor, which is to step the student through the planning process by a sequence of menus. This is not a totally satisfactory solution because students find the overhead associated with processing the menus to be high relative to the actual planning. Therefore, we do not work students through these planning menus unless they give evidence of having problems with the planning process.

Approximately 40 percent of the 1,000 productions model correct generation of code, and the residual productions model various bugs. The bugs are largely gathered by empirical observation of student errors. A current research project concerns the origin of such bugs. Obviously, a theory of bug origin relates strongly to a production-system learning theory.

9.2 Production Learning

To this point we have discussed how we use our production-system model to organize the tutorial interactions. However, the success of the tutorial interaction depends on both the accuracy of the model and the actual instuctional activities in which the tutor engages. This is predicated on our theory of production-system learning. Since there is considerable variation in learning theories, I will review the basic premises of the theory I subscribe to before considering the pedagogical application.

Learning begins with formal instruction. Consider this small fragment of instruction from Winston and Horn (1984, p. 24):

The value returned by CAR is the first element of the list given as its argument:

```
(CAR '(FAST COMPUTERS ARE NICE))
FAST
```

This is fundamentally declarative information. It does not directly tell one how to get the first element of a list or how to apply CAR and so contrasts with productions like

P1
IF the goal is to get the first element of a list
THEN write CAR,
and set a subgoal to code the list.

or

P2
IF the goal is to evaluate (CAR '(elem 1. . . .)),
THEN the answer is elem1.

The first claim of the learning theory is that the student has, coded as productions, various domain-general weak methods that enable the student to interpret declarative information such as in Winston and Horn (1984). So the student might have a means-end production like

G1
IF the goal is to obtain the element that bears a relation to
an argument
and an operation returns a value that bears the relation to
a structure if a precondition is satisfied,
THEN plan to use the operation
and set a subgoal to satisfy the precondition.

To understand how this production applies, assume the student has his goal encoded as

the goal is to get the first element of (a b c)

and the Winston and Horn instruction encoded as

CAR gets the first element of a list
if the list is the argument of CAR

Production G1 can evoke CAR to get the first of list (a b c) if we have the following binding of clauses:

1. "the goal is to get the element that bears a relation to an argument" matches to "the goal is to get the first element of (a b c),"

2. "an operation returns a value that bears the relation to a structure" matches to "CAR returns the first element of a list,"

3. "if a precondition is satisfied" matches to "if the list is the argument to CAR."

The production will then use CAR and set as a subgoal to make (a b c) an argument to CAR. Thus this production can interpret the declarative instruction to have the same effect as P1.

Another type of weak method that we have studied a great deal is analogy. It seems that in the domain of LISP programming, students like to solve problems by anology to other problems. Thus a student asked to get the first of the list (A B C) might look at the Winston and Horn example of (CAR '(FAST COMPUTERS ARE NICE)) and write

(CAR '(A B C))

by analogy.

We have also done some simulation work of other weak methods, in particular hill climbing. In each of our weak methods declarative knowledge is interpreted by productions to solve novel problems. The cost of interpretation of declarative knowledge by weak methods can be high. First, the requisite declarative knowledge must be held in working memory to guide the solution, posing a load on working memory. Second, the interpretive process is often very piecemeal, requiring a great many applications of productions.

Knowledge compilation is the name we give to the process that converts this interpretive use of declarative knowledge by general procedures into productions like P1 and P2 that directly perform the action. It has been discussed in detail elsewhere (Anderson 1986', Neves and Anderson 1981). There are two processes—one called *proceduralization* and the other, *composition*. Proceduralization involves the deletion of reference to declarative information and creation of domain-specific rules. The essential part of the declarative information is built into the resulting productions. So, rather than G1, which refers to relations in general, P1 concerns itself with first elements of a list. The second process, composition, collapses many productions into one. It is similar to ideas discussed by Rosenbloom and Newell (chapter 5) and Lewis (chapter 7) in this book. Composition also occurs to create *macro operators* out of basic operators. So, if we have one production to code CONS and another to code CAR, they can be composed together to create an operator that will insert the first element of one list into another.

The current state of the ACT learning theory is as notable for what it lacks as for what it contains. In particular, it lacks generalization and discrimination learning mechanisms, which had originally formed the inductive learning component of the theory. The story of their demise has been told elsewhere (Anderson 1986), but basically there has been an embarassing failure to get empirical evidence for their existence. We also decided that induction should be treated as a problem to be solved at the production level rather than the architectural level and have found that, by compiling solutions of inductive problems, we can produce productions that are generalizations and discriminations of original productions.

It would be useful to give an example of the difference between doing induction at the architectural level versus the production level. Consider, for instance, the task of learning when it is useful to make the vertical, or opposite, angle inference in geometry (Lewis and Anderson 1985). Among the production rules we want to learn is the following:

V1
IF $\angle 1$ and $\angle 2$ are opposite angles
and they are parts of triangles,
and there is a goal to prove the triangles congruent,
THEN conclude that the vertical angles are congruent.

The second and third clauses are not part of the legal definition of the vertical angles postulate but rather are problem features that predict the usefulness of the vertical angle inference. These features are not directly taught, but students must induce them. There are two ways to arrive at these heuristic features. One is compare cases of success and failure with automatic induction mechanisms such as were proposed in Anderson (1982) and Langley (chapter 3). This would be done at the architectural level. In contrast, if this were done at the production level, the student might consciously set as a goal to determine the features that predict the usefulness of the vertical angle inference. The student can bring problem-solving procedures to bear in answering this question and try to solve this just as he might try to figure out the identity of a murderer in a mystery. Chaining backward in the logical structure of the proof, he might see that the vertical angle inference enabled the congruent triangle inference and so form the declarative proposition:

vertical angle inferences help prove triangle congruence.

This fact could then be evoked in deciding whether to make a vertical angle inference later on. Compiling the steps of the decision that led to this later vertical angle inference would produce the desired rule V1. In contrast to the architectural level, this production level induction presumes that students would have conscious, declarative access to their inductions. This is one of the results of Lewis and Anderson (1985).

Besides knowledge compilation there is one other learning mechanism in the current ACT. This is the mechanism by which productions gain strength through practice. This strengthening mechanism accounts for the continued improvement of skill long after opportunity for compilation has ceased (Anderson 1982). It is a very simple learning mechanism but has important implications for tutoring.

Implications for Skill Acquisition

We turn now to the issue of what, according to the ACT theory, would impact on the growth of proficiency (speed and accuracy) with which a skill is manifested. We will be concerned with both learning factors that impact on the acquisition of a basic skill and performance factors that impact on how well that skill is executed. As we follow the development of a skill in the ACT theory, we find that there are relatively few such factors.

1. *Instruction.* The student has to get the requisite knowledge, but in most instructional situations that is not directly given. For instance, LISP instruction seldom tells students how to write recursive functions. This is something they have to figure out for themselves. It has been shown (Pirolli 1985) that students learn faster if they are told directly. This may seem obvious, but it has not had much effect on pedagogical practice. Most students induce recursive programming by analogy to examples.

More generally, whatever instruction the student receives will be encoded declaratively and will be interpreted by weak problem-solving procedures. Instruction is effective to the degree that it provides information that can be easily interpreted by the student's weak procedures.

2. *Correctness of declarative encoding.* Students may incorrectly represent the knowledge to which their weak methods are applied. For instance, consider the following statement of the side-angle-side postulate:

If two sides and an included angle of one triangle are congruent to the corresponding parts of another triangle, then the two triangles are congruent.

Students often interpret "included" to mean contained in the triangle, rather than contained between the two congruent sides. Any production compiled from this misunderstanding will be flawed. Similarly Pirolli and Anderson (1985) have argued that the major determinant of what is learned by anology from an example is how well students represent why the example solves the problem it does.

3. *Working memory limitations.* Assuming that instruction provides information in a useful declarative form and that it is correctly encoded, it has to be held in working memory in order to be compiled into production form. Any factor that increases the amount of information that must be held, or the time for which it must be held, will increase the likelihood of working memory failures. These working memory failures will result in incorrect compilations if certain details are missing, or in aborted compilations if the goal structure that holds the information together is lost. Thus, awkward instruction can result in failure by increasing load or comprehension time. Clearly, there is a premium in compacting the necessary instruction into its bare essentials. Also, one wants to avoid unnecessary working memory burdens in the actual problem solving.

Once productions have been compiled, they can be composed further into more effective macro operators. This requires holding in working memory the goal structures that indicate how the individual productions should be composed together to form the macro operator. Thus, working memory capacity can control the composition process.

Finally, working memory failures may cause correct productions to randomly misapply and produce errors. These are what Norman (1981) would classify as slips. Anderson and Jeffries (1986), looking at a population of undergraduates just learning LISP, concluded that the majority of their errors with basic concepts derived from working memory failures rather than fundamental mistakes.

4. *Production strength.* The strength of a production impacts on performance of a skill in multiple ways. Weak productions may fail to apply, producing permanent lapses until remediated by more instruction. Also, weak productions take longer in the ACT theory and so increase the period over which knowledge must be maintained in working memory for purposes of composition.

One of the surprising things to come out of our work with the LISP tutor is how very systematic the improvement of productions appears to be with practice. Figures 9.4 through 9.6 illustrate speedup in times for subjects to code actions corresponding to the firing of productions in our simulations

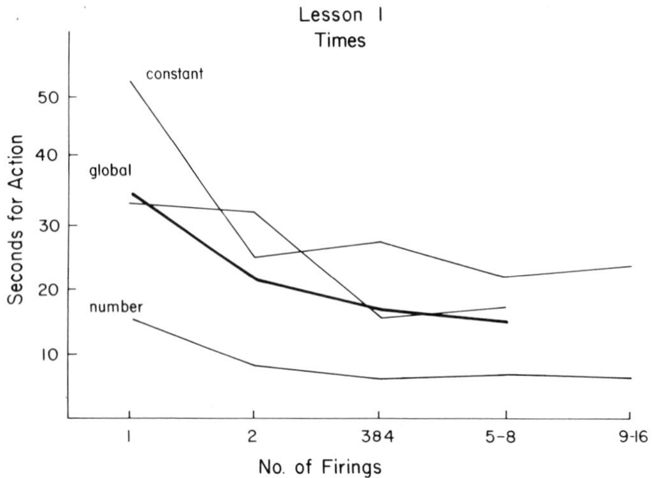

Figure 9.4
Times to perform actions corresponding to firings in the ideal model: constant = coding quoted constant; global = coding global variable; number = coding a number. The bold curve represents average. These data are for productions introduced in lesson 1.

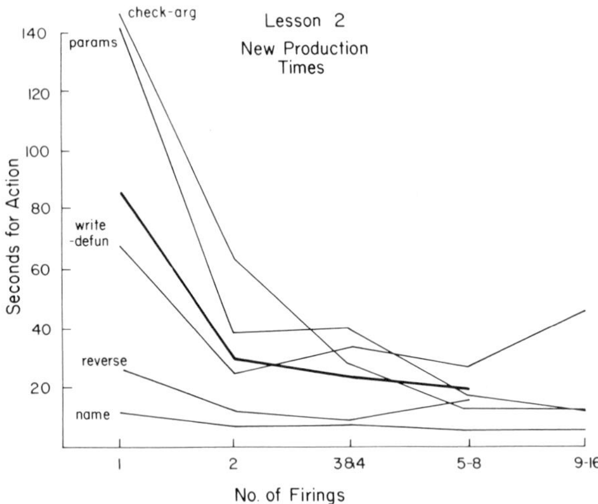

Figure 9.5
Lesson 2 times analogous to figure 9.4: arg = coding an argument to a function that is a parameter of a function definition; params = coding parameters of a function definition; reverse = coding function reverse; defun = coding function defun; name = coding name of function definition

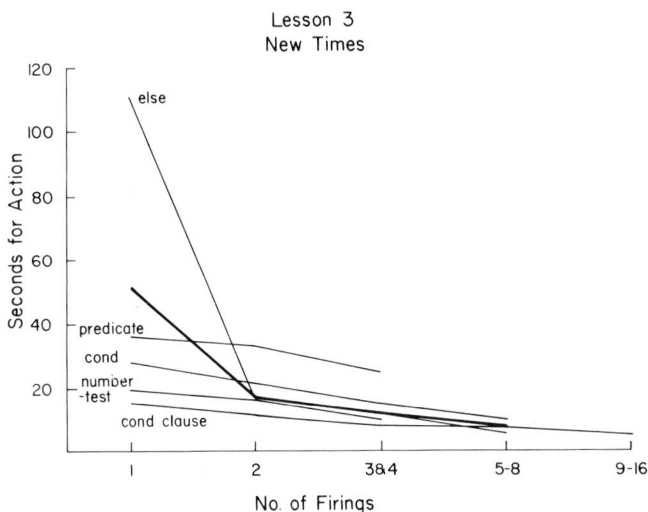

Figure 9.6
Lesson 3 times analogous to figure 9.4: else = coding *t* test in cond; predicate = coding predicate; cond = coding function cond; number test = coding numbers; cond clause = coding a clause in a cond

of their problem solving. Many of the productions in the LISP tutor have coding action associated with them. For instance, the production labeled *constant* produces the typing of a quoted constant like *'dog*. What we have plotted in these figures is the time for the student to type this action (measured from the last keystroke of the previous action to the last keystroke of this action). This is plotted as a function of the number of times that production fired in the simulation of the student. The three figures represent some newly introduced productions from each lesson. While the trace of individual production times show random perturbations, the overall pattern is clear: there is a rapid speedup from first to second execution, reflecting knowledge compilation, and then a slow strengthening process thereafter. A similar pattern is found in the error rates.

Tutorial Implications

Corresponding to each of these considerations are a set of implications for tutorial action:

1. *Instruction.* The first consideration about instruction is that it should be based on a production-system model of the target skill so that we know

what it is that we want to instruct. This is the basic presupposition of this chapter. One of the important features of an ACT production system is its goal structure, and it is essential that the student acquire the correct goal structure to control the problem solving. Finding a way to communicate the goal structure becomes a major issue in the design of a tutorial interface. It can be difficult because the goal structure is abstract and not easily described. In the LISP tutor we use various annotated symbols for various code structures.

In addition to basing instruction on a production-system analysis and emphasing communication of goal structures, there are a number of other general recommendations to make about the design of instructional activities. It makes sense to provide the instruction in the context where it should be used to maximize the probability that the student will retrieve and try to use the knowledge. Also, it makes sense to provide that knowledge in a form that can be most easily used by weak methods. For instance, we try to fashion our instruction to take the form of rules for means-ends solutions or of examples for use by analogy.

2. *Correctness of declarative encodings.* Unfortunately ACT theory does not provide *per se* any guidance about how to design instruction to minimize possibilities of misunderstanding. This is largely a language comprehension (and to some degree a graph comprehension) issue for which there is no ACT model, although in principle and with great effort we could create a production-system model for comprehension. We have instead developed a set of heuristics that seem to optimize communication. One of the principal heuristics is to minimize what we say.

Of course, the second line of defense against misunderstandings is to be able to remediate them when they occur. So far, we have simply catalogued observed confusions and associated appropriate instruction with them. Other work such as Buggy (Brown and VanLehn 1982) has tried to come up with a generative theory of the origins of these confusions. One approach is to try to enumerate the possible syntactic variations on correct rules, which certainly seems possible in domains like LISP. The other approach is to predictively generate the bugs. To the extent that these bugs have their origin in language comprehension, that seems like a hopeless goal, however.

3. *Working memory limitations.* The obvious pedagogical cure to working memory problems is to minimize unnecessary load. One way we try to achieve this in the LISP tutor is by doing syntactic checking. It also follows

that immediate feedback on errors is important because this limits the amount of time and information over which a student must integrate to learn. The nature of the feedback is important in that it should inform the student why there was an error, but not say what the correct answer is. If it gives away the correct answer, the student will compile a production to copy the answer rather than one to generate the answer when the answer is not given. The error messages generated by the LISP tutor have this quality of giving the right amount of information without giving away the answer.

Another aspect of working memory limitation that the tutor must deal with is the slips that produce errors but do not reflect fundamental misconceptions. These can be remediated by direct correction rather than the debugging process of pointing out the error and asking the student to correct it himself. This is because there is no fundamental error that needs correction. Unfortunately, slips and fundamental misconceptions often generate the same surface behavior. Rather than trying to diagnose which it is, the LISP tutor remediates all as if they were fundamental bugs. We intend to use a student model in future versions of the tutor to decide the appropriate remedial action. That is, if the student has displayed successful use of the production with some consistency, we will assume the current error is a slip.

One might question why slips should be corrected at all, given they do not reflect a fundamental misconception in need of remediation. The problem is that a flawed solution confounds later steps of problem solving and instruction. Students believe the slips they put down on paper or on the screen and begin to take erroneous actions based on them.

4. *Production strength.* The principal implication of considerations of production strength is that problems should be given in order to practice productions. However, this leaves open the questions of what is enough practice and how that practice should be distributed. We need to balance the following three considerations: First, as long as the student is making errors in a production, it needs practice. Second, too much practice in one session is not helpful because of the massing of practice. There is consistent evidence that further within-session practice on a piece of knowledge becomes valueless. Third, between sessions the subject may have forgotten and may need remedial practice.

To truly optimize performance would require making complex computations about the interaction of production strength and activation in the

ACT model. However, the important observation is that at this level of description of memory phenomena, ACT is nearly indiscriminable from many other memory theories, and we might as well select a computationally tractable theory. Therefore, we intend to do our problem selection on the basis of the three-state memory model (Atkinson 1972), which has already proved quite successful in dealing with the three considerations just mentioned. The three-state model assumes that a production can be in a permanent state, a temporary state, or a no-knowledge state. One can go from the no-knowledge state to the temporary or permanent state, and one can drop back from the temporary to the no-knowledge state. To use this model, one simply calculates Bayesian estimates of the probability of a production being in each of the states.

The assumption is that probability of transiting to the permanent state from a no-knowledge state is maximum when the surrounding productions have been performed correctly. Therefore, our problem selection algorithm favors problems that present unlearned productions in familiar context because this is what will maximize probability of learning new productions.

9.3 Production Learning and Tutoring: Concluding Remarks

What needs to be stressed is the very simple view that this framework depicts of the nature of skill acquisition and the tutoring of a skill. In particular, to tutor a skill optimally, we need to do the following:

1. Perform a task analysis to identify the productions that a student must acquire.
2. Find a form of instruction—presentation of examples, statement of abstract rules, and so forth—that the student's weak methods can use to solve the problems.
3. Give the student enough practice to compile and strengthen these rules.
4. Monitor the student's progress and only introduce new rules when the old rules have achieved a sufficient degree of strength that they no longer interfere with the acquisition of new rules.

To help recognize how simple an instructional strategy is implied by this learning theory, it is interesting to consider just two of the factors that are not important according to it, but which are accorded importance in other plausible learning theories:

1. According to this theory the learning of separate productions is independent, and we should not see, as one might intuitively expect, clusters of productions (e.g., productions for coding arithmetic expressions in LISP) behaving alike and so reflecting some fundamental misconceptions. In fact, statistical analyses of the data gathered with the LISP tutor suggest individual productions are learned independently.

2. Many learning theories would suggest that problem sequence is important. For instance, discrimination learning mechanisms would suggest that juxtaposing problems that involve similar but different productions, such as for coding LIST and CONS. This would enable acquisition of discriminating features. In contrast, the current ACT theory assumes nothing about problem sequence is special, except that it is important to minimize the number of new productions to be learned simultaneously, as we noted earlier. We have done only a little exploration of problem sequence with our tutor, but so far have gotten only null results, consistent with the ACT theory.

As another piece of evidence for the simplicity of the learning theory, note that it is not necessary to run a dynamic simulation of the learning processes in order to do tutoring. Rather, the tutor has compiled into its behavior all the pedagogical implications of the learning theory. The theory implies that productions are basically acquired through practice, and the only purpose of a tutor is to increase the effectiveness of that practice.

A number of decades ago, S-R theory was rejected in psychology because it implied that knowledge was nothing but the accumulation of S-R bonds, and an accounting of the number of S-R bonds necessary to produce interesting behavior came up with an astronomical number. Production systems provide a computationally more powerful framework than S-R theory. Production systems like ACT are more structured, with goals, weak methods and knowledge compilation. However, given that more powerful framework, it may be that knowledge (or at least problem-solving skill) is just the accumulation of production rules. A modified empiricism may still be feasible. Although I would not want to claim definitive results, our tutoring work is basically putting this modified empiricism to test.

Notes

The research reported in this paper was supported by Contract No. N00014-84-K-0064 from the Office of Navel Research and Grant No. IST-83-18629 from the National Science Foundation

References

Anderson, J. R. 1982. Acquisition of proof skills in geometry. In J. G. Carbonell. R. Michalski, and T. Mitchell (eds.), *Machine Learning, An Artificial Intelligence Approach*. Palo Alto, Calif. Tioga Publishing.

Anderson, J. R. 1982. Acquisition of Cognitive Skill. *Psychological Review* 89, 369–406.

Anderson, J. R. 1983. *The Architecture of Cognition*. Cambridge, Mass. Harvard University Press.

Anderson, J. R. 1985. *Skill acquisition: Compilation of weak-method problem solutions*. Office of Naval Research Technical Report. Carnegie-Mellon University.

Anderson, J. R. 1986. Knowledge compilation: The general learning mechanism. In R. Michalski, J. Carbonnell, and T. Mitchell (eds.), *Machine LearningII*. Palo Alto, Calif. Tioga Publishing.

Anderson, J. R., and Jeffries, R. 1986. Novice LISP errors: Undetected losses of information from working memory. *Human-Computer Interaction*, forthcoming.

Anderson, J. R., Boyle, C. F., and Yost, G. 1985. The Geometry Tutor. *Proceedings of IJCAI-85*. Los Angeles, Calif.

Anderson, J. R., Farrell, R., and Sauers, R. 1984. Learning to program in LISP. *Cognitive Science* 8, 87–129.

Atkinson. R. C. 1972. Optimizing the learning of second-language vocabulary. *Journal of Experimental Psychology* 96, 124–129.

Lewis, M. W., and Anderson, J. R. 1985. Discrimination of operator schemata in problem solving: Learning from examples. *Cognitive Psychology* 17, 26–65.

Neves, D. M., and Anderson, J. R. 1981. Knowledge compilation: Mechanisms for the automatization of cognitive skills. In J. R. Anderson (ed.). *Cognitive Skills and Their Acquisition*. Hillsdale, N.J.: Lawrence Erlbaum Associates.

Norman, D. A. 1981. Categorization of action slips. *Psychological Review* 88, 1–15.

Pirolli, P. L., and Anderson, J. R. 1985. The role of learning from examples in the acquisition of recursive programming skill. *Canadian Journal of Psychology* 39, 240–272.

Reiser, B. J., Anderson, J. R., and Farrell, R. G. 1985. Dynamic student modelling in an intelligent tutor for LISP programming. *Proceedings of IJCAI-85*. Los Angeles, Calif.

Winston, P. H., and Horn, B. K. P. 1984. *LISP* 2nd ed. Reading, Mass. Addison-Wesley.

Author Index

Subject Index